NON-CIRCULATING

English / Spanish
Inglés / Español

THE OXFORD
Picture
Dictionary

NORMA SHAPIRO AND JAYME ADELSON-GOLDSTEIN

Translated by Techno-Graphics & Translations, Inc.

Oxford University Press

Oxford University Press
198 Madison Avenue, New York, NY 10016 USA
Great Clarendon Street, Oxford OX2 6DP England

Oxford New York
Auckland Bangkok Buenos Aires Cape Town Chennai
Dar es Salaam Delhi Hong Kong Istanbul Karachi Kolkata
Kuala Lumpur Madrid Melbourne Mexico City Mumbai
Nairobi São Paulo Shanghai Taipei Tokyo Toronto

OXFORD is a trademark of Oxford University Press.

Library of Congress Cataloging-in-Publication Data

Shapiro, Norma.
    The Oxford picture dictionary : English / Spanish
Norma Shapiro and Jayme Adelson-Goldstein; translation
by Techno-Graphics and Translations, Inc.
            p.   cm.
    Includes bibliographical references and index.
    ISBN 0-19-435188-2
    1. Picture dictionaries, Spanish.   2. Picture dictionaries,
    English.   3. English language — Dictionaries—Spanish.
I. Adelson-Goldstein, Jayme.   II. Title.
PC4629.S53   1998   97-43652
423'.61—dc21

No unauthorized photocopying.

Translation reviewed by Mary-Anne Vetterling and Karen Davy
Editorial Manager: Susan Lanzano
Art Director: Lynn Luchetti
Senior Editor: Eliza Jensen
Senior Production Editor: Pat O'Neill
Senior Designer: Susan P. Brorein
Art Buyer: Tracy A. Hammond
Production Services by: Techno-Graphics and Translations, Inc.
Cover design by Silver Editions

Printing (last digit): 10 9

Printed in China

Illustrations by: David Aikins, Doug Archer, Craig Attebery,
Garin Baker, Sally Bensusen, Eliot Bergman, Mark Bischel, Dan
Brown / Artworks NY, Roy Douglas Buchman, George Burgos /
Larry Dodge, Carl Cassler, Mary Chandler, Robert Crawford, Jim
DeLapine, Judy Francis, Graphic Chart and Map Co., Dale
Gustafson, Biruta Akerbergs Hansen, Marcia Hartsock, C.M.I.,
David Hildebrand, The Ivy League of Artists, Inc. / Judy
Degraffenreid, The Ivy League of Artists, Inc. / Tom Powers, The
Ivy League of Artists, Inc. / John Rice, Pam Johnson, Ed
Kurtzman, Narda Lebo, Scott A. MacNeill / MACNEILL &
MACINTOSH, Andy Lendway / Deborah Wolfe Ltd., Jeffrey
Mangiat, Suzanne Mogensen, Mohammad Mansoor, Tom
Newsom, Melodye Benson Rosales, Stacey Schuett, Rob
Schuster, James Seward, Larry Taugher, Bill Thomson, Anna
Veltfort, Nina Wallace, Wendy Wassink-Ackison, Michael
Wepplo, Don Wieland
Thanks to Mike Mikos for his preliminary architectural sketches
of several pieces.

References
Boyer, Paul S., Clifford E. Clark, Jr., Joseph F. Kett, Thomas L.
Purvis, Harvard Sitkoff, Nancy Woloch *The Enduring Vision: A
History of the American People*, Lexington, Massachusetts: D.C.
Heath and Co., 1990.

Grun, Bernard, *The Timetables of History: A Horizontal Linkage
of People and Events,* (based on Werner Stein's Kulturfahrplan)
New York: A Touchstone Book, Simon and Schuster, 1946,
1963, 1975, 1979.

Statistical Abstract of the United States: 1996, 116th Edition,
Washington, DC: US Bureau of the Census, 1996.

The World Book Encyclopedia, Chicago: World Book Inc., a
Scott Fetzer Co., 1988 Edition.

Toff, Nancy, Editor-in-Chief, *The People of North America*
(Series), New York: Chelsea House Publishers, Main Line
Books, 1988.

Trager, James, *The People's Chronology, A Year-by-Year Record
of Human Events from Prehistory to the Present,* New York:
Henry Holt Reference Book, 1992.

Acknowledgments

The publisher and authors would like to thank the following people for reviewing the manuscript and/or participating in focus groups as the book was being developed:

Ana Maria Aguilera, Lubie Alatriste, Ann Albarelli, Margaret Albers, Sherry Allen, Fiona Armstrong, Ted Auerbach, Steve Austen, Jean Barlow, Sally Bates, Sharon Batson, Myra Baum, Mary Beauparlant, Gretchen Bitterlin, Margrajean Bonilla, Mike Bostwick, Shirley Brod, Lihn Brown, Trish Brys-Overeem, Lynn Bundy, Chris Bunn, Carol Carvel, Leslie Crucil, Jill DeLa Llata, Robert Denheim, Joshua Denk, Kay Devonshire, Thomas Dougherty, Gudrun Draper, Sara Eisen, Lynda Elkins, Ed Ende, Michele Epstein, Beth Fatemi, Andra R. Fawcett, Alice Fiedler, Harriet Fisher, James Fitzgerald, Mary Fitzsimmons, Scott Ford, Barbara Gaines, Elizabeth Garcia Grenados, Maria T. Gerdes, Penny Giacalone, Elliott Glazer, Jill Gluck de la Llata, Javier Gomez, Pura Gonzales, Carole Goodman, Joyce Grabowski, Maggie Grennan, Joanie Griffin, Sally Hansen, Fotini Haritos, Alice Hartley, Fernando Herrera, Ann Hillborn, Mary Hopkins, Lori Howard, Leann Howard, Pamela Howard, Rebecca Hubner, Jan Jarrell, Vicki Johnson, Michele Kagan, Nanette Kafka, Gena Katsaros, Evelyn Kay, Greg Keech, Cliff Ker, Gwen Kerner-Mayer, Marilou Kessler, Patty King, Linda Kiperman, Joyce Klapp, Susan Knutson, Sandy Kobrine, Marinna Kolaitis, Donna Korol, Lorraine Krampe, Karen Kuser, Andrea Lang, Nancy Lebow, Tay Lesley, Gale Lichter, Sandie Linn, Rosario Lorenzano, Louise Louie, Cheryl Lucas, Ronna Magy, Juanita Maltese, Mary Marquardsen, Carmen Marques Rivera, Susan McDowell, Alma McGee, Jerry McLeroy, Kevin McLure, Joan Meier, Patsy Mills, Judy Montague, Vicki Moore, Eneida Morales, Glenn Nadelbach, Elizabeth Neblett, Kathleen Newton, Yvonne Nishio, Afra Nobay, Rosa Elena Ochoa, Jean Owensby, Jim Park, John Perkins, Jane Pers, Laura Peskin, Maria Pick, Percy Pleasant, Selma Porter, Kathy Quinones, Susan Ritter, Martha Robledo, Maureen Rooney, Jean Rose, David Ross, Julietta Ruppert, Lorraine Ruston, Susan Ryan, Frederico Salas, Leslie Salmon, Jim Sandifer, Linda Sasser, Lisa Schreiber, Mary Segovia, Abe Shames, Debra Shaw, Stephanie Shipp, Pat Singh, Mary Sklavos, Donna Stark, Claire Cocoran Stehling, Lynn Sweeden, Joy Tesh, Sue Thompson, Christine Tierney, Laura Topete, Carmen Villanueva, Laura Webber, Renée Weiss, Beth Winningham, Cindy Wislofsky, Judy Wood, Paula Yerman.

A special thanks to Marna Shulberg and the students of the Saticoy Branch of Van Nuys Community Adult School.

We would also like to thank the following individuals and organizations who provided their expertise:

Carl Abato, Alan Goldman, Dr. Larry Falk, Caroll Gray, Henry Haskell, Susan Haskell, Los Angeles Fire Department, Malcolm Loeb, Barbara Lozano, Lorne Dubin, United Farm Workers.

Authors' Acknowledgments

Throughout our careers as English language teachers, we have found inspiration in many places—in the classroom with our remarkable students, at schools, conferences, and workshops with our fellow teachers, and with our colleagues at the ESL Teacher Institute. We are grateful to be part of this international community.

We would like to sincerely thank and acknowledge Eliza Jensen, the project's Senior Editor. Without Eliza, this book would not have been possible. Her indomitable spirit, commitment to clarity, and unwavering advocacy allowed us to realize the book we envisioned.

Creating this dictionary was a collaborative effort and it has been our privilege to work with an exceptionally talented group of individuals who, along with Eliza Jensen, make up the Oxford Picture Dictionary team. We deeply appreciate the contributions of the following people:

Lynn Luchetti, Art Director, whose aesthetic sense and sensibility guided the art direction of this book,

Susan Brorein, Senior Designer, who carefully considered the design of each and every page,

Klaus Jekeli, Production Editor, who pored over both manuscript and art to ensure consistency and accuracy, and

Tracy Hammond, Art Buyer, who skillfully managed thousands of pieces of art and reference material.

We also want to thank Susan Mazer, the talented artist who was by our side for the initial problem-solving and Mary Chandler who also lent her expertise to the project.

We have learned much working with Marjorie Fuchs, Lori Howard, and Renée Weiss, authors of the dictionary's ancillary materials. We thank them for their on-going contributions to the dictionary program.

We must make special mention of Susan Lanzano, Editorial Manager, whose invaluable advice, insights, and queries were an integral part of the writing process.

This book is dedicated to my husband, Neil Reichline, who has encouraged me to take the road less traveled, and to my sons, Eli and Alex, who have allowed me to sit at their baseball games with my yellow notepad. —NS

This book is lovingly dedicated to my husband, Gary and my daughter, Emily Rose, both of whom hugged me tight and let me work into the night. —JAG

A Letter to the Teacher

Welcome to The Oxford Picture Dictionary.

This comprehensive vocabulary resource provides you and your students with over 3,700 words, each defined by engaging art and presented in a meaningful context. *The Oxford Picture Dictionary* enables your students to learn and use English in all aspects of their daily lives. The 140 key topics cover home and family, the workplace, the community, health care, and academic studies. The topics are organized into 12 thematic units that are based on the curriculum of beginning and low-intermediate level English language coursework. The word lists of the dictionary include both single word entries and verb phrases. Many of the prepositions and adjectives are presented in phrases as well, demonstrating the natural use of words in conjunction with one another.

The Oxford Picture Dictionary uses a variety of visual formats, each suited to the topic being represented. Where appropriate, word lists are categorized and pages are divided into sections, allowing you to focus your students' attention on one aspect of a topic at a time.

Within the word lists:

- nouns, adjectives, prepositions, and adverbs are numbered,

- verbs are bolded and identified by letters, and

- targeted prepositions and adjectives within phrases are bolded.

The dictionary includes a variety of exercises and self access tools that will guide your students towards accurate and fluent use of the new words.

- Exercises at the bottom of the pages provide vocabulary development through pattern practice, application of the new language to other topics, and personalization questions.

- An alphabetical index assists students in locating all words and topics in the dictionary.

- A phonetic listing for each word in the index and a pronunciation guide give students the key to accurate pronunciation.

- A verb index of all the verbs presented in the dictionary provides students with information on the present, past, and past participle forms of the verbs.

The Oxford Picture Dictionary is the core of *The Oxford Picture Dictionary Program* which includes a *Dictionary Cassette,* a *Teacher's Book* and its companion *Focused Listening Cassette, Beginning* and *Intermediate Workbooks, Classic Classroom Activities* (a photocopiable activity book), *Overhead Transparencies,* and *Read All About It 1* and *2.* Bilingual editions of *The Oxford Picture Dictionary* are available in Spanish, Chinese, Vietnamese, and many other languages.

TEACHING THE VOCABULARY

Your students' needs and your own teaching philosophy will dictate how you use *The Oxford Picture Dictionary* with your students. The following general guidelines, however, may help you adapt the dictionary's pages to your particular course and students. (For topic-specific, step-by-step guidelines and activities for presenting and practicing the vocabulary on each dictionary page see the *Oxford Picture Dictionary Teacher's Book.*)

Preview the topic

A good way to begin any lesson is to talk with students to determine what they already know about the topic. Some different ways to do this are:

- Ask general questions related to the topic;

- Have students brainstorm a list of words they know from the topic; or

- Ask questions about the picture(s) on the page.

Present the vocabulary

Once you've discovered which words your students already know, you are ready to focus on presenting the words they need. Introducing 10–15 new words in a lesson allows students to really learn the new words. On pages where the word lists are longer, and students are unfamiliar with any of the words, you may wish to introduce the words by categories or sections, or simply choose the words you want in the lesson.

Here are four different presentation techniques. The techniques you choose will depend on the topic being studied and the level of your students.

- Say each new word and describe or define it within the context of the picture.

- Demonstrate verbs or verb sequences for the students, and have volunteers demonstrate the actions as you say them.

- Use Total Physical Response commands to build comprehension of the vocabulary: *Put the pencil on your book. Put it on your notebook. Put it on your desk.*

- Ask a series of questions to build comprehension and give students an opportunity to say the new words:

► Begin with *yes/no* questions. *Is #16 chalk?* (yes)

► Progress to *or* questions. *Is #16 chalk or a marker?* (chalk)

► Finally ask *Wh* questions.

What can I use to write on this paper? (a marker/ Use a marker.)

Check comprehension

Before moving on to the practice stage, it is helpful to be sure all students understand the target vocabulary. There are many different things you can do to check students' understanding. Here are two activities to try:

• Tell students to open their books and point to the items they hear you say. Call out target vocabulary at random as you walk around the room checking to see if students are pointing to the correct pictures.

• Make true/false statements about the target vocabulary. Have students hold up two fingers for true, three fingers for false. *You can write with a marker.* [two fingers] *You raise your notebook to talk to the teacher.* [three fingers]

Take a moment to review any words with which students are having difficulty before beginning the practice activities.

Practice the vocabulary

Guided practice activities give your students an opportunity to use the new vocabulary in meaningful communication. The exercises at the bottom of the pages are one source of guided practice activities.

• **Talk about...** This activity gives students an opportunity to practice the target vocabulary through sentence substitutions with meaningful topics.

    e.g. **Talk about your feelings.**

    I feel <u>happy</u> when I see my friends.

• **Practice...** This activity gives students practice using the vocabulary within common conversational functions such as making introductions, ordering food, making requests, etc.

    e.g. **Practice asking for things in the dining room.**

    Please pass <u>the platter</u>.

    May I have <u>the creamer</u>?

    Could I have <u>a fork</u>, please?

• **Use the new language.** This activity asks students to brainstorm words within various categories, or may

ask them to apply what they have learned to another topic in the dictionary. For example, on *Colors*, page 12, students are asked to look at *Clothing I*, pages 64–65, and name the colors of the clothing they see.

• **Share your answers.** These questions provide students with an opportunity to expand their use of the target vocabulary in personalized discussion. Students can ask and answer these questions in whole class discussions, pair or group work, or they can write the answers as journal entries.

Further guided and communicative practice can be found in the *Oxford Picture Dictionary Teacher's Book* and in *Classic Classroom Activities*. The *Oxford Picture Dictionary Beginning* and *Intermediate Workbooks* and *Read All About It 1* and *2* provide your students with controlled and communicative reading and writing practice.

We encourage you to adapt the materials to suit the needs of your classes, and we welcome your comments and ideas. Write to us at:

Oxford University Press
ESL Department
198 Madison Avenue
New York, NY 10016

Jayme Adelson-Goldstein

Norma Shapiro

A Letter to the Student

Dear Student of English,

Welcome to *The Oxford Picture Dictionary*. The more than 3,700 words in this book will help you as you study English.

Each page in this dictionary teaches about a specific topic. The topics are grouped together in units. All pages in a unit have the same color and symbol. For example, each page in the Food unit has this symbol:

On each page you will see pictures and words. The pictures have numbers or letters that match the numbers or letters in the word lists. Verbs (action words) are identified by letters and all other words are identified by numbers.

How to find words in this book

- Use the Table of Contents, pages ix–xi.
  Look up the general topic you want to learn about.

- Use the Index, pages 173–205.
  Look up individual words in alphabetical (A–Z) order.

- Go topic by topic.
  Look through the book until you find something that interests you.

How to use the Index

When you look for a word in the index this is what you will see:

the word   the number (or letter) in the word list

apples [ăp/əlz] **50**–4

the pronunciation   the page number

If the word is on one of the maps, pages 122–125, you will find it in the Geographical Index on pages 206–208.

How to use the Verb Guide

When you want to know the past form of a verb or its past participle form, look up the verb in the verb guide. The regular verbs and their spelling changes are listed on pages 170–171. The simple form, past form, and past participle form of irregular verbs are listed on page 172.

Workbooks

There are two workbooks to help you practice the new words:
The Oxford Picture Dictionary Beginning and *Intermediate Workbooks*.

As authors and teachers we both know how difficult English can be (and we're native speakers!). When we wrote this book, we asked teachers and students from the U.S. and other countries for their help and ideas. We hope their ideas and ours will help you. Please write to us with your comments or questions at:

Oxford University Press
ESL Department
198 Madison Avenue
New York, NY 10016

We wish you success!

Jayme Adelson-Goldstein   *Norma Shapiro*

Unas palabras para el alumno

Querido estudiante de inglés,

Bienvenido al *The Oxford Picture Dictionary*. Los más de 3,700 vocablos incluidos en este libro le serán de gran utilidad en su estudio del idioma inglés.

Cada página de este diccionario le enseña un tema específico. Los temas están agrupados en unidades. Las páginas de cada unidad se distinguen por un color y un símbolo determinado. Por ejemplo, todas las páginas en la unidad sobre Alimentos están marcadas con este símbolo:

En todas las páginas hay imágenes y palabras. Cada imagen tiene números o letras que corresponden a los números o letras en las listas de palabras. Los verbos (palabras que expresan una acción) se identifican por letras y todas las demás palabras, por números.

Cómo buscar una palabra en este diccionario

- Utilice el Indice temático (pp. ix–xi).
  Busque allí el tema general que le interesa.

- Utilice el Indice alfabético (pp. 173–205).
  Busque allí palabras individuales ordenadas alfabéticamente (de la A a la Z).

- Pase de un tema a otro.
  Hojee el libro hasta dar con un tema que le interese.

Cómo utilizar el Indice alfabético

Al buscar una palabra en el índice alfabético usted verá lo siguiente:

la palabra   el número (o letra) en la lista de palabras

apples [ăp/əlz] **50**–4

la pronunciación   el número de la página

Si la palabra se encuentra sobre uno de los mapas (pp. 122–125), entonces la hallará en el Indice geográfico en las páginas 206–208.

Cómo utilizar la Guía de verbos

Si desea saber el tiempo pasado o el participio de un verbo determinado, busque éste en la guía de verbos. Los verbos regulares y sus cambios ortográficos se listan en las páginas 170–171. La forma simple, el pasado y el participio pasado de los verbos irregulares aparecen en la página 172.

Libros de trabajo

Existen también dos libros de trabajo que le servirán para practicar las palabras aprendidas; *The Oxford Picture Dictionary Beginning* y *Intermediate Workbooks*.

Como autoras y maestras, ambas sabemos lo difícil que puede ser el inglés (¡y en nuestro caso se trata de nuestra lengua materna!). Cuando escribimos este libro, solicitamos ayuda e ideas a varios maestros y estudiantes de los Estados Unidos y otros países. Esperamos que esas ideas y las nuestras lo ayuden también a usted. Asimismo, lo invitamos a que nos envíe sus comentarios o preguntas a la siguiente dirección:

Oxford University Press
ESL Department
198 Madison Avenue
New York, NY 10016

¡Mucho éxito!

Jayme Adelson-Goldstein   *Norma Shapiro*

Contents   Indice temático

1. Everyday Language   Lenguaje cotidiano

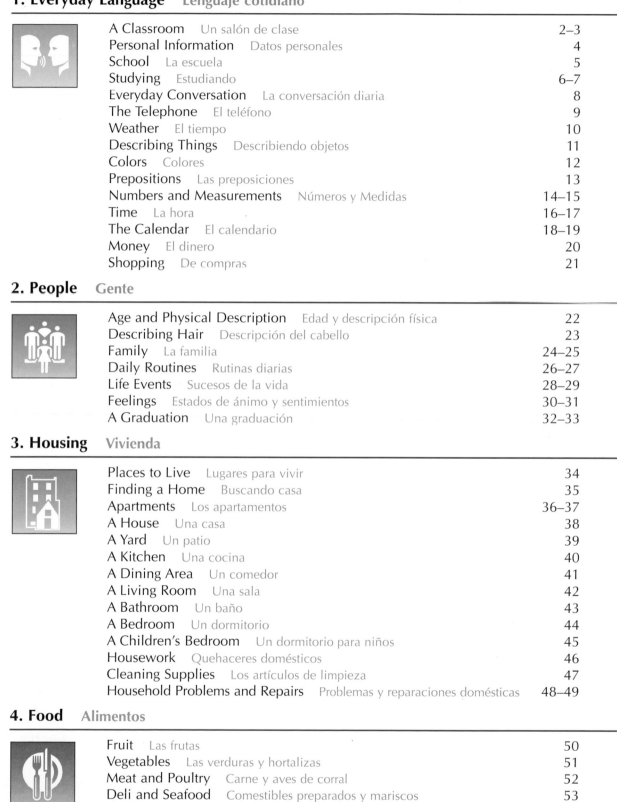

A Classroom Un salón de clase	2–3
Personal Information Datos personales	4
School La escuela	5
Studying Estudiando	6–7
Everyday Conversation La conversación diaria	8
The Telephone El teléfono	9
Weather El tiempo	10
Describing Things Describiendo objetos	11
Colors Colores	12
Prepositions Las preposiciones	13
Numbers and Measurements Números y Medidas	14–15
Time La hora	16–17
The Calendar El calendario	18–19
Money El dinero	20
Shopping De compras	21

2. People   Gente

Age and Physical Description Edad y descripción física	22
Describing Hair Descripción del cabello	23
Family La familia	24–25
Daily Routines Rutinas diarias	26–27
Life Events Sucesos de la vida	28–29
Feelings Estados de ánimo y sentimientos	30–31
A Graduation Una graduación	32–33

3. Housing   Vivienda

Places to Live Lugares para vivir	34
Finding a Home Buscando casa	35
Apartments Los apartamentos	36–37
A House Una casa	38
A Yard Un patio	39
A Kitchen Una cocina	40
A Dining Area Un comedor	41
A Living Room Una sala	42
A Bathroom Un baño	43
A Bedroom Un dormitorio	44
A Children's Bedroom Un dormitorio para niños	45
Housework Quehaceres domésticos	46
Cleaning Supplies Los artículos de limpieza	47
Household Problems and Repairs Problemas y reparaciones domésticas	48–49

4. Food   Alimentos

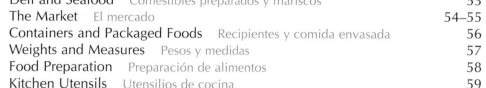

Fruit Las frutas	50
Vegetables Las verduras y hortalizas	51
Meat and Poultry Carne y aves de corral	52
Deli and Seafood Comestibles preparados y mariscos	53
The Market El mercado	54–55
Containers and Packaged Foods Recipientes y comida envasada	56
Weights and Measures Pesos y medidas	57
Food Preparation Preparación de alimentos	58
Kitchen Utensils Utensilios de cocina	59

Contents   Indice temático

Fast Food   Comida rápida   60
A Coffee Shop Menu   El menú de un café   61
A Restaurant   Un restaurante   62–63

5. Clothing   Ropa

Clothing I   La ropa I   64–65
Clothing II   La ropa II   66
Clothing III   La ropa III   67
Shoes and Accessories   Los zapatos y los accesorios   68–69
Describing Clothes   Descripción de la ropa   70–71
Doing the Laundry   Lavar la ropa / hacer la colada   72
Sewing and Alterations   Costura y arreglos   73

6. Health   Salud

The Body   El cuerpo   74–75
Personal Hygiene   La higiene personal   76–77
Symptoms and Injuries   Los síntomas y las lesiones   78
Illnesses and Medical Conditions   Las enfermedades y los padecimientos   79
Health Care   La atención médica   80–81
Medical Emergencies   Las emergencias médicas   82
First Aid   Los primeros auxilios   83
Clinics   Las clínicas   84
Medical and Dental Exams   Los exámenes médicos y dentales   85
A Hospital   Un hospital   86–87

7. Community   La comunidad

City Streets   Las calles de la ciudad   88–89
An Intersection   Una intersección   90–91
A Mall   Un centro comercial   92–93
A Childcare Center   Una guardería infantil   94–95
U.S. Mail   El servicio de correo de los EE.UU.   96
A Bank   Un banco   97
A Library   Una biblioteca   98
The Legal System   El sistema legal   99
Crime   La delincuencia   100
Public Safety   La seguridad pública   101
Emergencies and Natural Disasters   Emergencias y desastres naturales   102–103

8. Transportation   Medios de transporte

Public Transportation   El transporte público   104
Prepositions of Motion   Preposiciones de movimiento   105
Cars and Trucks   Automóviles y camiones   106
Directions and Traffic Signs   Direcciones y señales de tráfico   107
Parts of a Car and Car Maintenance   Las partes y el mantenimiento
    del auto   108–109
An Airport   Un aeropuerto   110
A Plane Trip   Un viaje en avión   111

9. Areas of Study   El estudio

Types of Schools   Tipos de escuela   112
English Composition   La composición en inglés   113
U.S. History   La historia de los EE.UU.   114–115

U.S. Government and Citizenship   El gobierno y la ciudadanía
   estadounidenses   116
Geography   La geografía   117
Mathematics   Las matemáticas   118
Science   Las ciencias   119
Music   La música   120
More School Subjects   Más materias escolares   121
North America and Central America   Norte y Centroamérica   122–123
The World   El mundo   124–125
Energy and the Environment   La energía y el medioambiente   126
The Universe   El universo   127

10. Plants and Animals   Plantas y animales

Trees and Plants   Árboles y plantas   128
Flowers   Flores   129
Marine Life, Amphibians, and Reptiles   Vida marina, anfibios y reptiles   130–131
Birds, Insects, and Arachnids   Pájaros, insectos y arácnidos   132
Domestic Animals and Rodents   Animales domésticos y roedores   133
Mammals   Mamíferos   134–135

11. Work   Trabajo

Jobs and Occupations, A–H   Empleos y profesiones   136–137
Jobs and Occupations, H–W   Empleos y profesiones   138–139
Job Skills   Destrezas laborales   140
Job Search   En busca de trabajo   141
An Office   Una oficina   142–143
Computers   Las computadoras   144
A Hotel   Un hotel   145
A Factory   Una fábrica   146
Job Safety   La seguridad en el lugar de trabajo   147
Farming and Ranching   La agricultura y la ganadería   148
Construction   La construcción   149
Tools and Building Supplies   Herramientas y materiales de construcción   150–151

12. Recreation   Recreación

Places to Go   Lugares para pasear   152
The Park and Playground   El parque y el patio de recreo   153
Outdoor Recreation   Recreación al aire libre   154
The Beach   La playa   155
Sports Verbs   Verbos utilizados en los deportes   156–157
Team Sports   Deportes en equipo   158
Individual Sports   Deportes individuales   159
Winter Sports and Water Sports   Deportes de invierno y acuáticos   160
Sports Equipment   Equipo deportivo   161
Hobbies and Games   Pasatiempos y juegos   162–163
Electronics and Photography   Electrónica y fotografía   164–165
Entertainment   Entretenimiento   166–167
Holidays   Días feriados   168
A Party   Una fiesta   169
Verb Guide   Guía de verbos   170
Index   Indice   173
Geographical Index   Indice geográfico   206

A Classroom   Un salón de clase

1. chalkboard
la pizarra

3. student
el estudiante

5. teacher
la maestra/la profesora

7. chair/seat
la silla/el asiento

2. screen
la pantalla

4. overhead projector
el retroproyector

6. desk
el escritorio

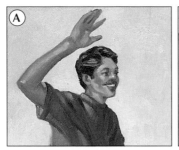

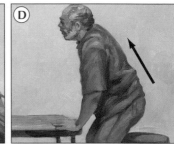

A. Raise your hand.
Levante la mano.

B. Talk to the teacher.
Hable con la maestra.

C. Listen to a cassette.
Escuche un casete.

D. Stand up.
Póngase de pie.

E. Sit down./Take a seat.
Siéntese./Tome asiento.

F. Point to the picture.
Señale el dibujo.

G. Write on the board.
Escriba en la pizarra.

H. Erase the board.
Borre la pizarra.

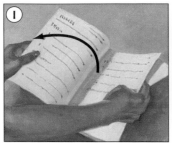

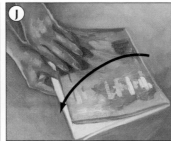

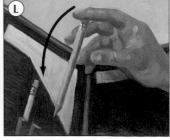

I. Open your book.
Abra el libro.

J. Close your book.
Cierre el libro.

K. Take out your pencil.
Saque el lápiz.

L. Put away your pencil.
Guarde el lápiz.

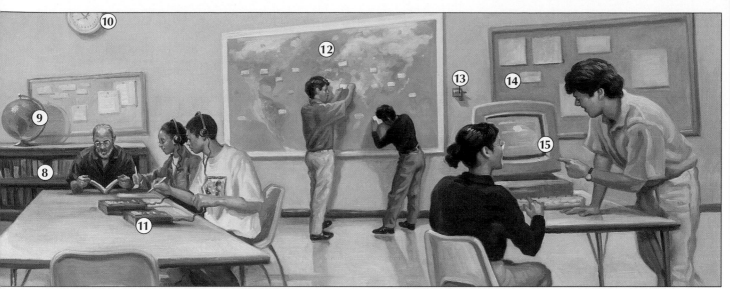

8. bookcase
el librero

9. globe
el globo terráqueo

10. clock
el reloj

11. cassette player
el tocacintas

12. map
el mapa

13. pencil sharpener
el sacapuntas

14. bulletin board
la cartelera

15. computer
la computadora

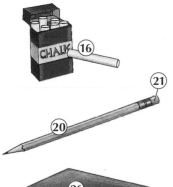

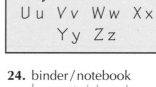

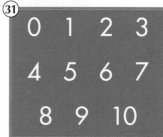
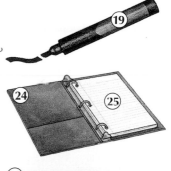

16. chalk
la tiza/el gis

17. chalkboard eraser
el borrador para pizarra

18. pen
el bolígrafo/la pluma

19. marker
el marcador

20. pencil
el lápiz

21. pencil eraser
la goma de borrar

22. textbook
el libro de texto

23. workbook
el cuaderno de trabajo

24. binder/notebook
la carpeta/el cuaderno

25. notebook paper
el papel para cuaderno

26. spiral notebook
el cuaderno de espiral

27. ruler
la regla

28. dictionary
el diccionario

29. picture dictionary
el diccionario gráfico

30. the alphabet
el alfabeto

31. numbers
los números

Use the new language.

1. Name three things you can open.

2. Name three things you can put away.

3. Name three things you can write with.

Share your answers.

1. Do you like to raise your hand?

2. Do you ever listen to cassettes in class?

3. Do you ever write on the board?

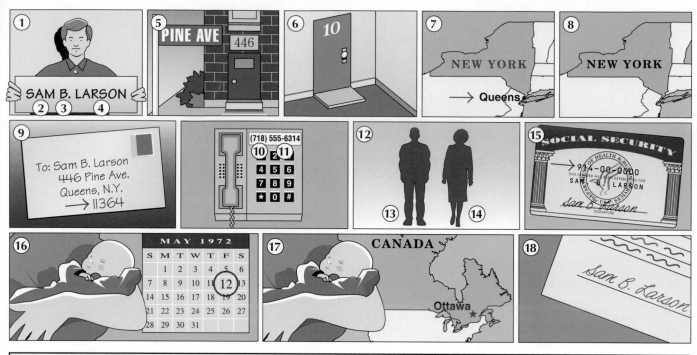

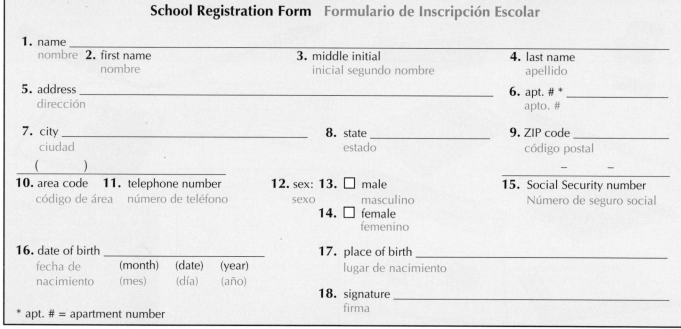

School Registration Form Formulario de Inscripción Escolar

1. name _____
nombre **2.** first name   **3.** middle initial   **4.** last name
        nombre   inicial segundo nombre   apellido

5. address _____ **6.** apt. # * _____
dirección   apto. #

7. city _____ **8.** state _____ **9.** ZIP code _____
ciudad   estado   código postal

(_____) _____   _____ – _____

10. area code **11.** telephone number   **12.** sex: **13.** ☐ male   **15.** Social Security number
código de área número de teléfono   sexo   masculino   Número de seguro social
                                               14. ☐ female
                                                       femenino

16. date of birth _____   **17.** place of birth _____
fecha de   (month) (date) (year)   lugar de nacimiento
nacimiento   (mes)   (día)   (año)
                                          18. signature _____
                                                  firma

* apt. # = apartment number

A. Spell your name.
Deletree su nombre.

B. Fill out a form.
Llene un formulario.

C. Print your name.
Escriba su nombre

D. Sign your name.
Firme.

Talk about yourself.

My first name is _Sam_.

My last name is spelled _L-A-R-S-O-N_.

I come from _Ottawa_.

Share your answers.

1. Do you like your first name?

2. Is your last name from your mother? father? husband?

3. What is your middle name?

1. classroom el salón de clase	**7.** lockers los roperos	**13.** principal's office la oficina del director
2. teacher el profesor/el maestro	**8.** rest rooms los baños	**14.** principal el director
3. auditorium el auditorio	**9.** gym el gimnasio	**15.** counselor's office la oficina del consejero
4. cafeteria la cafetería/el cafetín	**10.** bleachers las gradas	**16.** counselor el consejero
5. lunch benches los bancos para almorzar	**11.** track la pista	**17.** main office la oficina principal
6. library la biblioteca	**12.** field el campo	**18.** clerk el empleado

More vocabulary

instructor: teacher

coach: gym teacher

administrator: principal or other school supervisor

Share your answers.

1. Do you ever talk to the principal of your school?

2. Is there a place for you to eat at your school?

3. Does your school look the same as or different from the one in the picture?

5

Studying   Estudiando

Dictionary work   Uso del diccionario

A. Look up a word.
Busque una palabra.

B. Read the word.
Lea la palabra.

C. Say the word.
Diga la palabra.

D. Repeat the word.
Repita la palabra.

E. Spell the word.
Deletree la palabra.

F. Copy the word.
Copie la palabra.

Work with a partner   Trabaje con un compañero

G. Ask a question.
Haga una pregunta.

H. Answer a question.
Conteste una pregunta.

I. Share a book.
Comparta un libro.

J. Help your partner.
Ayude a su compañero.

Work in a group   Trabaje en grupo

K. Brainstorm a list.
Elabore una lista de ideas.

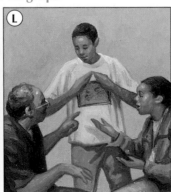

L. Discuss the list.
Discuta la lista.

M. Draw a picture.
Haga un dibujo.

N. Dictate a sentence.
Dicte una oración.

6

Class work   El trabajo en clase

O. Pass out the papers.
Distribuya las hojas.

P. Talk with each other.
Hable con sus compañeros.

Q. Collect the papers.
Recoja las hojas.

Follow directions   Siga las instrucciones

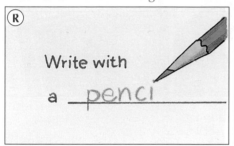

R. Fill in the blank.
Llene el espacio en blanco.

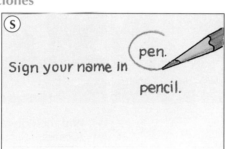

S. Circle the answer.
Encierre en un círculo la respuesta.

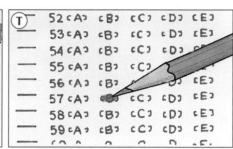

T. Mark the answer sheet.
Marque la hoja de respuestas.

U. Cross out the word.
Tache la palabra.

V. Underline the word.
Subraye la palabra.

W. Put the words **in order.**
Ponga las palabras **en orden.**

X. Match the items.
Seleccione la pareja.

Y. Check your work.
Revise su trabajo.

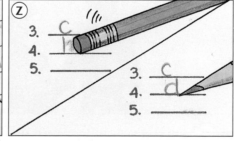

Z. Correct the mistake.
Corrija el error.

Share your answers.

1. Do you like to work in groups?

2. Do you like to share books?

3. Do you like to answer questions?

4. Is it easy for you to talk with your classmates?

5. Do you always check your work?

6. Do you cross out your mistakes or erase them?

Everyday Conversation   La conversación diaria

A. greet someone
saludar a alguien

B. begin a conversation
iniciar una conversación

C. end the conversation
terminar la conversación

D. introduce yourself
presentarse

E. make sure you **understand**
verificar lo que oye

F. introduce your friend
presentar a su amigo

G. compliment your friend
hacer un cumplido a su amigo

H. thank your friend
agradecer a su amigo

I. apologize
disculparse

Practice introductions.

Hi, I'm <u>Sam Jones</u> and this is my friend, <u>Pat Green</u>.

Nice to meet you. I'm <u>Tomas Garcia</u>.

Practice giving compliments.

That's a great <u>sweater</u>, <u>Tomas</u>.

Thanks <u>Pat</u>. I like your <u>shoes</u>.

Look at **Clothing I,** pages **64–65** for more ideas.

8

 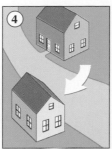  

1. telephone/phone
el teléfono
2. receiver
el auricular
3. cord
el cable
4. local call
la llamada local
5. long-distance call
la llamada de larga distancia
6. international call
la llamada internacional
7. operator
la operadora
8. directory assistance (411)
el servicio de directorio (411)
9. emergency service (911)
el servicio de emergencia (911)
10. phone card
la tarjeta telefónica
11. pay phone
el teléfono público
12. cordless phone
el teléfono inalámbrico
13. cellular phone
el teléfono celular
14. answering machine
la contestadora
15. telephone book
la guía telefónica/el directorio telefónico
16. pager
el buscapersonas

Using a pay phone   Usando el teléfono público

A. **Pick up** the receiver.
Levante el auricular
B. **Listen** for the dial tone.
Espere el tono de marcar.
C. **Deposit** coins.
Deposite monedas.

D. **Dial** the number.
Marque el número.
E. **Leave** a message.
Deje un mensaje.
F. **Hang up** the receiver.
Cuelgue el auricular.

More vocabulary

When you get a person or place that you didn't want to call, we say you have the **wrong number.**

Share your answers.

1. What kinds of calls do you make?
2. How much does it cost to call your country?
3. Do you like to talk on the telephone?

Temperature
Temperatura

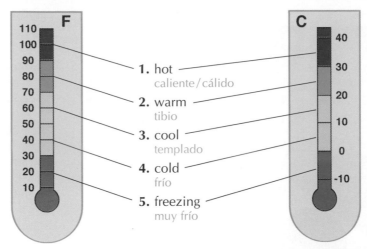

F
110
100
90
80
70
60
50
40
30
20
10

Degrees
Fahrenheit

C
40
30
20
10
0
-10

Degrees
Celsius

1. hot
   caliente/cálido
2. warm
   tibio
3. cool
   templado
4. cold
   frío
5. freezing
   muy frío

6. sunny/clear	7. cloudy	8. raining	9. snowing
soleado/despejado	nublado	lloviendo	nevando

10. windy	13. icy	16. thunderstorm	19. hail
con viento	helado	la tormenta	el granizo
11. foggy	14. smoggy	17. lightning	20. snowstorm
neblinoso	con esmog	el relámpago	la tormenta de nieve
12. humid	15. heat wave	18. hailstorm	21. dust storm
húmedo	la ola de calor	la granizada	la tormenta de polvo

Language note: *it is, there is*

For **1–14** we use,　*It's _cloudy_.*

For **15–21** we use,　*There's _a heat wave_.*
　　　　　　　　　　There's _lightning_.

Talk about the weather.

Today it's _hot_. It's _98 degrees_.

Yesterday it was _warm_. It was _85 degrees_.

1. **little** hand
   la mano **pequeña**
2. **big** hand
   la mano **grande**

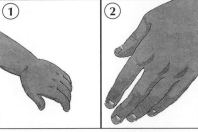

13. **heavy** box
    la caja **pesada**
14. **light** box
    la caja **liviana**

3. **fast** driver
   el chofer **rápido**
4. **slow** driver
   el chofer **lento**

15. **neat** closet
    el clóset **ordenado**
16. **messy** closet
    el clóset
    desordenado

5. **hard** chair
   la silla **dura**
6. **soft** chair
   la silla **blanda**

17. **good** dog
    el perro **bueno**
18. **bad** dog
    el perro **malo**

7. **thick** book/
   fat book
   el libro
   grueso / gordo
8. **thin** book
   el libro **delgado**

19. **expensive** ring
    el anillo **caro**
20. **cheap** ring
    el anillo **barato**

9. **full** glass
   el vaso **lleno**
10. **empty** glass
    el vaso **vacío**

21. **beautiful** view
    la vista **hermosa**
22. **ugly** view
    la vista **fea**

11. **noisy** children/
    loud children
    los niños
    ruidosos
12. **quiet** children
    los niños
    tranquilos

23. **easy** problem
    el problema **fácil**
24. **difficult** problem/
    hard problem
    el problema **difícil**

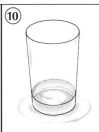

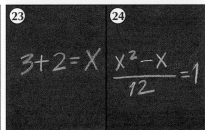

Use the new language.

1. Name three things that are thick.
2. Name three things that are soft.
3. Name three things that are heavy.

Share your answers.

1. Are you a slow driver or a fast driver?
2. Do you have a neat closet or a messy closet?
3. Do you like loud or quiet parties?

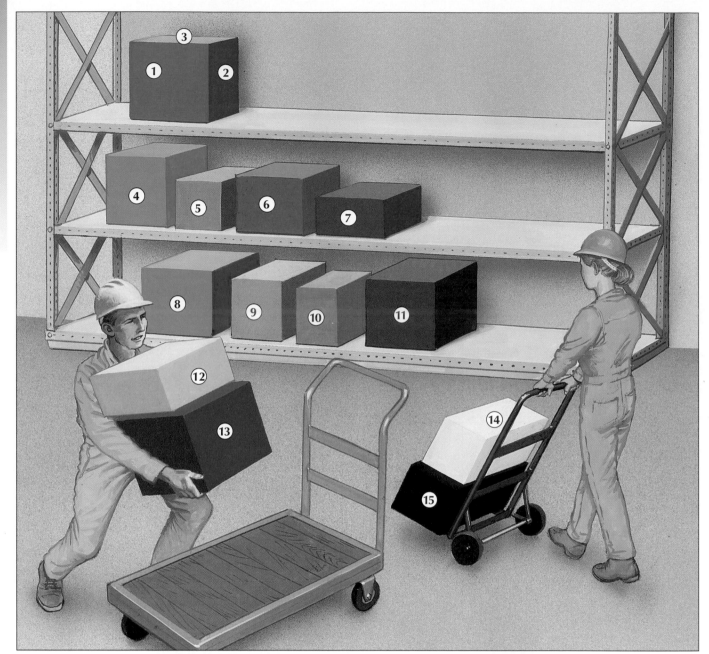

1. blue	6. orange	11. brown
azul	anaranjado/color naranja	marrón/café
2. dark blue	7. purple	12. yellow
azul oscuro	morado	amarillo
3. light blue	8. green	13. red
azul claro	verde	rojo
4. turquoise	9. beige	14. white
azul turquesa	beige	blanco
5. gray	10. pink	15. black
gris	rosado	negro

Use the new language.

Look at **Clothing I,** pages **64–65.**

Name the colors of the clothing you see.

That's a dark blue suit.

Share your answers.

1. What colors are you wearing today?

2. What colors do you like?

3. Is there a color you don't like? What is it?

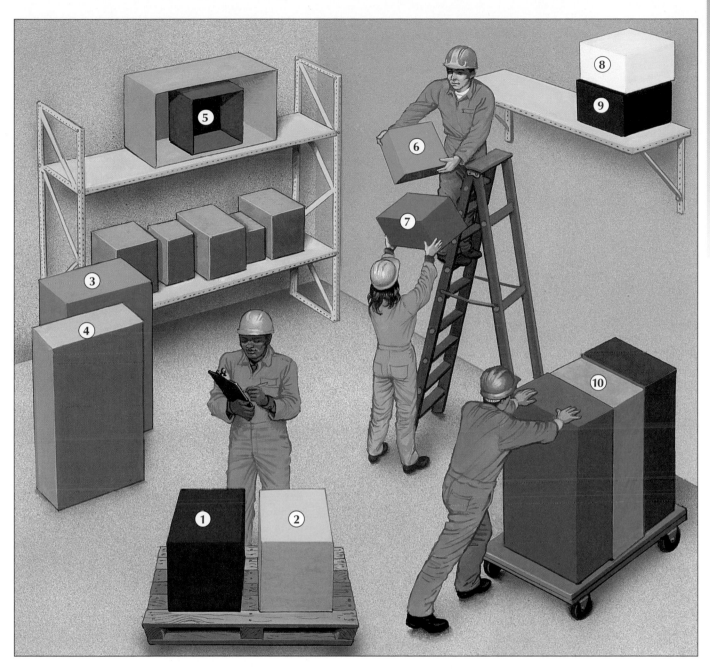

1. The red box is **next to** the yellow box, **on the left.**
La caja roja está **al lado de** la caja amarilla, **a la izquierda.**

2. The yellow box is **next to** the red box, **on the right.**
La caja amarilla está **al lado de** la caja roja, **a la derecha.**

3. The turquoise box is **behind** the gray box.
La caja azul turquesa está **detrás de** la caja gris.

4. The gray box is **in front of** the turquoise box.
La caja gris está **en frente de** la caja azul turquesa.

5. The dark blue box is **in** the beige box.
La caja azul oscuro está **dentro de** la caja beige.

6. The green box is **above** the orange box.
La caja verde está **encima de** la caja anaranjada.

7. The orange box is **below** the green box.
La caja anaranjada está **debajo de** la caja verde.

8. The white box is **on** the black box.
La caja blanca está **sobre** la caja negra.

9. The black box is **under** the white box.
La caja negra está **debajo de** la caja blanca.

10. The pink box is **between** the purple box and the brown box.
La caja rosada está **entre** la caja morada y la caja marrón.

More vocabulary

near: in the same area
*The white box is **near** the black box.*

far from: not near
*The red box is **far from** the black box.*

| HOME | 1 | 8 |
| VISITOR | 2 | 2 |

SAN DIEGO
235 miles

Cardinals Cardinales

0 zero / cero	11 eleven / once	21 twenty-one / ventiuno	101 / one hundred one / ciento uno
1 one / uno	12 twelve / doce	22 twenty-two / veintidós	1,000 / one thousand / mil
2 two / dos	13 thirteen / trece	30 thirty / treinta	1,001 / one thousand one / mil uno
3 three / tres	14 fourteen / catorce	40 forty / cuarenta	10,000 / ten thousand / diez mil
4 four / cuatro	15 fifteen / quince	50 fifty / cincuenta	100,000 / one hundred thousand / cien mil
5 five / cinco	16 sixteen / dieciséis	60 sixty / sesenta	1,000,000 / one million / un millón
6 six / seis	17 seventeen / diecisiete	70 seventy / setenta	1,000,000,000 / one billion / mil millones
7 seven / siete	18 eighteen / dieciocho	80 eighty / ochenta	
8 eight / ocho	19 nineteen / diecinueve	90 ninety / noventa	
9 nine / nueve	20 twenty / veinte	100 one hundred / cien	
10 ten / diez			

Ordinals Ordinales

1st first / 1º primero	8th eighth / 8º octavo	15th fifteenth / 15º decimoquinto
2nd second / 2º segundo	9th ninth / 9º noveno	16th sixteenth / 16º decimosexto
3rd third / 3º tercero	10th tenth / 10º décimo	17th seventeenth / 17º decimoséptimo
4th fourth / 4º cuarto	11th eleventh / 11º decimoprimero	18th eighteenth / 18º decimoctavo
5th fifth / 5º quinto	12th twelfth / 12º decimosegundo	19th nineteenth / 19º decimonoveno
6th sixth / 6º sexto	13th thirteenth / 13º decimotercero	20th twentieth / 20º vigésimo
7th seventh / 7º séptimo	14th fourteenth / 14º decimocuarto	

Roman numerals Números romanos

I = 1	VII = 7	XXX = 30
II = 2	VIII = 8	XL = 40
III = 3	IX = 9	L = 50
IV = 4	X = 10	C = 100
V = 5	XV = 15	D = 500
VI = 6	XX = 20	M = 1,000

Fractions Fracciones

1. 1/8 one-eighth
un octavo

2. 1/4 one-fourth
un cuarto

3. 1/3 one-third
un tercio

4. 1/2 one-half
un medio

5. 3/4 three-fourths
tres cuartos

6. 1 whole
un entero

1 cup
3/4
2/3
1/2
1/3
1/4

Percents Porcentajes

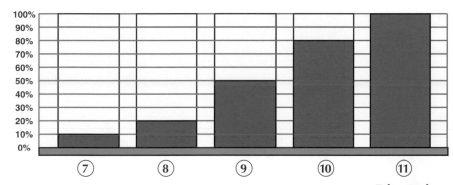

⑦ ⑧ ⑨ ⑩ ⑪

7. 10% ten percent
10% diez por ciento

8. 20% twenty percent
20% veinte por ciento

9. 50% fifty percent
50% cincuenta por ciento

10. 80% eighty percent
80% ochenta por ciento

11. 100% one hundred percent
100% cien por ciento

Dimensions Dimensiones

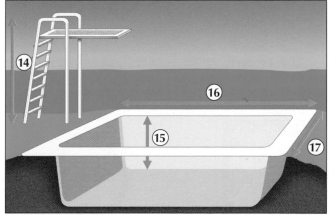

Measurement Medidas

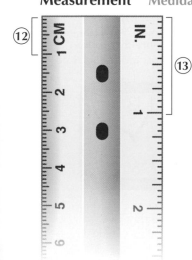

12. centimeter [cm]
centímetro [cm]

13. inch [in.]
pulgada [pulg.]

Equivalencies Equivalencias

1 inch = 2.54 centimeters
1 yard = .91 meters
1 mile = 1.6 kilometers

12 inches = 1 foot
3 feet   = 1 yard
1,760 yards = 1 mile

14. height
altura

15. depth
profundidad

16. length
largo

17. width
ancho

More vocabulary

measure: to find the size or amount of something

count: to find the total number of something

Share your answers.

1. How many students are in class today?

2. Who was the first person in class today?

3. How far is it from your home to your school?

Time La hora

1. second
el segundo

2. minute
el minuto

3. hour
la hora

A.M.

P.M.

4. 1:00
one o'clock
la una en punto

5. 1:05
one-oh-five
la una y cinco
five after one
la una y cinco

6. 1:10
one-ten
la una y diez
ten after one
la una y diez

7. 1:15
one-fifteen
la una y quince
a quarter after one
la una y cuarto

8. 1:20
one-twenty
la una y veinte
twenty after one
la una y veinte

9. 1:25
one twenty-five
la una y veinticinco
twenty-five after one
la una y veinticinco

10. 1:30
one-thirty
la una y treinta
half past one
la una y media

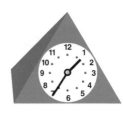

11. 1:35
one thirty-five
la una y treinta y cinco
twenty-five to two
veinticinco para las dos

12. 1:40
one-forty
la una y cuarenta
twenty to two
veinte para las dos

13. 1:45
one forty-five
la una y cuarenta y cinco
a quarter to two
un cuarto para las dos

14. 1:50
one-fifty
la una y cincuenta
ten to two
diez para las dos

15. 1:55
one fifty-five
la una y cincuenta y cinco
five to two
cinco para las dos

Talk about the time.

What time is it? It's 10:00 a.m.

What time do you wake up on weekdays? At 6:30 a.m.

What time do you wake up on weekends? At 9:30 a.m.

Share your answers.

1. How many hours a day do you study English?

2. You are meeting friends at 1:00. How long will you wait for them if they are late?

16. morning
la mañana

17. noon
el mediodía

18. afternoon
la tarde

19. evening
el anochecer

20. night
la noche

21. midnight
la medianoche

22. early
temprano

23. late
tarde

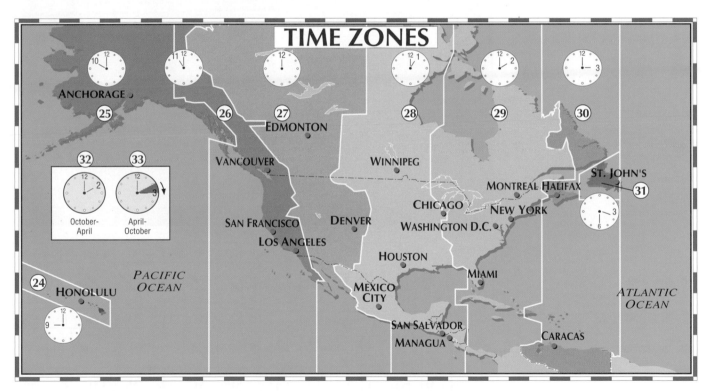

TIME ZONES

ANCHORAGE   **25**

26   **27**   EDMONTON

28   **29**   **30**

32   **33**
October-April   April-October

VANCOUVER

WINNIPEG

MONTREAL HALIFAX   ST. JOHN'S

31

CHICAGO   NEW YORK

SAN FRANCISCO   DENVER   WASHINGTON D.C.

LOS ANGELES

HOUSTON

24   HONOLULU   *PACIFIC OCEAN*

MIAMI

MEXICO CITY

ATLANTIC OCEAN

SAN SALVADOR
MANAGUA   CARACAS

24. Hawaii-Aleutian time
hora de Hawai-de las Aleutianas

25. Alaska time
hora de Alaska

26. Pacific time
hora del Pacífico

27. mountain time
hora de montaña

28. central time
hora del centro

29. eastern time
hora del este

30. Atlantic time
hora del Atlántico

31. Newfoundland time
hora de Terranova

32. standard time
hora estándar

33. daylight saving time
hora de verano

More vocabulary

on time: not early and not late
He's **on time.**

Share your answers.

1. When do you watch television? study? do housework?

2. Do you come to class on time? early? late?

The Calendar El calendario

Days of the week
Los días de la semana

1. Sunday
   domingo
2. Monday
   lunes
3. Tuesday
   martes
4. Wednesday
   miércoles
5. Thursday
   jueves
6. Friday
   viernes
7. Saturday
   sábado
8. year
   el año
9. month
   el mes
10. day
    el día
11. week
    la semana
12. weekdays
    los días de la semana
13. weekend
    el fin de semana
14. date
    la fecha
15. today
    hoy
16. tomorrow
    mañana
17. yesterday
    ayer
18. last week
    la semana pasada
19. this week
    esta semana
20. next week
    la semana próxima
21. every day
    todos los días
22. once a week
    una vez por semana
23. twice a week
    dos veces por semana
24. three times a week
    tres veces por semana

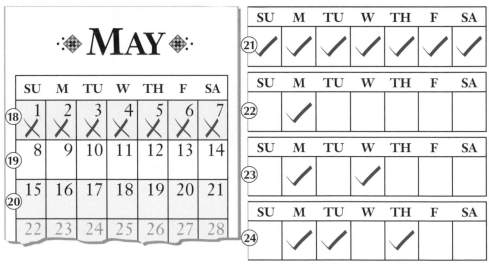

Talk about the calendar.
What's today's date? It's <u>March 10th</u>.
What day is it? It's <u>Tuesday</u>.
What day was yesterday? It was <u>Monday</u>.

Share your answers.
1. How often do you come to school?
2. How long have you been in this school?

2001

JAN (25)

SUN	MON	TUE	WED	THU	FRI	SAT
	1	2	3	4	5	6
7	8	9	10	11	12	13
14	15	16	17	18	19	20
21	22	23	24	25	26	27
28	29	30	31			

FEB (26)

SUN	MON	TUE	WED	THU	FRI	SAT
				1	2	3
4	5	6	7	8	9	10
11	12	13	14	15	16	17
18	19	20	21	22	23	24
25	26	27	28			

MAR (27)

SUN	MON	TUE	WED	THU	FRI	SAT
				1	2	3
4	5	6	7	8	9	10
11	12	13	14	15	16	17
18	19	20	21	22	23	24
25	26	27	28	29	30	31

APR (28)

SUN	MON	TUE	WED	THU	FRI	SAT
1	2	3	4	5	6	7
8	9	10	11	12	13	14
15	16	17	18	19	20	21
22	23	24	25	26	27	28
29	30					

MAY (29)

SUN	MON	TUE	WED	THU	FRI	SAT
		1	2	3	4	5
6	7	8	9	10	11	12
13	14	15	16	17	18	19
20	21	22	23	24	25	26
27	28	29	30	31		

JUN (30)

SUN	MON	TUE	WED	THU	FRI	SAT
					1	2
3	4	5	6	7	8	9
10	11	12	13	14	15	16
17	18	19	20	21	22	23
24	25	26	27	28	29	30

JUL (31)

SUN	MON	TUE	WED	THU	FRI	SAT
1	2	3	4	5	6	7
8	9	10	11	12	13	14
15	16	17	18	19	20	21
22	23	24	25	26	27	28
29	30	31				

AUG (32)

SUN	MON	TUE	WED	THU	FRI	SAT
			1	2	3	4
5	6	7	8	9	10	11
12	13	14	15	16	17	18
19	20	21	22	23	24	25
26	27	28	29	30	31	

SEP (33)

SUN	MON	TUE	WED	THU	FRI	SAT
						1
2	3	4	5	6	7	8
9	10	11	12	13	14	15
16	17	18	19	20	21	22
23/30	24	25	26	27	28	29

OCT (34)

SUN	MON	TUE	WED	THU	FRI	SAT
	1	2	3	4	5	6
7	8	9	10	11	12	13
14	15	16	17	18	19	20
21	22	23	24	25	26	27
28	29	30	31			

NOV (35)

SUN	MON	TUE	WED	THU	FRI	SAT
				1	2	3
4	5	6	7	8	9	10
11	12	13	14	15	16	17
18	19	20	21	22	23	24
25	26	27	28	29	30	

DEC (36)

SUN	MON	TUE	WED	THU	FRI	SAT
						1
2	3	4	5	6	7	8
9	10	11	12	13	14	15
16	17	18	19	20	21	22
23/30	24/31	25	26	27	28	29

Months of the year
Los meses del año

25. January
   enero
26. February
   febrero
27. March
   marzo
28. April
   abril
29. May
   mayo
30. June
   junio
31. July
   julio
32. August
   agosto
33. September
   septiembre
34. October
   octubre
35. November
   noviembre
36. December
   diciembre

Seasons
Las estaciones

MARCH 21

JUNE 21

SEPT. 21

DEC. 21

37. spring
   la primavera
38. summer
   el verano
39. fall
   el otoño
40. winter
   el invierno

JUNE 5 — TIM!

MARCH 2 — ANNIVERSARY

JULY 4 — INDEPENDENCE DAY — STATE BANK — CLOSED - JULY 4

APRIL 4 — EASTER SUNDAY

MAY 17 — DOCTOR 4:30

AUGUST

41. birthday
   el cumpleaños
42. anniversary
   el aniversario
43. legal holiday
   el día de fiesta oficial / el día feriado legal
44. religious holiday
   la fiesta religiosa
45. appointment
   la cita
46. vacation
   las vacaciones

Use the new language.
Look at the **ordinal numbers** on page **14**.
Use ordinal numbers to say the date.
It's June 5th. It's the fifth.

Talk about your birthday.
My birthday is in the winter.
My birthday is in January.
My birthday is on January twenty-sixth.

Money El dinero

Coins Las monedas

1. $.01 = 1¢
a penny / 1 cent
un centavo

2. $.05 = 5¢
a nickel / 5 cents
cinco centavos

3. $.10 = 10¢
a dime / 10 cents
diez centavos

4. $.25 = 25¢
a quarter / 25 cents
veinticinco centavos

5. $.50 = 50¢
a half dollar
medio dólar

6. $1.00
a silver dollar
un dólar de plata

Bills Los billetes

7. $1.00
a dollar
un dólar

8. $5.00
five dollars
cinco dólares

9. $10.00
ten dollars
diez dólares

10. $20.00
twenty dollars
veinte dólares

11. $50.00
fifty dollars
cincuenta dólares

12. $100.00
one hundred dollars
cien dólares

Ways to pay Formas de pagar

13. cash
el efectivo

14. personal check
el cheque personal

15. credit card
la tarjeta de crédito

16. money order
el giro postal

17. traveler's check
el cheque de viajero

More vocabulary

borrow: to get money from someone and return it later

lend: to give money to someone and get it back later

pay back: to return the money that you borrowed

Other ways to talk about money:

a dollar bill or *a one*

a five-dollar bill or *a five*

a ten-dollar bill or *a ten*

a twenty-dollar bill or *a twenty*

20

A. shop for
ir de compras para

B. sell
vender

C. pay for/**buy**
pagar / comprar

D. give
dar

E. keep
quedarse con

F. return
devolver

G. exchange
cambiar

1. price tag
la etiqueta del precio

2. regular price
el precio normal

3. sale price
el precio de oferta

4. bar code
el código de barra

5. receipt
el recibo

6. price/cost
el precio/el costo

7. sales tax
el impuesto de ventas

8. total
el total

9. change
el cambio

More vocabulary

When you use a credit card to shop, you get a **bill** in the mail. Bills list, in writing, the items you bought and the total you have to pay.

Share your answers.

1. Name three things you pay for every month.

2. Name one thing you will buy this week.

3. Where do you like to shop?

Age and Physical Description   Edad y descripción física

1. children los niños	**4.** 6-year-old boy el niño de 6 años	**7.** 13-year-old boy el muchacho de 13 años	**10.** woman la mujer
2. baby el bebé	**5.** 10-year-old girl la niña de 10 años	**8.** 19-year-old girl la muchacha de 19 años	**11.** man el hombre
3. toddler el niño pequeño	**6.** teenagers los adolescentes	**9.** adults los adultos	**12.** senior citizen el anciano/la anciana

 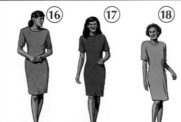 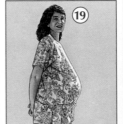 

13. young joven	**17.** average height de estatura promedio	**21.** average weight de peso promedio	**25.** physically challenged impedido(a)
14. middle-aged de edad media	**18.** short bajo(a)	**22.** thin/slim flaco(a)/delgado(a)	**26.** sight impaired/blind impedido visual/ciego(a)
15. elderly de edad avanzada	**19.** pregnant embarazada	**23.** attractive atractivo(a)	**27.** hearing impaired/deaf con problemas auditivos/sordo(a)
16. tall alto(a)	**20.** heavyset fornido(a)/corpulento(a)	**24.** cute atractivo(a)	

Talk about yourself and your teacher.

I am _young_, _average height_, and _average weight_.

My teacher is _a middle-aged_, _tall_, _thin_ man.

Use the new language.

Turn to **Hobbies and Games,** pages **162–163.**

Describe each person on the page.

He's _a heavyset_, _short_, _senior citizen_.

22

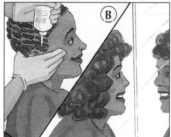

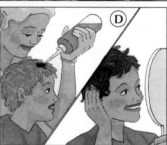

1. short hair
el cabello corto

2. shoulder-length hair
el cabello a la altura de
los hombros

3. long hair
el cabello largo

4. part
la raya

5. mustache
el bigote

6. beard
la barba

7. sideburns
las patillas

8. bangs
el flequillo/el fleco

9. straight hair
el cabello liso

10. wavy hair
el cabello ondulado

11. curly hair
el cabello rizado

12. bald
calvo

13. gray hair
las canas

14. red hair
pelirrojo(a)

15. black hair
el cabello negro

16. blond hair
el cabello rubio

17. brown hair
el cabello castaño

18. brush
el cepillo

19. scissors
las tijeras

20. blow dryer
el secador

21. rollers
los rizadores

22. comb
el peine/la peinilla

A. cut hair
cortar el cabello

B. perm hair
hacer la permanente

C. set hair
rizar el cabello

D. color hair/**dye** hair
teñir el cabello

More vocabulary

hair stylist: a person who cuts, sets, and perms hair

hair salon: the place where a hair stylist works

Talk about your hair.

My hair is _long_, _straight_, and _brown_.

I have _long_, _straight_, _brown_ hair.

When I was a child my hair was _short_, _curly_, and _blond_.

Family   La familia

Tom Lee's Family

1. grandparents
los abuelos

Min   *Lu*

2. grandmother
la abuela

3. grandfather
el abuelo

4. parents
los padres

Rose   *Chang*   *Helen*   *Daniel*

5. mother
la madre

6. father
el padre

10. aunt
la tía

11. uncle
el tío

Tom

Lily   *Alex*   *Emily*

8. sister
la hermana

9. brother
el hermano

12. cousin
la prima

7. (Min and Lu's)
grandson
El nieto
(de Min y Lu)

Berta   *Mario*   **Ana Garcia's
Family**

13. mother-in-law
la suegra

14. father-in-law
el suegro

Ana

Marta   *Carlos*   *Tito*

20. (Tito's) wife
la esposa
(de Tito)

15. sister-in-law
la cuñada

16. brother-in-law
el cuñado

19. husband
el esposo

Alice   *Eddie*   *Sara*   *Felix*

17. niece
la sobrina

18. nephew
el sobrino

21. daughter
la hija

22. son
el hijo

More vocabulary

Lily and Emily are Min and Lu's **granddaughters**.

Daniel is Min and Lu's **son-in-law**.

Ana is Berta and Mario's **daughter-in-law**.

Share your answers.

1. How many brothers and sisters do you have?

2. What number son or daughter are you?

3. Do you have any children?

24

Lisa Smith's Family

23. married
casados

Carol · Dan

Lisa

24. divorced
divorciados

25. single mother
la madre soltera

26. single father
el padre soltero

Rick · Carol

27. remarried
casados
nuevamente

Dan · Sue

Rick · Carol

28. stepfather
el padrastro

David

Mary

29. half brother
el medio hermano

30. half sister
la media hermana

Lisa

Dan · Sue

31. stepmother
la madrastra

Kim · Bill

32. stepsister
la hermanastra

33. stepbrother
el hermanastro

More vocabulary

Carol is Dan's **former wife**.

Sue is Dan's **wife**.

Dan is Carol's **former husband**.

Rick is Carol's **husband**.

Lisa is the **stepdaughter** of both Rick and Sue.

A. wake up
despertarse

B. get up
levantarse

C. take a shower
tomar una ducha

D. get dressed
vestirse

E. eat breakfast
desayunar

F. make lunch
preparar el almuerzo

G. take the children to school
llevar a los niños al colegio

H. take the bus to school
tomar el autobús para ir al colegio

I. drive to work/**go** to work
conducir al trabajo/**ir** al trabajo

J. be in school
estar en la escuela

K. work
trabajar

L. go to the market
ir al mercado

M. leave work
salir del trabajo

Grammar point: 3rd person singular

For **he** and **she**, we add **-s** or **-es** to the verb.

He/She wake**s** up.

He/She watch**es** TV.

These verbs are different (irregular):

be   He/She **is** in school at 10:00 a.m.

have   He/She **has** dinner at 6:30 p.m.

5:30 P.M. N O

6:00 P.M. P Q

6:30 P.M. R

7:30 P.M. S T

8:00 P.M. U V

8:30 P.M. W

10:30 P.M. X

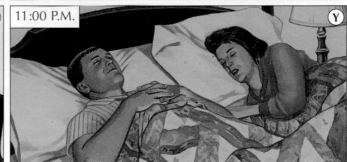

11:00 P.M. Y

N. clean the house
limpiar la casa

O. pick up the children
recoger a los niños

P. cook dinner
preparar la cena

Q. come home/**get** home
venir a la casa/**llegar** a la casa

R. have dinner
cenar

S. watch TV
mirar la tele

T. do homework
hacer la tarea

U. relax
descansar

V. read the paper
leer el periódico

W. exercise
hacer ejercicios

X. go to bed
acostarse

Y. go to sleep
dormirse

Talk about your daily routine.

I take _a shower_ in _the morning_.

I go to _school_ in _the evening_.

I go to _bed_ at _11 o'clock_.

Share your answers.

1. Who makes dinner in your family?

2. Who goes to the market?

3. Who goes to work?

A. be born
nacer

B. start school
empezar a ir al colegio

C. immigrate
inmigrar

D. graduate
graduarse

E. learn to drive
aprender a manejar

F. join the army
unirse al ejército/**alistarse**
en el ejército

G. get a job
conseguir empleo

H. become a citizen
convertirse en ciudadano

I. rent an apartment
alquilar un apartamento

J. go to college
ir a la universidad

K. fall in love
enamorarse

L. get married
casarse

Grammar point: past tense

start		
learn		
join	+ed	
rent		
travel		

immigrate		
graduate		
move	+d	
retire		
die		

These verbs are different (irregular):

be	— was	have — had
get	— got	buy — bought
become	— became	
go	— went	
fall	— fell	

 1960
 1967

M. have a baby
tener un bebé

N. travel
viajar

1971
1971

O. buy a house
comprar una casa

P. move
mudarse

1985
1997

Q. have a grandchild
tener un nieto/una nieta

R. die
morir

1. birth certificate
la partida/el acta de nacimiento
2. diploma
el diploma
3. Resident Alien card
la tarjeta de residente permanente

4. driver's license
la licencia de manejar
5. Social Security card
la tarjeta del seguro social
6. Certificate of Naturalization
el certificado de naturalización

7. college degree
el diploma universitario
8. marriage license
la licencia de matrimonio
9. passport
el pasaporte

More vocabulary

When a husband dies, his wife becomes a **widow**.
When a wife dies, her husband becomes a **widower**.
When older people stop working, we say they **retire**.

Talk about yourself.

I was born in 1968.
I learned to drive in 1987.
I immigrated in 1990.

Feelings Estados de ánimo y sentimientos

1. hot
   tener calor
2. thirsty
   tener sed
3. sleepy
   estar cansado(a)

4. cold
   tener frío
5. hungry
   tener hambre
6. full
   sentirse satisfecho(a)

7. comfortable
   cómodo(a)
8. uncomfortable
   incómodo(a)
9. disgusted
   sentir asco
10. calm
    tranquilo(a)
11. nervous
    nervioso(a)

12. in pain
    adolorido(a)
13. worried
    preocupado(a)
14. sick
    enfermo(a)
15. well
    bien
16. relieved
    aliviado(a)

17. hurt
    lastimado(a)
18. lonely
    solo(a)
19. in love
    enamorado(a)

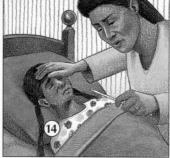

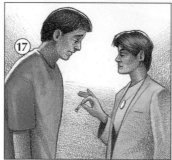

More vocabulary
furious: very angry
terrified: very scared
overjoyed: very happy

exhausted: very tired
starving: very hungry
humiliated: very embarrassed

Talk about your feelings.
I feel _happy_ when I see _my friends_.
I feel _homesick_ when I think about _my family_.

20. sad
   triste
21. homesick
   nostálgico(a)
22. proud
   orgulloso(a)

23. excited
   emocionado(a)
24. scared
   asustado(a)
25. embarrassed
   avergonzado(a)

26. bored
   aburrido(a)
27. confused
   confundido(a)
28. frustrated
   frustrado(a)

29. angry
   enojado(a)
30. upset
   molesto(a)

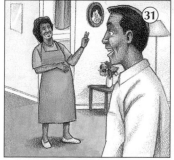

31. surprised
   sorprendido(a)
32. happy
   contento(a)
33. tired
   cansado(a)

Use the new language.

Look at **Clothing I,** page **64,** and answer the questions.

1. How does the runner feel?

2. How does the man at the bus stop feel?

3. How does the woman at the bus stop feel?

4. How do the teenagers feel?

5. How does the little boy feel?

A Graduation Una graduación

The Ceremony

1. graduating class
   los graduandos
2. gown
   la toga
3. cap
   el birrete
4. stage
   el escenario/el estrado

5. podium
   el podio
6. graduate
   el graduado
7. diploma
   el diploma
8. valedictorian
   la oradora estudiantil

9. guest speaker
   el orador invitado
10. audience
    el público
11. photographer
    el fotógrafo
A. **graduate**
   graduarse

B. **applaud / clap**
   aplaudir
C. **cry**
   llorar
D. **take** a picture
   tomar una foto
E. **give** a speech
   dar un discurso

Talk about what the people in the pictures are doing.

She is [tak**ing** a picture.
       giv**ing** a speech.
       smil**ing**.
       laugh**ing**.

He is [mak**ing** a toast.
      clap**ping**.

They are [graduat**ing**.
         hug**ging**.
         kiss**ing**.
         applaud**ing**.

The Party

12. caterer el encargado del banquete	**15.** banner la pancarta/la bandera	**18.** gifts los regalos	**H.** laugh reír
13. buffet el bufet/el ambigú	**16.** dance floor la pista de baile	**F.** kiss besar	**I.** make a toast brindar
14. guests los invitados	**17.** DJ (disc jockey) el DJ (el disc jockey)	**G.** hug abrazar	**J.** dance bailar

Share your answers.

1. Did you ever go to a graduation? Whose?

2. Did you ever give a speech? Where?

3. Did you ever hear a great speaker? Where?

4. Did you ever go to a graduation party?

5. What do you like to eat at parties?

6. Do you like to dance at parties?

33

Places to Live   Lugares para vivir

1. the city/an urban area
la ciudad/un área urbana

2. the suburbs
los suburbios/las afueras

3. a small town
un pueblo pequeño

4. the country/a rural area
el campo/un área rural

5. apartment building
el edificio de apartamentos

6. house
la casa

7. townhouse
la residencia urbana

8. mobile home
la casa rodante/la casa móvil

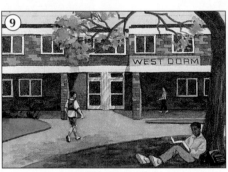

9. college dormitory
la residencia universitaria

10. shelter
el refugio

11. nursing home
el hogar de ancianos

12. ranch
la hacienda/el rancho

13. farm
la granja

More vocabulary

duplex house: a house divided into two homes

condominium: an apartment building where each apartment is owned separately

co-op: an apartment building owned by the residents

Share your answers.

1. Do you like where you live?

2. Where did you live in your country?

3. What types of housing are there near your school?

Renting an apartment   Alquilando un apartamento

A. look for a new apartment
buscar un nuevo apartamento

B. talk to the manager
hablar con el conserje

C. sign a rental agreement
firmar un contrato de alquiler/renta

D. move in
mudarse

E. unpack
desempacar

F. pay the rent
pagar el alquiler/la renta

Buying a house   Comprando una casa

G. talk to the Realtor
hablar con el agente de bienes raíces

H. make an offer
hacer una oferta

I. get a loan
obtener un préstamo

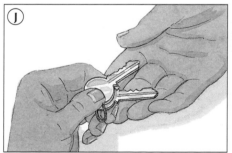

J. take ownership
asumir la propiedad

K. arrange the furniture
arreglar los muebles

L. pay the mortgage
pagar la hipoteca

More vocabulary

lease: a rental agreement for a specific period of time
utilities: gas, water, and electricity for the home

Practice talking to an apartment manager.

How much is the rent?
Are utilities included?
When can I move in?

35

Entrance

202

Apartment Aval.
2BD + 2BA
Sec. Sys.
555-4263

Laundry Room

Recreation Room

Garage

1. first floor
el primer piso

2. second floor
el segundo piso

3. third floor
el tercer piso

4. fourth floor
el cuarto piso

5. roof garden
el jardín aéreo

6. playground
el parque

7. fire escape
la salida de incendios

8. intercom/speaker
el intercomunicador

9. security system
el sistema de seguridad

10. doorman
el portero

11. vacancy sign
el letrero de "se alquila"

12. manager/superintendent
el conserje/el superintendente

13. security gate
la puerta/la reja de seguridad

14. storage locker
el maletero/el depósito de
almacenamiento

15. parking space
el espacio de estacionamiento

More vocabulary

rec room: a short way of saying **recreation room**

basement: the area below the street level of an apartment
or a house

Talk about where you live.

I live in <u>Apartment 3 near the entrance.</u>

I live in <u>Apartment 11 on the second floor near the fire</u>
<u>*escape.*</u>

16. swimming pool
la piscina/la alberca

17. balcony
el balcón

18. courtyard
el patio

19. air conditioner
el aire acondicionado

20. trash bin
el depósito de basura

21. alley
el callejón

22. neighbor
el vecino/la vecina

23. fire exit
la salida de incendios

24. trash chute
el conducto para basura

25. smoke detector
el detector de humo

26. stairway
las escaleras

27. peephole
el ojo mágico/la mirilla

28. door chain
la cadena para puerta

29. dead-bolt lock
el cerrojo de seguridad

30. doorknob
la perilla de la puerta

31. key
la llave

32. landlord
el arrendador/el dueño

33. tenant
el inquilino/el arrendatario

34. elevator
el elevador/el ascensor

35. stairs
las escaleras

36. mailboxes
los buzones

Grammar point: *there is, there are*

singular: *there is*   plural: *there are*

There is *a fire exit in the hallway.*

There are *mailboxes in the lobby.*

Talk about apartments.

My apartment has an elevator, a lobby, and a rec room.

My apartment doesn't have a pool or a garage.

My apartment needs air conditioning.

A House   Una casa

1. **floor plan**
   la planta

2. **backyard**
   el patio

3. **fence**
   la cerca

4. **mailbox**
   el buzón

5. **driveway**
   la entrada del garaje

6. **garage**
   el garaje

7. **garage door**
   la puerta del garaje

8. **screen door**
   la puerta mosquitero

9. **porch light**
   la luz del porche

10. **doorbell**
    el timbre

11. **front door**
    la puerta principal

12. **storm door**
    la contrapuerta

13. **steps**
    los escalones/los peldaños

14. **front walk**
    la vereda/el caminito

15. **front yard**
    el jardín

16. **deck**
    la terraza

17. **window**
    la ventana

18. **shutter**
    la persiana

19. **gutter**
    el canal/el canalón

20. **roof**
    el tejado/el techo

21. **chimney**
    la chimenea

22. **TV antenna**
    la antena de tele

More vocabulary

two-story house: a house with two floors

downstairs: the bottom floor

upstairs: the part of a house above the bottom floor

Share your answers.

1. What do you like about this house?

2. What's something you don't like about the house?

3. Describe the perfect house.

1. hedge
   el seto
2. hammock
   la hamaca
3. garbage can
   el recipiente de basura
4. leaf blower
   el soplador de hojas
5. patio furniture
   los muebles del patio
6. patio
   el patio
7. barbecue grill
   la parrilla

8. sprinkler
   el rociador
9. hose
   la manguera
10. compost pile
    la pila de abono
11. rake
    el rastrillo
12. hedge clippers
    las tijeras para setos
13. shovel
    la pala
14. trowel
    el desplantador

15. pruning shears
    las tijeras de podar
16. wheelbarrow
    la carretilla
17. watering can
    la regadera
18. flowerpot
    la maceta/el tiesto
19. flower
    la flor
20. bush
    el arbusto
21. lawn
    el césped

22. lawn mower
    la cortadora de césped
A. **weed** the flower bed
   quitar la maleza de las flores
B. **water** the plants
   regar las plantas
C. **mow** the lawn
   cortar el césped
D. **plant** a tree
   plantar un árbol
E. **trim** the hedge
   podar el seto
F. **rake** the leaves
   rastrillar las hojas

Talk about your yard and gardening.

I like to plant trees.

I don't like to weed.

I like/don't like to work in the yard/garden.

Share your answers.

1. What flowers, trees, or plants do you see in the picture? (Look at **Trees, Plants, and Flowers,** pages **128–129** for help.)
2. Do you ever use a barbecue grill to cook?

1. cabinet
el gabinete

2. paper towels
las toallas de papel

3. dish drainer
el escurridor de platos

4. dishwasher
el lavaplatos

5. garbage disposal
el triturador de
desperdicios

6. sink
el fregador/el fregadero

7. toaster
la tostadora/el tostador
de pan

8. shelf
el estante

9. refrigerator
el refrigerador/la nevera

10. freezer
el congelador

11. coffeemaker
la cafetera

12. blender
la licuadora

13. microwave oven
el horno microondas

14. electric can opener
el abrelatas eléctrico

15. toaster oven
el horno tostador

16. pot
la olla/la cacerola

17. teakettle
la tetera

18. stove
la estufa/la cocina

19. burner
la hornilla

20. oven
el horno

21. broiler
la parrilla

22. counter
el tope/el mostrador

23. drawer
el cajón/la gaveta

24. pan
la sartén

25. electric mixer
la batidora eléctrica

26. food processor
el procesador de
alimentos

27. cutting board
la tabla de cortar/picar

Talk about the location of kitchen items.

The toaster oven is *on the counter* *near the stove*.

The microwave is *above the stove*.

Share your answers.

1. Do you have a garbage disposal? a dishwasher?
a microwave?

2. Do you eat in the kitchen?

1. china cabinet
   la vitrina para la vajilla

2. set of dishes
   el juego de platos

3. platter
   el platón/el plato grande

4. ceiling fan
   el ventilador de techo

5. light fixture
   la lámpara

6. serving dish
   la fuente

7. candle
   la vela

8. candlestick
   el candelero

9. vase
   el florero

10. tray
    la bandeja/la charola

11. teapot
    la tetera

12. sugar bowl
    la azucarera

13. creamer
    la lechera

14. saltshaker
    el salero

15. pepper shaker
    el pimentero

16. dining room chair
    la silla del comedor

17. dining room table
    la mesa del comedor

18. tablecloth
    el mantel

19. napkin
    la servilleta

20. place mat
    el mantel individual

21. fork
    el tenedor

22. knife
    el cuchillo

23. spoon
    la cuchara

24. plate
    el plato

25. bowl
    el tazón/el plato hondo

26. glass
    el vaso

27. coffee cup
    la taza de café

28. mug
    la taza grande/el jarro

Practice asking for things in the dining room.

Please pass the platter.

May I have the creamer?

Could I have a fork, please?

Share your answers.

1. What are the women in the picture saying?

2. In your home, where do you eat?

3. Do you like to make dinner for your friends?

41

A Living Room   Una sala

1. bookcase
   el librero

2. basket
   la cesta

3. track lighting
   la luz móvil

4. lightbulb
   la bombilla/el foco

5. ceiling
   el techo

6. wall
   la pared

7. painting
   el cuadro

8. mantel
   la repisa de la chimenea

9. fireplace
   el hogar/la chimenea

10. fire
    el fuego

11. fire screen
    la pantalla de protección

12. logs
    los leños

13. wall unit
    la estantería

14. stereo system
    el estéreo/el equipo de
    sonido

15. floor lamp
    la lámpara de pie

16. drapes
    las cortinas

17. window
    la ventana

18. plant
    la planta

19. sofa/couch
    el sofá

20. throw pillow
    el cojín

21. end table
    la mesita

22. magazine holder
    el revistero

23. coffee table
    la mesa de centro

24. armchair/easy chair
    la butaca/el sillón

25. love seat
    el sofá para dos

26. TV (television)
    la tele (televisión)

27. carpet
    la alfombra

Use the new language.

Look at **Colors,** page **12,** and describe this room.

There is __a gray sofa__ and __a gray armchair__.

Talk about your living room.

In my living room I have __a sofa__, __two chairs__, and __a coffee table__.

I don't have __a fireplace__ or __a wall unit__.

1. hamper la cesta para la ropa	**8.** towel rack la repisa para toallas/ el toallero	**15.** toilet paper el papel higiénico	**22.** sink el lavamanos
2. bathtub la bañera	**9.** tile la porcelana/el azulejo	**16.** toilet brush el cepillo para el inodoro	**23.** soap el jabón
3. rubber mat la alfombra de goma/ el tapete de hule	**10.** showerhead el cabezal de la ducha	**17.** toilet el inodoro	**24.** soap dish la jabonera
4. drain el desagüe	**11.** (mini)blinds las (mini) persianas	**18.** mirror el espejo	**25.** wastebasket la papelera
5. hot water el agua caliente	**12.** bath towel la toalla de baño	**19.** medicine cabinet el gabinete de baño/ el botiquín	**26.** scale la balanza/ la báscula
6. faucet el grifo/la llave	**13.** hand towel la toalla de manos	**20.** toothbrush el cepillo de dientes	**27.** bath mat la alfombrilla para baño
7. cold water el agua fría	**14.** washcloth la toalla para frotarse	**21.** toothbrush holder el portacepillos	

More vocabulary

half bath: a bathroom without a shower or bathtub

linen closet: a closet or cabinet for towels and sheets

stall shower: a shower without a bathtub

Share your answers.

1. Do you turn off the water when you brush your teeth? wash your hair? shave?

2. Does your bathroom have a bathtub or a stall shower?

A Bedroom   Un dormitorio

1. mirror
   el espejo

2. dresser/bureau
   la cómoda

3. drawer
   la gaveta/el cajón

4. closet
   el clóset

5. curtains
   las cortinas

6. window shade
   la persiana

7. photograph
   la fotografía

8. bed
   la cama

9. pillow
   la almohada

10. pillowcase
    la funda

11. bedspread
    el cubrecama/la colcha

12. blanket
    la cobija/la manta

13. flat sheet
    la sábana

14. fitted sheet
    la sábana esquinera

15. headboard
    la cabecera

16. clock radio
    el radio reloj

17. lamp
    la lámpara

18. lampshade
    la pantalla de lámpara

19. light switch
    el interruptor de la luz

20. outlet
    el enchufe/el
    tomacorrientes

21. night table
    la mesita de noche

22. dust ruffle
    el volante

23. rug
    la alfombra

24. floor
    el piso

25. mattress
    el colchón

26. box spring
    el box spring/el muelle

27. bed frame
    el marco de la cama

Use the new language.

Describe this room. (See **Describing Things,** page **11,** for help.)

I see a soft pillow and a beautiful bedspread.

Share your answers.

1. What is your favorite thing in your bedroom?

2. Do you have a clock in your bedroom? Where is it?

3. Do you have a mirror in your bedroom? Where is it?

1. bunk bed
la litera

2. comforter
el edredón/la colcha

3. night-light
la luz de noche

4. mobile
el móvil

5. wallpaper
el papel tapiz

6. crib
la cuna

7. bumper pad
el protector

8. chest of drawers
el gavetero/la cómoda

9. baby monitor
el monitor para bebés

10. teddy bear
el osito

11. smoke detector
el detector de humo

12. changing table
la mesa para cambiar
pañales

13. diaper pail
el recipiente para pañales

14. dollhouse
la casa de muñecas

15. blocks
los bloques

16. ball
la pelota

17. picture book
el libro de dibujos

18. doll
la muñeca

19. cradle
la cuna mecedora

20. coloring book
el libro de pintar

21. crayons
los creyones

22. puzzle
el rompecabezas

23. stuffed animals
los animales de peluche

24. toy chest
el baúl para juguetes

Talk about where items are in the room.

The dollhouse is near _the coloring book_.

The teddy bear is on _the chest of drawers_.

Share your answers.

1. Do you think this is a good room for children? Why?

2. What toys did you play with when you were a child?

3. What children's stories do you know?

A. **dust** the furniture **sacudir** los muebles	**G.** **make** the bed **hacer** la cama	**M.** **wash** the dishes **lavar** los platos
B. **recycle** the newspapers **reciclar** los periódicos	**H.** **put away** the toys **guardar** los juguetes	**N.** **dry** the dishes **secar** los platos
C. **clean** the oven **limpiar** el horno	**I.** **vacuum** the carpet **aspirar** la alfombra	**O.** **wipe** the counter **limpiar** el mostrador/la barra
D. **wash** the windows **lavar** las ventanas	**J.** **mop** the floor **trapear/limpiar** el piso	**P.** **change** the sheets **cambiar** las sábanas
E. **sweep** the floor **barrer** el piso	**K.** **polish** the furniture **pulir** los muebles	**Q.** **take out** the garbage **sacar** la basura
F. **empty** the wastebasket **vaciar** la papelera	**L.** **scrub** the floor **restregar/fregar** el piso	

Talk about yourself.

I wash <u>the dishes</u> every day.

I change <u>the sheets</u> every week.

I never <u>dry the dishes</u>.

Share your answers.

1. Who does the housework in your family?

2. What is your favorite cleaning job?

3. What is your least favorite cleaning job?

1. feather duster
   el plumero

2. recycling bin
   el recipiente de reciclaje

3. oven cleaner
   el limpiador de hornos

4. rubber gloves
   los guantes de goma

5. steel-wool soap pads
   las esponjas de lana de acero

6. rags
   los trapos

7. stepladder
   la escalerilla

8. glass cleaner
   el limpiador de vidrios

9. squeegee
   el escurridor

10. broom
    la escoba

11. dustpan
    la pala/el recogedor

12. trash bags
    las bolsas para basura

13. vacuum cleaner
    la aspiradora

14. vacuum cleaner attachments
    los accesorios para aspiradora

15. vacuum cleaner bag
    la bolsa para aspiradora

16. wet mop
    la mopa/el trapeador

17. dust mop
    el sacudidor

18. furniture polish
    la cera para muebles

19. scrub brush
    el cepillo de frotar/de fregar

20. bucket/pail
    el cubo/el balde/la cubeta

21. dishwashing liquid
    el líquido lavaplatos

22. dish towel
    la toalla para platos

23. cleanser
    el limpiador

24. sponge
    la esponja

Practice asking for the items.

I want to <u>wash the windows</u>.

Please hand me <u>the squeegee</u>.

I have to <u>sweep the floor</u>.

Can you get me <u>the broom</u>, please?

1. The water heater is **not working**.
   El calentador de agua **no funciona**.

2. The power is **out**.
   No hay electricidad.

3. The roof is **leaking**.
   El techo **gotea**.

4. The wall is **cracked**.
   La pared está **agrietada**.

5. The window is **broken**.
   La ventana está **rota**.

6. The lock is **broken**.
   La cerradura está **estropeada**.

7. The steps are **broken**.
   Los escalones están **rotos**.

8. roofer
   el reparador de techos

9. electrician
   el electricista

10. repair person
    el reparador

11. locksmith
    el cerrajero

12. carpenter
    el carpintero

13. fuse box
    la caja de fusibles

14. gas meter
    el medidor de gas

Use the new language.

Look at **Tools and Building Supplies,** pages **150–151.**

Name the tools you use for household repairs.

I use a hammer and nails to fix a broken step.

I use a wrench to repair a dripping faucet.

15. The furnace is **broken**.
La caldera está **estropeada**.

16. The faucet is **dripping**.
El grifo / la llave **gotea.**

17. The sink is **overflowing**.
El lavamanos / el lavaplatos se **desborda.**

18. The toilet is **stopped up**.
El inodoro está **tapado.**

19. The pipes are **frozen**.
Los tuberías están **congeladas.**

20. plumber
el plomero

21. exterminator
el fumigador

Household pests

Las plagas domésticas

22. termite(s)
la(s) termita(s) / los comejenes

23. flea(s)
la(s) pulga(s)

24. ant(s)
la(s) hormiga(s)

25. cockroach(es)
la(s) cucaracha(s)

26. mice*
los ratones

27. rat(s)
la(s) rata(s)

*Note: *one mouse, two mice*

More vocabulary

fix: to repair something that is broken

exterminate: to kill household pests

pesticide: a chemical that is used to kill household pests

Share your answers.

1. Who does household repairs in your home?

2. What is the worst problem a home can have?

3. What is the most expensive problem a home can have?

TODAY

BANANAS 2lb/1.00

BLUEBERRIES 1.99 pint

1. grapes
las uvas

2. pineapples
las piñas

3. bananas
los plátanos

4. apples
las manzanas

5. peaches
los duraznos/los
melocotones

6. pears
las peras

7. apricots
los albaricoques

8. plums
las ciruelas

9. grapefruit
las toronjas

10. oranges
las naranjas

11. lemons
los limones

12. limes
las limas/los limones
verdes

13. tangerines
las naranjas mandarinas

14. avocadoes
los aguacates

15. cantaloupes
los melones

16. cherries
las cerezas

17. strawberries
las fresas

18. raspberries
las frambuesas

19. blueberries
los arándanos

20. papayas
las papayas/lechosas

21. mangoes
los mangos

22. coconuts
los cocos

23. nuts
las nueces

24. watermelons
las sandías

25. dates
los dátiles

26. prunes
las ciruelas pasas

27. raisins
las pasas

28. not ripe
verde

29. ripe
maduro(a)

30. rotten
podrido(a)/
pasado(a)

Language note: *a bunch of*

We say *a bunch of grapes* and *a bunch of bananas*.

Share your answers.

1. Which fruits do you put in a fruit salad?

2. Which fruits are sold in your area in the summer?

3. What fruits did you have in your country?

1. lettuce
   la lechuga

2. cabbage
   la col

3. carrots
   las zanahorias

4. zucchini
   la calabacita/el calabacín

5. radishes
   los rábanos

6. beets
   los betabeles/las remolachas

7. sweet peppers
   los pimientos morrones/los pimentones

8. chili peppers
   los chiles/los ajíes

9. celery
   el apio

10. parsley
    el perejil

11. spinach
    la espinaca

12. cucumbers
    los pepinos

13. squash
    la calabaza

14. turnips
    los nabos

15. broccoli
    el brócoli

16. cauliflower
    la coliflor

17. scallions
    las cebollitas

18. eggplants
    las berenjenas

19. peas
    los chícharos/los guisantes

20. artichokes
    las alcachofas

21. potatoes
    las papas

22. yams
    las batatas

23. tomatoes
    los tomates

24. asparagus
    los espárragos

25. string beans
    los ejotes/las judías verde

26. mushrooms
    los hongos

27. corn
    el maíz

28. onions
    las cebollas

29. garlic
    el ajo

Language note: *a bunch of, a head of*

We say *a bunch of carrots, a bunch of celery,* and *a bunch of spinach.*

We say *a head of lettuce, a head of cabbage,* and *a head of cauliflower.*

Share your answers.

1. Which vegetables do you eat raw? cooked?

2. Which vegetables need to be in the refrigerator?

3. Which vegetables don't need to be in the refrigerator?

Meat and Poultry   Carne y aves de corral

MEAT

Beef   Carne de res

1. roast beef
el rosbif

2. steak
el filete/el bistec

3. stewing beef
la carne para guisar

4. ground beef
la carne molida

5. beef ribs
las costillas de res

6. veal cutlets
las chuletas de ternera

7. liver
el hígado

8. tripe
el mondongo/la tripa

Pork   Carne de cerdo

9. ham
el jamón

10. pork chops
las chuletas de cerdo

11. bacon
el tocino

12. sausage
la salchicha

Lamb   Carne de cordero

13. lamb shanks
los jarretes de cordero

14. leg of lamb
la pierna de cordero

15. lamb chops
las chuletas de cordero

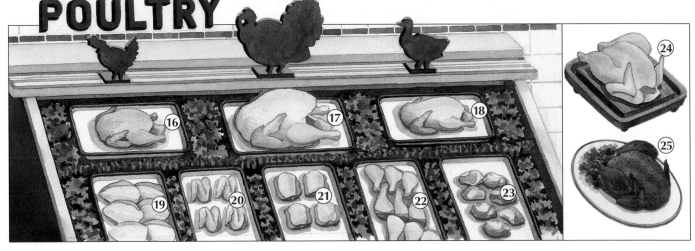

POULTRY

16. chicken
el pollo

17. turkey
el pavo

18. duck
el pato

19. breasts
las pechugas

20. wings
las alas

21. thighs
los muslos

22. drumsticks
las patas

23. gizzards
las mollejas

24. **raw** chicken
el pollo **crudo**

25. **cooked** chicken
el pollo **cocido**

More vocabulary

vegetarian: a person who doesn't eat meat

Meat and poultry without bones are called **boneless**.

Poultry without skin is called **skinless**.

Share your answers.

1. What kind of meat do you eat most often?

2. What kind of meat do you use in soup?

3. What part of the chicken do you like the most?

DELI

1. white bread
   el pan blanco

2. wheat bread
   el pan de trigo

3. rye bread
   el pan de centeno

4. smoked turkey
   el pavo ahumado

5. salami
   el salami

6. pastrami
   el pastrami

7. roast beef
   el rosbif

8. corned beef
   la cecina/la carne en conserva

9. American cheese
   el queso americano

10. cheddar cheese
    el queso cheddar

11. Swiss cheese
    el queso suizo

12. jack cheese
    el queso tipo jack

13. potato salad
    la ensalada de papas

14. coleslaw
    la ensalada de col fresca

15. pasta salad
    la ensalada de pasta

SEAFOOD

Fish Pescado

16. trout
    la trucha

17. catfish
    el bagre

18. whole salmon
    el salmón entero

19. salmon steak
    el bistec de salmón

20. halibut
    el halibut

21. filet of sole
    los filetes de lenguado

Shellfish Moluscos y crustáceos

22. crab
    el cangrejo

23. lobster
    la langosta

24. shrimp
    el camarón

25. scallops
    los escalopes

26. mussels
    los mejillones

27. oysters
    las ostras

28. clams
    las almejas

29. **fresh** fish
    el pescado **fresco**

30. **frozen** fish
    el pescado **congelado**

Practice ordering a sandwich.

I'd like _roast beef_ and _American cheese_ on _rye bread_.

Tell what you want on it.

Please put _tomato_, _lettuce_, _onions_, and _mustard_ on it.

Share your answers.

1. Do you like to eat fish?

2. Do you buy fresh or frozen fish?

1. bottle return
la devolución de
botellas

**2. meat and poultry
section**
la sección de carne y
aves de corral

3. shopping cart
el carrito

4. canned goods
los productos
enlatados

5. aisle
el pasillo

6. baked goods
los productos de
pastelería

7. shopping basket
la canasta

8. manager
el gerente

9. dairy section
la sección de
productos lácteos

10. pet food
la comida para mascotas

11. produce section
las verduras,
hortalizas y frutas

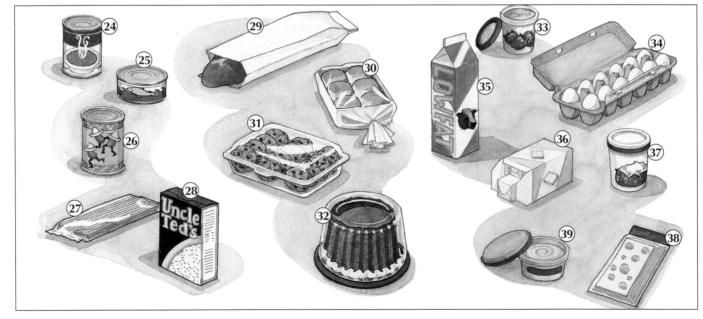

24. soup
la sopa

25. tuna
el atún

26. beans
los frijoles/las habichuelas

27. spaghetti
los espaguetis

28. rice
el arroz

29. bread
el pan

30. rolls
los panecillos

31. cookies
las galletas dulces

32. cake
el pastel/bizcocho

33. yogurt
el yogurt

34. eggs
los huevos

35. milk
la leche

36. butter
la mantequilla

37. sour cream
la crema agria

38. cheese
el queso

39. margarine
la margarina

12. frozen foods
la comida congelada

13. baking products
los productos para hacer
pastelerías

14. paper products
los productos de papel

15. beverages
las bebidas

16. snack foods
las botanas/las
meriendas

17. checkstand
la caja

18. cash register
la caja registradora

19. checker
la cajera/el cajero

20. line
la cola

21. bagger
la persona que empaca la
compra

22. paper bag
la bolsa de papel

23. plastic bag
la bolsa plástica

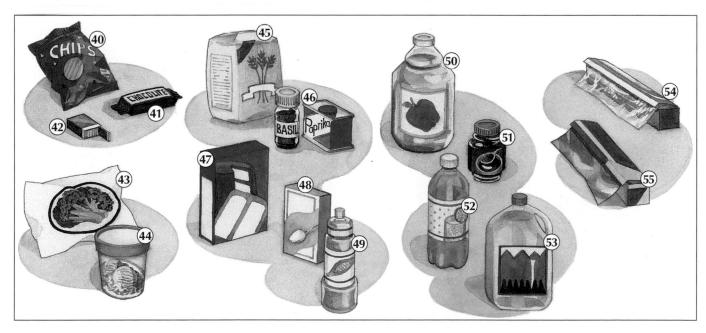

40. potato chips
las papas fritas de
bolsa/lata

41. candy bar
la barra de caramelo

42. gum
el chicle/la goma de
mascar

43. frozen vegetables
las verduras y hortalizas
congeladas

44. ice cream
el helado/la nieve/el
mantecado

45. flour
la harina

46. spices
las especias

47. cake mix
la mezcla para pastel

48. sugar
el azúcar

49. oil
el aceite

50. apple juice
el jugo de manzana

51. instant coffee
el café instantáneo

52. soda
el refresco

53. bottled water
el agua en botella

54. plastic wrap
el plástico para envolver

55. aluminum foil
el papel de aluminio

Containers and Packaged Foods   Recipientes y comida envasada

1. bottle
la botella

2. jar
el frasco

3. can
la lata

4. carton
el cartón

5. container
el recipiente

6. box
la caja

7. bag
la bolsa

8. package
el paquete

9. six-pack
el paquete de
media docena/
de seis

10. loaf
la hogaza

11. roll
el rollo

12. tube
el tubo

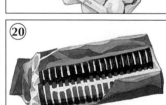

13. a bottle of soda
una botella de refresco

17. a container of cottage cheese
un recipiente de queso fresco

21. a six-pack of soda
media docena de refrescos

14. a jar of jam
un frasco de mermelada

18. a box of cereal
una caja de cereal

22. a loaf of bread
una hogaza de pan

15. a can of soup
una lata de sopa

19. a bag of flour
una bolsa de harina

23. a roll of paper towels
un rollo de toallas de papel

16. a carton of eggs
un cartón de huevos

20. a package of cookies
un paquete de galletas dulces

24. a tube of toothpaste
un tubo de pasta de dientes

Grammar point: *How much? How many?*

Some foods can be counted: *one apple, two apples.*

How many apples do you need? I need ***two*** apples.

Some foods cannot be counted, like liquids, grains, spices, or dairy foods. For these, count containers: *one box of rice, two boxes of rice.*

How much rice do you need? I need ***two boxes.***

A.

A. Measure the ingredients.
Medir los ingredientes.

B.

B. Weigh the food.
Pesar la comida.

C.
1 cup = 237 milliliters

C. Convert the measurements.
Convertir las medidas.

Liquid measures   Medidas para líquidos

| 1 fl. oz. | 1 c. | 1 pt. | 1 qt. | 1 gal. |

Dry measures   Medidas de volumen

    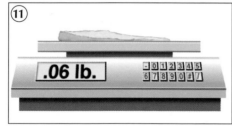

| 1 tsp. | 1 TBS. | 1/4 c. | 1/2 c. | 1 c. |

Weight   Peso

.06 lb.

1.00 lb.

1. a fluid ounce of water
una onza líquida de agua

2. a cup of oil
una taza de aceite

3. a pint of yogurt
una pinta de yogurt

4. a quart of milk
un cuarto de galón de leche

5. a gallon of apple juice
un galón de jugo de manzana

6. a teaspoon of salt
una cucharadita de sal

7. a tablespoon of sugar
una cucharada de azúcar

8. a 1/4 cup of brown sugar
un cuarto de taza de azúcar morena

9. a 1/2 cup of raisins
media taza de pasas

10. a cup of flour
una taza de harina

11. an ounce of cheese
una onza de queso

12. a pound of roast beef
una libra de rosbif

VOLUME
1 fl. oz. = 30 milliliters (ml.)
1 c. = 237 ml.
1 pt. = .47 liters (l.)
1 qt. = .95 l.
1 gal. = 3.79 l.

EQUIVALENCIES
3 tsp. = 1 TBS.	2 c. = 1 pt.
2 TBS. = 1 fl. oz.	2 pt. = 1 qt.
8 fl. oz. = 1 c.	4 qt. = 1 gal.

WEIGHT
1 oz. = 28.35 grams (g.)
1 lb. = 453.6 g.
2.205 lbs. = 1 kilogram
1 lb. = 16 oz.

Scrambled eggs   Huevos revueltos

A. Break 3 eggs.
Abra tres huevos.

B. Beat well.
Bata bien.

C. Grease the pan.
Engrase la sartén.

D. Pour the eggs into the pan.
Eche los huevos en la sartén.

E. Stir.
Revuelva.

F. Cook until done.
Cocine hasta que estén listos.

Vegetable casserole   Plato de verduras y hortalizas al horno

G. Chop the onions.
Corte las cebollas.

H. Sauté the onions.
Saltee las cebollas.

I. Steam the broccoli.
Cocine el brócoli al vapor.

J. Grate the cheese.
Ralle el queso.

K. Mix the ingredients.
Mezcle los ingredientes.

L. Bake at 350° for 45 minutes.
Hornee a 350° por 45 minutos.

Chicken soup   Sopa de pollo

M. Cut up the chicken.
Corte el pollo.

N. Peel the carrots.
Pele las zanahorias.

O. Slice the carrots.
Rebane las zanahorias.

P. Boil the chicken.
Hierva el pollo.

Q. Add the vegetables.
Añada las legumbres y las hortalizas.

R. Simmer for 1 hour.
Cocine a fuego lento durante una hora.

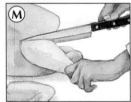

Five ways to cook chicken   Cinco formas de cocinar pollo

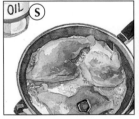

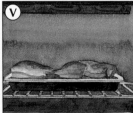
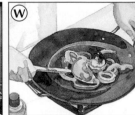

S. fry
freír

T. barbecue/grill
cocinar a la parrilla

U. roast
asar

V. broil
asar a la brasa

W. stir-fry
sofreír

Talk about the way you prepare these foods.

I _fry_ eggs.

I _bake_ potatoes.

Share your answers.

1. What are popular ways in your country to make rice? vegetables? meat?

2. What is your favorite way to cook chicken?

1. can opener
   el abrelatas

2. grater
   el rallador

3. plastic storage
   container
   el recipiente de plástico

4. steamer
   la olla/la cacerola a
   vapor

5. frying pan
   el/la sartén

6. pot
   la olla/la cacerola

7. ladle
   el cucharón

8. double boiler
   la cacerola doble

9. wooden spoon
   la cuchara de madera

10. garlic press
    la prensa para ajo

11. casserole dish
    el molde refractario

12. carving knife
    el cuchillo de trinchar

13. roasting pan
    la bandeja para asar

14. roasting rack
    la parrilla para asar

15. vegetable peeler
    el pelador de verduras y
    hortalizas

16. paring knife
    el cuchillo de pelar

17. colander
    el escurridor

18. kitchen timer
    el cronómetro de cocina

19. spatula
    la espátula

20. eggbeater
    el batidor de huevos

21. whisk
    el batidor

22. strainer
    la coladera

23. tongs
    las pinzas

24. lid
    la tapa

25. saucepan
    el cacillo/la olla

26. cake pan
    el molde para pastel

27. cookie sheet
    la hoja

28. pie pan
    el molde para torta/pay

29. pot holders
    las agarraderas

30. rolling pin
    el rodillo

31. mixing bowl
    el tazón para mezclar

Talk about how to use the utensils.

You use a peeler to peel potatoes.

You use a pot to cook soup.

Use the new language.

Look at **Food Preparation,** page **58.**

Name the different utensils you see.

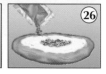

1. **hamburger**
   la hamburguesa

2. **french fries**
   las papas fritas

3. **cheeseburger**
   la hamburguesa con queso

4. **soda**
   el refresco

5. **iced tea**
   el té helado

6. **hot dog**
   el perro caliente

7. **pizza**
   la pizza

8. **green salad**
   la ensalada verde

9. **taco**
   el taco

10. **nachos**
    los nachos

11. **frozen yogurt**
    el yogurt helado

12. **milk shake**
    la malteada

13. **counter**
    el mostrador

14. **muffin**
    el panquecito

15. **doughnut**
    la dona

16. **salad bar**
    la barra de ensaladas

17. **lettuce**
    la lechuga

18. **salad dressing**
    el aderezo

19. **booth**
    el puesto

20. **straw**
    el popote/sorbeto

21. **sugar**
    el azúcar

22. **sugar substitute**
    el edulcorante artificial

23. **ketchup**
    la salsa catsup

24. **mustard**
    la mostaza

25. **mayonnaise**
    la mayonesa

26. **relish**
    la salsa de pepino

A. **eat**
   comer

B. **drink**
   beber

More vocabulary

donut: doughnut (spelling variation)

condiments: relish, mustard, ketchup, mayonnaise, etc.

Share your answers.

1. What would you order at this restaurant?

2. Which fast foods are popular in your country?

3. How often do you eat fast food? Why?

Breakfast

Lunch

Dinner

Desserts

Beverages

1. scrambled eggs
   los huevos revueltos

2. sausage
   la salchicha

3. toast
   la tostada

4. waffles
   los wafles

5. syrup
   el jarabe

6. pancakes
   los panqueques

7. bacon
   el tocino

8. grilled cheese sandwich
   el sandwich de queso a la plancha

9. chef's salad
   la ensalada del chef

10. soup of the day
    la sopa del día

11. mashed potatoes
    el puré de papas

12. roast chicken
    el pollo asado

13. steak
    el filete/el bistec

14. baked potato
    la papa asada

15. pasta
    la pasta

16. garlic bread
    el pan con ajo

17. fried fish
    el pescado frito

18. rice pilaf
    el pilaf de arroz

19. cake
    el pastel

20. pudding
    el pudín

21. pie
    el pay/la torta

22. coffee
    el café

23. decaf coffee
    el café descafeinado

24. tea
    el té

Practice ordering from the menu.

I'd like <u>a grilled cheese sandwich</u> and <u>some soup</u>.

I'll have <u>the chef's salad</u> and <u>a cup of decaf coffee</u>.

Use the new language.

Look at **Fruit,** page **50.**

Order a slice of pie using the different fruit flavors.

Please give me a slice of <u>apple</u> pie.

A Restaurant   Un restaurante

1. hostess
la anfitriona/el jefe de comedor

2. dining room
el comedor

3. menu
el menú

4. server/waiter
el mesero/camarero

5. patron/diner
el cliente

A. set the table
poner la mesa

B. seat the customer
sentar al cliente

C. pour the water
servir el agua

D. order from the menu
pedir del menú

E. take the order
tomar la orden

F. serve the meal
servir la comida

G. clear the table
recoger la mesa

H. carry the tray
llevar la bandeja

I. pay the check
pagar la cuenta

J. leave a tip
dejar una propina

More vocabulary

eat out: to go to a restaurant to eat

take out: to buy food at a restaurant and take it home
to eat

Practice giving commands.

Please <u>set the table</u>.

I'd like you to <u>clear the table</u>.

It's time to <u>serve the meal</u>.

6. server/waitress
la mesera/camarera

7. dessert tray
la charola de los postres

8. bread basket
la cesta para el pan

9. busperson
el ayudante del camarero

10. kitchen
la cocina

11. chef
el chef

12. dishroom
el cuarto de lavado

13. dishwasher
el lavaplatos

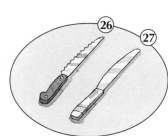

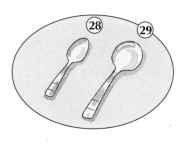

14. place setting
el lugar/el cubierto

15. dinner plate
el plato

16. bread-and-butter plate
el plato para el pan y la mantequilla

17. salad plate
el plato para ensalada

18. soup bowl
el tazón de sopa

19. water glass
el vaso de agua

20. wine glass
la copa de vino

21. cup
la taza

22. saucer
el platito/platillo

23. napkin
la servilleta

24. salad fork
el tenedor para ensalada

25. dinner fork
el tenedor

26. steak knife
el cuchillo para carne

27. knife
el cuchillo

28. teaspoon
la cucharita

29. soupspoon
la cuchara para sopa

Talk about how you set the table in your home.

The glass is on the right.

The fork goes on the left.

The napkin is next to the plate.

Share your answers.

1. Do you know anyone who works in a restaurant? What does he or she do?

2. In your opinion, which restaurant jobs are hard? Why?

1. **three-piece suit**
   el traje de tres piezas

2. **suit**
   el traje

3. **dress**
   el vestido

4. **shirt**
   la camisa

5. **jeans**
   los pantalones mezclilla / mahones

6. **sports coat**
   la chaqueta deportiva

7. **turtleneck**
   el cuello de tortuga

8. **slacks / pants**
   los pantalones

9. **blouse**
   la blusa

10. **skirt**
    la falda

11. **pullover sweater**
    el suéter cerrado / pulóver

12. **T-shirt**
    la camiseta

13. **shorts**
    los pantaloncillos

14. **sweatshirt**
    la sudadera

15. **sweatpants**
    los pants

More vocabulary:

outfit: clothes that look nice together

When clothes are popular, they are **in fashion.**

Talk about what you're wearing today and what you wore yesterday.

I'm wearing <u>a gray sweater</u>, <u>a red T-shirt</u>, and <u>blue jeans</u>.

Yesterday I wore <u>a green pullover sweater</u>, <u>a white shirt</u>, and <u>black slacks</u>.

16. jumpsuit
el juego de pants y sudadera

17. uniform
el uniforme

18. jumper
el vestido con peto y tirantes

19. maternity dress
el vestido de maternidad

20. knit shirt
la camiseta

21. overalls
el overol

22. tunic
el blusón

23. leggings
los leggings

24. vest
el chaleco

25. split skirt
la falda abierta

26. sports shirt
la camisa deportiva

27. cardigan sweater
el suéter de lana tejida

28. tuxedo
el esmoquin

29. evening gown
el vestido de noche

Use the new language.

Look at **A Graduation**, pages 32–33.

Name the clothes you see.

The man at the podium is wearing a suit.

Share your answers.

1. Which clothes in this picture are in fashion now?

2. Who is the best-dressed person in this line? Why?

3. What do you wear when you go to the movies?

1. hat el sombrero	**5.** gloves los guantes
2. overcoat el abrigo	**6.** cap la gorra
3. leather jacket la chaqueta de cuero	**7.** jacket la chamaca/chaqueta
4. wool scarf/muffler la bufanda de lana	

8. parka la parka/el abrigo de invierno	**12.** earmuffs las orejeras
9. mittens los guantes/mitones	**13.** down vest el chaleco relleno con plumas
10. ski cap el gorro para esquiar	**14.** ski mask la máscara de esquí
11. tights las medias de malla	**15.** down jacket la chaqueta rellena con plumas

16. umbrella el paraguas	**20.** trench coat la trinchera	**24.** windbreaker el rompevientos
17. raincoat la gabardina/el impermeable	**21.** sunglasses las gafas de sol	**25.** cover-up el albornoz/la bata de playa
18. poncho el poncho	**22.** swimming trunks el traje de baño	**26.** swimsuit/bathing suit el traje de baño
19. rain boots las botas para la lluvia	**23.** straw hat el sombrero de paja	**27.** baseball cap la gorra de béisbol

Use the new language.

Look at **Weather**, page **10**.

Name the clothing for each weather condition.

Wear a jacket when it's windy.

Share your answers.

1. Which is better in the rain, an umbrella or a poncho?

2. Which is better in the cold, a parka or a down jacket?

3. Do you have more summer clothes or winter clothes?

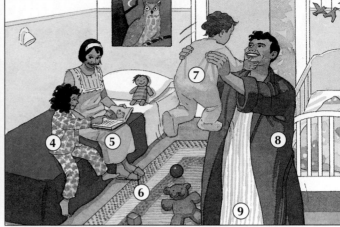

1. leotard
las mallas/el leotardo

2. tank top
la camiseta

3. bike shorts
los shorts de ciclista

4. pajamas
la pijama

5. nightgown
el camisón

6. slippers
las pantuflas

7. blanket sleeper
la cobija

8. bathrobe
la bata de baño

9. nightshirt
el camisón/la camisa de dormir

10. undershirt
la camiseta

11. long underwear
la ropa interior de invierno

12. boxer shorts
los boxers

13. briefs
los calzoncillos

14. athletic supporter/jockstrap
el soporte/suspensorio

15. socks
los calcetines

16. (bikini) panties
las pantis (bikinis)

17. briefs/underpants
las pantaletas

18. girdle
la faja

19. garter belt
el liguero

20. bra
el sostén

21. camisole
la camisola

22. full slip
el fondo entero

23. half slip
el medio fondo

24. knee-highs
las medias cortas

25. kneesocks
los calcetines hasta la rodilla

26. stockings
las medias largas

27. pantyhose
las pantimedias

More vocabulary

lingerie: underwear or sleepwear for women

loungewear: clothing (sometimes sleepwear) people wear around the home

Share your answers.

1. What do you wear when you exercise?

2. What kind of clothing do you wear for sleeping?

Shoes and Accessories   Los zapatos y los accesorios

1. salesclerk
el vendedor

2. suspenders
los tirantes

3. shoe department
el departamento de zapatos

4. silk scarves*
las chalinas de seda

5. hats
los sombreros/las pañoletas

12. sole
la suela

13. heel
el tacón

14. shoelace
el cordón

15. toe
la punta

16. pumps
los zapatos de tacón

17. high heels
los tacones altos

18. boots
las botas

19. loafers
los mocasines

20. oxfords
los zapatos de cordones/los
zapatos bajos/los choclos

21. hiking boots
las botas para excursión

22. tennis shoes
los zapatos tenis

23. athletic shoes
los zapatos para deporte

24. sandals
las sandalias

*Note: *one scarf, two scarves*

Talk about the shoes you're wearing today.
I'm wearing a pair of <u>white sandals</u>.

Practice asking a salesperson for help.
Could I try on these <u>sandals</u> in size <u>10</u>?
Do you have any <u>silk scarves</u>?
Where are <u>the hats</u>?

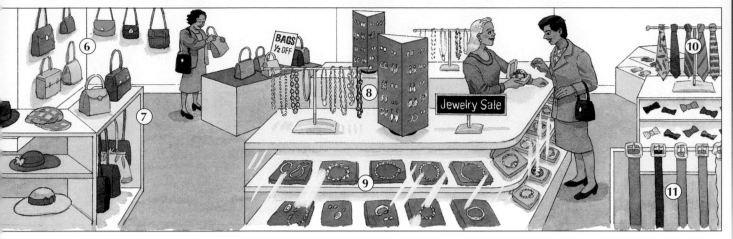

6. purses/handbags
las carteras

7. display case
el aparador/mostrador

8. jewelry
la joyería

9. necklaces
los collares

10. ties
las corbatas

11. belts
los cinturones/las correas

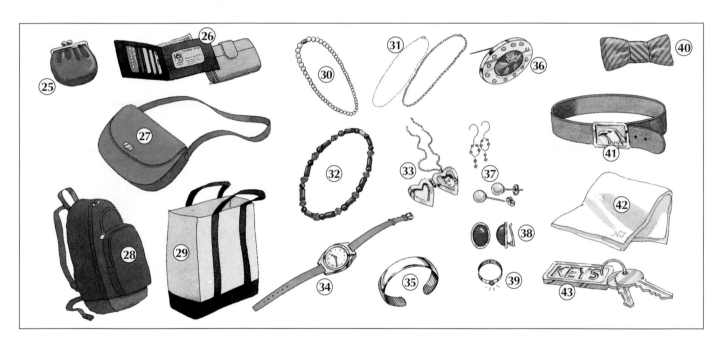

25. change purse
el monedero

26. wallet
la billetera

27. shoulder bag
la bolsa de colgar

28. backpack/bookbag
la mochila

29. tote bag
la bolsa

30. string of pearls
el collar de perlas

31. chain
la cadena

32. beads
las cuentas/los abalorios

33. locket
el relicario

34. (wrist)watch
el reloj (de pulsera)

35. bracelet
el brazalete/la pulsera

36. pin
el alfiler

37. pierced earrings
los aretes

38. clip-on earrings
los aretes

39. ring
el anillo

40. bow tie
la corbata de moño/lazo

41. belt buckle
la hebilla del cinturón

42. handkerchief
el pañuelo

43. key chain
el llavero

Share your answers.

1. Which of these accessories are usually worn by
women? by men?

2. Which of these do you wear every day?

3. Which of these would you wear to a job interview?
Why?

4. Which accessory would you like to receive as a
present? Why?

Describing Clothes   Descripción de la ropa

Sizes   Tallas

1. extra small
extra pequeño

2. small
pequeño

3. medium
mediano

4. large
grande

5. extra large
extra grande

Patterns   Diseños

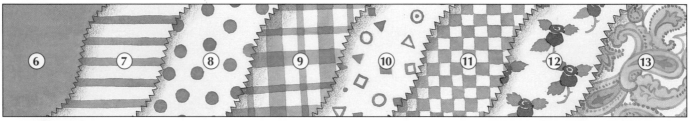

6. solid green
verde liso

7. striped
a rayas

8. polka-dotted
con lunares

9. plaid
con diseño de cuadros

10. print
estampado

11. checked
a cuadros

12. floral
con flores

13. paisley
cachemira

Types of material   Tipos de materiales

 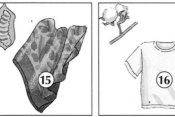 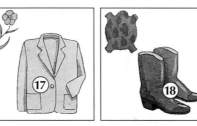

14. wool sweater
el suéter de **lana**

15. silk scarf
la bufanda de **seda**

16. cotton T-shirt
la camiseta de **algodón**

17. linen jacket
la chamarra de **lino**

18. leather boots
las botas de **cuero**

19. nylon stockings*
las medias de **nilón**

Problems   Problemas

  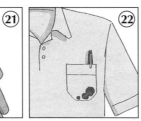 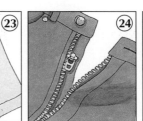

20. too small
demasiado pequeño

21. too big
demasiado grande

22. stain
la mancha

23. rip/tear
el rasgón/descosido

24. broken zipper
el cierre **estropeado**

25. missing button
falta un botón

*Note: Nylon, polyester, rayon, and plastic are synthetic materials.

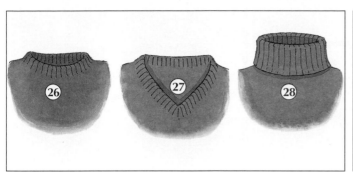

26. crewneck sweater
el suéter con **cuello de cisne**

27. V-neck sweater
el suéter con **cuello en V**

28. turtleneck sweater
el suéter **con cuello de tortuga**

29. sleeveless shirt
la camisa **sin mangas**

30. short-sleeved shirt
la camisa **de manga corta**

31. long-sleeved shirt
la camisa **de manga larga**

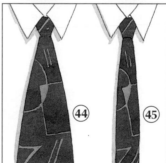

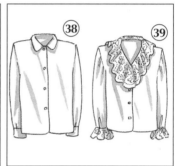

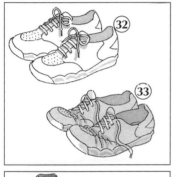

32. new shoes
los zapatos **nuevos**

33. old shoes
los zapatos **viejos**

34. long skirt
la falda **larga**

35. short skirt
la falda **corta**

36. formal dress
el vestido **formal**

37. casual dress
el vestido **casual / informal**

38. plain blouse
la blusa **lisa**

39. fancy blouse
la blusa **vistosa**

40. light jacket
la chaqueta **liviana**

41. heavy jacket
la chaqueta **gruesa**

42. loose pants / **baggy** pants
los pantalones **flojos / holgados**

43. tight pants
los pantalones **apretados / ceñidos**

44. wide tie
la corbata **ancha**

45. narrow tie
la corbata **estrecha**

46. low heels
los tacones / los tacos **bajos**

47. high heels
los tacones / los tacos **altos**

Talk about yourself.

I like <u>long-sleeved</u> shirts and <u>baggy</u> pants.

I like <u>short skirts</u> and <u>high heels</u>.

I usually wear <u>plain</u> clothes.

Share your answers.

1. What type of material do you usually wear in the summer? in the winter?

2. What patterns do you see around you?

3. Are you wearing casual or formal clothes?

Doing the Laundry Lavar la ropa/hacer la colada

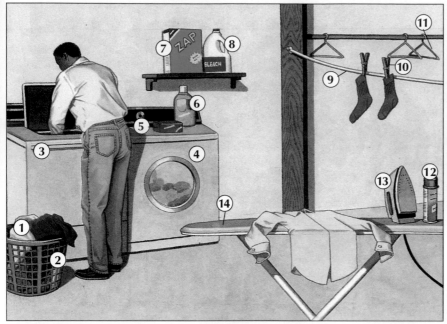

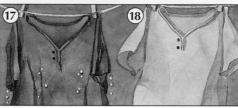

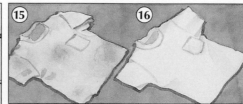

1. **laundry**
   la ropa sucia

2. **laundry basket**
   el cesto para la ropa sucia

3. **washer**
   la lavadora

4. **dryer**
   la secadora

5. **dryer sheets**
   las toallitas para la secadora

6. **fabric softener**
   el suavizante

7. **laundry detergent**
   el detergente para ropa

8. **bleach**
   el cloro

9. **clothesline**
   el tendedero/la cuerda

10. **clothespin**
    la pinza para ropa

11. **hanger**
    el gancho/la percha

12. **spray starch**
    el almidón para rociar

13. **iron**
    la plancha

14. **ironing board**
    la tabla para planchar

15. **dirty** T-shirt
    la camiseta **sucia**

16. **clean** T-shirt
    la camiseta **limpia**

17. **wet** T-shirt
    la camiseta **húmeda**

18. **dry** T-shirt
    la camiseta **seca**

19. **wrinkled** shirt
    la camisa **arrugada**

20. **ironed** shirt
    la camisa **planchada**

A. **Sort** the laundry.
   Separar la ropa.

B. **Add** the detergent.
   Añadir el detergente.

C. **Load** the washer.
   Llenar/Cargar la lavadora.

D. **Clean** the lint trap.
   Limpiar el filtro de pelusa.

E. **Unload** the dryer.
   Vaciar/Descargar la secadora.

F. **Fold** the laundry.
   Doblar la ropa.

G. **Iron** the clothes.
   Planchar la ropa.

H. **Hang up** the clothes.
   Colgar la ropa.

More vocabulary

dry cleaners: a business that cleans clothes using chemicals, not water and detergent

 wash in cold water only

 no bleach

line dry

dry-clean only, do not wash

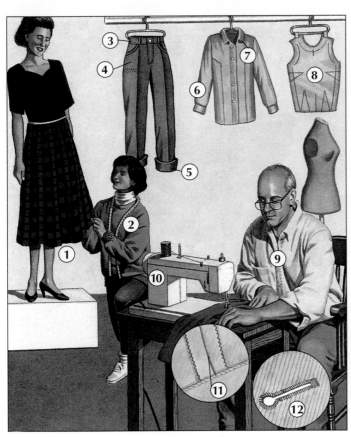

A. sew by hand
coser a mano

B. sew by machine
coser a máquina

C. lengthen
agrandar / bajarle / hacer
más largo(a)

D. shorten
acortar / subirle / hacer
más corto(a)

E. take in
meterle

F. let out
sacarle

1. hemline el dobladillo / el ruedo	**4.** pocket el bolsillo	**7.** collar el cuello	**10.** sewing machine la máquina de coser
2. dressmaker la modista	**5.** cuff el puño	**8.** pattern el patrón	**11.** seam la costura
3. waistband la pretina / el cinturón	**6.** sleeve la manga	**9.** tailor el sastre	**12.** buttonhole el ojal

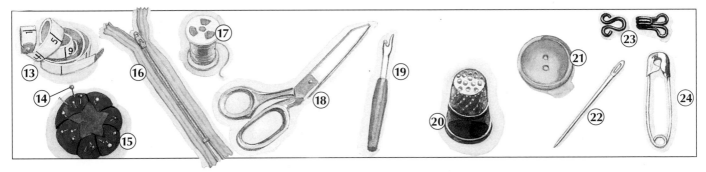

13. tape measure la cinta métrica	**16.** zipper el cierre	**19.** seam ripper el abrecosturas	**22.** needle la aguja
14. pin el alfiler	**17.** spool of thread el carrete de hilo	**20.** thimble el dedal	**23.** hook and eye el broche y corchete
15. pin cushion el alfiletero	**18.** (pair of) scissors (el par de) tijeras	**21.** button el botón	**24.** safety pin el alfiler de seguridad

More vocabulary

pattern maker: a person who makes patterns

garment worker: a person who works in a clothing factory

fashion designer: a person who makes original clothes

Share your answers.

1. Do you know how to use a sewing machine?
2. Can you sew by hand?

The Body El cuerpo

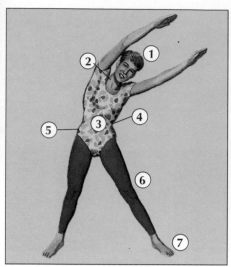

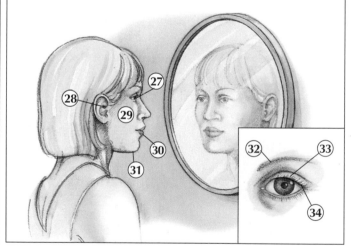

1. head
la cabeza

2. neck
el cuello

3. abdomen
el abdomen

4. waist
la cintura

5. hip
la cadera

6. leg
la pierna

7. foot
el pie

8. hand
la mano

9. arm
el brazo

10. shoulder
el hombro

11. back
la espalda

12. buttocks
las nalgas

13. chest
el pecho

14. breast
el seno/el pecho

15. elbow
el codo

16. thigh
el muslo

17. knee
la rodilla

18. calf
la pantorrilla

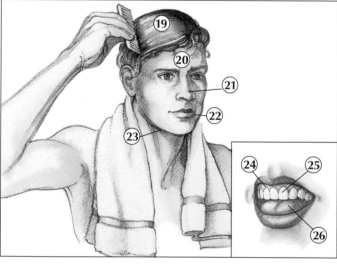

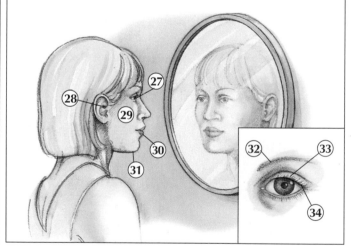

The face
La cara

19. hair
el pelo/el cabello

20. forehead
la frente

21. nose
la nariz

22. mouth
la boca

23. jaw
la quijada

24. gums
las encías

25. teeth
los dientes

26. tongue
la lengua

27. eye
el ojo

28. ear
la oreja

29. cheek
la mejilla/el cachete

30. lip
el labio

31. chin
la barbilla

32. eyebrow
la ceja

33. eyelid
el párpado

34. eyelashes
las pestañas

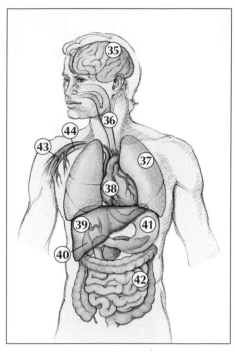

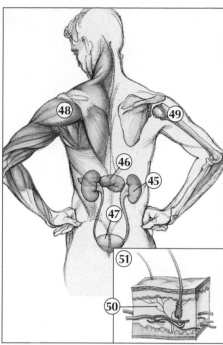

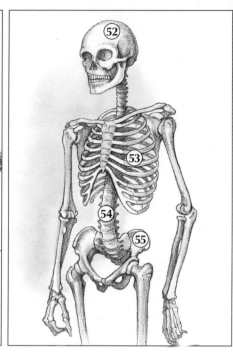

Inside the body
Dentro del cuerpo

35. brain
el cerebro

36. throat
la garganta

37. lung
el pulmón

38. heart
el corazón

39. liver
el hígado

40. gallbladder
la vesícula biliar

41. stomach
el estómago

42. intestines
los intestinos

43. artery
la arteria

44. vein
la vena

45. kidney
el riñón

46. pancreas
el páncreas

47. bladder
la vejiga

48. muscle
el músculo

49. bone
el hueso

50. nerve
el nervio

51. skin
la piel

The skeleton
El esqueleto

52. skull
el cráneo

53. rib cage
la caja toráxica

54. spinal column
la columna vertebral

55. pelvis
la pelvis

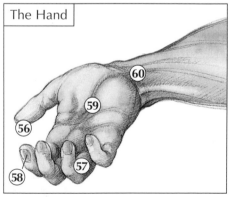

The Hand

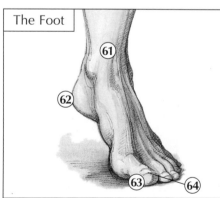

The Foot

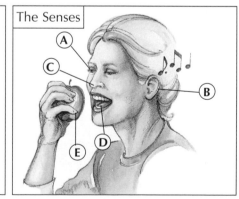

The Senses

56. thumb
el pulgar

57. fingers
los dedos

58. fingernail
la uña

59. palm
la palma

60. wrist
la muñeca

61. ankle
el tobillo

62. heel
el talón

63. toe
el dedo del pie

64. toenail
la uña del pie

A. see
ver

B. hear
oír

C. smell
oler

D. taste
probar

E. touch
tocar

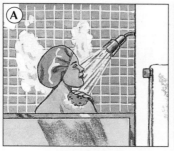

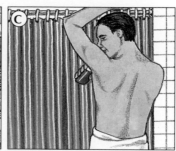

A. take a shower
darse una ducha/
bañarse/ducharse

B. bathe/take a bath
bañarse/tomar un baño

C. use deodorant
usar desodorante

D. put on sunscreen
ponerse protector solar

1. shower cap
la gorra de baño

2. soap
el jabón

3. bath powder/talcum powder
el talco

4. deodorant
el desodorante

5. perfume/cologne
el perfume/la colonia

6. sunscreen
el protector solar

7. body lotion
la crema para el cuerpo

8. moisturizer
la crema humectante

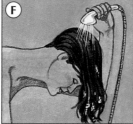

E. wash...hair
lavarse...el cabello

F. rinse...hair
enjuagarse...el cabello

G. comb...hair
peinarse

H. dry...hair
secarse...el cabello

I. brush...hair
cepillarse...el cabello

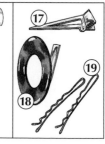

9. shampoo
el champú

10. conditioner
el acondicionador

11. hair gel
el gel para el cabello

12. hair spray
la laca

13. comb
el peine/la peinilla

14. brush
el cepillo

15. curling iron
las tenazas para el cabello/el rizador

16. blow dryer
el secador de cabello

17. hair clip
la pinza para el cabello

18. barrette
el broche

19. bobby pins
los pasadores/incaíbles/las horquillas

J. brush…teeth
cepillarse…los dientes

K. floss…teeth
usar hilo dental

L. gargle
hacer gárgara

M. shave
afeitarse

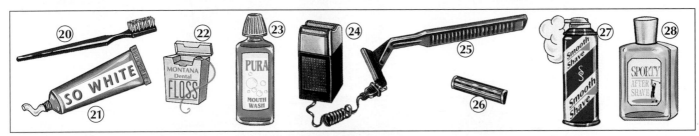

20. toothbrush
el cepillo de dientes

21. toothpaste
la pasta de dientes

22. dental floss
el hilo dental

23. mouthwash
el enjuague bucal

24. electric shaver
la rasuradora

25. razor
el rastrillo

26. razor blade
la hojilla/la navaja

27. shaving cream
la crema de afeitar

28. aftershave
la loción para después de afeitarse

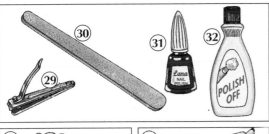

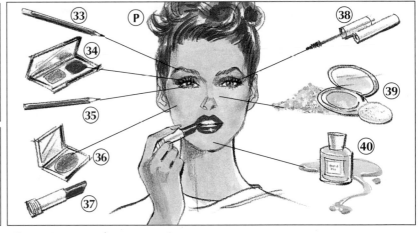

N. cut…nails
cortarse…las uñas

O. polish…nails
pulirse/pintarse… las uñas

P. put on…makeup
ponerse…maquillaje/**maquillarse**

29. nail clipper
el cortauñas

30. emery board
la lima

31. nail polish
la pintura/el esmalte de uñas

32. nail polish remover
la acetona/el removedor de esmalte de uñas

33. eyebrow pencil
el lápiz de cejas

34. eye shadow
la sombra

35. eyeliner
el delineador (de ojos)

36. blush/rouge
el rubor/el colorete

37. lipstick
el lápiz de labios

38. mascara
el rímel

39. face powder
el polvo facial

40. foundation
la base

More vocabulary

A product without perfume or scent is **unscented.**

A product that is better for people with allergies is **hypoallergenic.**

Share your answers.

1. What is your morning routine if you stay home? if you go out?

2. Do women in your culture wear makeup? How old are they when they begin to use it?

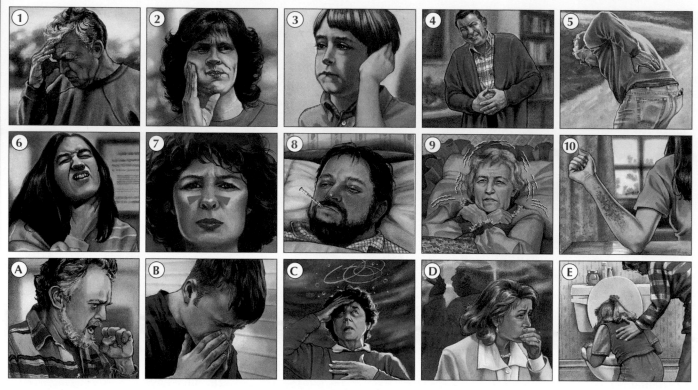

1. **headache**
   el dolor de cabeza

2. **toothache**
   el dolor de muelas

3. **earache**
   el dolor de oído

4. **stomachache**
   el dolor de estómago

5. **backache**
   el dolor de espalda

6. **sore throat**
   el dolor de garganta

7. **nasal congestion**
   la congestión nasal

8. **fever/temperature**
   la fiebre

9. **chills**
   los escalofríos

10. **rash**
    la erupción/el sarpullido

A. **cough**
   toser

B. **sneeze**
   estornudar

C. **feel** dizzy
   sentirse mareado

D. **feel** nauseous
   sentir/tener náuseas

E. **throw up/vomit**
   vomitar

11. **insect bite**
    la picadura de insecto

12. **bruise**
    el moretón/el morado/el cardenal

13. **cut**
    la cortada

14. **sunburn**
    la quemadura de sol

15. **blister**
    la ampolla

16. **swollen** finger
    el dedo **hinchado**

17. **bloody** nose
    la hemorragia nasal

18. **sprained** ankle
    el tobillo **torcido**

Use the new language.

Look at **Health Care**, pages **80–81**.

Tell what medication or treatment you would use for each health problem.

Share your answers.

1. For which problems would you go to a doctor? use medication? do nothing?

2. What do you do for a sunburn? for a headache?

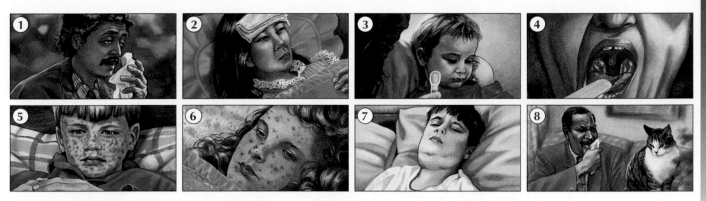

Common illnesses and childhood diseases Enfermedades comunes y de la infancia

1. cold
el resfriado

2. flu
la gripe

3. ear infection
la infección en el oído

4. strep throat
la infección de la garganta

5. measles
el sarampión

6. chicken pox
la varicela/la lechina

7. mumps
las paperas

8. allergies
las alergias

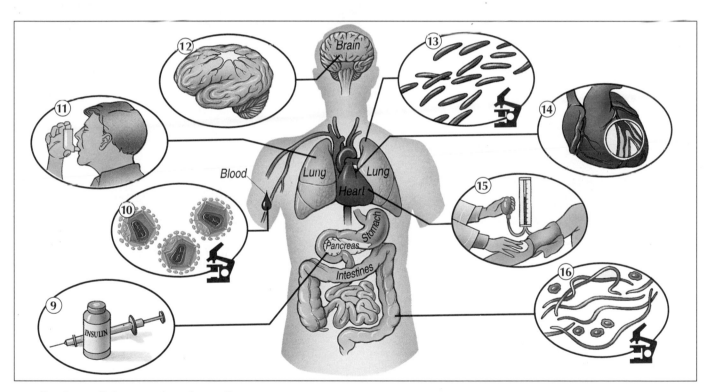

Medical conditions and serious diseases Enfermedades graves

9. diabetes
la diabetes

10. HIV (human immunodeficiency virus)
el VIH/el virus de la inmunodeficiencia humana

11. asthma
el asma

12. brain cancer
el cáncer del cerebro

13. TB (tuberculosis)
la tuberculosis

14. heart disease
las enfermedades cardíacas

15. high blood pressure
la hipertensión/la presión arterial alta

16. intestinal parasites
los parásitos intestinales

More vocabulary

AIDS (acquired immunodeficiency syndrome): a medical condition that results from contracting the HIV virus

influenza: flu

hypertension: high blood pressure

infectious disease: a disease that is spread through air or water

Share your answers.

Which diseases on this page are infectious?

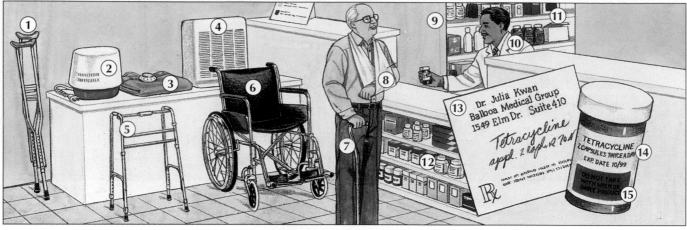

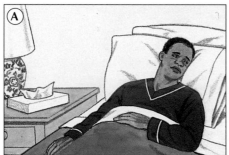

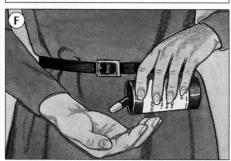

1. **crutches**
   las muletas

2. **humidifier**
   el humidificador

3. **heating pad**
   el parche de calor

4. **air purifier**
   el purificador de aire

5. **walker**
   la andadera

6. **wheelchair**
   la silla de ruedas

7. **cane**
   el bastón

8. **sling**
   el cabestrillo

9. **pharmacy**
   la farmacia

10. **pharmacist**
    el farmaceuta/el farmacéutico

11. **prescription medication**
    el medicamento prescrito

12. **over-the-counter medication**
    el medicamento de libre venta

13. **prescription**
    la prescripción/la receta

14. **prescription label**
    la etiqueta de la receta

15. **warning label**
    la etiqueta de advertencia

A. **Get** bed rest.
   Repose en cama.

B. **Drink** fluids.
   Tome líquidos.

C. **Change** your diet.
   Cambie su dieta.

D. **Exercise.**
   Haga ejercicios.

E. **Get** an injection.
   Inyéctese.

F. **Take** medicine.
   Tome medicina.

More vocabulary

dosage: how much medicine you take and how many times a day you take it

expiration date: the last day the medicine can be used

treatment: something you do to get better

Staying in bed, drinking fluids, and getting physical therapy are treatments.

An injection that stops a person from getting a serious disease is called **an immunization** or **a vaccination.**

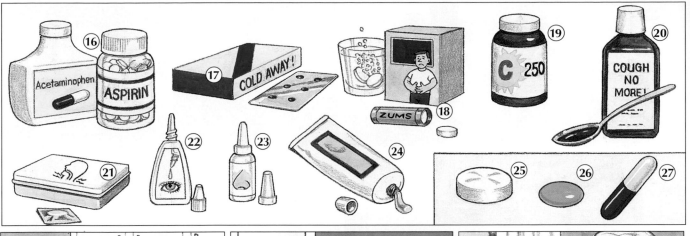

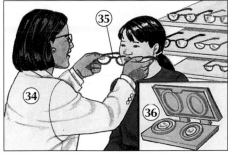

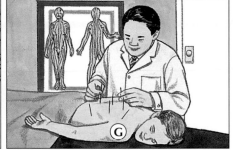

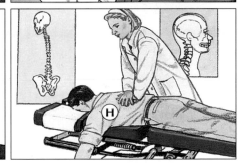

16. pain reliever
el analgésico

17. cold tablets
las pastillas para el resfriado

18. antacid
el antiácido

19. vitamins
las vitaminas

20. cough syrup
el jarabe para la tos

21. throat lozenges
las pastillas para la garganta

22. eyedrops
las gotas para los ojos

23. nasal spray
el rociador nasal

24. ointment
el ungüento

25. tablet
la tableta

26. pill
la pastilla

27. capsule
la cápsula

28. orthopedist
el ortopedista

29. cast
el yeso/la escayola

30. physical therapist
el fisioterapeuta

31. brace
la abrazadera

32. audiologist
el audiólogo

33. hearing aid
el audífono

34. optometrist
el optometrista/el optómetra

35. (eye)glasses
los lentes

36. contact lenses
los lentes de contacto

G. Get acupuncture.
Hágase acupuntura.

H. Go to a chiropractor.
Vaya a un quiropráctico.

Share your answers.

1. What's the best treatment for a headache? a sore throat? a stomachache? a fever?

2. Do you think vitamins are important? Why or why not?

3. What treatments are popular in your culture?

A. **be injured / be hurt**
   lastimarse / herirse

B. **be** unconscious
   estar inconsciente

C. **be** in shock
   estar en shock / choque

D. **have** a heart attack
   tener un ataque al corazón

E. **have** an allergic reaction
   tener una reacción alérgica

F. **get** an electric shock
   recibir una descarga eléctrica

G. **get** frostbite
   quemarse por el frío

H. **burn** (your)self
   quemar(se)

I. **drown**
   ahogarse

J. **swallow** poison
   envenenarse

K. **overdose** on drugs
   tomar una sobredosis de drogas

L. **choke**
   atragantarse / asfixiarse

M. **bleed**
   sangrar

N. **can't breathe**
   asfixiarse / no poder respirar

O. **fall**
   caerse

P. **break** a bone
   romperse un hueso

Grammar point: past tense

burn	— burned	choke	— choked	bleed	— bled
drown	— drowned	be	— was, were	can't	— couldn't
swallow	— swallowed	have	— had	fall	— fell
overdose	— overdosed	get	— got	break	— broke

82

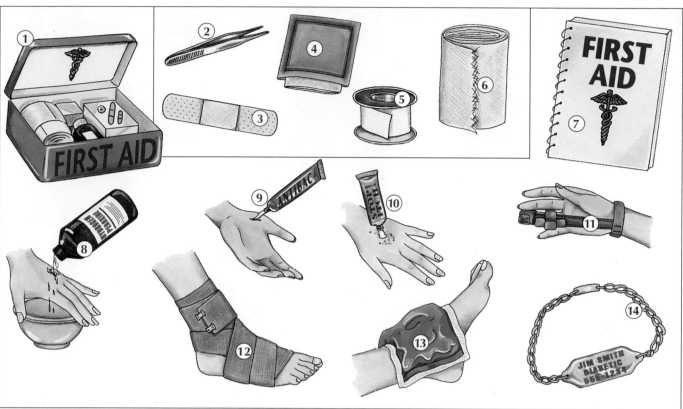

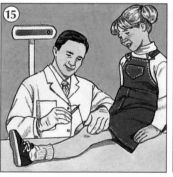
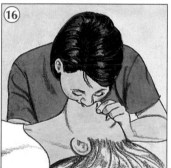

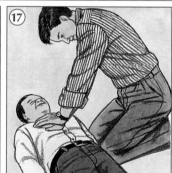

1. **first aid kit**
   el equipo de primeros auxilios

2. **tweezers**
   las pinzas

3. **adhesive bandage**
   la venda adhesiva

4. **sterile pad**
   el apósito estéril

5. **tape**
   el adhesivo

6. **gauze**
   la gasa

7. **first aid manual**
   el manual de primeros auxilios

8. **hydrogen peroxide**
   el agua oxigenada

9. **antibacterial ointment**
   el ungüento antibacterial

10. **antihistamine cream**
    la crema antihistamínica

11. **splint**
    la tablilla

12. **elastic bandage**
    el vendaje elástico

13. **ice pack**
    la bolsa de hielo

14. **medical emergency bracelet**
    la pulsera / el brazalete para
    casos de emergencias médicas

15. **stitches**
    los puntos

16. **rescue breathing**
    la respiración de boca a boca

17. **CPR (cardiopulmonary resuscitation)**
    RCP (la resucitación cardiopulmonar)

18. **Heimlich maneuver**
    la maniobra de Heimlich

Important Note: Only people who are properly trained should give stitches or do CPR.

Share your answers.

1. Do you have a First Aid kit in your home? Where can you buy one?

2. When do you use hydrogen peroxide? an elastic support bandage? antihistamine cream?

3. Do you know first aid? Where did you learn it?

Clinics   Las clínicas

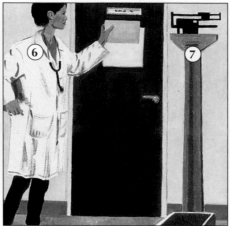

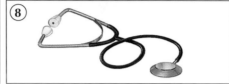

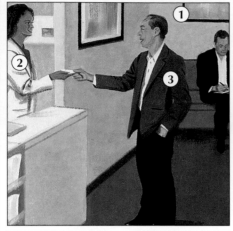

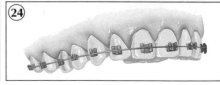

Medical clinic   La clínica

1. waiting room
la sala de espera

2. receptionist
el/la recepcionista

3. patient
el/la paciente

4. insurance card
la tarjeta del seguro

5. insurance form
la forma del seguro

6. doctor
el doctor/el médico

7. scale
la báscula

8. stethoscope
el estetoscopio

9. examining room
la sala de examen

10. nurse
la enfermera/el enfermero

11. eye chart
la escala tipográfica

12. blood pressure gauge
el medidor de presión

13. examination table
la mesa de examen

14. syringe
la jeringa

15. thermometer
el termómetro

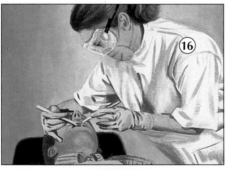
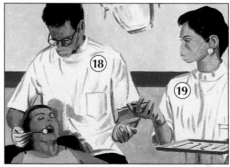

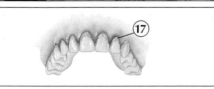

Dental clinic   La clínica odontológica

16. dental hygienist
el higienista dental

17. tartar
el sarro

18. dentist
el dentista

19. dental assistant
el ayudante del dentista

20. cavity
la caries

21. drill
la fresa/el taladro

22. filling
la amalgama

23. orthodontist
el ortodoncista

24. braces
los frenos/los frenillos

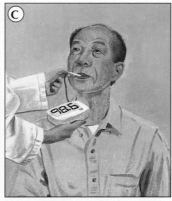

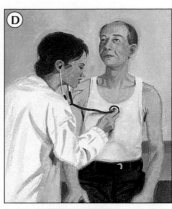

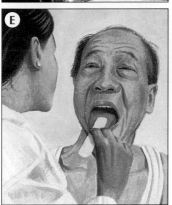

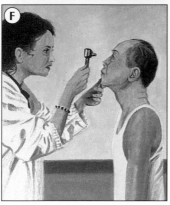

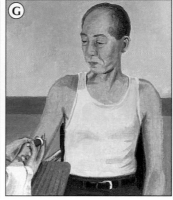

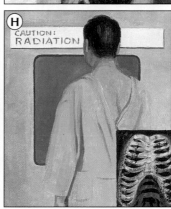

A. make an appointment
hacer / tomar una cita

B. check…blood pressure
verificar…la presión sanguínea

C. take…temperature
tomar…la temperatura

D. listen to…heart
escuchar…el corazón

E. look in…throat
mirar…la garganta

F. examine…eyes
examinar…los ojos

G. draw…blood
sacar…sangre

H. get an X ray
hacer / tomar una placa de rayos X

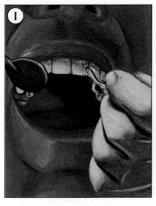

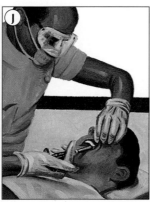

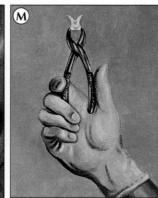

I. clean…teeth
limpiar…los dientes

J. give…a shot of anesthetic
poner…una inyección de
anestésico / **inyectar anestésico**

K. drill a tooth
taladrar un diente/una muela

L. fill a cavity
arreglar una caries

M. pull a tooth
sacar / extraer un diente/una muela

More vocabulary

get a checkup: to go for a medical exam

extract a tooth: to pull out a tooth

Share your answers.

1. What is the average cost of a medical exam in your area?

2. Some people are nervous at the dentist's office. What can they do to relax?

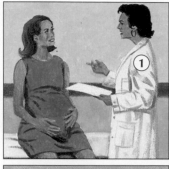

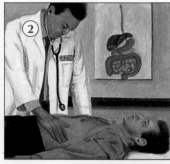

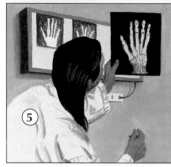
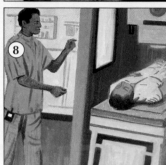
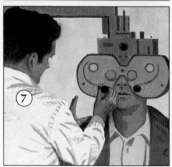

Hospital staff   El personal del hospital

1. obstetrician
   el obstetra

2. internist
   el internista

3. cardiologist
   el cardiólogo

4. pediatrician
   el pediatra

5. radiologist
   el radiólogo

6. psychiatrist
   el siquiatra

7. ophthalmologist
   el oftalmólogo

8. X-ray technician
   el técnico de rayos X

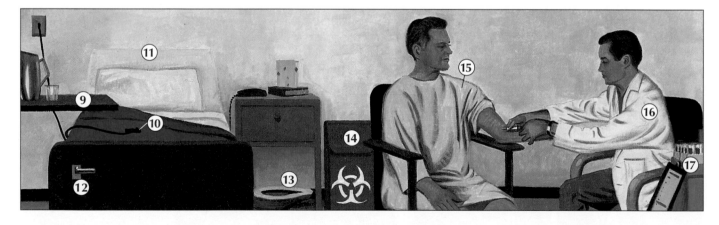

Patient's room   La habitación del paciente

9. bed table
   la mesa para la cama

10. call button
   el botón/el timbre para llamar

11. hospital bed
   la cama de hospital

12. bed control
   el control para la cama

13. bedpan
   la bacinilla

14. medical waste disposal
   el recipiente para desechos médicos

15. hospital gown
   la bata de hospital

16. lab technician
   el técnico de laboratorio

17. blood work/blood test
   el examen de sangre/sanguíneo

More vocabulary

nurse practitioner: a nurse licensed to give medical exams

specialist: a doctor who only treats specific medical problems

gynecologist: a specialist who examines and treats women

nurse midwife: a nurse practitioner who examines pregnant women and delivers babies

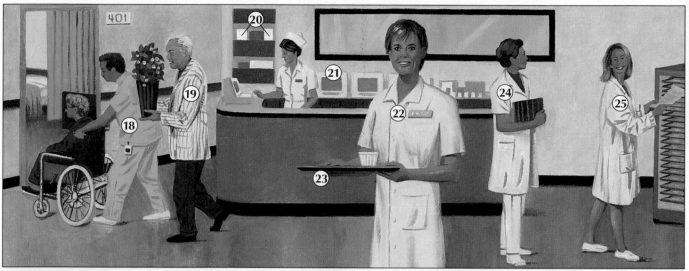

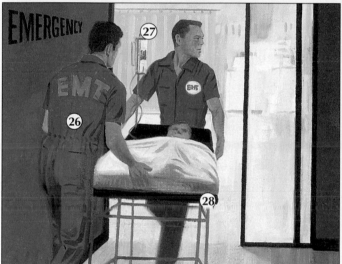

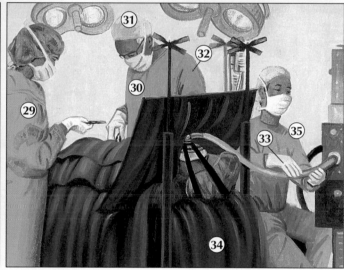

Nurse's station
El puesto de enfermeras

18. orderly
el camillero / el asistente del hospital

19. volunteer
el voluntario

20. medical charts
la historia médica / clínica

21. vital signs monitor
el monitor para signos vitales

22. RN (registered nurse)
la enfermera registrada

23. medication tray
la bandeja / la charola para medicamentos

24. LPN (licensed practical nurse)/ LVN (licensed vocational nurse)
el enfermero con licencia práctica / vocacional

25. dietician
la dietista

Emergency room
La sala de emergencia

26. emergency medical technician (EMT)
el técnico médico de emergencia

27. IV (intravenous drip)
el goteo intravenoso

28. stretcher / gurney
la camilla

Operating room
La sala de operaciones / El quirófano

29. surgical nurse
la enfermera quirúrgica

30. surgeon
el cirujano

31. surgical cap
el gorro de cirujano

32. surgical gown
la bata de cirujano

33. latex gloves
los guantes de látex

34. operating table
la mesa de operaciones

35. anesthesiologist
el anestesiólogo

Practice asking for the hospital staff.

Please get the nurse. I have a question for her.

Where's the anesthesiologist? I need to talk to her.

I'm looking for the lab technician. Have you seen him?

Share your answers.

1. Have you ever been to an emergency room? Who helped you?

2. Have you ever been in the hospital? How long did you stay?

City Streets   Las calles de la ciudad

1. **fire station**
   la estación de bomberos

2. **coffee shop**
   la cafetería

3. **bank**
   el banco

4. **car dealership**
   el lote de autos/la concesionaria
   de autos

5. **hotel**
   el hotel

6. **church**
   la iglesia

7. **hospital**
   el hospital

8. **park**
   el parque

9. **synagogue**
   la sinagoga

10. **theater**
    el teatro

11. **movie theater**
    el cine

12. **gas station**
    la gasolinera

13. **furniture store**
    la mueblería

14. **hardware store**
    la ferretería

15. **barber shop**
    la barbería

More vocabulary

skyscraper: a very tall office building

downtown/city center: the area in a city with the
city hall, courts, and businesses

Practice giving your destination.

I'm going to go <u>downtown</u>.

I have to go to <u>the post office</u>.

16. bakery
la panadería

17. city hall
el palacio municipal / la alcaldía

18. courthouse
el tribunal

19. police station
la comisaría / la estación de policía

20. market
el mercado

21. health club
el gimnasio

22. motel
el motel

23. mosque
la mezquita

24. office building
el edificio de oficinas

25. high-rise building
el rascacielos

26. parking garage
el estacionamiento / la cochera

27. school
la escuela

28. library
la biblioteca

29. post office
la oficina de correos

Practice asking for and giving the locations of buildings.

Where's the post office?

It's on Oak Street.

Share your answers.

1. Which of the places in this picture do you go to every week?

2. Is it good to live in a city? Why or why not?

3. What famous cities do you know?

89

1. **Laundromat**
la lavandería

2. **drugstore/pharmacy**
la botica/la farmacia

3. **convenience store**
la tienda de conveniencia

4. **photo shop**
la tienda de artículos para fotografía

5. **parking space**
el lugar para estacionar

6. **traffic light**
el semáforo

7. **pedestrian**
el peatón

8. **crosswalk**
el cruce peatonal

9. **street**
la calle

10. **curb**
el borde de la acera/de la banqueta

11. **newsstand**
el puesto de periódicos

12. **mailbox**
el buzón

13. **drive-thru window**
el servicio para automovilistas

14. **fast food restaurant**
el restaurante de comida rápida

15. **bus**
el autobús/el camión

A. **cross** the street
cruzar la calle

B. **wait** for the light
esperar a que cambie el semáforo

C. **drive** a car
manejar un automóvil

More vocabulary

neighborhood: the area close to your home

do errands: to make a short trip from your home to buy or pick up something

Talk about where to buy things.

You can buy <u>newspapers</u> at <u>a newsstand</u>.

You can buy <u>donuts</u> at <u>a donut shop</u>.

You can buy <u>food</u> at <u>a convenience store</u>.

16. bus stop
    la parada de autobús

17. corner
    la esquina

18. parking meter
    el parquímetro

19. motorcycle
    la motocicleta

20. donut shop
    la tienda de donas

21. public telephone
    el teléfono público

22. copy center/print shop
    el centro de copias/la imprenta

23. streetlight
    el farol/el poste de luz

24. dry cleaners
    la tintorería

25. nail salon
    el salón de uñas

26. sidewalk
    la acera/la banqueta

27. garbage truck
    el camión de la basura

28. fire hydrant
    la boca de incendio

29. sign
    el letrero

30. street vendor
    el vendedor ambulante

31. cart
    el carrito

D. **park** the car
   estacionar el auto/el coche

E. **ride** a bicycle
   andar en bicicleta

Share your answers.

1. Do you like to do errands?

2. Do you always like to go to the same stores?

3. Which businesses in the picture are also in your neighborhood?

4. Do you know someone who has a small business? What kind?

5. What things can you buy from a street vendor?

1. music store
   la tienda de música

2. jewelry store
   la joyería

3. candy store
   la dulcería

4. bookstore
   la librería

5. toy store
   la juguetería

6. pet store
   la tienda de mascotas

7. card store
   la tienda de tarjetas

8. optician
   la óptica

9. travel agency
   la agencia de viajes

10. shoe store
    la zapatería

11. fountain
    la fuente

12. florist
    la florería/la floristería

More vocabulary

beauty shop: hair salon

men's store: a store that sells men's clothing

dress shop: a store that sells women's clothing

Talk about where you want to shop in this mall.

Let's go to <u>the card store</u>.

I need to buy <u>a card</u> for Maggie's birthday.

13. department store
la tienda por departamentos

14. food court
la feria de comida rápida

15. video store
la tienda de videos

16. hair salon
la peluquería

17. maternity shop
la tienda de ropa de maternidad

18. electronics store
la tienda de aparatos electrónicos

19. directory
el directorio

20. ice cream stand
el puesto de helados

21. escalator
la escalera automática

22. information booth
la caseta de información

Practice asking for and giving the location of different shops.

Where's the maternity shop?

It's on the first floor, next to the hair salon.

Share your answers.

1. Do you like shopping malls? Why or why not?

2. Some people don't go to the mall to shop.
Name some other things you can do in a mall.

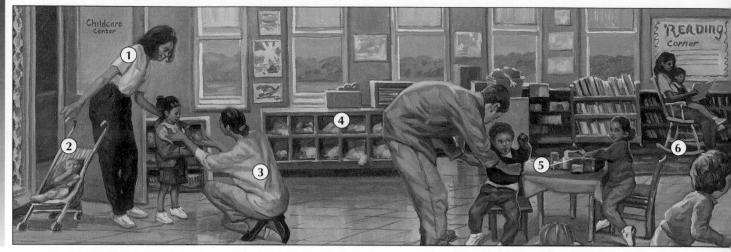

1. parent
el padre / la madre

2. stroller
el cochecito

3. childcare worker
el empleado de una guardería

4. cubby
la casilla

5. toys
los juguetes

6. rocking chair
la mecedora

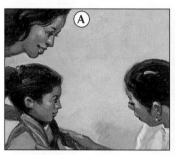

A. drop off
dejar

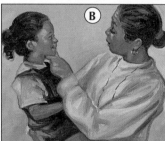

B. hold
aguantar.

C. nurse
amamantar

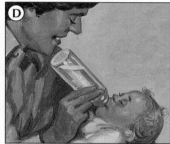

D. feed
dar de comer

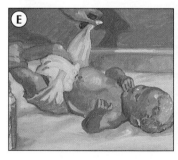

E. change diapers
cambiar los pañales

F. read a story
leer un cuento

G. pick up
levantar

H. rock
mecer

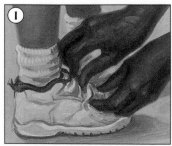

I. tie shoes
atar los cordones de los
zapatos

J. dress
vestir

K. play
jugar

L. take a nap
tomar / echar una siesta

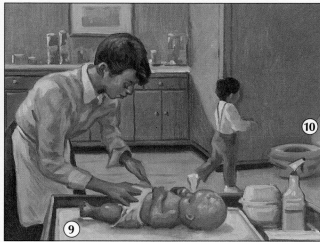

7. high chair
la silla alta

8. bib
el babero

9. changing table
la mesa para cambiar
pañales

10. potty seat
la bacinica

11. playpen
el corralito

12. walker
el andador

13. car safety seat
el asiento de seguridad
para el automóvil

14. baby carrier
el cargador

15. baby backpack
la mochila de bebé

16. carriage
el cochecito

17. wipes
las toallitas húmedas

18. baby powder
el talco para bebé

19. disinfectant
el desinfectante

20. disposable diapers
los pañales desechables

21. cloth diapers
los pañales de tela

22. diaper pins
los alfileres para pañales

23. diaper pail
la tina/el cesto para pañales

24. training pants
las braguitas de entrenamiento/
los calzoncitos de hule

25. formula
la fórmula

26. bottle
el biberón/la mamila

27. nipple
la mamadera/el chupón

28. baby food
el alimento para bebé

29. pacifier
el chupete/el chupón

30. teething ring
el anillo de dentición

31. rattle
la sonaja/el sonajero

1. **envelope**
   el sobre

2. **letter**
   la carta

3. **postcard**
   la postal

4. **greeting card**
   la tarjeta de felicitación

5. **package**
   el paquete

6. **letter carrier**
   el cartero

7. **return address**
   el remitente

8. **mailing address**
   la dirección del destinatario

9. **postmark**
   el matasellos

10. **stamp/postage**
    la estampilla/el timbre postal

11. **certified mail**
    el correo certificado

12. **priority mail**
    el correo prioritario

13. **air letter/aerogramme**
    el aerograma

14. **ground post/parcel post**
    el envío por vía terrestre

15. **Express Mail/overnight mail**
    el correo expreso/el correo urgente

A. **address** a postcard
   escribir la dirección en una postal

B. **send** it/**mail** it
   enviarla/ponerla en el correo

C. **deliver** it
   entregarla

D. **receive** it
   recibirla

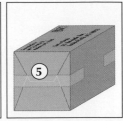

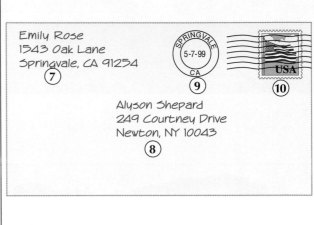

Emily Rose
1543 Oak Lane
Springvale, CA 91254

SPRINGVALE
5-7-99
CA

USA

Alyson Shepard
249 Courtney Drive
Newton, NY 10043

FRAGILE

EXPRESS MAIL
UNITED STATES POSTAL SERVICE

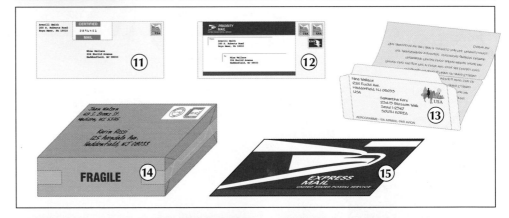

DEAR ELIZA,
...DOING WELL
THIS FALL,
...OOK FORWARD
...ING YOU
...AIN SOON,
LOVE, BOB

ELIZA JONE...
189 MAIN S...
SOUTH...
06...

1. teller
   el cajero
2. vault
   la bóveda
3. ATM (automated teller machine)
   el cajero automático
4. security guard
   el guardia

5. passbook
   la libreta de banco
6. savings account number
   el número de cuenta de ahorros
7. checkbook
   la chequera
8. checking account number
   el número de cuenta corriente
9. ATM card
   la tarjeta de cajero automático
10. monthly statement
    el estado de cuenta mensual
11. balance
    el balance
12. deposit slip
    el comprobante de depósito / la hoja de ingreso
13. safe-deposit box
    la caja de seguridad

Using the ATM machine   Uso del cajero automático

A. **Insert** your ATM card.
   Introduzca la tarjeta de cajero automático.
B. **Enter** your PIN number.*
   Escriba su clave en el teclado.
C. **Make** a deposit.
   Haga un depósito.

D. **Withdraw** cash.
   Retire el efectivo.
E. **Transfer** funds.
   Transfiera fondos.
F. **Remove** your ATM card.
   Retire la tarjeta de cajero automático.

*PIN: personal identification number

More vocabulary

overdrawn account: When there is not enough money in an account to pay a check, we say the account is overdrawn.

Share your answers.

1. Do you use a bank?
2. Do you use an ATM card?
3. Name some things you can put in a safe-deposit box.

A Library   Una biblioteca

1. **reference librarian**
   el bibliotecario de
   información

2. **reference desk**
   el mostrador de libros de
   consulta

3. **atlas**
   el atlas

4. **microfilm reader**
   el lector de microfilm

5. **microfilm**
   el microfilm

6. **periodical section**
   la sección de
   publicaciones periódicas

7. **magazine**
   la revista

8. **newspaper**
   el periódico

9. **online catalog**
   el fichero en
   computadora

10. **card catalog**
    el fichero de tarjetas

11. **media section**
    los medios audiovisuales

12. **audiocassette**
    el casete/la cinta
    de audio

13. **videocassette**
    el video/la cinta de
    video

14. **CD (compact disc)**
    el CD (el "compact disk")

15. **record**
    el disco

16. **checkout desk**
    el mostrador de
    préstamos

17. **library clerk**
    el bibliotecario

18. **encyclopedia**
    la enciclopedia

19. **library card**
    la tarjeta para uso de la
    biblioteca

20. **library book**
    el libro de la biblioteca

21. **title**
    el título

22. **author**
    el autor/la autora

More vocabulary

check a book out: to borrow a book from the library

nonfiction: real information, history or true stories

fiction: stories from the author's imagination

Share your answers.

1. Do you have a library card?

2. Do you prefer to buy books or borrow them from
   the library?

98

"You have the right to remain silent…"

"Bail is set at $20,000."

A. **arrest** a suspect
arrestar a un sospechoso

1. police officer
el oficial de policía/el policía

2. handcuffs
las esposas

B. **hire** a lawyer/**hire** an attorney
contratar a un abogado

3. guard
el guardia

4. defense attorney
el abogado defensor

C. **appear** in court
comparecer ante el tribunal

5. defendant
el acusado

6. judge
el juez

D. **stand trial**
ser juzgado

7. courtroom
la sala del tribunal

8. jury
el jurado

9. evidence
la evidencia/las pruebas

10. prosecuting attorney
el fiscal

11. witness
el testigo

12. court reporter
el escribiente/el secretario

13. bailiff
el alguacil

"Guilty."

"7 years."

E. **give** the verdict*
emitir el veredicto

F. **sentence** the defendant
sentenciar al acusado

G. **go** to jail/**go** to prison
ir a la cárcel/ir a prisión

14. convict
el condenado

H. **be released**
salir en libertad

*Note: There are two possible verdicts, "guilty" and "not guilty."

Share your answers.

1. What are some differences between the legal system in the United States and the one in your country?

2. Do you want to be on a jury? Why or why not?

1. **vandalism**
   el vandalismo

2. **gang violence**
   el pandillismo

3. **drunk driving**
   manejar en estado de embriaguez

4. **illegal drugs**
   las sustancias/drogas ilegales

5. **mugging**
   el ataque

6. **burglary**
   el robo

7. **assault**
   el asalto

8. **murder**
   el asesinato

9. **gun**
   la pistola

More vocabulary

commit a crime: to do something illegal

criminal: someone who commits a crime

victim: someone who is hurt or killed by someone else

Share your answers.

1. Is there too much crime on TV? in the movies?

2. Do you think people become criminals from watching crime on TV?

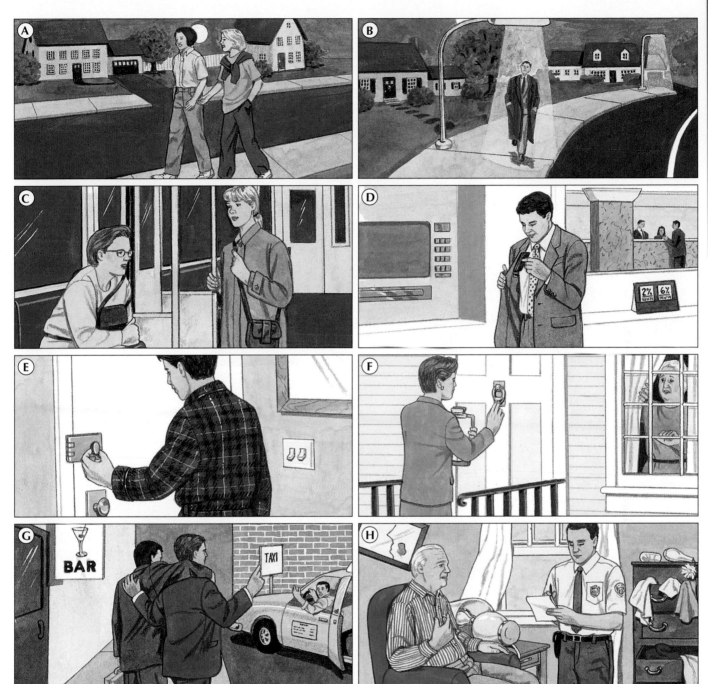

A. **Walk** with a friend.
Camine con un amigo.

B. **Stay** on well-lit streets.
Permanezca en calles bien iluminadas.

C. **Hold** your purse close to your body.
Mantenga el bolso cerca del cuerpo.

D. **Protect** your wallet.
Proteja la cartera/billetera.

E. **Lock** your doors.
Cierre las puertas con llave.

F. **Don't open** your door to strangers.
No abra la puerta a extraños.

G. **Don't drink** and **drive**.
No maneje en estado de embriaguez.

H. **Report** crimes to the police.
Denuncie los delitos a la policía.

More vocabulary

Neighborhood Watch: a group of neighbors who watch for criminals in their neighborhood

designated drivers: people who don't drink alcoholic beverages so that they can drive drinkers home

Share your answers.

1. Do you feel safe in your neighborhood?

2. Look at the pictures. Which of these things do you do?

3. What other things do you do to stay safe?

101

Emergencies and Natural Disasters Emergencias y desastres naturales

1. lost child
   el niño perdido

2. car accident
   el accidente automovilístico

3. airplane crash
   el accidente aéreo

4. explosion
   la explosión

5. earthquake
   el terremoto

6. mudslide
   el derrumbe

7. fire
   el incendio

8. firefighter
   el bombero

9. fire truck
   el camión de bomberos

Practice reporting a fire.

This is <u>Lisa Broad</u>. There is a fire.

The address is <u>323 Oak Street.</u>

Please send someone quickly.

Share your answers.

1. Can you give directions to your home if there is a fire?

2. What information do you give to the other driver if you are in a car accident?

102

10. drought
la sequía

11. blizzard
la ventisca

12. hurricane
el huracán

13. tornado
el tornado

14. volcanic eruption
la erupción volcánica

15. tidal wave
el maremoto

16. flood
la inundación

17. search and rescue team
las brigadas de búsqueda y rescate

Share your answers.

1. Which disasters are common in your area?
Which never happen?

2. What can you do to prepare for emergencies?

3. Do you have emergency numbers near your
telephone?

4. What organizations will help you in an emergency?

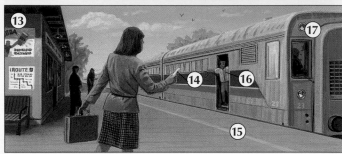

1. bus stop
   la parada de autobús
2. route
   la ruta
3. schedule
   el horario
4. bus
   el autobús
5. fare
   el pasaje
6. transfer
   el billete de transbordo

7. passenger
   el pasajero
8. bus driver
   el chofer de autobús
9. subway
   el metro/el tren
   subterráneo
10. track
    la vía férrea
11. token
    la ficha/el vale
12. fare card
    el boleto

13. train station
    la estación del tren
14. ticket
    el boleto/el billete
15. platform
    la plataforma
16. conductor
    el conductor
17. train
    el tren
18. taxi/cab
    el taxi

19. taxi stand
    la parada de taxis
20. taxi driver
    el chofer de taxi
21. meter
    el taxímetro
22. taxi license
    la licencia del taxi
23. ferry
    el ferry/el barco de
    transbordo

More vocabulary

hail a taxi: to get a taxi driver's attention by raising your hand

miss the bus: to arrive at the bus stop late

Talk about how you and your friends come to school.

I take _the bus_ to school.
You take _the train_.
We take _the subway_.

He _drives_ to school.
She _walks_ to school.
They _ride_ bikes.

1. under the bridge
debajo del puente

2. over the bridge
por encima del puente

3. across the water
al otro lado del agua

4. into the taxi
en el taxi

5. out of the taxi
fuera del taxi

6. onto the highway
a la autopista

7. off the highway
fuera de la autopista

8. down the stairs
escaleras abajo

9. up the stairs
escaleras arriba

10. around the corner
a la vuelta de la esquina

11. through the tunnel
a través del túnel/por el túnel

Grammar point: *into, out of, on, off*

We say, *get **into** a taxi or a car.*
But we say, *get **on** a bus, a train, or a plane.*

We say, *get **out of** a taxi or a car.*
But we say, *get **off** a bus, a train, or a plane.*

1. **subcompact**
   supercompacto

2. **compact**
   compacto

3. **midsize car**
   el automóvil mediano

4. **full-size car**
   el automóvil grande

5. **convertible**
   descapotable/convertible

6. **sports car**
   el automóvil deportivo

7. **pickup truck**
   la pickup/la camioneta

8. **station wagon**
   la camioneta

9. **SUV (sports utility vehicle)**
   el vehículo de doble tracción/la camioneta de servicio

10. **minivan**
    la miniván

11. **camper**
    el cámper

12. **dump truck**
    el camión de volteo

13. **tow truck**
    la grúa

14. **moving van**
    el camión de mudanza

15. **tractor trailer/semi**
    el camión semirremolque/el trailer

16. **cab**
    la cabina

17. **trailer**
    el remolque

More vocabulary

make: the name of the company that makes the car

model: the style of car

Share your answers.

1. What is your favorite kind of car?

2. What kind of car is good for a big family? for a single person?

Directions   Direcciones

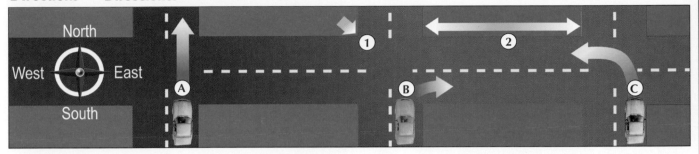

A. go straight
ir derecho

B. turn right
dar vuelta a la derecha

C. turn left
dar vuelta a la izquierda

1. corner
la esquina

2. block
la cuadra

Signs   Señales

3. stop
detenerse/pararse

4. do not enter/wrong way
no pasar/sentido contrario

5. speed limit
el límite de velocidad

6. one way
un solo sentido

7. U-turn OK
la vuelta en U permitida

8. no outlet/dead end
el callejón sin salida/la calle sin salida

9. right turn only
sólo giro a la derecha

10. pedestrian crossing
el cruce peatonal

11. railroad crossing
el cruce del ferrocarril

12. no parking
no estacionarse

13. school crossing
el cruce escolar

14. handicapped parking
el estacionamiento para minusválidos

More vocabulary

right-of-way: the right to go first

yield: to give another person or car the right-of-way

Share your answers.

1. Which traffic signs are the same in your country?

2. Do pedestrians have the right-of-way in your city?

3. What is the speed limit in front of your school? your home?

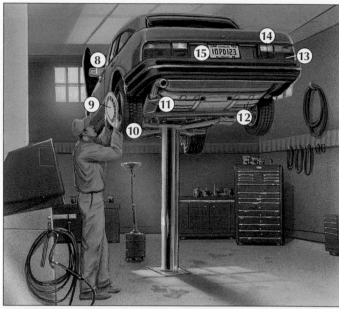

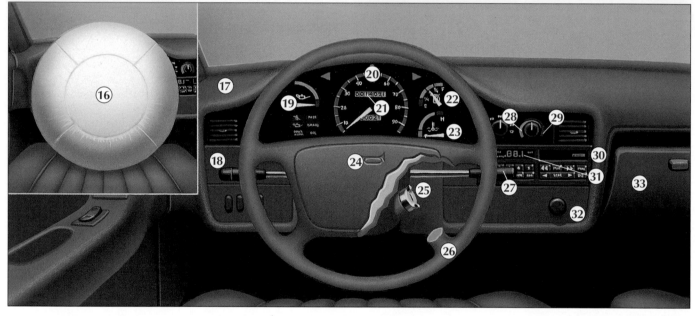

1. **rearview mirror**
   el espejo retrovisor

2. **windshield**
   el parabrisas

3. **windshield wipers**
   el limpiaparabrisas

4. **turn signal**
   la direccional

5. **headlight**
   la luz delantera

6. **hood**
   el capó/la capota

7. **bumper**
   el parachoques/la defensa

8. **sideview mirror**
   el espejo lateral

9. **hubcap**
   el tapacubos

10. **tire**
    el neumático/la llanta

11. **muffler**
    el silenciador

12. **gas tank**
    el tanque de gasolina

13. **brake light**
    la luz del freno

14. **taillight**
    la luz trasera

15. **license plate**
    la placa/la tablilla

16. **air bag**
    la bolsa de aire

17. **dashboard**
    el tablero

18. **turn signal**
    la direccional

19. **oil gauge**
    el medidor de aceite

20. **speedometer**
    el velocímetro/el tacómetro

21. **odometer**
    el odómetro

22. **gas gauge**
    el medidor de gasolina

23. **temperature gauge**
    el medidor de temperatura

24. **horn**
    el claxon/la bocina

25. **ignition**
    el arranque

26. **steering wheel**
    el volante

27. **gearshift**
    la palanca de velocidades

28. **air conditioning**
    el aire acondicionado

29. **heater**
    el calentador

30. **tape deck**
    el tocacintas

31. **radio**
    el radio

32. **cigarette lighter**
    el encendedor

33. **glove compartment**
    la guantera

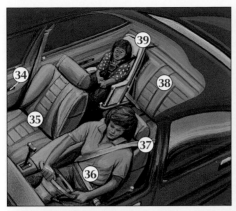

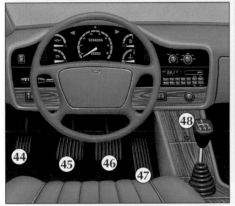

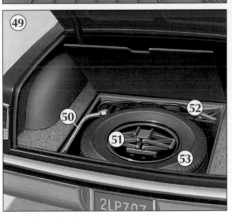

34. lock
el seguro

35. front seat
el asiento delantero

36. seat belt
el cinturón de seguridad

37. shoulder harness
el cinturón de hombro

38. backseat
el asiento trasero

39. child safety seat
el asiento para niños

40. fuel injection system
el sistema de inyección de combustible

41. engine
el motor

42. radiator
el radiador

43. battery
la batería

44. emergency brake
el freno de mano

45. clutch*
el clutch/el embrague

46. brake pedal
el pedal del freno

47. accelerator/gas pedal
el pedal del acelerador

48. stick shift
la palanca de velocidades

49. trunk
la cajuela/la maletera/el baúl

50. lug wrench
la llave de tuerca

51. jack
el gato hidráulico

52. jumper cables
los cables para pasar corriente

53. spare tire
el neumático/la llanta de repuesto

54. The car needs **gas**.
El auto necesita **gasolina.**

55. The car needs **oil**.
El auto necesita **aceite.**

56. The radiator needs **coolant**.
El radiador necesita **refrigerante.**

57. The car needs **a smog check**.
El auto necesita **una prueba de esmog.**

58. The battery needs **recharging**.
Hay que **recargar** la batería.

59. The tires need **air**.
Hay que **inflar** los neumáticos.

*Note: Standard transmission cars have a clutch; automatic transmission cars do not.

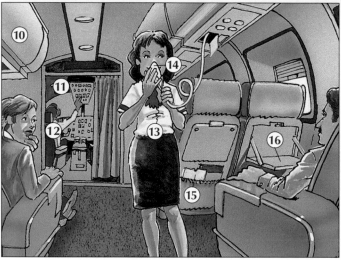

1. **airline terminal**
   la terminal de la línea aérea

2. **airline representative**
   el representante de la línea aérea

3. **check-in counter**
   el mostrador para registrarse

4. **arrival and departure monitors**
   los monitores de salidas y llegadas

5. **gate**
   la puerta

6. **boarding area**
   la zona de abordaje

7. **control tower**
   la torre de control

8. **helicopter**
   el helicóptero

9. **airplane**
   el avión

10. **overhead compartment**
    el compartimiento para el equipaje de mano

11. **cockpit**
    la cabina del piloto

12. **pilot**
    el piloto

13. **flight attendant**
    la aeromoza/la azafata

14. **oxygen mask**
    la máscara de oxígeno

15. **airsickness bag**
    la bolsa para mareos

16. **tray table**
    la mesita

17. **baggage claim area**
    la zona de entrega de equipaje

18. **carousel**
    el carrusel

19. **luggage carrier**
    el transporte de equipaje

20. **customs**
    la aduana

21. **customs officer**
    el agente aduanal

22. **declaration form**
    la declaración de aduana

23. **passenger**
    el pasajero

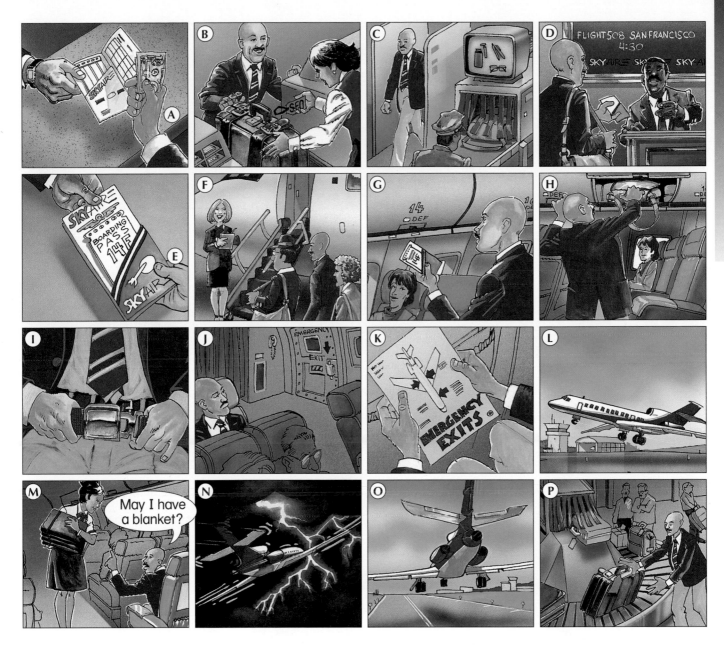

A. **buy** your ticket
    comprar el boleto

B. **check** your bags
    registrar el equipaje

C. **go through** security
    pasar por seguridad

D. **check in** at the gate
    presentarse en la puerta

E. **get** your boarding pass
    recibir la tarjeta de abordaje

F. **board** the plane
    abordar el avión

G. **find** your seat
    buscar su asiento

H. **stow** your carry-on bag
    guardar el equipaje de mano

I. **fasten** your seat belt
    abrocharse el cinturón de seguridad

J. **look for** the emergency exit
    buscar la salida de emergencia

K. **look at** the emergency card
    mirar la tarjeta sobre emergencias

L. **take off / leave**
    despegar / irse

M. **request** a blanket
    pedir una cobija / una manta / una frazada

N. **experience** turbulence
    experimentar turbulencias

O. **land / arrive**
    aterrizar / llegar

P. **claim** your baggage
    recoger el equipaje

More vocabulary

destination: the place the passenger is going

departure time: the time the plane takes off

arrival time: the time the plane lands

direct flight: a plane trip between two cities with no stops

stopover: a stop before reaching the destination, sometimes to change planes

Types of Schools   Tipos de escuela

1. public school
la escuela pública

2. private school
la escuela privada

3. parochial school
la escuela/el colegio parroquial

4. preschool
el jardín de niños/el
centro de enseñanza
preescolar

5. elementary school
la escuela primaria

6. middle school/
junior high school
la escuela intermedia

7. high school
la escuela secundaria

8. adult school
la escuela para adultos

9. vocational school/trade school
la escuela vocacional/de artes y
oficios/industrial

10. college/university
el colegio de enseñanza superior/
la universidad

Note: In the U.S. most children begin school at age 5 (in kindergarten)
and graduate from high school at 17 or 18.

More vocabulary

When students graduate from a college or university
they receive a **degree:**

Bachelor's degree — usually 4 years of study

Master's degree—an additional 1–3 years of study

Doctorate—an additional 3–5 years of study

community college: a two-year college where students
can get an Associate of Arts degree

graduate school: a school in a university where students
study for their master's and doctorates

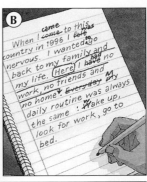

1. writing assignment
la tarea de redacción

A. Write a first draft.
Escriba un primer borrador.

B. Edit your paper.
Corrija su ensayo.

C. Get feedback.
Reciba comentarios.

D. Rewrite your paper.
Redacte nuevamente su ensayo.

E. Turn in your paper.
Entregue su ensayo.

2. paper/composition
el ensayo/la composición

My life in the U.S.

I arrived in this country in 1996. My family did not come with me. I was homesick, nervous, and a little excited. I had no job and no friends here. I lived with my aunt and my daily routine was always the same: get up, look for a job, go to bed. At night I remembered my mother's words to me, "Son, you can always come home!" I was homesick and scared, but I did not go home.

I started to study English at night. English is a difficult language and many times I was too tired to study. One teacher, Mrs. Armstrong, was very kind to me. She showed me many

3. title — el título
4. sentence — la oración
5. paragraph — el párrafo

Punctuation   La puntuación

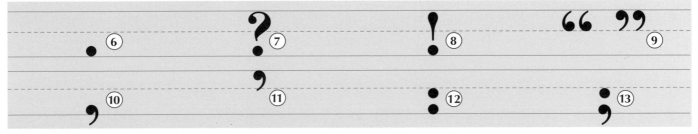

6. period — el punto
7. question mark — el signo de interrogación
8. exclamation mark — el signo de exclamación
9. quotation marks — las comillas
10. comma — la coma
11. apostrophe — el apóstrofo
12. colon — los dos puntos
13. semicolon — el punto y coma

U.S. History   La historia de los EE.UU.

Exploration	War	Immigration
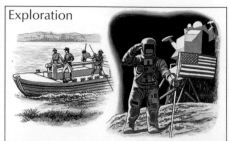		

| **Historical and Political Events**
Eventos históricos y políticos | **1492 →**
French, Spanish, English explorers
Exploradores franceses, españoles e ingleses | **1607–1750**
Colonies along Atlantic coast founded by Northern Europeans
Colonias a lo largo de la costa del Atlántico de inmigrantes procedentes del norte de Europa | **1619** 1st African slave sold in Virginia
Primeros esclavos africanos vendidos en Virginia
1653 1st Indian reservation in Virginia
1era Reservación India en Virginia |

Before 1700   **1700**

| **Immigration***
Inmigración | **1607**
1st English in Virginia
Primer inglés en Virginia | **1610**
Spanish at Santa Fe
Españoles en Santa Fe |

| **Population****
Población | Before 1700: Native American: 1,000,000+
Indígenas: 1,000,000+ | 1700: colonists: 250,000
colonos: 250,000 |

| **1803**
Louisiana Purchase
Compra de Luisiana | **1812**
War of 1812
Guerra de 1812 | **1820**
Missouri Compromise
Compromiso Missouri | **1830**
Indian Removal Act
Acta de Remoción de los Indios | **1835–1838**
Cherokee Trail of Tears
Senda de Lágrimas Cheroquí | **1846–1848**
U.S. war with Mexico
Guerra entre México y los EE.UU. |

1800   **1810**   **1820**   **1830**   **1840**

1815 →
Irish
Irlandeses

1800: citizens and free blacks: 5,300,000   slaves: 450,000
ciudadanos y negros libres: 5,300,000   esclavos: 450,000

| **1903**
1st *Model A* Ford car
Primer modelo de automóvil Ford | **1927**
1st sound pictures
Primeras películas sonoras | **1929**
stock market crashes
Caída de la Bolsa de Valores | **1939–1945**
World War II
Segunda Guerra Mundial | **1945**
United Nations
Las Naciones Unidas |

1st air flight
Primer vuelo aéreo

1914–1918
World War I
Primera Guerra Mundial

1920
women get vote
Las mujeres obtienen el derecho al voto

1930–1940
The Depression
La Depresión

1945
1st atomic bomb
Primera bomba atómica

1948–1985
The Cold War
La Guerra Fría

1900   **1910**   **1920**   **1930**   **1940**

1910 →
Mexicans
Mexicanos

1924
U.S. closes borders
EE.UU. cierra sus fronteras

1942–1945
Japanese internment
Internamiento de los japoneses

1945 →
Puerto Ricans
Puerto-rriqueños

1948
WW II refugees immigrate
Inmigración de refugiad de la Segunda Guerra Mundial

1900: 75,994,000

*Immigration dates indicate a time when large numbers of that group first began to immigrate to the U.S.
**All population figures before 1790 are estimates. Figures after 1790 are based on the official U.S. census.

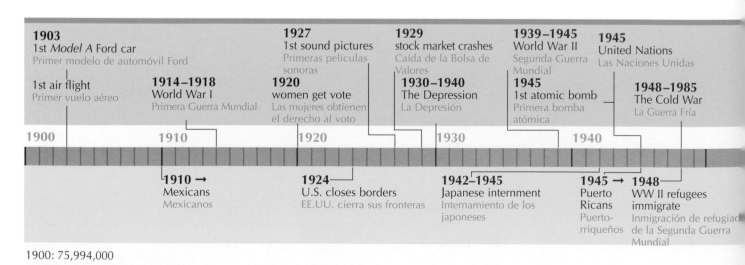

Movement

Election

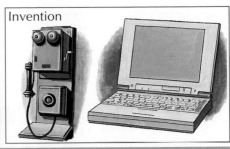

Invention

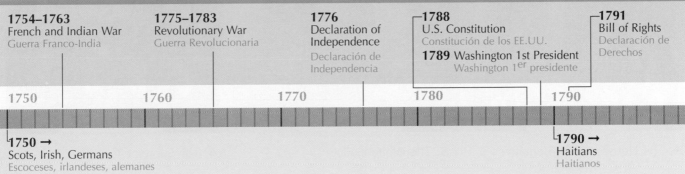

1754–1763
French and Indian War
Guerra Franco-India

1775–1783
Revolutionary War
Guerra Revolucionaria

1776
Declaration of
Independence
Declaración de
Independencia

1788
U.S. Constitution
Constitución de los EE.UU.

1789 Washington 1st President
Washington 1er presidente

1791
Bill of Rights
Declaración de
Derechos

1750   1760   1770   1780   1790

1750 →
Scots, Irish, Germans
Escoceses, irlandeses, alemanes

1790 →
Haitians
Haitianos

1750: Native American: 1,000,000 +   colonists and free blacks: 1,171,000   slaves: 200,000
Aborígenes: 1,000,000+   colonos y negros libres: 1,171,000   esclavos: 200,000

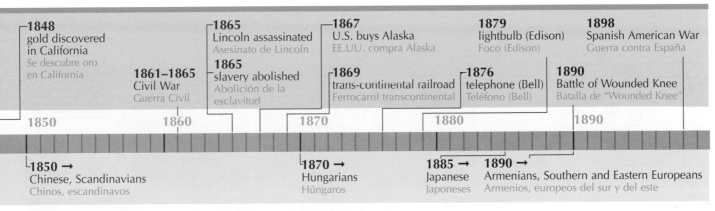

1848
gold discovered
in California
Se descubre oro
en California

1861–1865
Civil War
Guerra Civil

1865
Lincoln assassinated
Asesinato de Lincoln

1865
slavery abolished
Abolición de la
esclavitud

1867
U.S. buys Alaska
EE.UU. compra Alaska

1869
trans-continental railroad
Ferrocarril transcontinental

1879
lightbulb (Edison)
Foco (Edison)

1876
telephone (Bell)
Teléfono (Bell)

1898
Spanish American War
Guerra contra España

1890
Battle of Wounded Knee
Batalla de "Wounded Knee"

1850   1860   1870   1880   1890

1850 →
Chinese, Scandinavians
Chinos, escandinavos

1870 →
Hungarians
Húngaros

1885 →
Japanese
Japoneses

1890 →
Armenians, Southern and Eastern Europeans
Armenios, europeos del sur y del este

1850: 23,191,000

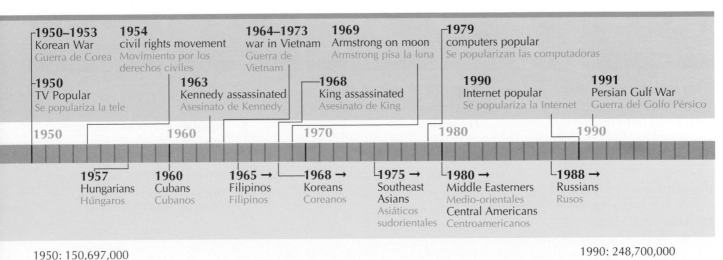

1950–1953
Korean War
Guerra de Corea

1954
civil rights movement
Movimiento por los
derechos civiles

1964–1973
war in Vietnam
Guerra de
Vietnam

1969
Armstrong on moon
Armstrong pisa la luna

1979
computers popular
Se popularizan las computadoras

1950
TV Popular
Se populariza la tele

1963
Kennedy assassinated
Asesinato de Kennedy

1968
King assassinated
Asesinato de King

1990
Internet popular
Se populariza la Internet

1991
Persian Gulf War
Guerra del Golfo Pérsico

1950   1960   1970   1980   1990

1957
Hungarians
Húngaros

1960
Cubans
Cubanos

1965 →
Filipinos
Filipinos

1968 →
Koreans
Coreanos

1975 →
Southeast
Asians
Asiáticos
sudorientales

1980 →
Middle Easterners
Medio-orientales
Central Americans
Centroamericanos

1988 →
Russians
Rusos

1950: 150,697,000   1990: 248,700,000

BRANCHES OF GOVERNMENT

Legislative

Executive

Judicial

1. The House of Representatives
La Cámara de Representantes

2. congresswoman/congressman
el/la congresista

3. The Senate
El Senado

4. senator
el senador

5. The White House
La Casa Blanca

6. president
el presidente

7. vice president
el vicepresidente

8. The Supreme Court
La Corte Suprema

9. chief justice
el presidente de la Corte Suprema

10. justices
los jueces

Citizenship application requirements
Requisitos para la solicitud de ciudadanía

A. **be** 18 years old
tener 18 años de edad

B. **live** in the U.S. for five years
vivir en los EE.UU. por cinco años

C. **take** a citizenship test
presentar un examen de ciudadanía

Rights and responsibilities
Derechos y responsabilidades

D. **vote**
votar

E. **pay** taxes
pagar impuestos

F. **register** with Selective Service*
inscribirse en el ejército

G. **serve** on a jury
servir en un jurado

H. **obey** the law
obedecer/acatar las leyes

***Note:** All males 18 to 26 who live in the U.S. are required to register with Selective Service.

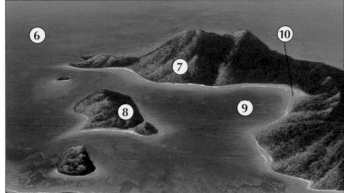

1. rain forest
   el bosque húmedo/la
   selva tropical húmeda

2. waterfall
   la cascada/el salto de
   agua/la catarata

3. river
   el río

4. desert
   el desierto

5. sand dune
   la duna

6. ocean
   el océano

7. peninsula
   la península

8. island
   la isla

9. bay
   la bahía

10. beach
    la playa

11. forest
    el bosque

12. shore
    la orilla

13. lake
    el lago

14. mountain peak
    el pico/la cima de la
    montaña

15. mountain range
    la cordillera/la sierra

16. hills
    las colinas

17. canyon
    el cañón

18. valley
    el valle

19. plains
    el llano/la llanura

20. meadow
    la pradera/el prado

21. pond
    el estanque/la charca

More vocabulary

a body of water: a river, lake, or ocean

stream/creek: a very small river

Talk about where you live and where you like to go.

I live in a valley. There is a lake nearby.

I like to go to the beach.

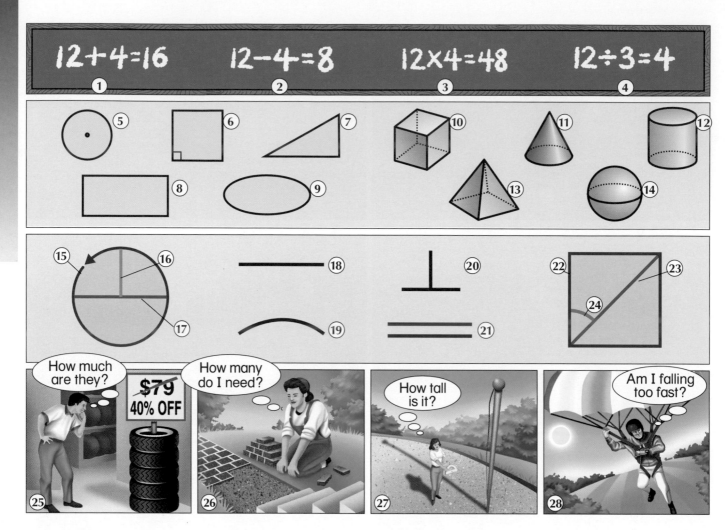

Operations
Las operaciones matemáticas

1. addition
   la suma

2. subtraction
   la resta

3. multiplication
   la multiplicación

4. division
   la división

Shapes
Las figuras geométricas

5. circle
   el círculo

6. square
   el cuadrado

7. triangle
   el triángulo

8. rectangle
   el rectángulo

9. oval/ellipse
   el óvalo/la elipse

Solids
Los sólidos

10. cube
    el cubo

11. cone
    el cono

12. cylinder
    el cilindro

13. pyramid
    la pirámide

14. sphere
    la esfera

Parts of a circle
Las partes de un círculo

15. circumference
    la circunferencia

16. radius
    el radio

17. diameter
    el diámetro

Lines
Las líneas

18. straight
    la recta

19. curved
    la curva

20. perpendicular
    la perpendicular

21. parallel
    la paralela

Parts of a square
Las partes de un cuadrado

22. side
    el lado

23. diagonal
    la diagonal

24. angle
    el ángulo

Types of math
Los tipos de matemáticas

25. algebra
    el álgebra

26. geometry
    la geometría

27. trigonometry
    la trigonometría

28. calculus
    el cálculo

More vocabulary

total: the answer to an addition problem

difference: the answer to a subtraction problem

product: the answer to a multiplication problem

quotient: the answer to a division problem

pi (π): the number when you divide the circumference of a circle by its diameter (approximately = 3.14)

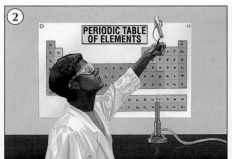

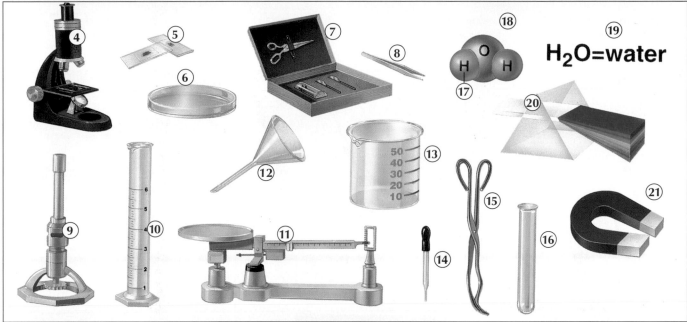

H₂O=water

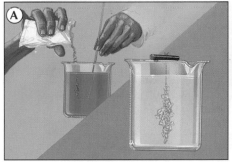

1. biology
la biología

2. chemistry
la química

3. physics
la física

4. microscope
el microscopio

5. slide
la platina

6. petri dish
la cápsula de Petri

7. dissection kit
el juego de disección

8. forceps
las pinzas / las tenazas

9. Bunsen burner
el mechero de Bunsen

10. graduated cylinder
el cilindro graduado

11. balance
la balanza

12. funnel
el embudo

13. beaker
el vaso de laboratorio

14. dropper
el gotero

15. crucible tongs
las tenazas para crisol

16. test tube
el tubo de ensayo

17. atom
el átomo

18. molecule
la molécula

19. formula
la fórmula

20. prism
el prisma

21. magnet
el imán

A. **do** an experiment
hacer un experimento

B. **observe**
observar

C. **record** results
anotar los resultados

119

Music La música

A. **play** an instrument
tocar un instrumento

B. **sing** a song
cantar una canción

1. orchestra
la orquesta

2. rock band
la banda de rock

Woodwinds

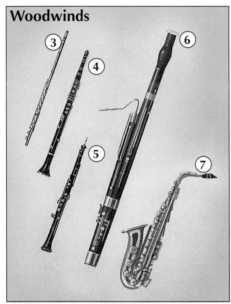

Strings

Brass

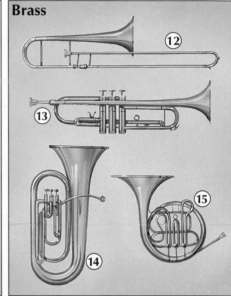

Percussion

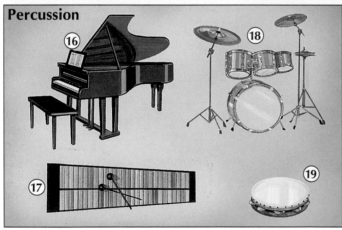

Other Instruments

3. flute
la flauta

4. clarinet
el clarinete

5. oboe
el oboe

6. bassoon
el fagot

7. saxophone
el saxofón

8. violin
el violín

9. cello
el violoncelo

10. bass
el bajo

11. guitar
la guitarra

12. trombone
el trombón

13. trumpet/horn
la trompeta/el corno

14. tuba
la tuba

15. French horn
el corno francés

16. piano
el piano

17. xylophone
el xilófono

18. drums
la batería

19. tambourine
la pandereta/el pandero

20. electric keyboard
el teclado electrónico

21. accordion
el acordeón

22. organ
el órgano

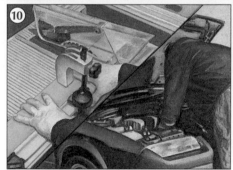

1. art
   el arte

2. business education
   la educación de negocios

3. chorus
   el coro

4. computer science
   las ciencias de la computación

5. driver's education
   los cursos de manejo

6. economics
   la economía

7. English as a second language
   el inglés como segundo idioma

8. foreign language
   el idioma extranjero

9. home economics
   la economía doméstica/las ciencias domésticas

10. industrial arts/shop
    las artes industriales

11. PE (physical education)
    la educación física

12. theater arts
    las artes teatrales

More vocabulary

core course: a subject students have to take

elective: a subject students choose to take

Share your answers.

1. What are your favorite subjects?
2. In your opinion, what subjects are most important? Why?
3. What foreign languages are taught in your school?

ARCTIC OCEAN

ATLANTIC OCEAN

GREENLAND

Baffin Bay

Labrador Sea

Queen Elizabeth Islands

Beaufort Sea

Alaska (US)

Gulf of Alaska

CANADA

Yukon Territory

Northwest Territories

British Columbia

Alberta

Saskatchewan

Manitoba

Ontario

Québec

Hudson Bay

Newfoundland

Gulf of St. Lawrence

Prince Edward Island

Nova Scotia

New Brunswick

Maine

OTTAWA

UNITED STATES OF AMERICA

Washington

Oregon

Idaho

Montana

Wyoming

Nevada

Utah

California

Arizona

New Mexico

Colorado

North Dakota

South Dakota

Nebraska

Kansas

Oklahoma

Minnesota

Iowa

Missouri

Arkansas

Wisconsin

Michigan

Michigan

Illinois

Indiana

Ohio

Kentucky

Tennessee

New York

Pennsylvania

West Virginia

Virginia

North Carolina

South Carolina

Vermont

New Hampshire

Massachusetts

Rhode Island

Connecticut

New Jersey

Delaware

Maryland

WASHINGTON, D.C.

BERMUDA

Hawaii (US)

① ② ③ ④ ⑤ ⑥ ⑦ ⑧ ⑨ ⑩ ⑪

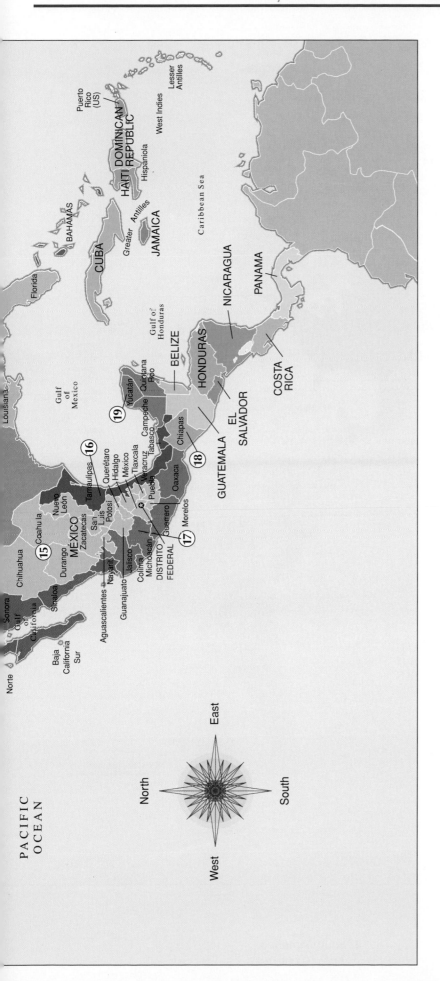

Regions of Canada
Regiones de Canadá

1. Northern Canada
Canadá del Norte

2. British Columbia
Colombia Británica/Columbia Británica

3. The Prairie Provinces
Las Provincias de las praderas

4. Ontario
Ontario

5. Québec
Quebec

6. The Atlantic Provinces
Las Provincias del Atlántico

Regions of the United States
Regiones de los Estados Unidos

7. The Pacific States/the West Coast
Los estados del Pacífico/la costa oeste

8. The Rocky Mountain States
Los estados de las Montañas Rocosas

9. The Midwest
El mediooeste

10. The Mid-Atlantic States
Los estados del centro del Atlántico

11. New England
Nueva Inglaterra

12. The Southwest
El suroeste

13. The Southeast/the South
El sureste/el sur

Regions of Mexico
Regiones de México

14. The Pacific Northwest
El noroeste del Pacífico

15. The Plateau of Mexico
El altiplano de México

16. The Gulf Coastal Plain
La planicie de la costa del Golfo

17. The Southern Uplands
Las mesetas del Sur

18. The Chiapas Highlands
Las regiones montañosas de Chiapas

19. The Yucatan Peninsula
La península de Yucatán

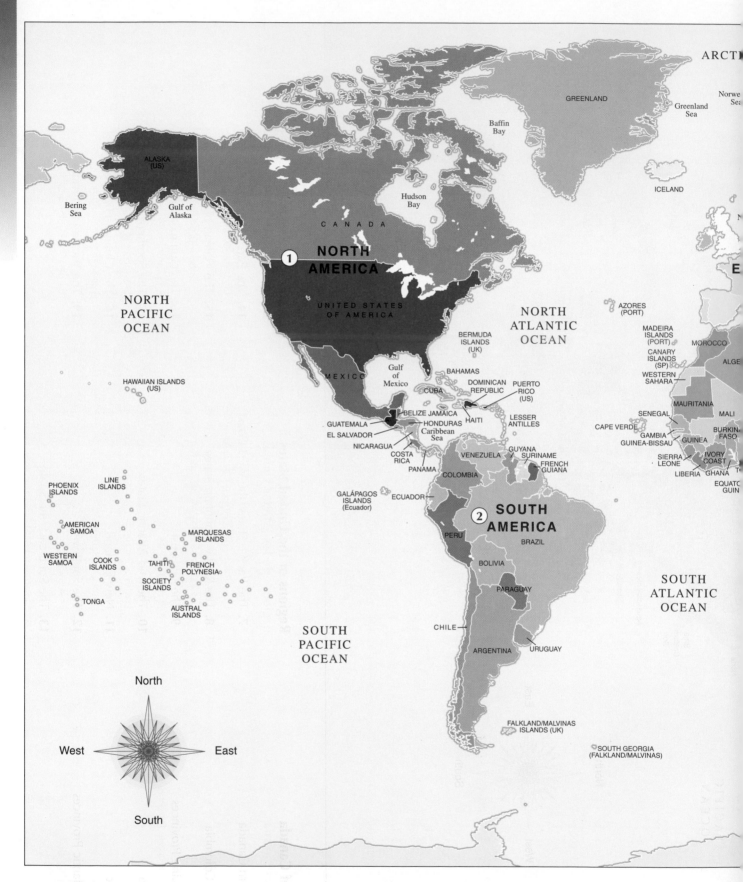

Continents
Los continentes

1. North America
América del Norte

2. South America
América del Sur

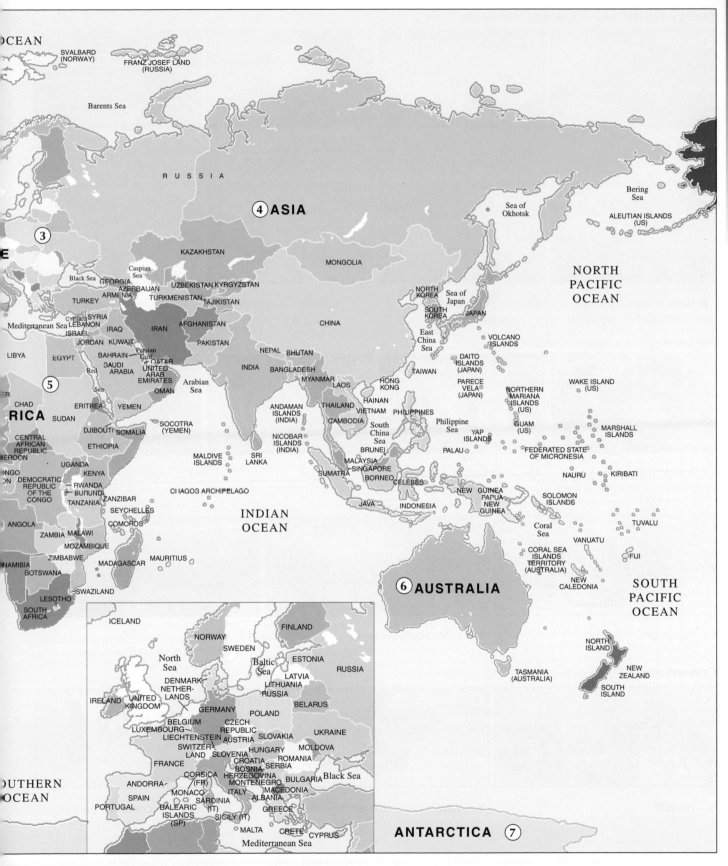

OCEAN

SVALBARD
(NORWAY)

FRANZ JOSEF LAND
(RUSSIA)

Barents Sea

R U S S I A

④ ASIA

③

⑤

E

Black Sea

Caspian
Sea

KAZAKHSTAN

MONGOLIA

GEORGIA
AZERBAIJAN
ARMENIA
TURKEY

UZBEKISTAN KYRGYZSTAN
TURKMENISTAN
TAJIKISTAN

Sea of
Okhotsk

Bering
Sea

ALEUTIAN ISLANDS
(US)

NORTH
PACIFIC
OCEAN

CYPRUS SYRIA
Mediterranean Sea LEBANON
ISRAEL
JORDAN KUWAIT
LIBYA
EGYPT
BAHRAIN
SAUDI
ARABIA
RICA

IRAQ
IRAN
AFGHANISTAN
PAKISTAN
Persian
Gulf QATAR
UNITED
ARAB
EMIRATES
Red
OMAN
Sea

CHINA

NORTH
KOREA
SOUTH
KOREA

Sea of
Japan

JAPAN

East
China
Sea

TAIWAN

VOLCANO
ISLANDS

DAITO
ISLANDS
(JAPAN)

PARECE
VELA
(JAPAN)

WAKE ISLAND
(US)

NORTHERN
MARIANA
ISLANDS
(US)

NEPAL BHUTAN
INDIA BANGLADESH
Arabian
Sea
MYANMAR LAOS

CHAD
SUDAN
ERITREA
YEMEN
DJIBOUTI SOMALIA
ETHIOPIA

SOCOTRA
(YEMEN)

ANDAMAN
ISLANDS
(INDIA)

NICOBAR
ISLANDS
(INDIA)

THAILAND
CAMBODIA

HAINAN
VIETNAM
PHILIPPINES

HONG
KONG

South
China
Sea

Philippine
Sea
YAP
ISLANDS

GUAM
(US)

MARSHALL
ISLANDS

FEDERATED STATE
OF MICRONESIA

MEROON
UGANDA
KENYA

MALDIVE
ISLANDS

SRI
LANKA

BRUNEI
MALAYSIA
SINGAPORE

PALAU

NAURU

KIRIBATI

CONGO
ON

DEMOCRATIC
REPUBLIC
OF THE
CONGO
RWANDA
BURUNDI
TANZANIA
ZANZIBAR

CHAGOS ARCHIPELAGO

SUMATRA
BORNEO
CELEBES

NEW GUINEA
PAPUA
NEW
GUINEA

SOLOMON
ISLANDS

SEYCHELLES

ANGOLA
ZAMBIA MALAWI
MOZAMBIQUE
ZIMBABWE
NAMIBIA
BOTSWANA
LESOTHO
SWAZILAND
SOUTH
AFRICA

COMOROS

MAURITIUS

JAVA
INDONESIA

INDIAN
OCEAN

MADAGASCAR

Coral
Sea

CORAL SEA
ISLANDS
TERRITORY
(AUSTRALIA)

TUVALU

VANUATU

FIJI

NEW
CALEDONIA

⑥ AUSTRALIA

SOUTH
PACIFIC
OCEAN

NORTH
ISLAND

TASMANIA
(AUSTRALIA)

NEW
ZEALAND
SOUTH
ISLAND

ICELAND

NORWAY
SWEDEN

FINLAND

North
Sea
DENMARK
NETHER-
LANDS

Baltic
Sea

ESTONIA
LATVIA
LITHUANIA
RUSSIA

RUSSIA

IRELAND
UNITED
KINGDOM
GERMANY
POLAND
BELGIUM
LUXEMBOURG
LIECHTENSTEIN
SWITZER-
LAND
FRANCE
CZECH
REPUBLIC
AUSTRIA SLOVAKIA
SLOVENIA
HUNGARY
CROATIA
BELARUS
UKRAINE
MOLDOVA
ROMANIA

OUTHERN
OCEAN

ANDORRA
SPAIN
PORTUGAL
MONACO
SARDINIA
(IT)
BALEARIC
ISLANDS
(SP)
CORSICA
(FR)
ITALY
BOSNIA
HERZEGOVINA
MONTENEGRO
ALBANIA
SICILY (IT)
SERBIA
BULGARIA
MACEDONIA
GREECE
MALTA
CRETE
Mediterranean Sea
CYPRUS
Black Sea

ANTARCTICA ⑦

3. Europe
Europa

4. Asia
Asia

5. Africa
África

6. Australia
Australia

7. Antarctica
Antártida

Energy and the Environment   La energía y el medioambiente

Energy resources   Los recursos energéticos

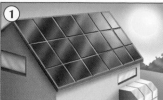

1. solar energy
la energía solar

2. wind
el viento

3. natural gas
el gas natural

4. coal
el carbón

5. hydroelectric power
la energía hidroeléctrica

6. oil/petroleum
el petróleo

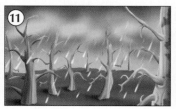

7. geothermal energy
la energía geotérmica

8. nuclear energy
la energía nuclear

Pollution   La contaminación

9. hazardous waste
los desechos peligrosos

10. air pollution/smog
la contaminación del
aire/el esmog, el neblumo

11. acid rain
la lluvia ácida

12. water pollution
la contaminación
del agua

13. radiation
la radiación

14. pesticide poisoning
el envenenamiento con insecticidas

15. oil spill
el derrame de petróleo

Conservation   La preservación/la conservación

A. **recycle**
reciclar

B. **save** water/**conserve** water
ahorrar agua/**conservar** agua

C. **save** energy/**conserve** energy
ahorrar energía/**conservar** energía

Share your answers.

1. How do you heat your home?

2. Do you have a gas stove or an electric stove?

3. What are some ways you can save energy when it's cold?

4. Do you recycle? What products do you recycle?

5. Does your market have recycling bins?

The Solar System

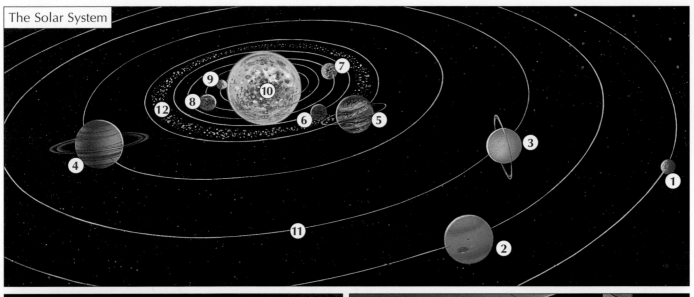

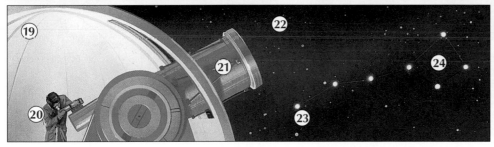

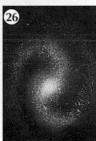

The planets
Los planetas

1. Pluto
   Plutón

2. Neptune
   Neptuno

3. Uranus
   Urano

4. Saturn
   Saturno

5. Jupiter
   Júpiter

6. Mars
   Marte

7. Earth
   Tierra

8. Venus
   Venus

9. Mercury
   Mercurio

10. sun
    el sol

11. orbit
    la órbita

12. asteroid belt
    la zona de asteroides

13. new moon
    la luna nueva

14. crescent moon
    la media luna

15. quarter moon
    el cuarto menguante

16. full moon
    la luna llena

17. astronaut
    el astronauta

18. space station
    la estación espacial

19. observatory
    el observatorio

20. astronomer
    el astrónomo

21. telescope
    el telescopio

22. space
    el espacio

23. star
    la estrella

24. constellation
    la constelación

25. comet
    el cometa

26. galaxy
    la galaxia

More vocabulary

lunar eclipse: when the earth is between the sun and the moon

solar eclipse: when the moon is between the earth and the sun

Share your answers.

1. Do you know the names of any constellations?

2. How do you feel when you look up at the night sky?

3. Is the night sky in the U.S. the same as in your country?

Trees and Plants   Árboles y plantas

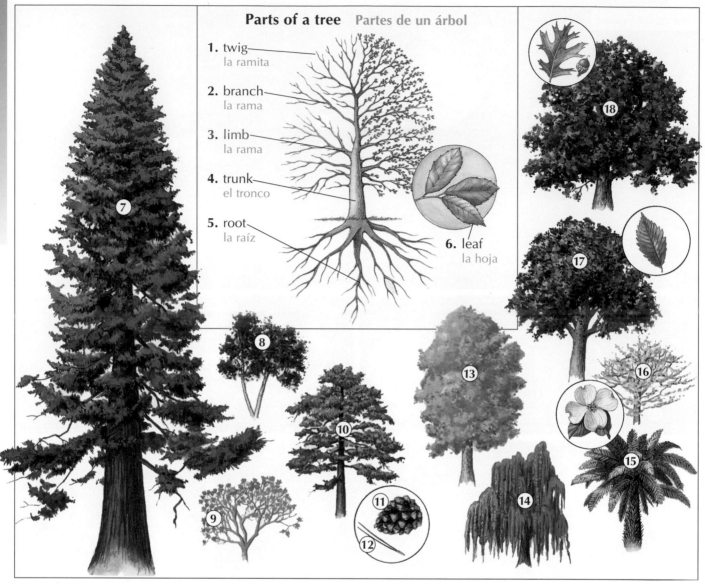

Parts of a tree   Partes de un árbol

1. twig
   la ramita
2. branch
   la rama
3. limb
   la rama
4. trunk
   el tronco
5. root
   la raíz
6. leaf
   la hoja

7. redwood la secoya	**10.** pine el pino	**13.** maple el arce	**16.** dogwood el cornejo/el cerezo silvestre
8. birch el abedul	**11.** pinecone la piña/el cono	**14.** willow el sauce	**17.** elm el olmo
9. magnolia la magnolia	**12.** needle la aguja	**15.** palm la palma	**18.** oak el roble

Plants   Plantas

19. holly el acebo	**21.** cactus el cactus	**23.** poison oak el árbol de las pulgas	**25.** poison ivy la hiedra venenosa
20. berries las bayas	**22.** vine la enredadera	**24.** poison sumac el zumaque venenoso	

Parts of a flower   Partes de una flor

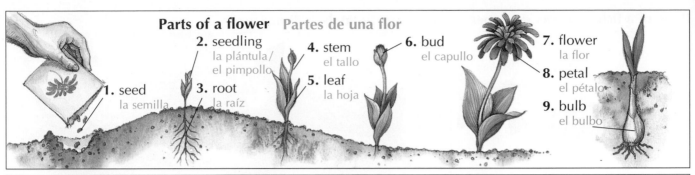

1. seed
la semilla

2. seedling
la plántula/
el pimpollo

3. root
la raíz

4. stem
el tallo

5. leaf
la hoja

6. bud
el capullo

7. flower
la flor

8. petal
el pétalo

9. bulb
el bulbo

10. sunflower el girasol	**15.** rose la rosa	**20.** iris el lirio	**25.** crocus el azafrán
11. tulip el tulipán	**16.** gardenia la gardenia	**21.** jasmine el jazmín	**26.** daffodil el narciso atrompetado/trompón
12. hibiscus el hibisco	**17.** orchid la orquídea	**22.** violet la violeta	**27.** bouquet el ramo/el ramillete
13. marigold la maravilla/el clavelón	**18.** carnation el clavel	**23.** poinsettia la flor de Nochebuena/ la pascua	**28.** thorn la espina
14. daisy la margarita	**19.** chrysanthemum el crisantemo	**24.** lily la azucena/el lirio	**29.** houseplant la planta para interiores

Marine Life, Amphibians, and Reptiles   Vida marina, anfibios y reptiles

Parts of a fish   Partes de un pez

Sea animals   Fauna marina

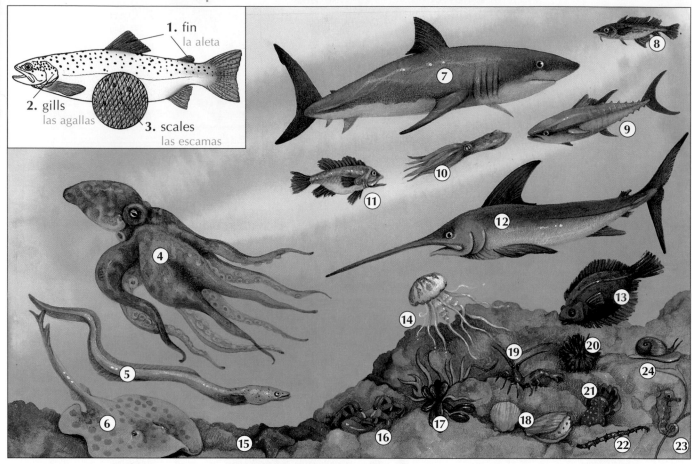

1. fin
la aleta

2. gills
las agallas

3. scales
las escamas

4. octopus el pulpo	**11.** bass el róbalo/la perca	**18.** scallop la venera/el escalope
5. eel la anguila	**12.** swordfish el pez espada	**19.** shrimp el camarón
6. ray la raya	**13.** flounder el lenguado	**20.** sea urchin el erizo de mar
7. shark el tiburón	**14.** jellyfish la medusa	**21.** sea anemone el anémona de mar
8. cod el bacalao/el abadejo	**15.** starfish la estrella de mar	**22.** worm la lombriz/el gusano
9. tuna el atún	**16.** crab el cangrejo	**23.** sea horse el caballo de mar
10. squid el calamar	**17.** mussel el mejillón	**24.** snail el caracol

Amphibians   Anfibios

25. frog
la rana

26. newt
la salamandra acuática/
el tritón

27. salamander
la salamandra

28. toad
el sapo

Sea mammals   Mamíferos marinos

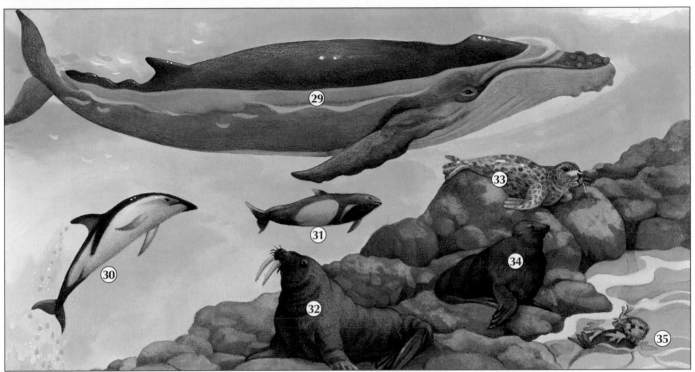

29. whale
la ballena

30. dolphin
el delfín

31. porpoise
la marsopa

32. walrus
la morsa

33. seal
la foca

34. sea lion
el león marino

35. otter
la nutria

Reptiles   Reptiles

36. alligator
el caimán

37. crocodile
el cocodrilo

38. rattlesnake
la serpiente de cascabel

39. garter snake
la culebra americana no
venenosa

40. cobra
la cobra

41. lizard
la lagartija

42. turtle
la tortuga

Birds, Insects, and Arachnids Pájaros, insectos y arácnidos

Parts of a bird Partes de un pájaro

1. beak/bill
   el pico
2. wing
   el ala
3. nest
   el nido
4. claw
   la garra
5. feather
   la pluma

6. owl
   el búho/la lechuza
7. blue jay
   el arrendajo azul/el grajo azul
8. sparrow
   el gorrión

9. woodpecker
   el pájaro carpintero
10. eagle
    el águila
11. hummingbird
    el colibrí/el picaflor

12. penguin
    el pingüino
13. duck
    el pato
14. goose
    el ganso

15. peacock
    el pavo real
16. pigeon
    la paloma
17. robin
    el petirrojo

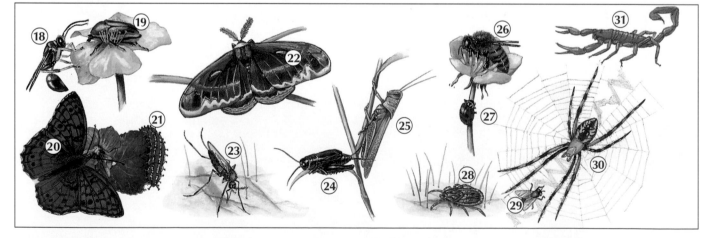

18. wasp
    la avispa
19. beetle
    el escarabajo
20. butterfly
    la mariposa
21. caterpillar
    la oruga

22. moth
    la mariposa nocturna/la polilla
23. mosquito
    el mosquito
24. cricket
    el grillo

25. grasshopper
    el saltamontes
26. honeybee
    la abeja melífera
27. ladybug
    la mariquita/la catarinita

28. tick
    la garrapata
29. fly
    la mosca
30. spider
    la araña
31. scorpion
    el escorpión

Farm animals   Animales de la granja

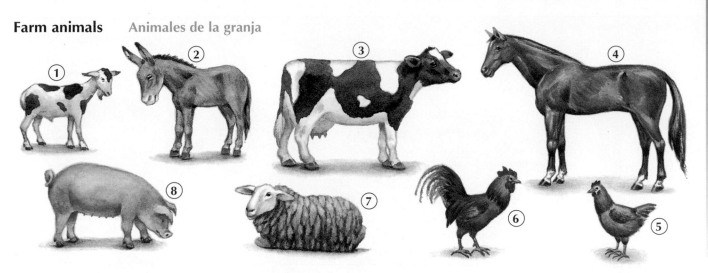

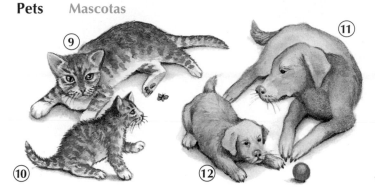

1. goat
la cabra

2. donkey
el burro

3. cow
la vaca

4. horse
el caballo

5. hen
la gallina

6. rooster
el gallo

7. sheep
la oveja

8. pig
el cerdo/el puerco/el cochino

Pets   Mascotas

9. cat
el gato

10. kitten
el gatito

11. dog
el perro

12. puppy
el cachorro

13. rabbit
el conejo

14. guinea pig
el conejillo de Indias

15. parakeet
el periquito

16. goldfish
la carpa dorada

Rodents   Roedores

17. mouse
el ratón

18. rat
la rata

19. gopher
la tuza

20. chipmunk
la ardilla listada

21. squirrel
la ardilla

22. prairie dog
la marmota de las praderas

More vocabulary

Wild animals live, eat, and raise their young away from people, in the forests, mountains, plains, etc.

Domesticated animals work for people or live with them.

Share your answers.

1. Do you have any pets? any farm animals?

2. Which of these animals are in your neighborhood? Which are not?

133

1. **moose**
   el alce

2. **mountain lion**
   el puma

3. **coyote**
   el coyote

4. **opossum**
   el opossum/la zarigüeya

5. **wolf**
   el lobo

6. **buffalo/bison**
   el búfalo/el bisonte

7. **bat**
   el murciélago

8. **armadillo**
   el armadillo

9. **beaver**
   el castor

10. **porcupine**
    el puerco espín

11. **bear**
    el oso

12. **skunk**
    el zorrillo/la mofeta

13. **raccoon**
    el mapache

14. **deer**
    el venado

15. **fox**
    el zorro

16. **antler**
    la cornamenta del ciervo

17. **hoof**
    la pezuña

18. **whiskers**
    los bigotes

19. **coat/fur**
    la lana/la piel

20. **paw**
    la garra/la pata

21. **horn**
    el cuerno

22. **tail**
    la cola

23. **quill**
    la púa

24. anteater
el oso hormiguero

25. leopard
el leopardo

26. llama
la llama

27. monkey
el mono

28. chimpanzee
el chimpancé

29. rhinoceros
el rinoceronte

30. gorilla
el gorila

31. hyena
la hiena

32. baboon
el mandril

33. giraffe
la jirafa

34. zebra
la cebra

35. antelope
el antílope

36. lion
el león

37. tiger
el tigre

38. camel
el camello

39. panther
la pantera

40. orangutan
el orangután

41. panda
el panda

42. elephant
el elefante

43. hippopotamus
el hipopótamo

44. kangaroo
el canguro

45. koala
el koala

46. platypus
el ornitorrinco

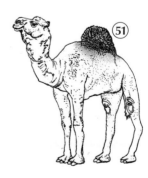

47. trunk
la trompa

48. tusk
el colmillo

49. mane
la crin/la melena

50. pouch
la bolsa

51. hump
la joroba

Jobs and Occupations, A–H   Empleos y profesiones

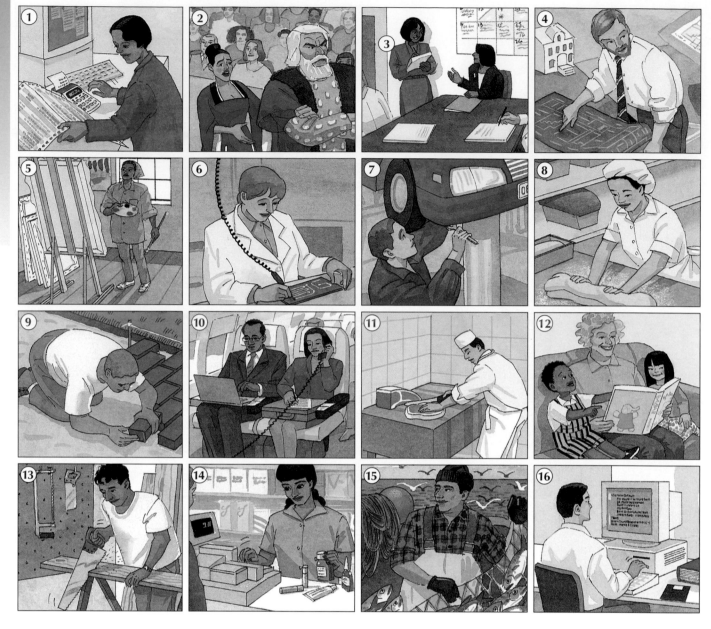

1. accountant
la contadora

2. actor
el actor/la actriz

3. administrative assistant
la asistente administrativo

4. architect
el arquitecto

5. artist
el artista

6. assembler
el montador

7. auto mechanic
el mecánico de automóviles

8. baker
el panadero

9. bricklayer
el albañil

10. businessman/businesswoman
el hombre/la mujer de negocios

11. butcher
el carnicero

12. caregiver/baby-sitter
la niñera

13. carpenter
el carpintero

14. cashier
la cajera

15. commercial fisher
el pescador comercial

16. computer programmer
el programador de computadoras

Use the new language.

1. Who works outside?

2. Who works inside?

3. Who makes things?

4. Who uses a computer?

5. Who wears a uniform?

6. Who sells things?

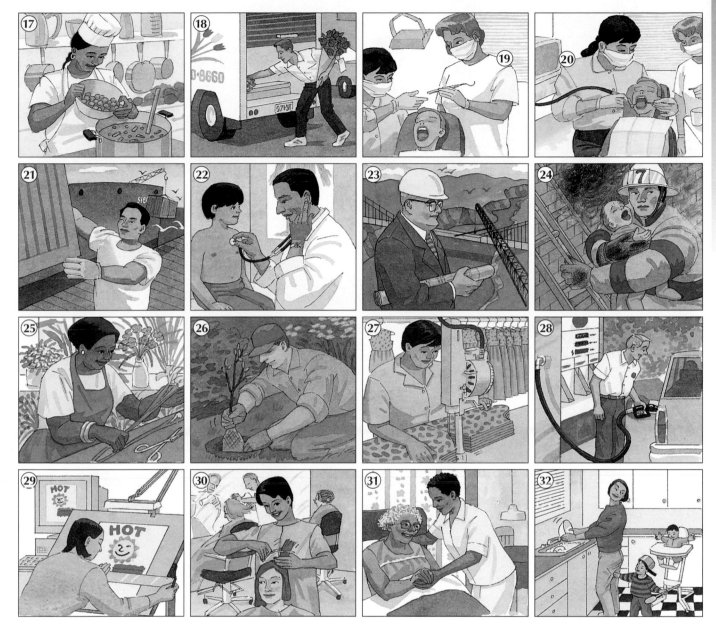

17. cook
    la cocinera

18. delivery person
    el repartidor

19. dental assistant
    la asistente dental

20. dentist
    la dentista

21. dockworker
    el trabajador portuario/el estibador

22. doctor
    el doctor/el médico

23. engineer
    el ingeniero

24. firefighter
    el bombero

25. florist
    la florista

26. gardener
    el jardinero

27. garment worker
    la empleada de una fábrica de ropa

28. gas station attendant
    el dependiente de la gasolinera

29. graphic artist
    el artista gráfico

30. hairdresser
    la peluquera

31. home attendant
    la empleada doméstica

32. homemaker
    el ama de casa

Share your answers.

1. Do you know people who have some of these jobs? What do they say about their work?

2. Which of these jobs are available in your city?

3. For which of these jobs do you need special training?

137

33. housekeeper
el ama de llaves

34. interpreter/translator
el intérprete/el traductor

35. janitor/custodian
el conserje/el guardián

36. lawyer
el abogado

37. machine operator
el operador de maquinaria

38. messenger/courier
el mensajero

39. model
la modelo

40. mover
el empleado de una casa de mudanzas

41. musician
el músico

42. nurse
la enfermera

43. painter
el pintor

44. police officer
la oficial de policía

45. postal worker
la empleada de correos

46. printer
el impresor

47. receptionist
la recepcionista

48. repair person
el reparador/el mecánico de reparaciones

Talk about each of the jobs or occupations.

She's a housekeeper. She works in a hotel.
He's an interpreter. He works for the government.

She's a nurse. She works with patients.

49. reporter
el reportero

50. salesclerk / salesperson
el dependiente / el vendedor

51. sanitation worker
el empleado de servicios de la
higiene pública

52. secretary
la secretaria

53. server
la camarera

54. serviceman / servicewoman
el militar / la mujer militar

55. stock clerk
el empleado de almacén

56. store owner
la dueña de tienda

57. student
la estudiante

58. teacher / instructor
la maestra / la instructora

59. telemarketer
la persona que realiza
ventas por teléfono

60. travel agent
el agente de viajes

61. truck driver
el camionero

62. veterinarian
la doctora en veterinaria

63. welder
el soldador

64. writer / author
el escritor / el autor

Talk about your job or the job you want.

What do you do?

I'm <u>a salesclerk.</u> I work in <u>a store.</u>

What do you want to do?

I want to be <u>a veterinarian.</u> I want to work with
<u>animals.</u>

A. **assemble** components
ensamblar componentes

B. **assist** medical patients
ayudar a los pacientes

C. **cook**
cocinar

D. **do** manual labor
hacer labores manuales

E. **drive** a truck
conducir un camión

F. **operate** heavy machinery
operar maquinaria pesada

G. **repair** appliances
reparar electrodomésticos

H. **sell** cars
vender automóviles

I. **sew** clothes
coser ropa

J. **speak** another language
hablar otro idioma

K. **supervise** people
supervisar a las personas

L. **take care** of children
cuidar niños

M. **type**
escribir a máquina

N. **use** a cash register
usar una caja registradora

O. **wait on** customers
atender a los clientes

P. **work** on a computer
trabajar en una computadora

More vocabulary

act: to perform in a play, movie, or TV show

fly: to pilot an airplane

teach: to instruct, to show how to do something

Share your answers.

1. What job skills do you have? Where did you learn them?

2. What job skills do you want to learn?

A. **talk** to friends
hablar con los amigos

B. **look** at a job board
mirar un tablero donde se anuncian trabajos

C. **look** for a help wanted sign
buscar un letrero de "se solicita ayuda"

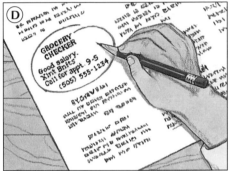

D. **look** in the classifieds
buscar en los anuncios clasificados

E. **call** for information
llamar para información

F. **ask** about the hours
preguntar sobre el horario

G. **fill out** an application
llenar una solicitud

H. **go** on an interview
ir a una entrevista

I. **talk** about your experience
comentar sobre su experiencia

J. **ask** about benefits
preguntar sobre las prestaciones/los beneficios

K. **inquire** about the salary
preguntar acerca del salario

L. **get hired**
ser contratado

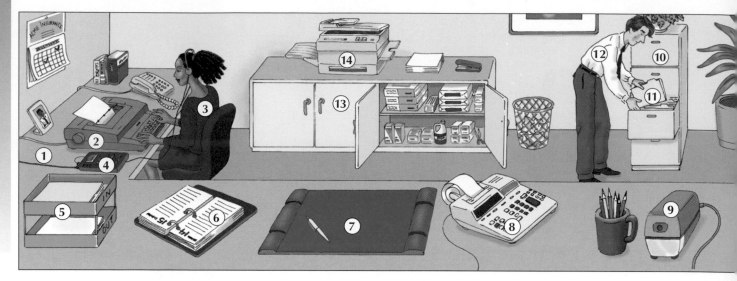

1. **desk**
   el escritorio

2. **typewriter**
   la máquina de escribir

3. **secretary**
   la secretaria

4. **microcassette transcriber**
   la micrograbadora de transcripción

5. **stacking tray**
   la bandeja apilable

6. **desk calendar**
   el calendario para escritorio

7. **desk pad**
   el cartapacio para escritorio

8. **calculator**
   la calculadora

9. **electric pencil sharpener**
   el sacapuntas eléctrico

10. **file cabinet**
    el archivero/el fichero

11. **file folder**
    la carpeta de archivos

12. **file clerk**
    el archivista

13. **supply cabinet**
    el gabinete de artículos de oficina

14. **photocopier**
    la fotocopiadora

A. **take** a message
   tomar un mensaje

B. **fax** a letter
   enviar una carta por fax

C. **transcribe** notes
   transcribir notas

D. **type** a letter
   escribir una carta a máquina

E. **make** copies
   hacer copias

F. **collate** papers
   cotejar documentos

G. **staple**
   engrapar

H. **file** papers
   archivar documentos

Practice taking messages.

Hello. My name is <u>Sara Scott</u>. Is <u>Mr. Lee</u> in?

  Not yet. Would you like to leave a message?

Yes. Please ask <u>him</u> to call me at <u>555-4859</u>.

Share your answers.

1. Which office equipment do you know how to use?
2. Which jobs does a file clerk do?
3. Which jobs does a secretary do?

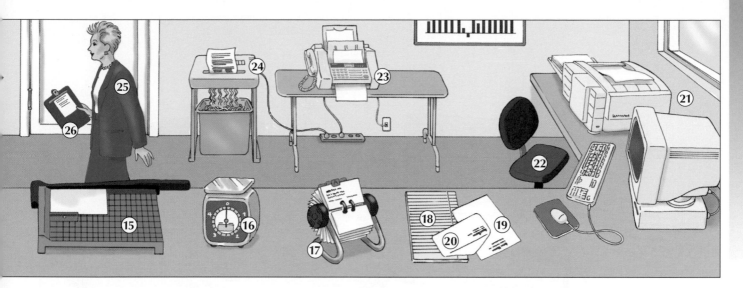

15. paper cutter
el cortapapeles/la guillotina

16. postal scale
la máquina franqueadora

17. rotary card file
el tarjetero

18. legal pad
el cuaderno de tamaño legal

19. letterhead paper
el papel membretado

20. envelope
el sobre

21. computer workstation
la estación de trabajo con
computadora

22. swivel chair
la silla giratoria

23. fax machine
la máquina de fax/el fax

24. paper shredder
la trituradora de papeles

25. office manager
la jefa de oficina

26. clipboard
la tablilla con sujetapapeles

27. appointment book
la libreta de citas/
la agenda

28. stapler
la engrapadora/la
grapadora

29. staple
la grapa

30. organizer
el organizador

31. typewriter cartridge
la cinta para máquina
de escribir

32. mailer
el envase especial para
remitir un objeto por correo

33. correction fluid
el líquido corrector

34. Post-it notes
el block de notas con
hojas adhesivas

35. label
la etiqueta

36. notepad
la libreta de notas/la
libreta para taquigrafía

37. glue
el engrudo/la pega

38. rubber cement
el cemento de goma

39. clear tape
la cinta adhesiva
transparente

40. rubber stamp
el sello de goma

41. ink pad
la almohadilla de tinta

42. packing tape
la cinta adhesiva para empacar

43. pushpin
la tachuela

44. paper clip
el clip/el sujetapapeles

45. rubber band
la liga elástica

Use the new language.

1. Which items keep things together?

2. Which items are used to mail packages?

3. Which items are made of paper?

Share your answers.

1. Which office supplies do students use?

2. Where can you buy them?

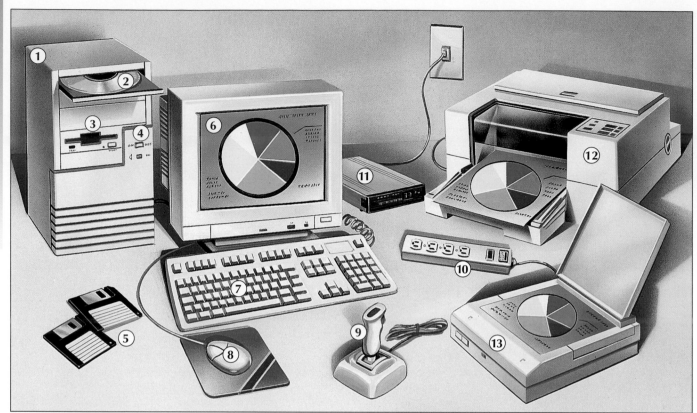

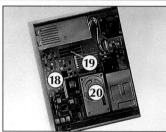

Hardware
Equipo y accesorios

1. CPU (central processing unit)
la unidad central de procesamiento

2. CD-ROM disc
el disco CD-ROM

3. disk drive
la unidad de disco

4. power switch
el conmutador

5. disk/floppy
el disco/el disco flexible

6. monitor/screen
el monitor/la pantalla

7. keyboard
el teclado

8. mouse
el ratón

9. joystick
la palanca de juegos

10. surge protector
el protector de sobrevoltaje

11. modem
el módem

12. printer
la impresora

13. scanner
el explorador

14. laptop
la computadora portátil

15. trackball
la bola de señalización

16. cable
el cable

17. port
el puerto

18. motherboard
la placa matriz

19. slot
la ranura

20. hard disk drive
la unidad de disco duro

Software
El software/los programas

21. program/application
el programa/la aplicación

22. user's manual
el manual

More vocabulary

data: information that a computer can read

memory: how much data a computer can hold

speed: how fast a computer can work with data

Share your answers.

1. Can you use a computer?

2. How did you learn? in school? from a book? by yourself?

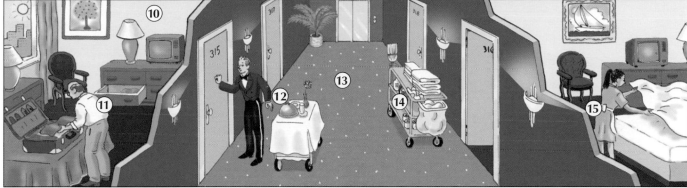

1. valet parking
   el servicio de estacionamiento

2. doorman
   el portero

3. lobby
   el vestíbulo

4. bell captain
   el capitán de botones

5. bellhop
   el botones

6. luggage cart
   el carrito de maletas

7. gift shop
   la tienda de regalos

8. front desk
   la recepción

9. desk clerk
   el recepcionista

10. guest room
    la habitación de los huéspedes

11. guest
    el huésped

12. room service
    el servicio en la habitación

13. hall
    el pasillo

14. housekeeping cart
    el carrito de la limpieza

15. housekeeper
    el ama de llaves

16. pool
    la alberca/piscina

17. pool service
    el servicio en la alberca/piscina

18. ice machine
    la máquina de hielo

19. meeting room
    la sala de conferencias

20. ballroom
    el salón de bailes

More vocabulary

concierge: the hotel worker who helps guests find restaurants and interesting places to go

service elevator: an elevator for hotel workers

Share your answers.

1. Does this look like a hotel in your city? Which one?
2. Which hotel job is the most difficult?
3. How much does it cost to stay in a hotel in your city?

1. **front office**
   la dirección/la oficina principal

2. **factory owner**
   el dueño de la fábrica

3. **designer**
   el diseñador

4. **time clock**
   el reloj registrador/
   el marcador de tiempo

5. **line supervisor**
   el supervisor de la cadena/de línea

6. **factory worker**
   el obrero

7. **parts**
   las piezas

8. **assembly line**
   la cadena de montaje/la línea de
   ensamblaje

9. **warehouse**
   la bodega/el almacén

10. **order puller**
    el encargado de pedidos

11. **hand truck**
    la carretilla de mano

12. **conveyor belt**
    la cinta transportadora

13. **packer**
    el empacador

14. **forklift**
    el elevador de carga

15. **shipping clerk**
    el dependiente encargado del
    despacho de mercadería

16. **loading dock**
    el muelle de carga

A. design
diseñar

B. manufacture
fabricar

C. ship
despachar

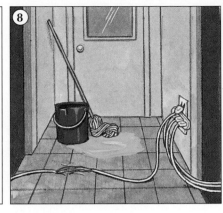

1. electrical hazard
el peligro de tipo eléctrico

2. flammable
inflamable

3. poison
el veneno

4. corrosive
el corrosivo

5. biohazard
el peligro por sustancias biológicas

6. radioactive
radiactivo

7. hazardous materials
los materiales peligrosos

8. dangerous situation
la situación de peligro

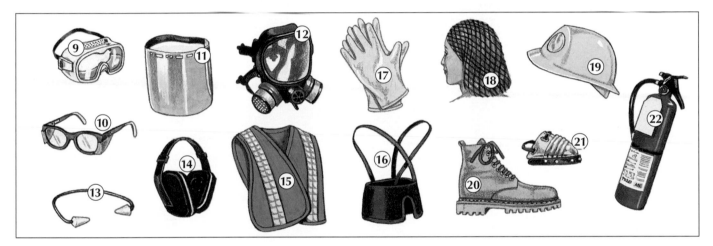

9. safety goggles
las gafas protectoras

10. safety glasses
las antiparras/las gafas de seguridad

11. safety visor
la visera de seguridad

12. respirator
el respirador

13. earplugs
los tapones de oído

14. safety earmuffs
las orejeras de protección

15. safety vest
el chaleco de protección

16. back support
el soporte para la espalda

17. latex gloves
los guantes de látex

18. hair net
la redecilla para el cabello

19. hard hat
el casco protector

20. safety boot
la bota de protección

21. toe guard
la protección para los dedos de pies

22. fire extinguisher
el extintor de incendios

23. careless
descuidado

24. careful
cuidadoso

Farming and Ranching La agricultura y la ganadería

Crops Las siembras

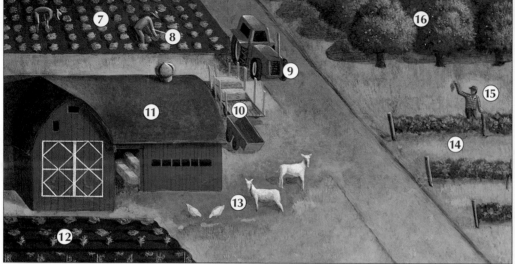

1. **rice**
   el arroz

2. **wheat**
   el trigo

3. **soybeans**
   los frijoles de soya

4. **corn**
   el maíz

5. **alfalfa**
   la alfalfa

6. **cotton**
   el algodón

7. **field**
   el campo

8. **farmworker**
   el trabajador agrícola

9. **tractor**
   el tractor

10. **farm equipment**
    el equipo para trabajar
    en el campo

11. **barn**
    la granja

12. **vegetable garden**
    la hortaliza/huerta

13. **livestock**
    el ganado

14. **vineyard**
    la viña

15. **farmer/grower**
    el agricultor/el cultivador

16. **orchard**
    el huerto

17. **corral**
    el corral

18. **hay**
    el heno

19. **fence**
    la cerca

20. **hired hand**
    el mozo de campo/el
    peón de labranza

21. **steers/cattle**
    los novillos/el ganado

22. **rancher**
    el ganadero

A. **plant**
   sembrar

B. **harvest**
   cosechar

C. **milk**
   ordeñar

D. **feed**
   alimentar

1. construction worker
   el obrero de la construcción

2. ladder
   la escalera

3. I beam/girder
   la viga/la viga maestra

4. scaffolding
   el andamiaje

5. cherry picker
   la grúa alzacarro

6. bulldozer
   el tractor nivelador

7. crane
   la grúa

8. backhoe
   la retroexcavadora

9. jackhammer/pneumatic drill
   el martillo perforador/el taladro
   neumático

10. concrete
    el cemento

11. bricks
    los ladrillos

12. trowel
    la paleta de albañil

13. insulation
    el aislamiento

14. stucco
    el estuco

15. window pane
    la hoja de vidrio

16. plywood
    la madera terciada/contrachapada

17. wood/lumber
    la madera/el madero

18. drywall
    el muro construido de piedras
    encajadas sin mezcla cohesiva

19. shingles
    las tejas de madera

20. pickax
    el azadón de pico

21. shovel
    la pala

22. sledgehammer
    el marrón

A. **paint**
   pintar

B. **lay** bricks
   colocar ladrillos

C. **measure**
   medir

D. **hammer**
   martillar

HAND TOOLS

HARDWARE

POWER TOOLS

SALE 50% OFF

1. hammer
el martillo

2. mallet
el mazo

3. ax
el hacha

4. handsaw
el serrucho

5. hacksaw
la sierra de arco

6. C-clamp
la abrazadera en
forma de C

7. pliers
los alicates

8. electric drill
el taladro eléctrico

9. power sander
la lijadora eléctrica

10. circular saw
la sierra circular

11. blade
la cuchilla

12. router
la buriladora/
el contorneador

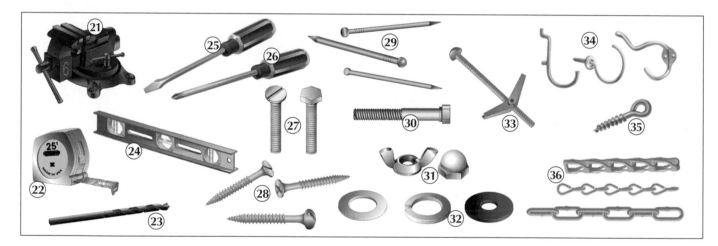

21. vise
el tornillo de banco/la
prensa de tornillo

22. tape measure
la cinta métrica

23. drill bit
la barrena

24. level
el nivel

25. screwdriver
el destornillador

26. Phillips screwdriver
el destornillador
de estrella

27. machine screw
el tornillo para máquina

28. wood screw
el tornillo para madera

29. nail
el clavo

30. bolt
el clavo

31. nut
la tuerca

32. washer
la arandela

33. toggle bolt
el tornillo articulado

34. hook
el gancho

35. eye hook
el gancho de ojo

36. chain
la cadena

Use the new language.

1. Which tools are used for plumbing?

2. Which tools are used for painting?

3. Which tools are used for electrical work?

4. Which tools are used for working with wood?

13. wire
el alambre

14. extension cord
el cordón prolongador / la
extensión

15. yardstick
la yarda

16. pipe
el tubo

17. fittings
los accesorios

18. wood
la madera

19. spray gun
la pistola rociadora

20. paint
la pintura

37. wire stripper
los alicates pelacables

38. electrical tape
la cinta de aislar /
la cinta aislante

39. flashlight
la linterna /
la lámpara de mano

40. battery
la pila

41. outlet
el enchufe / el
tomacorrientes

42. pipe wrench
la llave corrediza

43. wrench
la llave de tuerca

44. plunger
el punzón

45. paint pan
la bandeja de pintura

46. paint roller
el rodillo de pintar

47. paintbrush
la brocha

48. scraper
la espátula / el raspador

49. masking tape
la cinta adhesiva para
proteger bordes

50. sandpaper
el papel de lija

51. chisel
el cincel

52. plane
el cepillo

Use the new language.

Look at **Household Problems and Repairs,**
pages **48–49.**

Name the tools you use to fix the problems you see.

Share your answers.

1. Which tools do you have in your home?
2. Which tools can be dangerous to use?

151

Places to Go   Lugares para pasear

1. zoo
   el zoológico

2. animals
   los animales

3. zookeeper
   el encargado del zoológico

4. botanical gardens
   los jardines botánicos

5. greenhouse
   el invernadero

6. gardener
   el jardinero

7. art museum
   el museo de arte

8. painting
   la pintura

9. sculpture
   la escultura

10. the movies
    el cine

11. seat
    el asiento

12. screen
    la pantalla

13. amusement park
    el parque de diversiones

14. puppet show
    el espectáculo de marionetas

15. roller coaster
    la montaña rusa

16. carnival
    el carnaval

17. rides
    los paseos

18. game
    el juego

19. county fair
    la feria del condado

20. first place/first prize
    el primer lugar/el primer premio

21. exhibition
    la exhibición

22. swap meet/flea market
    el bazar/el mercado de pulgas

23. booth
    el quiosco/la caseta

24. merchandise
    la mercancía

25. baseball game
    el partido de béisbol

26. stadium
    el estadio

27. announcer
    el anunciador

Talk about the places you like to go.

I like <u>animals</u>, so I go to <u>the zoo</u>.

I like <u>rides</u>, so I go to <u>carnivals</u>.

Share your answers.

1. Which of these places is interesting to you?

2. Which rides do you like at an amusement park?

3. What are some famous places to go to in your country?

1. ball field
   el campo de béisbol

2. bike path
   el camino para bicicletas

3. cyclist
   el ciclista

4. bicycle/bike
   la bicicleta

5. jump rope
   la cuerda para saltar

6. duck pond
   el estanque para patos

7. tennis court
   la cancha de tenis

8. picnic table
   la mesa para comidas campestres

9. tricycle
   el triciclo

10. bench
    la banca

11. water fountain
    el bebedero/la fuente de agua

12. swings
    los columpios

13. slide
    la resbaladilla

14. climbing apparatus
    los aparatos de gimnasia

15. sandbox
    el cajón de arena

16. seesaw
    el subibaja

A. **pull** the wagon
   arrastrar el cochecito

B. **push** the swing
   empujar el columpio

C. **climb** on the bars
   trepar a las barras

D. **picnic/have** a picnic
   hacer una comida campestre

1. camping
   el campamento

2. boating
   el paseo en bote

3. canoeing
   el piragüismo

4. rafting
   el paseo en balsa

5. fishing
   la pesca

6. hiking
   la caminata/la excursión

7. backpacking
   ir de campamento

8. mountain biking
   el ciclismo de montañas

9. horseback riding
   la equitación/
   el paseo a caballo

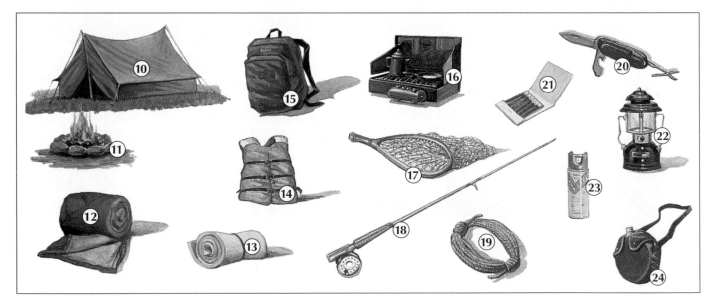

10. tent
    la tienda de campaña

11. campfire
    la hoguera/la fogata

12. sleeping bag
    el saco para dormir

13. foam pad
    el relleno de espuma

14. life vest
    el chaleco salvavidas

15. backpack
    la mochila

16. camping stove
    la cocina de campamento

17. fishing net
    la red de pescar

18. fishing pole
    la caña de pescar

19. rope
    la cuerda

20. multi-use knife
    el cuchillo multiusos

21. matches
    los cerillos/los fósforos

22. lantern
    la linterna

23. insect repellent
    el repelente de insectos

24. canteen
    la cantimplora

1. ocean/water
   el océano/el agua

2. fins
   las aletas

3. diving mask
   la careta de buzo

4. sailboat
   el velero

5. surfboard
   la tabla de surf/la tabla hawaiana

6. wave
   la ola

7. wet suit
   el traje de buzo

8. scuba tank
   el tanque de buceo

9. beach umbrella
   la sombrilla de playa

10. sand castle
    el castillo de arena

11. cooler
    la hielera/la nevera de playa

12. shade
    la sombra

13. sunscreen/sunblock
    el protector solar

14. beach chair
    la silla de playa

15. beach towel
    la toalla de playa

16. pier
    el muelle

17. sunbather
    el bañista

18. lifeguard
    el salvavidas

19. lifesaving device
    el dispositivo salvavidas

20. lifeguard station
    la estación del salvavidas

21. seashell
    el caracol/la concha

22. pail/bucket
    la pala/el cubo

23. sand
    la arena

24. rock
    la roca

More vocabulary

seaweed: a plant that grows in the ocean

tide: the level of the ocean. The tide goes in and out every twelve hours.

Share your answers.

1. Are there any beaches near your home?

2. Do you prefer to spend more time on the sand or in the water?

3. Where are some of the world's best beaches?

Sports Verbs   Verbos utilizados en los deportes

A. walk caminar	**E. catch** atrapar / cachar	**I. shoot** disparar	**M. tackle** atajar
B. jog trotar	**F. pitch** lanzar	**J. jump** saltar / brincar	
C. run correr	**G. hit** pegar	**K. dribble / bounce** driblar / regatear / rebotar	
D. throw arrojar / aventar	**H. pass** pasar	**L. kick** patear	

Practice talking about what you can do.

I can _swim_, but I can't _dive_.

I can _pass the ball_ well, but I can't _shoot_ too well.

Use the new language.

Look at **Individual Sports,** page **159**.

Name the actions you see people doing.

The man in number 18 is riding a horse.

N. **serve**
servir

O. **swing**
girar

P. **exercise / work out**
hacer ejercicios /
entrenar

Q. **stretch**
estirarse

R. **bend**
agacharse

S. **dive**
zambullirse / echar
clavados

T. **swim**
nadar

U. **ski**
esquiar

V. **skate**
patinar

W. **ride**
cabalgar

X. **start**
comenzar

Y. **race**
competir en una carrera

Z. **finish**
terminar

Share your answers.

1. What do you like to do?
2. What do you have difficulty doing?
3. How often do you exercise? Once a week? Two or three times a week? More? Never?
4. Which is more difficult, throwing a ball or catching it?

Team Sports Deportes en equipo

1. score
el tanteo/la puntuación

2. coach
el entrenador

3. team
el equipo

4. fan
el fanático

5. player
el jugador

6. official/referee
el oficial/el árbitro

7. basketball court
la cancha de baloncesto

8. basketball
el baloncesto

9. baseball
el béisbol

10. softball
el sófbol

11. football
el fútbol americano

12. soccer
el fútbol/el balompié

13. ice hockey
el hockey sobre hielo

14. volleyball
el vólibol/voleibol

15. water polo
el polo acuático

More vocabulary

captain: the team leader

umpire: in baseball, the name for the referee

Little League: a baseball league for children

win: to have the best score

lose: the opposite of win

tie: to have the same score as the other team

1. archery
   el tiro con arco

2. billiards/pool
   el billar

3. bowling
   el boliche

4. cycling/biking
   el ciclismo

5. fencing
   la esgrima

6. flying disc*
   el disco volador

7. golf
   el golf

8. gymnastics
   la gimnasia

9. inline skating
   el patinaje sobre ruedas

10. martial arts
    las artes marciales

11. racquetball
    el juego de raqueta

12. skateboarding
    el deporte de la patineta

13. table tennis/
    Ping-Pong™
    el tenis de mesa/el ping
    pong

14. tennis
    el tenis

15. weightlifting
    el levantamiento de
    pesas

16. wrestling
    la lucha

17. track and field
    el atletismo

18. horse racing
    el hipismo

*Note: One brand is Frisbee®
(Mattel, Inc.)

Talk about sports.

Which sports do you like?

  I like <u>tennis</u> but I don't like <u>golf</u>.

Share your answers.

1. Which sports are good for children to learn? Why?
2. Which sport is the most difficult to learn? Why?
3. Which sport is the most dangerous? Why?

Winter Sports and Water Sports   Deportes de invierno y acuáticos

1. downhill skiing
el esquí de descenso

2. snowboarding
el monopatinador de nieve

3. cross-country skiing
el esquí a campo traviesa/
la carrera de fondo

4. ice skating
el patinaje sobre hielo

5. figure skating
el patinaje artístico/de figuras

6. sledding
el viajar en trineo

7. waterskiing
el esquí acuático

8. sailing
el velerismo

9. surfing
el deporte de la tabla hawaiana/el
surfing

10. sailboarding
el surf a vela

11. snorkeling
el esnórquel

12. scuba diving
el buceo con escafandra

Use the new language.

Look at **The Beach,** page **155.**

Name the sports you see.

Share your answers.

1. Which sports are in the Winter Olympics?

2. Which sports do you think are the most exciting
to watch?

1. golf club
   el palo de golf

2. tennis racket
   la raqueta de tenis

3. volleyball
   la bola/la pelota de
   vólibol/voleibol

4. basketball
   la bola de baloncesto

5. bowling ball
   la bola de boliche

6. bow
   el arco

7. arrow
   la flecha

8. target
   el blanco

9. ice skates
   los patines de hielo

10. inline skates
    los patines de rueda

11. hockey stick
    el palo de hockey

12. soccer ball
    el balón de fútbol/
    de balompié

13. shin guards
    las espinilleras

14. baseball bat
    el bate de béisbol

15. catcher's mask
    la careta del receptor

16. uniform
    el uniforme

17. glove
    el guante

18. baseball
    la pelota de béisbol

19. weights
    las pesas

20. football helmet
    el casco de fútbol
    americano

21. shoulder pads
    las hombreras

22. football
    el balón de fútbol
    americano

23. snowboard
    el monopatinador de
    nieve

24. skis
    los esquíes

25. ski poles
    los bastones de esquí

26. ski boots
    las botas de esquí

27. flying disc*
    el disco volador

*Note: One brand is Frisbee®
(Mattel, Inc.)

Share your answers.

1. Which sports equipment is used for safety reasons?

2. Which sports equipment is heavy?

3. What sports equipment do you have at home?

Use the new language.

Look at **Individual Sports,** page **159.**

Name the sports equipment you see.

161

A. **collect** things
coleccionar objetos

B. **play** games
participar en juegos

C. **build** models
construir modelos
a escala

D. **do** crafts
hacer artesanías

1. video game system
el juego de video
(el sistema)

2. cartridge
el cartucho

3. board game
el juego de mesa

4. dice
los dados

5. checkers
las damas

6. chess
el ajedrez

7. model kit
el juego para construir
modelos a escala

8. glue
el pegamento

9. acrylic paint
la pintura de acrílico

10. figurine
la figurilla

11. baseball card
la tarjeta de béisbol

12. stamp collection
la colección de
estampillas/de timbres

13. coin collection
la colección de monedas

14. clay
la plastilina/plasticina

15. doll making kit
el juego para
hacer muñecas

16. woodworking kit
el juego de artesanía
en madera

Talk about how much time you spend on your hobbies.

I _do crafts_ all the time.

I _play chess_ sometimes.

I never _build models_.

Share your answers.

1. How often do you play video games? Often?
Sometimes? Never?

2. What board games do you know?

3. Do you collect anything? What?

E. paint pintar	**F. knit** tejer	**G. pretend** hacer creer / actuar	**H. play** cards **jugar** a los naipes

17. yarn
el hilo

18. knitting needles
las agujas de tejer

19. embroidery
el bordado

20. crochet
el tejido a gancho

21. easel
el caballete

22. canvas
el lienzo

23. paintbrush
el pincel

24. oil paint
la pintura de aceite/
al óleo

25. watercolor
las acuarelas

26. clubs
tréboles

27. diamonds
diamantes

28. spades
espadas/picas

29. hearts
corazones

30. paper doll
la muñeca de papel

31. action figure
el héroe de aventuras

32. model trains
los trenes a escala

Share your answers.

1. Do you like to play cards? Which games?

2. Did you pretend a lot when you were a child? What did you pretend to be?

3. Is it important to have hobbies? Why or why not?

4. What's your favorite game?

5. What's your hobby?

163

Electronics and Photography Electrónica y fotografía

1. clock radio
   el radio reloj

2. portable radio-cassette player
   el radio/el tocacintas portátil

3. cassette recorder
   la grabadora

4. microphone
   el micrófono

5. shortwave radio
   el radio de onda corta

6. TV (television)
   la televisión

7. portable TV
   el televisor portátil

8. VCR (videocassette recorder)
   la videograbadora

9. remote control
   el control remoto

10. videocassette
    el videocasete

11. speakers
    las bocinas/los altavoces

12. turntable
    el plato giratorio/el gira discos

13. tuner
    el sintonizador

14. CD player
    el tocador de disco compacto

15. personal radio-cassette player
    el radio/el tocacintas personal

16. headphones
    los audífonos

17. adapter
    el adaptador

18. plug
    el enchufe

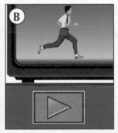

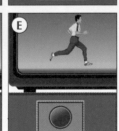
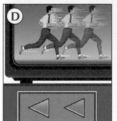

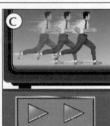

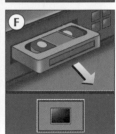

19. video camera
la cámara de video

20. tripod
el trípode/el tripié

21. camcorder
la cámara de video y audio

22. battery pack
el bloque de pilas secas

23. battery charger
el cargador de pilas

24. 35 mm camera
la cámara de 35 mm

25. zoom lens
el lente de zoom/el teleobjetivo

26. film
la película/el rollo de película

27. camera case
el estuche para la cámara

28. screen
la pantalla

29. carousel slide projector
el proyector de diapositivas
en forma de carrusel

30. slide tray
la bandeja para diapositivas

31. slides
las diapositivas

32. photo album
el álbum de fotografías

33. out of focus
fuera de foco

34. overexposed
sobreexpuesto

35. underexposed
expuesto insuficientemente

A. record
grabar

B. play
tocar

C. fast forward
adelantar

D. rewind
rebobinar

E. pause
pausar

F. stop and **eject**
detener y expulsar

Entertainment   Entretenimiento

Types of entertainment   Tipos de entretenimiento

1. film/movie
la película

2. play
la obra de teatro

3. television program
el programa de televisión

4. radio program
el programa de radio

5. stand-up comedy
la comedia

6. concert
el concierto

7. ballet
el ballet

8. opera
la ópera

Types of stories   Tipos de cuentos

9. western
una película del oeste/de vaqueros

10. comedy
la comedia

11. tragedy
la tragedia

12. science fiction story
el cuento de ciencia ficción

13. action story/adventure story
el cuento de acción/de aventuras

14. horror story
el cuento de horror

15. mystery
el misterio

16. romance
el romance

166

Types of TV programs Tipos de programas de tele

17. news
las noticias/el noticiero

18. sitcom (situation comedy)
la comedia de situaciones

19. cartoon
el dibujo animado

20. talk show
el programa de entrevistas

21. soap opera
la telenovela

22. nature program
el programa sobre la naturaleza

23. game show/quiz show
el programa de juegos/de preguntas

24. children's program
el programa infantil

25. shopping program
el programa de ventas/
las ventas por tele

26. serious book
el libro **serio**

27. funny book
el libro **cómico/chistoso**

28. sad book
el libro **triste**

29. boring book
el libro **aburrido**

30. interesting book
el libro **interesante**

1. **New Year's Day**
   el Día de Año Nuevo

2. **parade**
   el desfile

3. **confetti**
   el confeti

4. **Valentine's Day**
   el Día de los Enamorados

5. **card**
   la tarjeta

6. **heart**
   el corazón

7. **Independence Day/4th of July**
   el Día de la Independencia/
   el 4 de julio

8. **fireworks**
   los fuegos artificiales

9. **flag**
   la bandera

10. **Halloween**
    el Día de las Brujas

11. **jack-o'-lantern**
    la linterna hecha de una calabaza

12. **mask**
    la máscara/la careta/el antifaz

13. **costume**
    el disfraz

14. **candy**
    los dulces

15. **Thanksgiving**
    el Día de Acción de Gracias

16. **feast**
    la festividad

17. **turkey**
    el pavo/el guajolote

18. **Christmas**
    la Navidad

19. **ornament**
    el adorno

20. **Christmas tree**
    el árbol de Navidad

A. plan a party
planear una fiesta

B. invite the guests
invitar / convidar a los invitados

C. decorate the house
decorar la casa

D. wrap a gift
envolver un regalo

E. hide
esconderse

F. answer the door
abrir la puerta

G. shout "surprise!"
gritar "¡sorpresa!"

H. light the candles
encender las velas

I. sing "Happy Birthday"
cantar "las mañanitas"/
"Feliz cumpleaños"

J. make a wish
pedir un deseo

K. blow out the candles
apagar las velas

L. open the presents
abrir los regalos

Practice inviting friends to a party.

I'd love for you to come to my party <u>next week</u>.

Could <u>you and your friend</u> come to my party?

Would <u>your friend</u> like to come to a party I'm giving?

Share your answers.

1. Do you celebrate birthdays? What do you do?

2. Are there birthdays you celebrate in a special way?

3. Is there a special birthday song in your country?

Verb Guide

Verbs in English are either regular or irregular in the past tense and past participle forms.

Regular Verbs

The regular verbs below are marked 1, 2, 3, or 4 according to four different spelling patterns. (See page 172 for the **irregular verbs** which do not follow any of these patterns.)

Spelling Patterns for the Past and the Past Participle	*Example*		
1. Add **-ed** to the end of the verb.	**ASK**	→	**ASKED**
2. Add **-d** to the end of the verb.	**LIVE**	→	**LIVED**
3. Double the final consonant and add **-ed** to the end of the verb.	**DROP**	→	**DROPPED**
4. Drop the final y and add **-ied** to the end of the verb.	**CRY**	→	**CRIED**

The Oxford Picture Dictionary List of Regular Verbs

act (1)
add (1)
address (1)
answer (1)
apologize (2)
appear (1)
applaud (1)
arrange (2)
arrest (1)
arrive (2)
ask (1)
assemble (2)
assist (1)
bake (2)
barbecue (2)
bathe (2)
board (1)
boil (1)
borrow (1)
bounce (2)
brainstorm (1)
breathe (2)
broil (1)
brush (1)
burn (1)
call (1)
carry (4)
change (2)
check (1)
choke (2)
chop (3)
circle (2)
claim (1)
clap (3)
clean (1)
clear (1)
climb (1)
close (2)
collate (2)

collect (1)
color (1)
comb (1)
commit (3)
compliment (1)
conserve (2)
convert (1)
cook (1)
copy (4)
correct (1)
cough (1)
count (1)
cross (1)
cry (4)
dance (2)
design (1)
deposit (1)
deliver (1)
dial (1)
dictate (2)
die (2)
discuss (1)
dive (2)
dress (1)
dribble (2)
drill (1)
drop (3)
drown (1)
dry (4)
dust (1)
dye (2)
edit (1)
eject (1)
empty (4)
end (1)
enter (1)
erase (2)
examine (2)
exchange (2)

exercise (2)
experience (2)
exterminate (2)
fasten (1)
fax (1)
file (2)
fill (1)
finish (1)
fix (1)
floss (1)
fold (1)
fry (4)
gargle (2)
graduate (2)
grate (2)
grease (2)
greet (1)
grill (1)
hail (1)
hammer (1)
harvest (1)
help (1)
hire (2)
hug (3)
immigrate (2)
inquire (2)
insert (1)
introduce (2)
invite (2)
iron (1)
jog (3)
join (1)
jump (1)
kick (1)
kiss (1)
knit (3)
land (1)
laugh (1)
learn (1)

lengthen (1)
listen (1)
live (2)
load (1)
lock (1)
look (1)
mail (1)
manufacture (2)
mark (1)
match (1)
measure (2)
milk (1)
miss (1)
mix (1)
mop (3)
move (2)
mow (1)
need (1)
nurse (2)
obey (1)
observe (2)
open (1)
operate (2)
order (1)
overdose (2)
paint (1)
park (1)
pass (1)
pause (2)
peel (1)
perm (1)
pick (1)
pitch (1)
plan (3)
plant (1)
play (1)
point (1)
polish (1)
pour (1)
pretend (1)
print (1)
protect (1)

pull (1)
push (1)
race (2)
raise (2)
rake (2)
receive (2)
record (1)
recycle (2)
register (1)
relax (1)
remove (2)
rent (1)
repair (1)
repeat (1)
report (1)
request (1)
return (1)
rinse (2)
roast (1)
rock (1)
sauté (2)
save (2)
scrub (3)
seat (1)
sentence (2)
serve (2)
share (2)
shave (2)
ship (3)
shop (3)
shorten (1)
shout (1)
sign (1)
simmer (1)
skate (2)
ski (1)
slice (2)
smell (1)
sneeze (2)
sort (1)
spell (1)
staple (2)

start (1)
stay (1)
steam (1)
stir (3)
stir-fry (4)
stop (3)
stow (1)
stretch (1)
supervise (2)
swallow (1)
tackle (2)
talk (1)
taste (2)
thank (1)
tie (2)
touch (1)
transcribe (2)
transfer (3)
travel (1)
trim (3)
turn (1)
type (2)
underline (2)
unload (1)
unpack (1)
use (2)
vacuum (1)
vomit (1)
vote (2)
wait (1)
walk (1)
wash (1)
watch (1)
water (1)
weed (1)
weigh (1)
wipe (2)
work (1)
wrap (3)
yield (1)

Irregular Verbs

These verbs have irregular endings in the past and/or the past participle.

The Oxford Picture Dictionary List of Irregular Verbs

simple	past	past participle	simple	past	past participle
be	was	been	leave	left	left
beat	beat	beaten	lend	lent	lent
become	became	become	let	let	let
begin	began	begun	light	lit	lit
bend	bent	bent	make	made	made
bleed	bled	bled	pay	paid	paid
blow	blew	blown	picnic	picnicked	picnicked
break	broke	broken	put	put	put
build	built	built	read	read	read
buy	bought	bought	rewind	rewound	rewound
catch	caught	caught	rewrite	rewrote	rewritten
come	came	come	ride	rode	ridden
cut	cut	cut	run	ran	run
do	did	done	say	said	said
draw	drew	drawn	see	saw	seen
drink	drank	drunk	sell	sold	sold
drive	drove	driven	send	sent	sent
eat	ate	eaten	set	set	set
fall	fell	fallen	sew	sewed	sewn
feed	fed	fed	shoot	shot	shot
feel	felt	felt	sing	sang	sung
find	found	found	sit	sat	sat
fly	flew	flown	speak	spoke	spoken
get	got	gotten	stand	stood	stood
give	gave	given	sweep	swept	swept
go	went	gone	swim	swam	swum
hang	hung	hung	swing	swung	swung
have	had	had	take	took	taken
hear	heard	heard	teach	taught	taught
hide	hid	hidden	throw	threw	thrown
hit	hit	hit	wake	woke	woken
hold	held	held	wear	wore	worn
keep	kept	kept	withdraw	withdrew	withdrawn
lay	laid	laid	write	wrote	written

Index

Two numbers are shown after words in the index: the first refers to the page where the word is illustrated and the second refers to the item number of the word on that page. For example, cool [kōōl] **10**-3 means that the word *cool* is item number 3 on page 10. If only the bold page number appears, then that word is part of the unit title or subtitle, or is found somewhere else on the page. A bold number followed by ✦ means the word can be found in the exercise space at the bottom of that page.

Words or combinations of words that appear in **bold** type are used as verbs or verb phrases. Words used as other parts of speech are shown in ordinary type. So, for example, **file** (in bold type) is the verb *file*, while file (in ordinary type) is the noun *file*. Words or phrases in small capital letters (for example, HOLIDAYS) form unit titles.

Phrases and other words that form combinations with an individual word entry are often listed underneath it. Rather than repeating the word each time it occurs in combination with what is listed under it, the word is replaced by three dots (...), called an ellipsis. For example, under the word *bus*, you will find ...driver and ...stop meaning *bus driver* and *bus stop*. Under the word *store* you will find shoe... and toy..., meaning *shoe store* and *toy store*.

Pronunciation Guide

The index includes a pronunciation guide for all the words and phrases illustrated in the book. This guide uses symbols commonly found in dictionaries for native speakers. These symbols, unlike those used in pronunciation systems such as the International Phonetic Alphabet, tend to use English spelling patterns and so should help you to become more aware of the connections between written English and spoken English.

Consonants

[b] as in back [băk]	[k] as in key [kē]	[sh] as in shoe [shōō]
[ch] as in cheek [chēk]	[l] as in leaf [lēf]	[t] as in tape [tāp]
[d] as in date [dāt]	[m] as in match [măch]	[th] as in three [thrē]
[dh] as in this [dhĭs]	[n] as in neck [nĕk]	[v] as in vine [vīn]
[f] as in face [fās]	[ng] as in ring [rĭng]	[w] as in wait [wāt]
[g] as in gas [găs]	[p] as in park [pärk]	[y] as in yams [yămz]
[h] as in half [hăf]	[r] as in rice [rīs]	[z] as in zoo [zōō]
[j] as in jam [jăm]	[s] as in sand [sănd]	[zh] as in measure [mĕzh/ər]

Vowels

[ā] as in bake [bāk]	[ĭ] as in lip [lĭp]	[ow] as in cow [kow]
[ă] as in back [băk]	[ï] as in near [nïr]	[oy] as in boy [boy]
[ä] as in car [kär] or box [bäks]	[ō] as in cold [kōld]	[ŭ] as in cut [kŭt]
[ē] as in beat [bēt]	[ö] as in short [shört]	[ü] as in curb [kürb]
[ĕ] as in bed [bĕd]	or claw [klö]	[ə] as in above [ə bŭv/]
[ë] as in bear [bër]	[ōō] as in cool [kōōl]	
[ī] as in line [līn]	[ŏŏ] as in cook [kŏŏk]	

All the pronunciation symbols used are alphabetical except for the schwa [ə]. The schwa is the most frequent vowel sound in English. If you use the schwa appropriately in unstressed syllables, your pronunciation will sound more natural.

Vowels before [r] are shown with the symbol [¨] to call attention to the special quality that vowels have before [r]. (Note that the symbols [ä] and [ö] are also used for vowels not followed by [r], as in *box* or *claw*.) You should listen carefully to native speakers to discover how these vowels actually sound.

Stress

This index follows the system for marking stress used in many dictionaries for native speakers.

1. Stress is not marked if a word consisting of a single syllable occurs by itself.

2. Where stress is marked, two levels are distinguished:

a bold accent [/] is placed after each syllable with primary (or strong) stress, a light accent [/] is placed after each syllable with secondary (or weaker) stress.

In phrases and other combinations of words, stress is indicated for each word as it would be pronounced within the whole phrase or other unit. If a word consisting of a single syllable is stressed in the combinations listed below it, the accent mark indicating the degree of stress it has in the phrases (primary or secondary) is shown in parentheses. A hyphen replaces any part of a word or phrase that is omitted. For example, bus [bŭs(/–)] shows that the word *bus* is said with primary stress in the combinations shown below it. The word ...driver [–drī/vər], listed under *bus*, shows that *driver* has secondary stress in the combination *bus driver*: [bŭs/ drī/vər].

Syllable Boundaries

Syllable boundaries are indicated by a single space or by a stress mark.

Note: The pronunciations shown in this index are based on patterns of American English. There has been no attempt to represent all of the varieties of American English. Students should listen to native speakers to hear how the language actually sounds in a particular region.

Index

abdomen [ăb/də mən] **74**–3
above [ə bŭv/] **13**–6
accelerator [ĭk sĕl/ə rā/tər] **109**–47
ACCESSORIES [ĭk sĕs/ə rēz] **68–69**
accident [ăk/sə dənt] **102**–2
accordion [ə kör/dē ən] **120–21**
accountant [ə kown/tnt] **136**–1
acid rain [ăs/əd rān/] **126**–11
across [ə krös/] **105**–3
acrylic paint [ə krĭl/ĭk pānt/] **162**–9
act [ăkt] **140** ✦
action [ăk/shən]
...figure [–fĭg/yər] **163**–31
...story [–stör/ē] **166**–13
actor [ăk/tər] **136**–2
acupuncture [ăk/yə pŭngk/chər] **81**–G
adapter [ə dăp/tər] **164**–18
add [ăd] **58**–Q, **72**–B
addition [ə dĭsh/ən] **118**–1
address [ə drĕs/] **96**–A
address [ə drĕs/, ă/drĕs] **4–5, 96**–7,8
adhesive bandage [əd hē/sĭv băn/dĭj] **83**–3
administrative assistant [əd mĭn/ə strā/tĭv ə sĭs/tənt] **136**–3
administrator [əd mĭn/ə strā/tər] **5** ✦
adults [ə dŭlts/, ăd/ŭlts] **22**–9
adult school [ə dŭlt/ skool/, ăd/ŭlt–] **112**–8
adventure story [əd vĕn/chər stör/ē] **166**–13
aerogramme [ĕr/ə grăm/] **96**–13
afternoon [ăf/tər noon/] **17**–18
aftershave [ăf/tər shāv/] **77**–28
AGE AND PHYSICAL DESCRIPTION [āj/ ən fĭz/ĭ kəl
dĭ skrĭp/shən] **22**
AIDS (acquired immunodeficiency syndrome) [ādz] **79** ✦
air [ĕr(/–)] **109**–59
...bag [–băg/] **108**–16
...conditioner [–kən dĭsh/ə nər] **37**–19
...conditioning [–kən dĭsh/ə nĭng] **108**–28
...letter [–lĕt/ər] **96**–13
...pollution [–pə loo/shən] **126**–10
...purifier [–pyoor/ə fī ər] **80**–4
airline [ĕr/līn/]
...representative [–rĕp rĭ zĕn/tə tĭv] **110**–2
...terminal [–tür/mə nəl] **110**–1
airplane [ĕr/plān/] **110**–9
...crash [–krăsh/] **102**–3
AIRPORT [ĕr/pört/] **110**
airsickness bag [ĕr/sĭk/nəs băg/] **110**–15
aisle [īl] **54**–5
Alaska time [ə lăs/kə tīm/] **17**–25
alfalfa [ăl făl/fə] **148**–5
algebra [ăl/jə brə] **118**–25
allergies [ăl/ər jēz] **79**–8
alley [ăl/ē] **37**–21
alligator [ăl/ə gā/tər] **131**–36
alphabet [ăl/fə bĕt/] **3**–30
ALTERATIONS [öl/tə rā/shənz] **73**
aluminum foil [ə loo/mə nəm foyl/] **55**–55
a.m. [ā/ĕm/] **16** ✦
American cheese [ə mĕr/ə kən chēz/] **53**–9
AMPHIBIANS [ăm fĭb/ē ənz] **130–131**
amusement park [ə myooz/mənt pärk/] **152**–13
anesthesiologist [ăn/əs thē/zē ăl/ə jĭst] **87**–35
angle [ăng/gəl] **118**–24
angry [ăng/grē] **31**–29
animals [ăn/ə məlz] **152**–2
ANIMALS, DOMESTIC [də mĕs/tĭk ăn/ə məlz] **133**

ankle [ăng/kəl] **75**–61, **78**–18
anniversary [ăn/ə vür/sə rē] **19**–42
announcer [ə nown/sər] **152**–27
answer [ăn/sər]
...a question [–ə kwĕs/chən] **6**–H
...the door [–dhə dör/] **169**–F
answering machine [ăn/sə rĭng mə shēn/] **9**–14
answer sheet [ăn/sər shēt/] **7**–T
antacid [ănt ăs/əd] **81**–18
anteater [ănt/ē/tər] **135**–24
antelope [ăn/tə lōp/] **135**–35
antibacterial ointment [ăn/tē băk tïr/ē əl oynt/mənt] **83**–9
antihistamine cream [ăn/tĭ hĭs/tə mēn krēm/] **83**–10
antler [ănt/lər] **134**–16
ants [ănts] **49**–24
apartment [ə pärt/mənt]
...building [–bĭl/dĭng] **34**–5
...number [–nŭm/bər] **4**–6
APARTMENTS [ə pärt/mənts] **36–37**
apologize [ə päl/ə jīz/] **8**–I
apostrophe [ə päs/trə fē] **113**–11
appear in court [ə pïr/ ĭn kört/] **99**–C
applaud [ə plöd/] **32**–B
apple juice [ăp/əl joos/] **55**–50, **57**–5
apples [ăp/əlz] **50**–4
application [ăp/lə kā/shən] **144**–21
appointment [ə poynt/mənt] **19**–45, **85**
...book [–book/] **143**–27
apricots [ăp/rə kăts/] **50**–7
April [ā/prəl] **19**–28
archery [är/chə rē] **159**–1
architect [är/kə tĕkt/] **136**–4
area [ĕr/ē ə] **34**–(1, 4)
area code [ĕr/ē ə kōd/] **4**–10
arm [ärm] **74**–9
armadillo [är/mə dĭl/ō] **134**–8
armchair [ärm/chër/] **42**–24
around [ə rownd/] **105**–10
arrange [ə rānj/] **35**–K
arrest [ə rĕst/] **99**–A
arrival and departure monitors
[ə rī/vəl ən dĭ pär/chər män/ə tərz] **110**–4
arrival time [ə rī/vəl tīm/] **111** ✦
arrive [ə rīv/] **111**–O
arrow [ăr/ō] **161**–7
art [ärt] **121**–1
artery [är/tə rē] **75**–43
artichokes [är/tə chōks/] **51**–20
artist [är/tĭst] **136**–5
art museum [ärt/ myoo zē/əm] **152**–7
ask [ăsk(/–)]
...about benefits [–ə bowt/ bĕn/ə fĭts] **141**–J
...about the hours [–ə bowt/ dhē ow/ərz] **141**–F
...a question [–ə kwĕs/chən] **6**–G
asparagus [ə spăr/ə gəs] **51**–24
assault [ə sölt/] **100**–7
assemble [ə sĕm/bəl] **140**–A
assembler [ə sĕm/blər] **136**–6
assembly line [ə sĕm/blē līn/] **146**–8
assist [ə sĭst/] **140**–B
Associate of Arts (AA) [ə sō/shē ĭt əv ärts/, –sē ĭt–] /
[ā/ā/] **112** ✦
asteroid belt [ăs/tə royd bĕlt/] **127**–12
asthma [ăz/mə] **79**–11
astronaut [ăs/trə nöt/] **127**–17
astronomer [ə strän/ə mər] **127**–20

athletic [ăth lĕt/ĭk]
...shoes [–sho͞oz/] **68**–23
...supporter [–sə pör/tər] **67**–14
Atlantic time [ət lăn/tĭk tīm/] **17**–30
atlas [ăt/ləs] **98**–3
ATM (automated teller machine) [ā/tē/ĕm/] **97**–3
ATM card [ā/tē/ĕm/ kärd/] **97**–9
atom [ăt/əm] **119**–17
attorney [ə tür/nē] **99**–4
attractive [ə trăk/tĭv] **22**–23
audience [ö/dē əns] **32**–10
audiocassette [ö/dē ō kə sĕt/] **98**–12
audiologist [ö/dē äl/ə jĭst] **81**–32
auditorium [ö/də tör/ē əm] **5**–3
August [ö/gəst] **19**–32
aunt [ănt] **24**–10
author [ö/thər] **98**–22, **139**–64
automatic transmission
   [ö/tə măt/ĭk tränz mĭsh/ən, –trăns–] **109**
auto mechanic [ö/tō mə kăn/ĭk] **136**–7
average [ăv/rĭj]
...height [–hīt/] **22**–17
...weight [–wāt/] **22**–21
avocadoes [ä/və kä/dŏz, ăv/ə–] **50**–14
ax [ăks] **150**–3
baboon [bă bo͞on/] **135**–32
baby [bā/bē] **22**–2
...backpack [–băk/păk/] **95**–15
...carrier [–kăr/ē ər] **95**–14
...food [–fo͞od/] **95**–28
...monitor [–măn/ə tər] **45**–9
...powder [–pow/dər] **95**–18
baby-sitter [bā/bē sĭt/ər] **136**–12
Bachelor's degree [băch/lərz də grē/] **112** ✦
back [băk(/–)] **74**–11
...support [–sə pört/] **147**–16
backache [băk/āk/] **78**–5
backhoe [băk/hō/] **149**–8
backpack [băk/păk/] **69**–28, **95**–15, **154**–15
backpacking [băk/păk/ĭng] **154**–7
backseat [băk/sēt/] **109**–38
backyard [băk/yärd/] **38**–2
bacon [bā/kən] **52**–11, **61**–7
bad [băd] **11**–18
bag [băg] (market) **55**–22, 23, **56**–7, 19 (purse) **69**–27, 28, 29
baggage claim area [băg/ĭj klām/ ër/ē ə] **110**–17
bagger [băg/ər] **55**–21
baggy [băg/ē] **71**–42
bag of flour [băg/ əv flow/ər] **56**–19
bags (luggage) [băgz] **111**–B
bailiff [bā/ləf] **99**–13
bake [bāk] **58**–L
baked [bākt(/–)]
...goods [–go͞odz/] **54**–6
...potato [–pə tā/tō] **61**–14
baker [bā/kər] **136**–8
bakery [bā/kə rē] **89**–16
baking products [bā/kĭng präd/ŭkts] **55**–13
balance [băl/əns] (bank) **97**–11, (science) **119**–11
balcony [băl/kə nē] **37**–17
bald [böld] **23**–12
ball [böl] **45**–16, **161**–3, 4, 5, 12, 18, 22
ballet [bă lā/] **166**–7
ball field [böl/ fēld/] **153**–1
ballroom [böl/ro͞om/] **145**–20

bananas [bə năn/əz] **50**–3
bandage [băn/dĭj] **83**–3, 12
bangs [băngz] **23**–8
BANK [băngk] **97**
bank [băngk] **88**–3
banner [băn/ər] **33**–15
barbecue [bär/bĭ kyo͞o/] **58**–T
barbecue grill [bär/bĭ kyo͞o grĭl/] **39**–7
barber shop [bär/bər shäp/] **88**–15
bar code [bär/ kōd/] **21**–4
barn [bärn] **148**–11
barrette [bə rĕt/] **76**–18
baseball [bās/böl] **158**–9, **161**–18
...bat [–băt/] **161**–14
...cap [–kăp/] **66**–27
...card [–kärd/] **162**–11
...game [–gām/] **152**–25
basement [bās/mənt] **36** ✦
basket [băs/kət] **42**–2
basketball [băs/kət böl/] **158**–8, **161**–4
...court [–kört/] **158**–7
bass (fish) [băs] **130**–11
bass (instrument) [bās] **120**–10
bassoon [bə so͞on/] **120**–6
bat [băt] (animal) **134**–7, (baseball) **161**–14
bath [băth(/–)]
...mat [–măt/] **43**–27
...powder [–pow/dər] **76**–3
...towel [–tow/əl] **43**–12
bathe [bādh] **76**–B
bathing suit [bā/dhĭng so͞ot/] **66**–26
bathrobe [băth/rōb/] **67**–8
BATHROOM [băth/ro͞om/] **43**
bathtub [băth/tŭb/] **43**–2
battery [băt/ə rē] (car) **109**–43, (flashlight) **151**–40
...charger [–chär/jər] **165**–23
...pack [–păk/] **165**–22
bay [bā] **117**–9
be [bē]
...18 years old [–ā/tēn/ yïrz/ ōld/] **116**–A
...**born** [–börn/] **28**–A
...**hurt** [–hürt/] **82**–A
...**injured** [–ĭn/jərd] **82**–A
...in school [–ĭn sko͞ol/] **26**–J
...in shock [–ĭn shäk/] **82**–C
...released [–rĭ lēst/] **99**–H
...unconscious [–ŭn kän/shəs] **82**–B
BEACH [bēch] **155**
beach [bēch(/–)] **117**–10
...chair [–chër/] **155**–14
...towel [–tow/əl] **155**–15
...umbrella [–ŭm brĕl/ə] **155**–9
beads [bēdz] **69**–32
beak [bēk] **132**–1
beaker [bē/kər] **119**–13
beam [bēm] **149**–3
beans [bēnz] **51**–25, **54**–26
bear [bër] **134**–11
beard [bïrd] **23**–6
beat [bēt] **58**–B
beautiful [byo͞o/tə fəl] **11**–21
beauty shop [byo͞o/tē shäp/] **92** ✦
beaver [bē/vər] **134**–9
become a citizen [bĭ kŭm/ ə sĭt/ə zən] **28**–H
bed [bĕd(/–)] **44**–8

Index

...control [–kən trōl/] **86**–12
...frame [–frām/] **44**–27
...table [–tā/bəl] **86**–9
bedpan [bĕd/păn/] **86**–13
BEDROOM [bĕd/rōōm/] **44**
bedspread [bĕd/sprĕd/] **44**–11
Beef [bēf] **52**
beef ribs [bēf/ rĭbz/] **52**–5
beetle [bēt/l] **132**–19
beets [bēts] **51**–6
begin [bĭ gĭn/] **8**–B
behind [bĭ hīnd/] **13**–3
beige [bāzh] **12**–9
bell captain [bĕl/ kăp/tən] **145**–4
bellhop [bĕl/hăp/] **145**–5
below [bĭ lō/] **13**–7
belt buckle [bĕlt/ bŭk/əl] **69**–41
belts [bĕlts] **69**–11
bench [bĕnch] **153**–10
bend [bĕnd] **157**–R
berries [bĕr/ēz] **128**–20
between [bĭ twēn/] **13**–10
beverages [bĕv/rə jəz] **55**–15, **61**
bib [bĭb] **95**–8
bicycle [bī/sĭ kəl] **153**–4
big [bĭg] **11**–2
bike [bīk(/–)] **153**–4
...path [–păth/] **153**–2
...shorts [–shörts/] **67**–3
biking [bī/kĭng] **159**–4
bikini panties [bə kē/nē păn/tēz] **67**–16
bill (bird) [bĭl] **132**–1
bill (invoice) [bĭl] **21** ✦
billiards [bĭl/yərdz] **159**–2
billion [bĭl/yən] **14**
bills (paper money) [bĭlz] **20, 20** ✦
bin [bĭn] **37**–20
binder [bīn/dər] **3**–24
biohazard [bī/ō hăz/ərd] **147**–5
biology [bī äl/ə jē] **119**–1
birch [bürch] **128**–8
BIRDS, INSECTS, AND ARACHNIDS
[bürdz/ ĭn/sĕkts ən ə răk/nĭdz] **132**
birth certificate [bürth/ sər tĭf/ə kət] **29**–1
birthday [bürth/dā/] **19**–41, **169**–I
bison [bī/sən] **134**–6
black [blăk(/–)] **12**–15
...hair [–hër/] **23**–15
bladder [blăd/ər] **75**–47
blade [blād] **150**–11
blanket [blăng/kət] **44**–12
...sleeper [–slē/pər] **67**–7
bleach [blēch] **72**–8
bleachers [blē/chərz] **5**–10
bleed [blēd] **82**–M
blender [blĕn/dər] **40**–12
blind [blīnd] **22**–26
blinds [blīndz] **43**–11
blister [blĭs/tər] **78**–15
blizzard [blĭz/ərd] **103**–11
block [blăk] **107**–2
blocks [blăks] **45**–15
blond [bländ] **23**–16
blood [blŭd(/–)] **79**–15
...pressure gauge [–prĕsh/ər gāj/] **84**–12

...test [–tĕst/] **86**–17
...work [–würk/] **86**–17
bloody nose [blŭd/ē nōz/] **78**–17
blouse [blows] **64**–9
blow dryer [blō/ drī/ər] **23**–20, **76**–16
blow out [blō/ owt/] **169**–K
blue [blōō] **12**–1
blueberries [blōō/bĕr/ēz] **50**–19
blue jay [blōō/ jā/] **132**–7
blush [blŭsh] **77**–36
board game [börd/ gām/] **162**–3
boarding area [bör/dĭng ër/ē ə] **110**–6
board the plane [börd/ dhə plān/] **111**–F
boating [bō/tĭng] **154**–2
bobby pins [bäb/ē pĭnz/] **76**–19
BODY [bäd/ē] **74**–75
body lotion [bäd/ē lō/shən] **76**–7
body of water [bäd/ē əv wö/tər] **117** ✦
boil [boyl] **58**–P
bolt [bōlt] **37**–29, **150**–30, 33
bone [bōn] (body) **75**–49, (broken) **82**–P
boneless [bōn/ləs] **52** ✦
bookbag [bōōk/băg/] **69**–28
bookcase [bōōk/kās/] **3**–8, **42**–1
bookstore [bōōk/stör/] **92**–4
booth [bōōth] **60**–19, **152**–23
boots [bōōts] **68**–18
bored [börd] **31**–26
boring [bör/ĭng] **167**–29
borrow [bär/ō, bör/ō] **20** ✦
botanical gardens [bə tăn/ĭ kəl gär/dnz] **152**–4
bottle [bät/l] **56**–1, **95**–26
...of soda [–əv sō/də] **56**–13
bottled water [bät/ld wö/tər] **55**–53
bottle return [bät/l rĭ türn/] **54**–1
bounce [bowns] **156**–K
bouquet [bō kā/, bōō–] **129**–27
bow [bō] **161**–6
bowl [bōl] **41**–25
bowling [bō/lĭng] **159**–3
...ball [–böl/] **161**–5
bow tie [bō/ tī/] **69**–40
box [bäks(/–)] **56**–6
...of cereal [–əv sïr/ē əl] **56**–18
...spring [–sprĭng/] **44**–26
boxer shorts [bäk/sər shörts/] **67**–12
boy [boy] **22**–4, 7
bra [brä] **67**–20
brace [brās] **81**–31
bracelet [brās/lət] **69**–35, **83**–14
braces [brā/səz] **84**–24
brain [brān(/–)] **75**–35
...cancer [–kăn/sər] **79**–12
brainstorm [brān/störm/] **6**–K
brake [brāk(/–)]
...light [–līt/] **108**–13
...pedal [–pĕd/l] **109**–46
branch [brănch] **128**–2
Branches of government [brăn/chəz əv gŭv/ər mənt] **116**
Brass [brăs] **120**
bread [brĕd(/–)] **53**–1, 2, 3, **54**–29
...basket [–băs/kət] **63**–8
bread-and-butter plate [brĕd/ n bŭt/ər plāt/] **63**–16
break [brāk(/–)]
...a bone [–ə bōn/] **82**–P

...three eggs [–thrē/ ĕgz/] **58**–A
Breakfast [brĕk/fəst] **61**
breast (body) [brĕst] **74**–14
breasts (chicken) [brĕsts] **52**–19
bricklayer [brĭk/lā/ər] **136**–9
bricks [brĭks] **149**–11
bridge [brĭj] **105**–2
briefs [brēfs] **67**–13, 17
broccoli [bräk/ə lē] **51**–15, **58**–I
broil [broyl] **58**–V
broiler [broy/lər] **40**–21
broken [brō/kən] **48**–5, 6, 7, **49**–15, **70**–24
broom [broōm] **47**–10
brother [brŭdh/ər] / [–brŭdh/ər] **24**–9
    half... [hăf/–] **25**–29
brother-in-law [brŭdh/ər ĭn lö/] **24**–16
brown [brown(/–)] **12**–11
    ...hair [–hër/] **23**–17
bruise [broōz] **78**–12
brush [brŭsh(/–)]
    ...hair [–hër/] **76**–I
    ...teeth [–tēth/] **77**–J
brush [(–)brŭsh(/)] **23**–18, **76**–14
    paint... [pānt/–] **151**–47, **163**–23
    scrub... [skrŭb/–] **47**–19
    toilet... [toy/lət–] **43**–16
bucket [bŭk/ət] **47**–20, **155**–22
buckle [bŭk/əl] **69**–41
bud [bŭd] **129**–6
buffalo [bŭf/ə lō] **134**–6
buffet [bə fā/] **33**–13
building [bĭl/dĭng] **34**–5
BUILDING SUPPLIES [bĭl/dĭng sə plīz/] **150**–**151**
build models [bĭld/ mäd/lz] **162**–C
bulb [bŭlb] **129**–9
bulldozer [boōl/dō/zər] **149**–6
bulletin board [boōl/ə tn börd/] **3**–14
bumper [bŭm/pər] **108**–7
bumper pad [bŭm/pər păd/] **45**–7
bunk [bŭngk] **45**–1
Bunsen burner [bŭn/sən bür/nər] **119**–9
bureau [byoōr/ō] **44**–2
burglary [bür/glə rē] **100**–6
burner [bür/nər] **40**–19
burn (your)self [bürn/ (yər)sĕlf/] **82**–H
bus [bŭs(/–)] **90**–15, **104**–4
    ...driver [–drī/vər] **104**–8
    ...stop [–stäp/] **91**–16, **104**–1
bush [boōsh] **39**–20
business education [bĭz/nəs ĕj ə kā/shən] **121**–2
businessman [bĭz/nəs măn/] **136**–10
businesswoman [bĭz/nəs woōm/ən] **136**–10
busperson [bŭs/pür/sən] **63**–9
butcher [boōch/ər] **136**–11
butter [bŭt/ər] **54**–36
butterfly [bŭt/ər flī/] **132**–20
buttocks [bŭt/əks] **74**–12
button [bŭt/n] **73**–21
buttonhole [bŭt/n hōl/] **73**–12
buy [bī(/–)] **21**–C
    ...a house [–ə hows/] **29**–O
    ...your ticket [–yər tĭk/ət] **111**–A
Buying a house [bī/ĭng ə hows/] **35**
cab [kăb] **104**–18, **106**–16
cabbage [kăb/ĭj] **51**–2

cabinet [kăb/ə nət] **40**–1
cable [kā/bəl] **144**–16
cactus [kăk/təs] **128**–21
cafeteria [kăf/ə tïr/ē ə] **5**–4
cake [kāk(/–)] **54**–32, **61**–19
    ...mix [–mĭks/] **55**–47
    ...pan [–păn/] **59**–26
calculator [kăl/kyə lā/tər] **142**–8
calculus [kăl/kyə ləs] **118**–28
CALENDAR [kăl/ən dər] **18**–**19**
calf [kăf] **74**–18
call [köl] **141**–E
call button [köl/ bŭt/n] **86**–10
calm [käm] **30**–10
camcorder [kăm/kör/dər] **165**–21
camel [kăm/əl] **135**–38
camera [kăm/rə] **165**–19, 24, 27
    ...case [–kās/] **165**–27
camisole [kăm/ə sōl/] **67**–21
camper [kăm/pər] **106**–11
campfire [kămp/fīr/] **154**–11
camping [kăm/pĭng] **154**–1
    ...stove [–stōv/] **154**–16
can [kăn(/–)] **56**–3
    ...of soup [–əv soōp/] **56**–15
    ...opener [–ō/pə nər] **40**–14, **59**–1
cancer [kăn/sər] **79**–12
candle [kăn/dl] **41**–7
candles [kăn/dlz] **169**–H, K
candlestick [kăn/dl stĭk/] **41**–8
candy [kăn/dē] **55**–41, **168**–14
    ...bar [–bär/] **55**–41
    ...store [–stör/] **92**–3
cane [kān] **80**–7
canned goods [kănd/ goōdz/] **54**–4
canoeing [kə noō/ĭng] **154**–3
cantaloupes [kăn/tə lōps/] **50**–15
can't breathe [kănt/ brēdh/] **82**–N
canteen [kăn tēn/] **154**–24
canvas [kăn/vəs] **163**–22
canyon [kăn/yən] **117**–17
cap [kăp] (graduation) **32**–3, (clothing) **66**–6
capsule [kăp/səl] **81**–27
captain [kăp/tən] **158** ✦
car [kär(/–)]
    ...accident [–ăk/sə dənt] **102**–2
    ...dealership [–dē/lər shĭp] **88**–4
    ...safety seat [–sāf/tē sēt/] **95**–13
card [kärd(/–)] **96**–4, **168**–5
    ...catalog [–kăt/l ög, –äg] **98**–10
    ...store [–stör/] **92**–7
cardigan sweater [kär/də gən swĕt/ər] **65**–27
Cardinals [kärd/nəlz] **14**
cardiologist [kär/dē äl/ə jĭst] **86**–3
cards [kärdz] **163**–H
careful [kër/fəl] **147**–24
caregiver [kër/gĭv/ər] **136**–12
careless [kër/ləs] **147**–23
CAR MAINTENANCE [kär/ mān/tn əns] **108**–**109**
carnation [kär nā/shən] **129**–18
carnival [kär/nə vəl] **152**–16
carousel [kär/ə sĕl/] **110**–18
carousel slide projector [kär/ə sĕl/ slīd/ prə jĕk/tər] **165**–29
carpenter [kär/pən tər] **48**–12, **136**–13
carpet [kär/pət] **42**–27

carriage [kăr/ĭj] **95**–16
carrots [kăr/əts] **51**–3
carry [kăr/ē] **62**–H
carry-on bag [kăr/ē än băg/, –ön–] **111**–H
CARS AND TRUCKS [kärz/ ən trŭks/] **106**
cart [kärt] **54**–3, **91**–31
carton [kär/tn] **56**–4
 …of eggs [–əv ĕgz/] **56**–16
cartoon [kär tōōn/] **167**–19
cartridge [kär/trĭj] / [–kär/trĭj] **162**–2
 typewriter… [tīp/rī/tər–] **143**–31
carving knife [kär/vĭng nīf/] **59**–12
cash [kăsh(/–)] **20**–13, **97**–D
 …register [–rĕj/ə stər] **55**–18, **140**–N
cashier [kă shïr/] **136**–14
casserole dish [kăs/ə rōl dĭsh/] **59**–11
cassette [kə sĕt/]
 …player [–plā/ər] **3**–11, **164**–2, 15
 …recorder [–rĭ kör/dər] **164**–3
cast [kăst] **81**–29
casual [kăzh/ōō əl] **71**–37
cat [kăt] **133**–9
catch [kăch] **156**–E
catcher's mask [kăch/ərz măsk/] **161**–15
caterer [kā/tər ər] **33**–12
caterpillar [kăt/ə pĭl/ər, kăt/ər–] **132**–21
catfish [kăt/fĭsh/] **53**–17
cattle [kăt/l] **148**–21
cauliflower [kö/lĭ flow/ər, kä/–] **51**–16
cavity [kăv/ə tē] **84**–20
C-clamp [sē/klămp/] **150**–6
CD (compact disc) [sē/dē/] **98**–14
 …player [–plā/ər] **164**–14
 …ROM disc [–räm/ dĭsk/] **144**–2
ceiling [sē/lĭng] **42**–5
 …fan [–făn/] **41**–4
celery [sĕl/ə rē] **51**–9
cello [chĕl/ō] **120**–9
cellular phone [sĕl/yə lər fōn/] **9**–13
Celsius [sĕl/sē əs] **10**
cent [sĕnt] **20**–1
centimeter (cm) [sĕn/tə mē/tər] **15**–12
CENTRAL AMERICA [sĕn/trəl ə mĕr/ə kə] **122**–**123**
central time [sĕn/trəl tīm/] **17**–28
cents [sĕnts] **20**–2, 3, 4
cereal [sïr/ē əl] **56**–18
Ceremony [sĕr/ə mō/nē] **32**
Certificate of Naturalization
 [sər tĭf/ə kət əv năch/rə lə zā/shən] **29**–6
certified mail [sür/tə fīd/ māl] **96**–11
chain [chān] (hardware) **37**–28, **150**–36, (jewelry) **69**–31
chair [(–)chër(/)] **2**–7
 dining room… [dī/nĭng rōōm/–] **41**–16
 easy… [ē/zē–] **42**–24
 high… [hī/–] **95**–7
 rocking… [räk/ĭng–] **94**–6
 swivel… [swĭv/əl–] **143**–22
chalk [chök] **3**–16
chalkboard [chök/börd/] **2**–1
 …eraser [–ĭ rā/sər] **3**–17
change [chānj(/–)] **21**–9
 …purse [–pürs/] **69**–25
change [chānj(/–)]
 …diapers [–dī/pərz] **94**–E
 …the sheets [–dhə shēts/] **46**–P

…your diet [–yər dī/ət] **80**–C
changing table [chān/jĭng tā/bəl] **45**–12, **95**–9
cheap [chēp] **11**–20
check [chĕk(/–)]
 …blood pressure [–blŭd/ prĕsh/ər] **85**–B
 …your bags [–yər băgz/] **111**–B
 …your work [–yər würk/] **7**–Y
checkbook [chĕk/bōōk/] **97**–7
checked [chĕkt] **70**–11
checker [chĕk/ər] **55**–19
checkers [chĕk/ərz] **162**–5
check in [chĕk/ ĭn/] **111**–D
check-in counter [chĕk/ĭn kown/tər] **110**–3
checking account number [chĕk/ĭng ə kownt/ nŭm/bər] **97**–8
check out [chĕk/ owt/] **98** ✦
checkout desk [chĕk/owt dĕsk/] **98**–16
checkstand [chĕk/stănd/] **55**–17
cheddar cheese [chĕd/ər chēz/] **53**–10
cheek [chēk] **74**–29
cheese [chēz] **53**–9, 10, 11, 12, **54**–38
cheeseburger [chēz/bür/gər] **60**–3
chef [shĕf] **63**–11
chef's salad [shĕfs/ săl/əd] **61**–9
chemistry [kĕm/ə strē] **119**–2
cherries [chĕr/ēz] **50**–16
cherry picker [chĕr/ē pĭk/ər] **149**–5
chess [chĕs] **162**–6
chest (body) [chĕst] **74**–13
chest of drawers [chĕst/ əv drörz/] **45**–8
chicken [chĭk/ən] **52**–16, **61**–12
 …soup [–sōōp/] **58**
chicken pox [chĭk/ən päks/] **79**–6
Chief Justice [chēf/ jŭs/təs] **116**–9
CHILDCARE CENTER [chīld/kër sĕn/tər] **94**–**95**
childcare worker [chīld/kër wür/kər] **94**–3
Childhood diseases [chīld/hōōd dĭ zē/zəz] **79**
children [chĭl/drən] **11**–11, 12, **22**–1
CHILDREN'S BEDROOM [chĭl/drənz bĕd/rōōm] **45**
children's program [chĭl/drənz prō/grăm] **167**–24
child safety seat [chīld/ sāf/tē sēt/] **109**–39
chili peppers [chĭl/ē pĕp/ərz] **51**–8
chills [chĭlz] **78**–9
chimney [chĭm/nē] **38**–21
chimpanzee [chĭm/păn zē/] **135**–28
chin [chĭn] **74**–31
china cabinet [chī/nə kăb/ə nət] **41**–1
chipmunk [chĭp/mŭngk/] **133**–20
chiropractor [kī/rə prăk/tər] **81**–H
chisel [chĭz/əl] **151**–51
choke [chōk] **82**–L
chop [chäp] **58**–G
chorus [kör/əs] **121**–3
Christmas [krĭs/məs] **168**–18
 …tree [–trē/] **168**–20
chrysanthemum [krĭ săn/thə məm] **129**–19
church [chürch] **88**–6
cigarette lighter [sĭg/ə rĕt/ lī/tər, sĭg/ə rĕt–] **108**–32
circle [sür/kəl] **7**–5
circle [sür/kəl] **118**–5
circular saw [sür/kyə lər sö/] **150**–10
circumference [sər kŭm/frəns] **118**–15
Citizen application requirements
 [sĭt/ə zən ăp/lə kā/shən rĭ kwïr/mənts] **116**
CITIZENSHIP [sĭt/ə zən shĭp/] **116**
city [sĭt/ē] **34**–1

...center [–sĕn/tər] **88** ✦
...hall [–höl/] **89**–17
CITY STREETS [sĭt/ē strēts/] **88**–89
claim your baggage [klām/ yər băg/ĭj] **111**–P
clams [klămz] **53**–28
clap [klăp] **32**–B
clarinet [klăr/ə nĕt/] **120**–4
CLASSROOM [klăs/rōōm/] **2**–3
classroom [klăs/rōōm/] **5**–1
Class work [klăs/ würk/] **7**
claw [klö] **132**–4
clay [klā] **162**–14
clean [klēn] (household) **27**–N, **46**–C, **72**–D, (teeth) **85**–I
clean [klēn] **72**–16
CLEANING SUPPLIES [klē/nĭng sə plīz/] **47**
cleanser [klĕn/zər] **47**–23
clear [klïr(/–)] **10**–6
...tape [–tāp/] **143**–39
clear [klïr] **62**–G
clear [klïr] **10**–6
clerk [(–)klürk(/)] **5**–18
  desk... [dĕsk/–] **145**–8
  file... [fīl/–] **142**–12
  library... [lī/brër ē–] **98**–17
  shipping... [shĭp/ĭng–] **146**–15
  stock... [stäk/–] **139**–55
climb [klīm] **153**–C
climbing apparatus [klī/mĭng ăp ə răt/əs] **153**–14
CLINICS [klĭn/ĭks] **84**
clipboard [klĭp/börd/] **143**–26
clip-on earrings [klĭp/än ïr/ĭngz, –ön–] **69**–38
clock [kläk(/–)] **3**–10
...radio [–rā/dē ō] **44**–16, **164**–1
close [klōz] **2**–J
closet [kläz/ət] **11**–15, 16, **43** ✦, **44**–4
cloth diapers [klöth/ dī/pərz] **95**–21
clothesline [klōz/līn/] **72**–9
clothespin [klōz/pĭn/] **72**–10
CLOTHING I, II, III [klō/dhĭng] **64**–67
cloudy [klow/dē] **10**–7
clubs [klŭbz] **163**–26
clutch [klŭch] **109**–45
coach [kōch] **5** ✦, **158**–2
coal [kōl] **126**–4
coat [kōt] (clothing) **66**, (animal) **134**–19
cobra [kō/brə] **131**–40
cockpit [käk/pĭt/] **110**–11
cockroaches [käk/rō/chəz] **49**–25
coconuts [kō/kə nŭts/] **50**–22
cod [käd] **130**–8
coffee [kö/fē] **55**–51, **61**–22
...cup [–kŭp/] **41**–27
...shop [–shäp/] **88**–2
...table [–tā/bəl] **42**–23
instant... [ĭn/stənt–] **55**–51
coffeemaker [kö/fē mā/kər] **40**–11
COFFEE SHOP MENU [kö/fē shäp/ mĕn/yōō] **61**
coin collection [koyn/ kə lĕk/shən] **162**–13
Coins [koynz] **20**
colander [käl/ən dər] **59**–17
cold [kōld] (weather) **10**–4, (feeling) **30**–4
cold (illness) [kōld(/–)] **79**–1
...tablets [–tăb/ləts] **81**–17
cold water [kōld/ wö/tər] **43**–7
coleslaw [kōl/slö/] **53**–14

collar [käl/ər] **73**–7
collate [kō/lāt/, kə lāt/] **142**–F
collect [kə lĕkt/]
  ...the papers [–dhə pā/pərz] **7**–Q
  ...things [–thĭngz/] **162**–D
collection [kə lĕk/shən] **162**–12, 13
college [käl/ĭj] **112**–10
  ...degree [–də grē/] **29**–7
  ...dormitory [–dör/mə tör/ē] **34**–9
  community... [kə myōō/nə tē–] **112** ✦
cologne [kə lōn/] **76**–5
colon [kō/lən] **113**–12
color hair [kŭl/ər hër/] **23**–D
coloring book [kŭl/ə rĭng bŏŏk/] **45**–20
COLORS [kŭl/ərz] **12**
comb...hair [kōm/ hër/] **76**–G
comb [kōm] **23**–22, **76**–13
comedy [käm/ə dē] **166**–10
come home [kŭm/ hōm/] **27**–Q
comet [käm/ət] **127**–25
comfortable [kŭmf/tə bəl, –tər–] **30**–7
comforter [kŭm/fər tər] **45**–2
comma [käm/ə] **113**–10
commercial fisher [kə mür/shəl fĭsh/ər] **136**–15
commit a crime [kə mĭt/ ə krīm/] **100** ✦
Common illnesses and childhood diseases
  [käm/ən ĭl/nə səz ən chīld/hŏŏd dĭ zē/zəz] **79**
community college [kə myōō/nə tē käl/ĭj] **112** ✦
compact [käm/păkt] **106**–2
compact disc (CD) [käm/păkt dĭsk/] **98**–14
compliment [käm/plə mĕnt/] **8**–G
components [kəm pō/nənts] **140**–A
composition [käm/pə zĭsh/ən] **113**–2
compost pile [käm/pōst pīl/] **39**–10
computer [kəm pyōō/tər] **3**–15
  ...programmer [–prō/grăm ər] **136**–16
  ...science [–sī/əns] **121**–4
  ...workstation [–würk/stā/shən] **143**–21
COMPUTERS [kəm pyōō/tərz] **144**
concert [kän/sərt] **166**–6
concierge [kän/sē ërzh/, kōn/–] **145** ✦
concrete [käng/krēt, kän krēt/] **149**–10
condiments [kän/də mənts] **60** ✦
conditioner [kən dĭsh/ə nər] **76**–10
condominium [kän/də mĭn/ē əm] **34** ✦
conductor [kən dŭk/tər] **104**–16
cone [kōn] **118**–11
confetti [kən fĕt/ē] **168**–3
confused [kən fyōōzd/] **31**–27
congestion [kən jĕs/chən] **78**–7
Congressman [käng/grəs mən] **116**–2
Congresswoman [käng/grəs wŏŏm/ən] **116**–2
Conservation [kän/sər vā/shən] **126**
conserve [kən sürv/] **126**–B, C
constellation [kän/stə lā/shən] **127**–24
CONSTRUCTION [kən strŭk/shən] **149**
construction worker [kən strŭk/shən wür/kər] **149**–1
contact lenses [kän/tăkt lĕn/zəz] **81**–36
container [kən tā/nər] **56**–5, **59**–3
  ...of cottage cheese [–əv kät/ĭj chēz/] **56**–17
CONTAINERS AND PACKAGED FOODS
  [kən tā/nərz ən păk/ĭjd fōōdz/] **56**
Continents [kän/tə nənts] **124**
control tower [kən trōl/ tow/ər] **110**–7
convenience store [kən vēn/yəns stör/] **90**–3

Index

CONVERSATION, EVERYDAY [ĕv/rē dā/ kän/vər sā/shən] **8**
convertible [kən vür/tə bəl] **106**–5
convert the measurements
   [kən vürt/ dhə mĕzh/ər mənts] **57**–C
conveyor belt [kən vā/ər bĕlt/] **146**–12
convict [kən vĭkt/] **99**–14
cook [kŏok] **27**–P, **58**–F, **140**–C
cook [kŏok] **137**–17
cooked chicken [kŏokt/ chĭk/ən] **52**–25
cookies [kŏok/ēz] **54**–31, **56**–20
cookie sheet [kŏok/ē shēt/] **59**–27
cool [kŏol] **10**–3
coolant [kŏo/lənt] **109**–56
cooler [kŏo/lər] **155**–11
co-op [kō/äp/] **34** ✦
copy [käp/ē] **6**–F
copy center [käp/ē sĕn/tər] **91**–22
cord [körd] **9**–3, **151**–14
cordless phone [körd/ləs fōn/] **9**–12
core course [kör/ körs/] **121** ✦
corn [körn] **51**–27, **148**–4
corned beef [körnd/ bēf/] **53**–8
corner [kör/nər] **91**–17, **105**–10, **107**–1
corral [kə răl/] **148**–17
correct [kə rĕkt/] **7**–Z
correction fluid [kə rĕk/shən flŏo/əd] **143**–33
corrosive [kə rō/sĭv] **147**–4
cost [köst] **21**–6
costume [käs/tŏom] **168**–13
cottage cheese [kät/ĭj chēz/] **56**–17
cotton [kät/n] **70**–16, **148**–6
couch [kowch] **42**–19
cough [köf] **78**–A
cough syrup [köf/ sĭr/əp, –sür/–] **81**–20
counselor [kown/slər] **5**–16
counselor's office [kown/slərz ö/fəs] **5**–15
count [kownt] **15** ✦
counter [kown/tər] **40**–22, **46**–O, **60**–13, **80**–12, **110**–3
country [kŭn/trē] **34**–4
county fair [kown/tē fër/] **152**–19
courier [kür/ē ər, kŏor/–] **138**–38
court [kört(/–)] **99**–C
   ...reporter [–rĭ pör/tər] **99**–12
courthouse [kört/hows/] **89**–18
courtroom [kört/rŏom/] **99**–7
courtyard [kört/yärd/] **37**–18
cousin [kŭz/ən] **24**–12
cover-up [kŭv/ər ŭp/] **66**–25
cow [kow] **133**–3
coyote [kī ō/tē, kī/ōt/] **134**–3
CPR (cardiopulmonary resuscitation) [sē/pē/är/] **83**–17
CPU (central processing unit) [sē/pē/yŏo/] **144**–1
crab [krăb] **53**–22, **130**–16
cracked [krăkt] **48**–4
cradle [krād/l] **45**–19
crane [krān] **149**–7
crash [krăsh] **102**–3
crayons [krā/änz] **45**–21
creamer [krē/mər] **41**–13
credit card [krĕd/ət kärd/] **20**–15
creek [krēk, krĭk] **117** ✦
crescent moon [krĕs/ənt mŏon/] **127**–14
crewneck sweater [krŏo/nĕk/ swĕt/ər] **71**–26
crib [krĭb] **45**–6
cricket [krĭk/ət] **132**–24

CRIME [krīm] **100**
criminal [krĭm/ə nəl] **100** ✦
crochet [krō shā/] **163**–20
crocodile [kräk/ə dīl/] **131**–37
crocus [krō/kəs] **129**–25
Crops [kräps] **148**
cross-country skiing [krös/kŭn/trē skē/ĭng] **160**–3
cross out [krös/ owt/] **7**–U
cross the street [krös/ dhə strēt/] **90**–A
crosswalk [krös/wök/] **90**–8
crucible tongs [krŏo/sə bəl tängz/, –töngz/] **119**–15
crutches [krŭch/əz] **80**–1
cry [krī] **32**–C
cubby [kŭb/ē] **94**–4
cube [kyŏob] **118**–10
cucumbers [kyŏo/kŭm bərz] **51**–12
cuff [kŭf] **73**–5
cup [kŭp(/–)] **63**–21
   ...of flour [–əv flow/ər] **57**–10
   ...of oil [–əv oyl/] **57**–2
curb [kürb] **90**–10
curling iron [kür/lĭng ī/ərn] **76**–15
curly [kür/lē] **23**–11
curtains [kür/tnz] **44**–5
curved [kürvd] **118**–19
custodian [kŭ stō/dē ən] **138**–35
customs [kŭs/təmz] **110**–20
   ...officer [–ö/fə sər] **110**–21
cut [kŭt] **23**–A, **77**–N
cut [kŭt] **78**–13
cute [kyŏot] **22**–24
cutting board [kŭt/ĭng börd/] **40**–27
cut up [kŭt/ ŭp/] **58**–M
cycling [sī/klĭng] **159**–4
cyclist [sī/klĭst] **153**–3
cylinder [sĭl/ən dər] **118**–12
daffodil [dăf/ə dĭl] **129**–26
DAILY ROUTINES [dā/lē rŏo tēnz/] **26**–**27**
dairy section [dër/ē sĕk/shən] **54**–9
daisy [dā/zē] **129**–14
dance [dăns] **33**–J
dance floor [dăns/ flör/] **33**–16
dangerous situation [dān/jər əs sĭch/ŏo ā/shən] **147**–8
dark blue [därk/ blŏo/] **12**–2
dashboard [dăsh/börd/] **108**–17
data [dā/tə, dăt/ə] **144** ✦
date [dāt(/–)] **18**–14
   ...of birth [–əv bürth/] **4**–16
dates (fruit) [dāts] **50**–25
daughter [dö/tər] **24**–21
daughter-in-law [dö/tər ĭn lö/] **24** ✦
day [dā] **18**–10
daylight saving time [dā/līt/ sā/vĭng tīm/] **17**–33
Days of the week [dāz/ əv dhə wēk/] **18**
dead-bolt lock [dĕd/bōlt/ läk/] **37**–29
dead end [dĕd/ĕnd/] **107**–8
deaf [dĕf] **22**–27
decaf coffee [dē/kăf/ kö/fē] **61**–23
December [dĭ sĕm/bər] **19**–36
deck [dĕk] **38**–16
declaration form [dĕk/lə rā/shən förm/] **110**–22
decorate [dĕk/ə rāt/] **169**–C
deer [dïr] **134**–14
defendant [dĭ fĕn/dənt] **99**–5
defense attorney [dĭ fĕns/ ə tür/nē] **99**–4

degree [də grē′] **29**–7, **112** ✦
degrees [də grēz′]
…Celsius [–sĕl′sē əs] **10**
…Fahrenheit [–făr′ən hīt′] **10**
DELI AND SEAFOOD [dĕl′ē ən sē′fōod′] **53**
deliver [də lĭv′ər] **96**–C
delivery person [də lĭv′ə rē pür′sən] **137**–18
dental [dĕn′təl]
…assistant [–ə sĭs′tənt] **84**–19, **137**–19
…floss [–flös′, –fläs′] **77**–22
…hygienist [–hī jē′nĭst, –jĕn′ĭst] **84**–16
Dental clinic [dĕn′təl klĭn′ĭk] **84**
DENTAL EXAMS [dĕn′təl ĭg zămz′] **85**
dentist [dĕn′tĭst] **84**–18, **137**–20
deodorant [dē ō′dər ənt] **76**–4
department store [dĭ pärt′mənt stör′] **93**–13
departure time [dĭ pür′chər tīm′] **111** ✦
deposit [dĭ päz′ət] **9**–C
deposit [dĭ päz′ət] **97**–C
…slip [–slĭp′] **97**–12
depth [dĕpth] **15**–15
DESCRIBING CLOTHES [dĭ skrī′bĭng klōz′] **70–71**
DESCRIBING HAIR [dĭ skrī′bĭng hër′] **23**
DESCRIBING THINGS [dĭ skrī′bĭng thĭngz′] **11**
desert [dĕz′ərt] **117**–4
design [dĭ zīn′] **146**–A
designated drivers [dĕz′ĭg nā′təd drī′vərz] **101** ✦
designer [dĭ zī′nər] **146**–3
desk [dĕsk′–)] **2**–6, **142**–1
…calendar [–kăl′ən dər] **142**–6
…clerk [–klürk′] **145**–9
…pad [–păd′] **142**–7
dessert tray [dĭ zürt′ trā′] **63**–7
destination [dĕs′tə nā′shən] **111** ✦
diabetes [dī′ə bē′tēz, –təs] **79**–9
diagonal [dī ăg′ə nəl, –ăg′nəl] **118**–23
dial [dī′əl] **9**–D
dial tone [dī′əl tōn′] **9**–B
diameter [dī ăm′ə tər] **118**–17
diamonds [dī′məndz] **163**–27
diaper [dī′pər]
…pail [–pāl′] **45**–13, **95**–23
…pins [–pĭnz′] **95**–22
dice [dīs] **162**–4
dictate [dĭk′tāt] **6**–N
dictionary [dĭk′shə nër/ē] **3**–28
Dictionary work [dĭk′shə nër ē würk′] **6**
die [dī] **29**–R
dietician [dī′ə tĭsh′ən] **87**–25
difference [dĭf′rəns] **118** ✦
difficult [dĭf′ĭ kŭlt′] **11**–24
dime [dīm] **20**–3
Dimensions [də mĕn′shənz] **15**
diner [dī′nər] **62**–5
DINING AREA [dī′nĭng ër/ē ə] **41**
dining room [dī′nĭng rōom′] **62**–2
…chair [–chër′] **41**–16
…table [–tā′bəl] **41**–17
dinner [dĭn′ər]
…fork [–förk′] **63**–25
…plate [–plāt′] **63**–15
diploma [də plō′mə] **29**–2, **32**–7
direct flight [də rĕkt′ flīt′, dī–] **111** ✦
Directions [də rĕk′shənz, dī–] **107**

DIRECTIONS AND TRAFFIC SIGNS
[də rĕk′shənz ən trăf′ĭk sīnz′, dī–] **107**
directory [də rĕk′tə rē, dī–] **9**–8, **93**–19
directory assistance (411) [də rĕk′tə rē ə sĭs′təns, dī–] **9**–8
dirty [dür′tē] **72**–15
discuss [dĭ skŭs′] **6**–L
disgusted [dĭ skŭs′təd] **30**–9
dish [dĭsh(′–)]
…drainer [–drā′nər] **40**–3
…towel [–tow′əl] **47**–22
dishroom [dĭsh′rōom′] **63**–12
dishwasher [dĭsh′wä′shər, –wö′–] (machine) **40**–4, (person) **63**–13
dishwashing liquid [dĭsh′wä′shĭng lĭk′wəd, –wö′–] **47**–21
disinfectant [dĭs′ən fĕk′tənt] **95**–19
disk [dĭsk(′–)] **144**–5
…drive [–drīv′] **144**–3
display case [dĭ splā′ kās′] **69**–7
disposable diapers [dĭ spō′zə bəl dī′pərz] **95**–20
dissection kit [dĭ sĕk′shən kĭt′, dī–] **119**–7
dive [dīv] **157**–5
diving mask [dī′vĭng măsk′] **155**–3
division [də vĭzh′ən] **118**–4
divorced [də vörst′] **25**–24
DJ (disc jockey) [dē′jā′] / [dĭsk′ jäk′ē] **33**–17
do [dōo(′–)]
…an experiment [–ən ĭk spër′ə mənt] **119**–A
…crafts [–krăfts′] **162**–A
…errands [–ĕr′əndz] **90** ✦
…homework [–hōm′würk′] **27**–T
…manual labor [–măn′yōo əl lā′bər] **140**–D
dockworker [däk′wür/kər] **137**–21
doctor [däk′tər] **84**–6, **137**–22
Doctorate [däk′tər ət] **112** ✦
dog [dög] **11**–17, 18, **133**–11
dogwood [dög′wōod′] **128**–16
DOING THE LAUNDRY [dōo′ĭng dhə lön′drē] **72**–2
doll [däl] **45**–18
dollar [däl′ər] **20**–7
dollhouse [däl′hows′] **45**–14
doll making kit [däl′ mā′kĭng kĭt′] **162**–15
dolphin [däl′fən, döl′–] **131**–30
DOMESTIC ANIMALS AND RODENTS
[də mĕs′tĭk ăn′ə məlz ən rōd′nts] **133**
domesticated animals [də mĕs′tə kā′təd ăn′ə məlz] **133** ✦
donkey [däng′kē, dŭng′–, döng′–] **133**–2
do not enter [dōo′ nät′ ĕn′tər] **107**–4
do not wash [dōo′ nät′ wäsh′, –wösh′] **72** ✦
don't [dōnt(′–)]
…**drink** and **drive** [–drĭngk′ ən drīv′] **101**–G
…**open** [–ō′pən] **101**–F
donut shop [dō′nŭt shäp′] **91**–20
doorbell [dör′bĕl′] **38**–10
door chain [dör′ chān′] **37**–28
doorknob [dör′näb′] **37**–30
doorman [dör′măn′] **36**–10, **145**–2
dosage [dō′sĭj] **80** ✦
double boiler [dŭb′əl boy′lər] **59**–8
doughnut [dō′nŭt] **60**–15, **60** ✦
down (feathers) [down(′–)]
…jacket [–jăk′ət] **66**–15
…vest [–vĕst′] **66**–13
down (preposition) [down] **105**–8
downhill skiing [down′hĭl′ skē′ĭng] **160**–1
downstairs [down′stërz′] **38** ✦

Index

downtown [down/town/] **88** ✦
drain [drān] **43**–4
drapes [drāps] **42**–16
draw a picture [drö/ ə pĭk/chər] **6**–M
draw blood [drö/ blŭd/] **85**–G
drawer [drör] **40**–23, **44**–3
dress [(–)drĕs(/)] **64**–3
   maternity... [mə tür/nə tē–] **65**–19
dress [drĕs] **94**–J
dresser [drĕs/ər] **44**–2
dressmaker [drĕs/mā/kər] **73**–2
dress shop [drĕs/ shäp/] **92** ✦
dribble [drĭb/əl] **156**–K
drill [drĭl(/–)] **84**–21, **150**–8, 23
   ...bit [–bĭt/] **150**–23
drill a tooth [drĭl/ ə tooth/] **85**–K
drink [drĭngk(/–)] / [–drĭngk/] **60**–B
   ...fluids [–floo/ədz] **80**–B
   don't... [dōnt/–] **101**–G
dripping [drĭp/ĭng] **49**–16
drive [drīv] **26**–I, **90**–C, **140**–E
drive (computer) [drīv] **144**–3, 20
driver's [drī/vərz]
   ...education [–ĕj/ə kā/shən] **121**–5
   ...license [–lī/səns] **29**–4
drive-thru window [drīv/throo/ wĭn/dō] **90**–13
driveway [drīv/wā/] **38**–5
drop off [dräp/ öf/] **94**–A
dropper [dräp/ər] **119**–14
drought [drowt] **103**–10
drown [drown] **82**–I
drugs [drŭgz] **100**–4
drugstore [drŭg/stör/] **90**–2
drums [drŭmz] **120**–18
drumsticks [drŭm/stĭks/] **52**–22
drunk driving [drŭngk/ drī/vĭng] **100**–3
dry [drī(/–)]
   ...hair [–hër/] **76**–H
   ...the dishes [–dhə dĭsh/əz] **46**–N
dry [drī] **72**–18
dry-clean [drī/klēn/] **72** ✦
dry cleaners [drī/ klē/nərz] **72** ✦, **91**–24
dryer [drī/ər] **72**–4
   ...sheets [–shēts/] **72**–5
Dry measures [drī/ mĕzh/ərz] **57**
drywall [drī/wöl/] **149**–18
duck [dŭk(/–)] **52**–18, **132**–13
   ...pond [–pänd/] **153**–6
dump truck [dŭmp/ trŭk/] **106**–12
duplex house [doo/plĕks hows/] **34** ✦
dust [dŭst] **46**–A
dust [dŭst(/–)]
   ...mop [–mäp/] **47**–17
   ...ruffle [–rŭf/əl] **44**–22
   ...storm [–störm/] **10**–21
dustpan [dŭst/pän/] **47**–11
dye hair [dī/ hër/] **23**–D
eagle [ē/gəl] **132**–10
ear [ïr(/–)] **74**–28
   ...infection [–ĭn fĕk/shən] **79**–3
earache [ïr/āk/] **78**–3
early [ür/lē] **17**–22
earmuffs [ïr/mŭfs/] (outdoor) **66**–12, (safety) **147**–14
earplugs [ïr/plŭgz/] **147**–13
earrings [ïr/ĭngz] **69**–37

Earth [ürth] **127**–7
earthquake [ürth/kwāk/] **102**–5
easel [ē/zəl] **163**–21
east [ēst] **107, 123, 124**
eastern time [ē/stərn tīm/] **17**–29
easy [ē/zē] **11**–23
   ...chair [–chër/] **42**–24
eat [ēt(/–)] **60**–B
   ...breakfast [–brĕk/fəst] **26**–E
eat out [ēt/ owt/] **62** ✦
eclipse [ĭ klĭps/]
   lunar... [loo/nər–] **127** ✦
   solar... [sō/lər–] **127** ✦
economics [ĕk/ə näm/ĭks, ē/kə–] **121**–6
edit [ĕd/ət] **113**–B
eel [ēl] **130**–5
eggbeater [ĕg/bē/tər] **59**–20
eggplants [ĕg/plănts/] **51**–18
eggs [(–)ĕgz(/)] **54**–34
   scrambled... [skrăm/bəld–] **61**–1
eight [āt] **14**
eighteen [ā/tēn/] **14**
eighteenth [ā/tēnth/] **14**
eighth [ātth, āth] **14, 15**–1
eighty [ā/tē] **14, 15**–10
eject [ĭ jĕkt/] **165**–F
elastic bandage [ĭ lăs/tĭk băn/dĭj] **83**–12
elbow [ĕl/bō] **74**–15
elderly [ĕl/dər lē] **22**–15
Election [ĭ lĕk/shən] **115**
elective [ĭ lĕk/tĭv] **121** ✦
electric [ĭ lĕk/trĭk]
   ...can opener [–kăn/ ō/pə nər] **40**–14
   ...drill [–drĭl/] **150**–8
   ...keyboard [–kē/börd/] **120**–20
   ...mixer [–mĭk/sər] **40**–25
   ...pencil sharpener [–pĕn/səl shär/pə nər] **142**–9
   ...shaver [–shā/vər] **77**–24
electrical [ĭ lĕk/trĭ kəl] **151**–38
   ...hazard [–hăz/ərd] **147**–1
   ...tape [–tāp/] **151**–38
electrician [ĭ lĕk trĭsh/ən] **48**–9
ELECTRONICS AND PHOTOGRAPHY
   [ĭ lĕk trän/ĭks ən fə täg/rə fē] **164**–**165**
electronics store [ĭ lĕk trän/ĭks stör/] **93**–18
elementary school [ĕl/ə mĕn/trē skool/] **112**–5
elephant [ĕl/ə fənt] **135**–42
elevator [ĕl/ə vā/tər] **37**–34, **145** ✦
eleven [ĭ lĕv/ən] **14**
eleventh [ĭ lĕv/ənth] **14**
ellipse [ĭ lĭps/] **118**–9
elm [ĕlm] **128**–17
embarrassed [ĭm băr/əst] **31**–25
embroidery [ĭm broy/də rē] **163**–19
EMERGENCIES AND NATURAL DISASTERS [ĭ mür/jən sēz ən
   năch/rəl dĭ zăs/tərz, –năch/ər əl–] **102**–**103**
emergency [ĭ mür/jən sē]
   ...brake [–brāk/] **109**–44
   ...card [–kärd/] **111**–K
   ...exit [–ĕg/zət, –ĕk/sət] **111**–J
   ...medical technician (EMT)
      [–mĕd/ĭ kəl tĕk nĭsh/ən] / [ē/ĕm/tē/] **87**–26
   ...service (911) [–sür/vəs] **9**–9
Emergency room [ĭ mür/jən sē room/] **87**
emery board [ĕm/ə rē börd/, ĕm/rē–] **77**–30

empty [ĕmp/tē] **46**–F
empty [ĕmp/tē] **11**–10
encyclopedia [ĭn sī/klə pē/dē ə] **98**–18
end table [ĕnd/ tā/bəl] **42**–21
end the conversation [ĕnd/ dhə kän/vər sā/shən] **8**–C
ENERGY AND THE ENVIRONMENT
[ĕn/ər jē ən dhē ĭn vī/rən mənt, –vī/ərn–] **126**
Energy resources [ĕn/ər jē rē/sör səz, –rĭ sör/səz] **126**
engine [ĕn/jən] **109**–41
engineer [ĕn/jə nïr/] **137**–23
English as a second language
[ĭng/glĭsh əz ə sĕk/ənd lăng/gwĭj] **121**–7
ENGLISH COMPOSITION [ĭng/glĭsh käm/pə zĭsh/ən] **113**
ENTERTAINMENT [ĕn/tər tān/mənt] **166**–**167**
enter your PIN number [ĕn/tər yər pĭn/ nŭm/bər] **97**–B
entrance [ĕn/trəns] **36** ✦
Entryway [ĕn/trē wā/] **37**
envelope [ĕn/və lōp/] **96**–1, **143**–20
ENVIRONMENT [ĭn vī/rən mənt, –vī/ərn–] **126**
Equivalents [ĭ kwĭv/ə lənts] **15**
erase [ĭ rās/] **2**–H
eraser [ĭ rā/sər] **3**–21
escalator [ĕs/kə lā/tər] **93**–21
evening [ēv/nĭng] **17**–19
...gown [–gown/] **65**–29
every day [ĕv/rē dā/] **18**–21
EVERYDAY CONVERSATION [ĕv/rē dā/ kän/vər sā/shən] **8**
evidence [ĕv/ə dəns] **99**–9
examination table [ĭg zăm/ə nā/shən tā/bəl] **84**–13
examine [ĭg zăm/ən] **85**–F
examining room [ĭg zăm/ə nĭng rōōm/] **84**–9
exchange [ĭks chānj/] **21**–G
excited [ĭk sī/təd] **31**–23
exclamation mark [ĕk/sklə mā/shən märk/] **113**–8
Excuse me. [ĭk skyōōz/ mē] **8**
Executive [ĭg zĕk/yə tĭv] **116**
exercise [ĕk/sər sīz/] **27**–W, **80**–D, **157**–P
exhausted [ĭg zö/stəd] **30** ✦
exhibition [ĕk/sə bĭsh/ən] **152**–21
expensive [ĭk spĕn/sĭv] **11**–19
experience turbulence [ĭk spïr/ē əns tür/byə ləns] **111**–N
expiration date [ĕk/spə rā/shən dāt/] **80** ✦
Exploration [ĕk/splə rā/shən] **114**
explosion [ĭk splō/zhən] **102**–4
Express Mail [ĭk sprĕs/ māl/] **96**–15
extension cord [ĭk stĕn/shən körd/] **151**–14
exterminate [ĭk stür/mə nāt/] **49** ✦
exterminator [ĭk stür/mə nā/tər] **49**–21
extra [ĕk/strə]
...large [–lärj/] **70**–5
...small [–smöl/] **70**–1
extract a tooth [ĭk străkt/ ə tōōth/] **85** ✦
eye [ī(/–)] / [–ī/] **73**–23, **74**–27
...chart [–chärt/] **84**–11
...glasses [–glăs/əz] **81**–35
...hook [–hōōk/] **150**–35
...shadow [–shăd/ō] **77**–34
hook and... [hōōk/ ən–] **73**–23
eyebrow [ī/brow/] **74**–32
...pencil [–pĕn/səl] **77**–33
eyedrops [ī/dräps/] **81**–22
eyelashes [ī/lăsh/əz] **74**–34
eyelid [ī/lĭd/] **74**–33
eyeliner [ī/lī/nər] **77**–35
fabric softener [făb/rĭk sö/fə nər] **72**–6

Face [fās] **74**, **77**
face powder [fās/ pow/dər] **77**–39
FACTORY [făk/tə rē, –trē] **146**
factory [făk/tə rē, –trē]
...owner [–ō/nər] **146**–2
...worker [–wür/kər] **146**–6
fall [föl] **82**–O
fall [föl] **19**–39
fall in love [föl/ ĭn lŭv/] **28**–K
FAMILY [făm/lē, făm/ə lē] **24**–**25**
fan [făn] (appliance) **41**–4, (person) **158**–4
fancy [făn/sē] **71**–39
fare [fër(/–)] **104**–5
...card [–kärd/] **104**–12
far from [fär/ frŭm/, –frəm] **13** ✦
farm [färm(/–)] **34**–13
...equipment [–ĭ kwĭp/mənt] **148**–10
Farm animals [färm/ ăn/ə məlz] **133**
farmer [fär/mər] **148**–15
FARMING AND RANCHING [fär/mĭng ən răn/chĭng] **148**
farmworker [färm/wür/kər] **148**–8
fashion designer [făsh/ən dĭ zī/nər] **73** ✦
fast [făst] **11**–3
fasten your seat belt [făs/ən yər sēt/ bĕlt/] **111**–I
FAST FOOD [făst/ fōōd/] **60**
fast food restaurant [făst/ fōōd/ rĕs/tə rənt, –ränt] **90**–14
fast forward [făst/ för/wərd] **165**–C
fat [făt] **11**–7
father [fä/dhər] **24**–6
father-in-law [fä/dhər ĭn lö/] **24**–14
faucet [fö/sət] **43**–6, **49**–16
fax [făks] **142**–B
fax machine [făks/ mə shēn/] **143**–23
feast [fēst] **168**–16
feather [fĕdh/ər] **132**–3
...duster [–dŭs/tər] **47**–1
February [fĕb/yōō ër/ē, fĕb/rōō–] **19**–26
feed [fēd] **94**–D, **148**–D
feel [fēl(/–)]
...dizzy [–dĭz/ē] **78**–C
...nauseous [–nö/shəs, –zē əs] **78**–D
FEELINGS [fē/lĭngz] **30**–**31**
feet [fēt] **15** ✦
female [fē/māl/] **4**–14
fence [fĕns] **38**–3, **148**–19
fencing [fĕn/sĭng] **159**–5
ferry [fër/ē] **104**–23
fever [fē/vər] **78**–8
fiction [fĭk/shən] **98**, **166**
field [fēld] (school) **5**–12, (farm) **148**–7, (sports) **159**–17
fifteen [fĭf/tēn/] **14**
fifteenth [fĭf/tēnth/] **14**
fifth [fĭfth] **14**
fifty [fĭf/tē] **14**
...dollars [–däl/ərz] **20**–11
...percent [–pər sĕnt/] **15**–9
figure skating [fĭg/yər skā/tĭng] **160**–5
figurine [fĭg/yə rēn/] **162**–10
file [fīl] **142**–H
file [fīl(/–)]
...cabinet [–kăb/ə nət] **142**–10
...clerk [–klürk/] **142**–12
...folder [–fōl/dər] **142**–11
filet of sole [fĭ lā/ əv sōl/] **53**–21
fill a cavity [fĭl/ ə kăv/ə tē] **85**–L

Index

fill in the blank [fĭl/ ĭn dhə blăngk/] 7–R
fill out [fĭl/ owt/] / [fĭl/ owt/–]
...a form [–ə förm/] 4–B
...an application [–ən ăp/lə kā/shən] 141–G
filling [fĭl/ĭng] 84–22
film [fĭlm] (camera) 165–26, (movie) 166–1
fin [fĭn] 130–1
find your seat [fīnd/ yər sēt/] 111–G
FINDING A HOME [fīn/dĭng ə hōm/] 35
fingernail [fĭng/gər nāl/] 75–58
fingers [fĭng/gərz] 75–57
finish [fĭn/ĭsh] 157–Z
fins [fĭnz] 155–2
fire [fīr(/–)] 42–10, 102–7
...escape [–ĭ skāp/] 36–7
...exit [–ĕg/zət, –ĕk/sət] 37–23
...extinguisher [–ĭk stĭng/gwĭ shər] 147–22
...hydrant [–hī/drənt] 91–28
...screen [–skrēn/] 42–11
...station [–stā/shən] 88–1
...truck [–trŭk/] 102–9
firefighter [fīr/fī/tər] 102–8, 137–24
fireplace [fīr/plās/] 42–9
fireworks [fīr/würks/] 168–8
first [fürst(/–)] 14
...draft [–drăft/] 113–A
...floor [–flör/] 36–1
...name [–nām/] 4–2
...place [–plās/] 152–20
...prize [–prīz/] 152–20
FIRST AID [fürst/ ād/] 83
first aid [fürst/ ād/]
...kit [–kĭt/] 83–1
...manual [–măn/yoō əl] 83–7
Fish [fĭsh] 53
fish [fĭsh] 61–17, 130–12, 14, 15
fishing [fĭsh/ĭng] 154–5
...net [–nĕt/] 154–17
...pole [–pōl/] 154–18
fitted sheet [fĭt/əd shēt/] 44–14
fittings [fĭt/ĭngz] 151–17
five [fīv(/–)] 14–5, 20
...after one [–ăf/tər wŭn/] 16–5
...to two [tə toō/] 16–15
Five ways to cook chicken [fīv/ wāz/ tə koōk/ chĭk/ən] 58
fix [fĭks] 49 ✦
flag [flăg] 168–9
flammable [flăm/ə bəl] 147–2
flashlight [flăsh/līt/] 151–39
flat sheet [flăt/ shēt/] 44–13
flea market [flē/ mär/kət] 152–22
fleas [flēz] 49–23
flight attendant [flīt/ ə tĕn/dənt] 110–13
flood [flŭd] 103–16
floor [flör(/–)] / [–flör/] 44–24
...lamp [–lămp/] 42–15
...plan [–plăn/] 38–1
dance... [dăns/–] 33–16
floppy [flăp/ē] 144–5
floral [flör/əl] 70–12
florist [flör/ĭst] 92–12, 137–25
floss [flös, fläs] 77–K
flounder [flown/dər] 130–13
flour [flow/ər] 55–45, 57–10
flower [flow/ər] 39–19, 129–7

...bed [–bĕd/] 39–A
...pot [–pät/] 39–18
Parts of a... [pärts/ əv ə–] 129
FLOWERS [flow/ərz] 129
flu [floō] 79–2
fluid ounce [floō/əd owns/] 57–1
flute [floōt] 120–3
fly [flī] 140 ✦
fly [flī] 132–29
flying disc [flī/ĭng dĭsk/] 159–6, 161–27
foam pad [fōm/ păd/] 154–13
foggy [fö/gē, fäg/ē–] 10–11
fold [fōld] 72–F
Follow directions [fäl/ō də rek/shənz, –dī–] 7
food [foōd(/–)]
...court [–kört/] 93–14
...processor [–prä/sĕ sər] 40–26
FOOD PREPARATION [foōd/ prĕp ə rā/shən] 58
Foot [foōt] 75
foot [foōt] (measurement) 15 ✦, (body) 74–7
football [foōt/böl/] 158–11, 161–22
...helmet [–hĕl/mət] 161–20
forceps [för/səps, –sĕps] 119–8
forehead [för/əd, –hĕd/, fär/–] 74–20
foreign language [för/ən lăng/gwĭj, fär/–] 121–8
forest [för/əst, fär/–] 117–11
fork [förk] 41–21, 63–24, 25, ✦
forklift [förk/lĭft/] 146–14
form [(–)förm(/)]
declaration... [dĕk/lə rā/shən–] 110–22
registration... [rĕj/ə strā/shən–] 4
formal [för/məl] 71–36
former husband [för/mər hŭz/bənd] 25 ✦
former wife [för/mər wīf/] 25 ✦
formula [för/myə lə] 95–25, 119–19
forty [för/tē] 14, 16–12
foundation [fown dā/shən] 77–40
fountain [fown/tn] / [–fown/tn] 92–11
water... [wö/tər–] 153–11
four [för] 14
fourteen [för/tēn/] 14
fourteenth [för/tēnth/] 14
fourth [förth(/–)] 14, 15–2
...floor [–flör/] 36–4
fox [fäks] 134–15
Fractions [frăk/shənz] 15
freezer [frē/zər] 40–10
freezing [frē/zĭng] 10–5
french fries [frĕnch/ frīz/] 60–2
French horn [frĕnch/ hörn/] 120–15
fresh [frĕsh] 53–29
Friday [frī/dā, –dē] 18–6
fried [frīd] 61–17
frog [frög, fräg] 130–25
front... [frŭnt(/–)]
...desk [–dĕsk/] 145–8
...door [–dör/] 38–11
...office [–ö/fəs] 146–1
...seat [–sēt/] 109–35
...walk [–wök/] 38–14
...yard [–yärd/] 38–15
frozen [frō/zən]
...fish [–fĭsh/] 53–30
...foods [–foōdz/] 55–12
...vegetables [–vĕj/tə bəlz] 55–43

…yogurt [–yō/gərt] **60**–11
FRUIT [fro͞ot] **50**
frustrated [frŭs/trā/təd] **31**–28
fry [frī] **58**–5
frying pan [frī/ĭng păn/] **59**–5
fuel injection system [fyo͞o/əl ĭn jĕk/shən sĭs/təm] **109**–40
full [fo͞ol] (not empty) **11**–9, (satisfied) **30**–6
full [fo͞ol(/–)]
…moon [–mo͞on/] **127**–16
…slip [–slĭp/] **67**–22
full-size car [fo͞ol/sīz/ kär/] **106**–4
funnel [fŭn/əl] **119**–12
funny [fŭn/ē] **167**–27
fur [für] **134**–19
furious [fyo͝or/ē əs] **30** ✦
furniture [für/nĭ chər] / [–für/nĭ chər] **35**–K
…polish [–päl/ĭsh] **47**–18
…store [–stör/] **88**–13
patio… [păt/ē ō–] **39**–5
fuse box [fyo͞oz/ bäks/] **48**–13
galaxy [găl/ək sē] **127**–26
gallbladder [göl/blăd/ər] **75**–40
gallon [găl/ən] **57**–5
game [gām(/–)] **152**–18
…show [–shō/] **167**–23
GAMES [gām(/–)] **162**–163
gang violence [găng/ vī/ə ləns] **100**–2
garage [gə räzh/, –räj/] / [–gə räzh/, –räj/] **36, 38**–6
…door [–dör/] **38**–7
garbage [gär/bĭj] **46**–Q
…can [–kăn/] **39**–3
…disposal [–dĭ spō/zəl] **40**–5
…truck [–trŭk/] **91**–27
garden [gär/dn] (vegetable) **148**–12, (botanical) **152**–4
gardener [gärd/nər, gär/dn ər] **137**–26, **152**–6
gardenia [gär dēn/yə] **129**–16
gargle [gär/gəl] **77**–L
garlic [gär/lĭk] **51**–29
…bread [–brĕd/] **61**–16
…press [–prĕs/] **59**–10
garment worker [gär/mənt wür/kər] **73** ✦, **137**–27
garter belt [gär/tər bĕlt/] **67**–19
garter snake [gär/tər snāk/] **131**–39
gas [găs(/–)] / [–găs/] **109**–54
…gauge [–gāj/] **108**–22
…meter [–mē/tər] **48**–14
…pedal [–pĕd/l] **109**–47
…station [–stā/shən] **88**–12, **137**–28
…station attendant [–stā/shən ə tĕn/dənt] **137**–28
…tank [–tăngk/] **108**–12
natural… [năch/rəl–, năch/ər əl–] **126**–3
gate [gāt] (garage) **36**, (airport) **110**–5, **111**–D
gauge [gāj] **84**–12, **108**–19, 22, 23
gauze [göz] **83**–6
gearshift [gĭr/shĭft/] **108**–27
GEOGRAPHY [jē ăg/rə fē] **117**
geometry [jē äm/ə trē] **118**–26
geothermal energy [jē/ō thür/məl ĕn/ər jē] **126**–7
get [gĕt(/–)]
…a checkup [–ə chĕk/ŭp/] **85** ✦
…acupuncture [–ăk/yə pŭngk/chər] **81**–G
…a job [–ə jäb/] **28**–G
…a loan [–ə lōn/] **35**–1
…an electric shock [–ən ĭ lĕk/trĭk shäk/] **82**–F
…an injection [–ən ĭn jĕk/shən] **80**–E

…an X ray [–ən ĕks/ rā/] **85**–H
…bed rest [–bĕd/ rĕst/] **80**–A
…feedback [–fēd/băk/] **113**–C
…frostbite [–fröst/bīt/] **82**–G
…home [–hōm/] **27**–Q
…your boarding pass [–yər bör/dĭng păs/] **111**–E
get dressed [gĕt/ drĕst/] **26**–D
get hired [gĕt/ hīrd/] **141**–L
get married [gĕt/ măr/ēd] **28**–L
get up [gĕt/ ŭp/] **26**–B
gift [gĭft(/–)] **169**–D
…shop [–shäp/] **145**–7
gifts [gĭfts] **33**–18
gills [gĭlz] **130**–2
giraffe [jə răf/] **135**–33
girder [gür/dər] **149**–3
girdle [gür/dl] **67**–18
girl [gürl] **22**–5, 8
give [gĭv(/–)] **21**–D
…a shot of anesthetic [–ə shät/ əv ăn/əs thet/ĭk] **85**–J
…a speech [–ə spēch/] **32**–E
…the verdict [–dhə vür/dĭkt] **99**–E
gizzards [gĭz/ərdz] **52**–23
glass [glăs(/–)] **11**–9, 10, **41**–26, **63**–19, 20, ✦
…cleaner [–klē/nər] **47**–8
glasses [glăs/əz] **81**–35
globe [glōb] **3**–9
glove [glŭv(/–)] **161**–17
…compartment [–kəm pärt/mənt] **108**–33
gloves [glŭvz] **66**–5
glue [glo͞o] **143**–37, **162**–8
go [gō(/–)]
…on an interview [–än ən ĭn/tər vyo͞o/, –ön–] **141**–H
…straight [–strāt/] **107**–A
…through security [–thro͞o sĭ kyo͝or/ə tē] **111**–C
…to a chiropractor [–to͞o ə kī/rə prăk/tər] **81**–H
…to bed [–tə bĕd/] **27**–X
…to college [–tə käl/ĭj] **28**–J
…to jail [–tə jāl/] **99**–G
…to prison [–tə prĭz/ən] **99**–G
…to sleep [–tə slēp/] **27**–Y
…to the market [–tə dhə mär/kət] **26**–L
…to work [–tə würk/] **26**–I
goat [gōt] **133**–1
goggles [gäg/əlz] **147**–9
goldfish [gōld/fĭsh/] **133**–16
golf [gälf(/–), gölf(/–)] **159**–7
…club [–klŭb/] **161**–1
good [go͝od] **11**–17
good-bye [go͝od bī/, gə–] **8**
goose [go͞os] **132**–14
gopher [gō/fər] **133**–19
gorilla [gə rĭl/ə] **135**–30
gown [gown] **32**–2, **65**–29
graduate [grăj/o͞o āt/] **28**–D, **32**–A
graduate [grăj/o͞o ət] **32**–6
…school [–sko͞ol/] **112** ✦
graduated cylinder [grăj/o͞o ā/təd sĭl/ən dər] **119**–10
graduating class [grăj/o͞o ā/tĭng klăs/] **32**–1
GRADUATION [grăj/o͞o ā/shən] **32**–33
grams [grămz] **57** ✦
grandchild [grăn/chīld/, grănd/–] **29**–Q
granddaughters [grăn/dö/tərz] **24** ✦
grandfather [grăn/fä/dhər, grănd/–] **24**–3
grandmother [grăn/mŭdh/ər, grănd/–] **24**–2

Index

grandparents [grăn/pĕr/ənts, grănd/–] 24–1
grandson [grăn/sŭn/, grănd/–] 24–7
grapefruit [grāp/frōōt/] 50–9
grapes [grāps] 50–1
graphic artist [grăf/ĭk är/tĭst] 137–29
grasshopper [grăs/hăp/ər] 132–25
grate [grāt] 58–J
grater [grā/tər] 59–2
gray [grā(/–)] 12–5
...hair [–hĕr/] 23–13
grease [grēs] 58–C
green [grēn] 12–8
greenhouse [grēn/hows/] 152–5
green salad [grēn/ săl/əd] 60–8
greeting card [grē/tĭng kärd/] 96–4
greet someone [grēt/ sŭm/wŭn] 8–A
grill [grĭl] 58–T
grilled cheese sandwich [grĭld/ chēz/ săn/wĭch, –sănd/–] 61–8
ground beef [grownd/ bēf/] 52–4
ground post [grownd/ pōst/] 96–14
grower [grō/ər] 148–15
guard [gärd] 97–4, 99–3
guest [gĕst(/–)] 32–9, 145–11
...room [–rōōm/] 145–10
...speaker [–spē/kər] 32–9
guests [gĕsts] 33–14, 169–B
guilty [gĭl/tē] 99
guinea pig [gĭn/ē pĭg/] 133–14
guitar [gĭ tär/] 120–11
gum [gŭm] 55–42
gums [gŭmz] 74–24
gun [gŭn] 100–9
gurney [gür/nē] 87–28
gutter [gŭt/ər] 38–19
gym [jĭm] 5–9
gymnastics [jĭm năs/tĭks] 159–8
gynecologist [gī/nə käl/ə jĭst] 86 ✦
hacksaw [hăk/sö/] 150–5
hail [hāl] 10–19
hail a taxi [hāl/ ə tăk/sē] 104 ✦
hailstorm [hāl/störm/] 10–18
hair [hĕr(/–)] 23, 74–19
...clip [–klĭp/] 76–17
...gel [–jĕl/] 76–11
...net [–nĕt/] 147–18
...salon [–sə län/] 23 ✦, 93–16
...spray [–sprā/] 76–12
...stylist [–stī/lĭst] 23 ✦
hairdresser [hĕr/drĕs/ər] 137–30
half [hăf(/–)] 15–4, 16–10, 20–5
...bath [–băth/] 43 ✦
...brother [–brŭdh/ər] 25–29
...cup of raisins [–kŭp/ əv rā/zənz] 57–9
...past one [–păst/ wŭn/] 16
...sister [–sĭs/tər] 25–30
...slip [–slĭp/] 67–23
halibut [hăl/ə bət] 53–20
hall [höl] 89–17, 145–13
Halloween [hăl/ə wēn/, häl/–] 168–10
Hallway [höl/wā/] 37
ham [hăm] 52–9
hamburger [hăm/bür/gər] 60–1
hammer [hăm/ər] 149–D
hammer [hăm/ər] 150–1
hammock [hăm/ək] 39–2

hamper [hăm/pər] 43–1
Hand [hănd] 75
hand [hănd(/–)] 2, 11, 74–8
...towel [–tow/əl] 43–13
...truck [–trŭk/] 146–11
handbags [hănd/băgz/] 69–6
handcuffs [hănd/kŭfs/] 99–2
handicapped parking [hăn/dē kăpt pär/kĭng] 107–14
handkerchief [hăng/kər chĭf, –chēf/] 69–42
handsaw [hănd/sö/] 150–4
hanger [hăng/ər] 72–11
hang up [hăng/ ŭp/] / [hăng/ ŭp/–]
...the clothes [–dhə klōz/] 72–H
...the receiver [–dhə rĭ sē/vər] 9–F
happy [hăp/ē] 31–32
Happy Birthday [hăp/ē bürth/dā] 169
hard [härd] (surface) 11–5, (difficult) 11–24
hard [härd(/–)]
...disk drive [–dĭsk/ drīv/] 144–20
...hat [–hăt/] 147–19
Hardware [härd/wĕr/] 144
hardware [härd/wĕr/] 150
...store [–stör/] 88–14
harvest [här/vəst] 148–B
hat [hăt] 66–1
hats [hăts] 68–5
have [hăv(/–)]
...a baby [–ə bā/bē] 29–M
...a grandchild [–ə grăn/chīld/, grănd/–] 29–Q
...a heart attack [–ə härt/ ə tăk/] 82–D
...an allergic reaction [–ən ə lür/jĭk rē ăk/shən] 82–E
...a picnic [–ə pĭk/nĭk] 153–D
...dinner [–dĭn/ər] 27–R
Hawaii-Aleutian time [hə wī/ē ə lōō/shən tīm/] 17–24
hay [hā] 148–18
hazardous [hăz/ər dəs]
...materials [–mə tïr/ē əlz] 147–7
...waste [–wāst/] 126–9
head [hĕd] 74–1
headache [hĕd/āk/] 78–1
headboard [hĕd/börd/] 44–15
headlight [hĕd/līt/] 108–5
headphones [hĕd/fōnz/] 164–16
HEALTH CARE [hĕlth/ kĕr/] 80–81
health [hĕlth(/–)]
...club [–klŭb/] 89–21
...insurance card [–ĭn shōōr/əns kärd/] 84
hear [hïr] 75–B
hearing aid [hïr/ĭng ād/] 81–33
hearing impaired [hïr/ĭng ĭm përd/] 22–27
heart (symbol) [härt] 168–6
heart (body) [härt(/–)] 75–38, 79–14
...disease [–dĭ zēz/] 79–14
listen to... [lĭs/ən tə–] 85–D
hearts [härts] 163–29
heater [hē/tər] 48–1, 108–29
heating pad [hē/tĭng păd/] 80–3
heat wave [hēt/ wāv/] 10–15
heavy [hĕv/ē] 11–13, 71–41
...machinery [–mə shē/nə rē] 140–F
heavyset [hĕv/ē sĕt/] 22–20
hedge [hĕj(/–)] 39–1
...clippers [–klĭp/ərz] 39–12
heel [hēl] (shoe) 68–13, (foot) 75–62
height [hīt] 15–14, 22

Heimlich maneuver [hīm/lĭk mə noo/vər] **83**–18
helicopter [hĕl/ə kăp/tər] **110**–8
Hello. [hə lō/, hĕ–] **8**
help [hĕlp] **6**–J
help wanted sign [hĕlp/ wän/təd sīn/, –wön/–] **141**–C
hemline [hĕm/līn/] **73**–1
hen [hĕn] **133**–5
Hi! [hī] **8**
hibiscus [hī bĭs/kəs, hĭ–] **129**–12
hide [hīd] **169**–E
high [hī(/–)]
…chair [–chër/] **95**–7
…heels [–hēlz/] **68**–17, **71**–47
high blood pressure [hī/ blŭd/ prĕsh/ər] **79**–15
high-rise building [hī/rīz/ bĭl/dĭng] **89**–25
high school [hī/ skool/] **112**–7
hiking [hī/kĭng] **154**–6
…boots [–boots/] **68**–21
hills [hĭlz] **117**–16
hip [hĭp] **74**–5
hippopotamus [hĭp/ə pät/ə məs] **135**–43
hire [hīr] **99**–B
hired hand [hīrd/ hănd/] **148**–20
hit [hĭt] **156**–G
HIV (human immunodeficiency virus) [ăch/ī/vē/]
[hyoo/mən ĭm/yə nō dĭ fĭsh/ən sē vī/rəs] **79**–10
HOBBIES AND GAMES [häb/ēz ən gāmz/] **162–163**
hockey stick [häk/ē stĭk/] **161**–11
hold [hōld] **94**–B, **101**–C
holiday [häl/ə dā/] **19**–43, 44
HOLIDAYS [häl/ə dāz/] **168**
holly [häl/ē] **128**–19
home [hōm(/–)]
…attendant [–ə tĕn/dənt] **137**–31
…economics [–ĕk/ə näm/ĭks, –ē/kə–] **121**–9
homemaker [hōm/mā/kər] **137**–32
homesick [hōm/sĭk/] **31**–21
honeybee [hŭn/ē bē/] **132**–26
hood [hood] **108**–6
hoof [hoof] **134**–17
hook [hook(/–)] **150**–34, 35
…and eye [–ən ī/] **73**–23
horn [hörn] (car) **108**–24, (music) **120**–13, (animal) **134**–21
horror story [hör/ər stör/ē, här/–] **166**–14
horse [hörs(/–)] **133**–4
…racing [–rā/sĭng] **159**–18
horseback riding [hörs/băk rī/dĭng] **154**–9
hose [hōz] **39**–9
HOSPITAL [häs/pĭ tl] **86–87**
hospital [häs/pĭ tl] **88**–7
…bed [–bĕd/] **86**–11
…gown [–gown/] **86**–15
Hospital staff [häs/pĭ tl stăf/] **86**
hostess [hō/stəs] **62**–1
hot [hät] (weather) **10**–1, (feeling) **30**–1
hot dog [hät/ dög/] **60**–6
HOTEL [hō tĕl/] **145**
hotel [hō tĕl/] **88**–5
hot water [hät/ wö/tər] **43**–5
hour [ow/ər] **16**–3
HOUSE [hows] **38**
house [(–)hows(/)] **34**–6
buy a… [bī/ ə–] **29**–O
clean the… [klēn/ dhə–] **27**–N
Household Pests [hows/hōld/ pĕsts/] **49**

HOUSEHOLD PROBLEMS AND REPAIRS
[hows/hōld/ präb/ləmz ən rĭ përz/] **48–49**
housekeeper [hows/kē/pər] **138**–33, **145**–15
housekeeping cart [hows/kē/pĭng kärt/] **145**–14
House of Representatives [hows/ əv rĕp/rĭ zĕn/tə tĭvz] **116**–1
houseplant [hows/plănt/] **129**–29
HOUSEWORK [hows/würk/] **46**
hubcap [hŭb/kăp/] **108**–9
hug [hŭg] **33**–G
humid [hyoo/məd] **10**–12
humidifier [hyoo mĭd/ə fī/ər] **80**–2
humiliated [hyoo mĭl/ē ā/təd] **30** ✦
hummingbird [hŭm/ĭng bürd/] **132**–11
hump [hŭmp] **135**–51
hundred [hŭn/drəd] **14**
hungry [hŭng/grē] **30**–5
hurricane [hür/ə kān/] **103**–12
hurt [hürt] (feeling) **30**–17, (medical) **82**–A
husband [hŭz/bənd] **24**–19
hydrant [hī/drənt] **91**–28
hydroelectric power [hī/drō ĭ lĕk/trĭk pow/ər] **126**–5
hydrogen peroxide [hī/drə jən pə räk/sīd] **83**–8
hyena [hī ē/nə] **135**–31
hygienist [hī jē/nĭst, –jĕn/ĭst] **84**–16
hypertension [hī/pər tĕn/shən] **79** ✦
hypoallergenic [hī/pō ăl/ər jĕn/ĭk] **77** ✦
I beam [ī/ bēm/] **149**–3
ice [īs(/–)]
…hockey [–häk/ē] **158**–13
…machine [–mə shēn/] **145**–18
…pack [–păk/] **83**–13
…skates [–skāts/] **161**–9
…skating [–skā/tĭng] **160**–4
ice cream [īs/ krēm/] **55**–44
ice cream stand [īs/ krēm stănd/] **93**–20
iced tea [īst/ tē/] **60**–5
icy [ī/sē] **10**–13
ignition [ĭg nĭsh/ən] **108**–25
illegal drugs [ĭ lē/gəl drŭgz/] **100**–4
ILLNESSES AND MEDICAL CONDITIONS
[ĭl/nə səz ən mĕd/ĭ kəl kən dĭsh/ənz] **79**
immigrate [ĭm/ə grāt/] **28**–C
Immigration [ĭm/ə grā/shən] **114**
immunization [ĭm/yə nə zā/shən] **80** ✦
in [ĭn] **13**–5
…fashion [–făsh/ən] **64** ✦
…front of [–frŭnt/ əv] **13**–4
…love [–lŭv/] **28**–K, **30**–19
…pain [–pān/] **30**–12
…shock [–shäk/] **82**
inch (in.) [ĭnch] **15**–13
Independence Day [ĭn/də pĕn/dəns dā/] **168**–7
INDIVIDUAL SPORTS [ĭn/də vĭj/oo əl spörts/] **159**
industrial arts [ĭn dŭs/trē əl ärts/] **121**–10
infectious disease [ĭn fĕk/shəs dĭ zēz/] **79** ✦
influenza [ĭn/floo ĕn/zə] **79** ✦
information booth [ĭn/fər mā/shən booth/] **93**–22
ingredients [ĭn grē/dē ənts] **58**–K
INJURIES [ĭn/jə rēz] **78**
ink pad [ĭngk/ păd/] **143**–41
inline [ĭn/līn/]
…skates [–skāts/] **161**–10
…skating [–skā/tĭng] **159**–9
inquire about the salary [ĭn kwīr/ ə bowt/ dhə săl/ə rē] **141**–K
insect [ĭn/sĕkt]

Index

...bite [–bīt/] **78**–11
...repellent [–rĭ pĕl/ənt] **154**–23
INSECTS [ĭn/sĕkts] **132**
insert [ĭn sürt/] **97**–A
Inside the body [ĭn/sīd/ dhə bäd/ē] **75**
instant coffee [ĭn/stənt kö/fē] **55**–51
instructor [ĭn strŭk/tər] **5** ✦, **139**–58
instrument [ĭn/strə mənt] **120**–A
insulation [ĭn/sə lā/shən] **149**–13
insurance [ĭn shoor/əns]
...card [–kärd/] **84**–4
...form [–förm/] **84**–5
intercom [ĭn/tər käm/] **36**–8
interesting [ĭn/trə stĭng, ĭn/tə rĕs/tĭng] **167**–30
international call [ĭn/tər näsh/ə nəl köl/] **9**–6
internist [ĭn/tür/nĭst] **86**–2
interpreter [ĭn tür/prə tər] **138**–34
INTERSECTION [ĭn/tər sĕk/shən] **90–91**
interview [ĭn/tər vyoo/] **141**–H
intestinal parasites [ĭn tĕs/tə nəl păr/ə sīts/] **79**–16
intestines [ĭn tĕs/tənz] **75**–42
into [ĭn/too, –tə] **105**–4
introduce [ĭn/trə doos/] **8**–D, F
Invention [ĭn vĕn/shən] **115**
invite [ĭn vīt/] **169**–B
iris [ī/rəs] **129**–20
iron [ī/ərn] **72**–G
iron [ī/ərn] **72**–13
ironed shirt [ī/ərnd shürt/] **72**–20
ironing board [ī/ər nĭng börd/] **72**–14
island [ī/lənd] **117**–8
IV (intravenous drip) [ī/vē/] / [ĭn/trə vē/nəs drĭp/] **87**–27
jack [jăk] **109**–53
jack cheese [jăk/ chēz/] **53**–12
jacket [jăk/ət] **66**–7
jack hammer [jăk/ hăm/ər] **149**–9
jack-o'-lantern [jăk/ə lăn/tərn] **168**–11
jam [jăm] **56**–14
janitor [jăn/ə tər] **138**–3
January [jăn/yoo ër/ē] **19**–25
jar [jär(/–)] **56**–2
...of jam [–əv jăm/] **56**–14
jasmine [jăz/mən] **129**–21
jaw [jö] **74**–23
jeans [jēnz] **64**–5
jellyfish [jĕl/ē fĭsh/] **130**–14
jewelry [joo/əl rē] **69**–8
...store [–stör/] **92**–2
job [jäb(/–)] / [–jäb/]
...board [–börd/] **141**–B
get a... [gĕt/ ə–] **28**–G
JOB SAFETY [jäb/ sāf/tē] **147**
JOB SEARCH [jäb/ sürch/] **141**
JOB SKILLS [jäb/ skĭlz/] **140**
JOBS AND OCCUPATIONS A–H [jäbz/ ən äk/yə pā/shənz] **136–137**
JOBS AND OCCUPATIONS H–W [jäbz/ ən äk/yə pā/shənz] **138–139**
jockstrap [jäk/străp/] **67**–14
jog [jäg] **156**–B
join the army [joyn/ dhē är/mē] **28**–F
joystick [joy/stĭk/] **144**–9
judge [jŭj] **99**–6
Judicial [joo dĭsh/əl] **116**
July [joo lī/] **19**–31, **168**–7
jump [jŭmp] **156**–J

jumper [jŭm/pər] **65**–18
jumper cables [jŭm/pər kā/bəlz] **109**–52
jump rope [jŭmp/ rōp/] **153**–5
jumpsuit [jŭmp/soot/] **65**–16
June [joon] **19**–30
junior high school [joon/yər hī/ skool] **112**–6
Jupiter [joo/pə tər] **127**–5
jury [joor/ē] **99**–8, **116**
Justices [jŭs/tə səz] **116**–10
kangaroo [kăng/gə roo/] **135**–44
keep [kēp] **21**–E
ketchup [kĕch/əp, kăch/–] **60**–23
key [kē(/–)] **37**–31
...chain [–chān/] **69**–43
keyboard [kē/börd/] **120**–20, **144**–7
kick [kĭk] **156**–L
kidney [kĭd/nē] **75**–45
kilometers [kĭ läm/ə tərz, kĭl/ə mē/tərz] **15** ✦
kiss [kĭs] **33**–F
KITCHEN [kĭch/ən] **40**
kitchen [kĭch/ən] **63**–10
...timer [–tī/mər] **59**–18
KITCHEN UTENSILS [kĭch/ən yoo tĕn/səlz] **59**
kitten [kĭt/n] **133**–10
knee [nē(/–)] **74**–17
...socks [–säks/] **67**–25
knee-highs [nē/hīz/] **67**–24
knife [(–)nīf(/)] **41**–22, **63**–27
carving... [kär/vĭng–] **59**–12
multi-use... [mŭl/tē yoos/–, mŭl/tī–] **154**–20
paring... [për/ĭng–] **59**–16
knit [nĭt] **163**–F
knit shirt [nĭt/ shürt/] **65**–20
knitting needles [nĭt/ĭng nēd/lz] **163**–18
koala [kō ä/lə] **135**–45
label [lā/bəl] / [–lā/bəl] **143**–35
prescription... [prĭ skrĭp/shən–] **80**–14
lab technician [lăb/ tĕk nĭsh/ən] **86**–16
ladder [lăd/ər] **149**–2
ladle [lād/l] **59**–7
ladybug [lā/dē bŭg/] **132**–27
lake [lāk] **117**–13
lamb [lăm(/–)] **52**–13, 14, 15
...chops [–chäps/] **52**–15
...shanks [–shăngks/] **52**–13
lamp [lămp] **42**–15, **44**–17
lampshade [lămp/shād/] **44**–18
land [lănd] **111**–O
landlord [lănd/lörd/] **37**–32
language [lăng/gwĭj]
English as a second... [ĭng/glĭsh əz ə sĕk/ənd–] **141**–7
foreign... [för/ən–, fär/–] **141**–8
speak another... [spēk/ ə nä/thər] **140**–J
use the new... [yooz/ thə noo/–] **143** ✦
lantern [lăn/tərn] **154**–22
laptop [lăp/täp/] **144**–14
large [lärj] **70**–4
last [lăst(/–)]
...name [–nām/] **4**–4
...week [–wēk/] **18**–18
late [lāt] **17**–23
latex gloves [lā/tĕks glŭvz/] **87**–33, **147**–17
laugh [lăf] **33**–H
Laundromat [lön/drə măt/] **90**–1
laundry [lön/drē] **72**–1

...basket [–băs/kət] **72**–2
...detergent [–dĭ tür/jənt] **72**–7
...room [–rōōm/] **36**
lawn [lön(/–)] **39**–21
...mower [–mō/ər] **39**–22
lawyer [lö/yər] **99**–B, **138**–36
lay bricks [lā/ brĭks/] **149**–B
leaf [lēf(/–)] **128**–6, **129**–5
...blower [–blō/ər] **39**–4
leaking [lē/kĭng] **48**–3
learn to drive [lürn/ tə drīv/] **28**–E
lease [lēs] **35** ✦
leather [lĕdh/ər]
...boots [–bōōts/] **70**–18
...jacket [–jăk/ət] **66**–3
leave [lēv(/–)] **111**–L
...a message [–ə mĕs/ĭj] **9**–E
...a tip [–ə tĭp/] **62**–J
...work [–würk/] **26**–M
left [lĕft] **13**–1
leg [lĕg(/–)] **74**–6
...of lamb [–əv lăm/] **52**–14
legal [lē/gəl]
...holiday [–häl/ə dā/] **19**–43
...pad [–păd/] **143**–18
LEGAL SYSTEM [lē/gəl sĭs/təm] **99**
leggings [lĕg/ĭngz] **65**–23
Legislative [lĕj/əs lā/tĭv] **116**
lemons [lĕm/ənz] **50**–11
lend [lĕnd] **20** ✦
length [lĕngkth] **15**–16
lengthen [lĕngk/thən] **73**–C
leopard [lĕp/ərd] **135**–25
leotard [lē/ə tärd/] **67**–1
let out [lĕt/ owt/] **73**–F
letter [lĕt/ər] / [–lĕt/ər] **96**–2, **142**–B, D
...carrier [–kăr/ē ər] **96**–6
air... [ër/–] **96**–13
letterhead paper [lĕt/ər hĕd pā/pər] **143**–19
lettuce [lĕt/əs] **51**–1, **60**–17
level [lĕv/əl] **150**–24
librarian [lī brër/ē ən] **98**–1
LIBRARY [lī/brër ē] **98**
library [lī/brër ē] **5**–6, **89**–28, **98**–17, 19, 20
...book [–bŏŏk/] **98**–20
...card [–kärd/] **98**–19
...clerk [–klürk/] **98**–17
license plate [lī/səns plāt/] **108**–15
lid [lĭd] **59**–24
LIFE EVENTS [līf/ ĭ vĕnts/] **28**–29
lifeguard [līf/gärd/] **155**–18
...station [–stā/shən] **155**–20
lifesaving device [līf/sā/vĭng dĭ vīs/] **155**–19
life vest [līf/ vĕst/] **154**–14
light [līt] **169**–H
light [līt] (weight) **11**–14, **71**–40, (color) **12**–3
light (appliance) [līt(/–)] / [–līt/]
...fixture [–fĭks/chər] **41**–5
...switch [–swĭch/] **44**–19
porch... [pörch/–] **38**–9
lightbulb [līt/bŭlb/] **42**–4
lightning [līt/nĭng] **10**–17
lily [lĭl/ē] **129**–24
limb [lĭm] **128**–3
limes [līmz] **50**–12

line [līn(/–)] / [–līn/] **55**–20
...supervisor [–sōō/pər vī zər] **146**–5
assembly... [ə sĕm/blē–] **146**–8
line dry [līn/ drī/] **72** ✦
linen [lĭn/ən] **70**–17
linen closet [lĭn/ən kläz/ət] **43** ✦
Lines [līnz] **118**
lingerie [län/zhə rā/, –jə–] **67** ✦
lion [lī/ən] **135**–36
lip [lĭp] **74**–30
lipstick [lĭp/stĭk/] **77**–37
Liquid measures [lĭk/wəd mĕzh/ərz] **57**
list [lĭst] **6**–L
listen [lĭs/ən] **2**–C, **85**–D
listen for the dial tone [lĭs/ən fər dhə dī/əl tōn/] **9**–B
liters [lē/tərz] **57** ✦
little [lĭt/l] **11**–1
Little League [lĭt/l lēg/] **158** ✦
live [lĭv] **116**–B
liver [lĭv/ər] (food) **52**–7, (body) **75**–39
livestock [līv/stäk/] **148**–13
LIVING ROOM [lĭv/ĭng rōōm/] **42**
lizard [lĭz/ərd] **131**–41
llama [lä/mə] **135**–26
loading dock [lō/dĭng däk/] **146**–16
load the washer [lōd/ dhə wä/shər, –wö/–] **72**–C
loaf [lōf(/–)] **56**–10
...of bread [–əv brĕd/] **56**–22
loafers [lō/fərz] **68**–19
loan [lōn] **35**–I
Lobby [läb/ē] **37**
lobby [läb/ē] **145**–3
lobster [läb/stər] **53**–23
local call [lō/kəl köl/] **9**–4
lock [läk] **101**–E
lock [läk] (house) **37**–29, **48**–6, (car) **109**–34
lockers [läk/ərz] **5**–7
locket [läk/ət] **69**–33
locksmith [läk/smĭth/] **48**–11
logs [lögz, lägz] **42**–12
lonely [lōn/lē] **30**–18
long [löng(/–)] **23**–3, **71**–34
...underwear [–ŭn/dər wër/] **67**–11
long-distance call [löng/dĭs/təns köl/] **9**–5
long-sleeved shirt [löng/slēvd/ shürt/] **71**–31
look at [lŏŏk/ ăt/, –ət] **111**–K, **141**–B
look for [lŏŏk/ för/] / [lŏŏk/ fər]
...a help wanted sign [–ə hĕlp/ wän/təd sīn/, –wön/–] **141**–C
...a new apartment [–ə nōō/ ə pärt/mənt] **35**–A
...the emergency exit
[–dhē ĭ mür/jən sē ĕg/zət, –ĕk/sət] **111**–J
look in [lŏŏk/ ĭn]
...the classifieds [–dhə klăs/ə fīdz/] **141**–D
...throat [–thrōt/] **85**–E
look up a word [lŏŏk/ ŭp ə würd/] **6**–A
loose [lōōs] **71**–42
lose [lōōz] **158** ✦
lost child [löst/ chīld/] **102**–1
loud [lowd] **11**–11
loungewear [lownj/wër/] **67** ✦
love [lŭv(/–)] **30**–19
...seat [–sēt/] **42**–25
low [lō] **71**–46
LPN (licensed practical nurse)
[ĕl/pē/ĕn/] / [lī/sənst prăk/tĭ kəl nürs/] **87**–24

Index

luggage [lŭg**/**ĭj]
   ...carrier [–kăr**/**ē ər] **110**–19
   ...cart [–kärt**/**] **145**–6
lug wrench [lŭg**/** rĕnch**/**] **109**–50
lumber [lŭm**/**bər] **149**–17, **151**
lunar eclipse [lo͞o**/**nər ĭ klĭps**/**] **127** ✦
lunch [lŭnch(**/**–)] **61**
   ...benches [–bĕn**/**chəz] **5**–5
lung [lŭng] **75**–37
LVN (licensed vocational nurse)
   [ĕl**/**vē**/**ĕn] / [lī**/**sənst vō kā**/**shə nəl nürs**/**] **87**–24
machine [mə shēn**/**]
   ...operator [–äp**/**ə rā tər] **138**–37
   ...screw [–skro͞o**/**] **150**–27
magazine [măg**/**ə zēn**/**, măg**/**ə zēn**/**] **98**–7
   ...holder [–hōl**/**dər] **42**–22
magnet [măg**/**nət] **119**–21
magnolia [măg nōl**/**yə] **128**–9
mailbox [māl**/**bäks**/**] **38**–4, **90**–12
mailboxes [māl**/**bäk**/**səz] **37**–36
mailer [mā**/**lər] **143**–32
mailing address [mā**/**lĭng ə drĕs**/**, –ă**/**drĕs] **96**–8
mail [māl**/** ĭt] **96**–B
main office [mān**/** ö**/**fəs] **5**–17
make [māk] **106** ✦
make [māk(**/**–)]
   ...a deposit [–ə dĭ päz**/**ət] **97**–C
   ...an appointment [–ən ə poynt**/**mənt] **85**–A
   ...an offer [–ən ö**/**fər] **35**–H
   ...a toast [–ə tōst**/**] **33**–I
   ...a wish [–ə wĭsh**/**] **169**–J
   ...copies [–käp**/**ēz] **142**–E
   ...lunch [–lŭnch**/**] **26**–F
   ...the bed [–dhə bĕd**/**] **46**–G
make sure you **understand**
   [māk**/** sho͞or**/** yo͞o ŭn**/**dər stănd**/**] **8**–E
male [māl] **4**–13
MALL [möl] **92**–93
mallet [măl**/**ət] **150**–2
MAMMALS [măm**/**əlz] **134**–135
Mammals, Sea [sē**/** măm**/**əlz] **131**
man [măn] **22**–11
manager [măn**/**ĭ jər] **35**–B, **36**–12, **54**–8, **143**–25
mane [mān] **135**–49
mangoes [măng**/**gōz] **50**–21
mantel [măn**/**təl] **42**–8
manual [măn**/**yo͞o əl] **144**–22
manual labor [măn**/**yo͞o əl lā**/**bər] **140**–D
manufacture [măn**/**yə făk**/**chər] **146**–B
map [măp] **3**–12
maple [mā**/**pəl] **128**–13
March [märch] **19**–27
margarine [mär**/**jər ən] **54**–39
marigold [mär**/**ə gōld**/**] **129**–13
MARINE LIFE, AMPHIBIANS, AND REPTILES
   [mə rēn**/** līf**/** ăm fĭb**/**ē ənz ən rĕp**/**tīlz] **130**–131
mark [märk] **7**–T
marker [mär**/**kər] **3**–19
MARKET [mär**/**kət] **54**–55
market [mär**/**kət] **89**–20
marriage license [măr**/**ĭj lī**/**səns] **29**–8
married [măr**/**ēd] **25**–23, **28**–L
Mars [märz] **127**–6
martial arts [mär**/**shəl ärts**/**] **159**–10
mascara [mă skăr**/**ə] **77**–38

mashed potatoes [măsht**/** pə tā**/**tōz] **61**–11
mask [măsk] **168**–12
masking tape [măs**/**kĭng tāp**/**] **151**–49
Master's degree [măs**/**tərz də grē**/**] **112** ✦
match [măch] **7**–X
matches [măch**/**əz] **154**–21
maternity dress [mə tür**/**nə tē drĕs**/**] **65**–19
maternity shop [mə tür**/**nə tē shäp**/**] **93**–17
MATHEMATICS [măth**/**ə măt**/**ĭks] **118**
mattress [mă**/**trəs] **44**–25
May [mā] **19**–29
mayonnaise [mā**/**ə nāz**/**, mā**/**ə nāz**/**] **60**–25
meadow [mĕd**/**ō] **117**–20
measles [mē**/**zəlz] **79**–5
measure [mĕzh**/**ər] **15** ✦, **149**–C
Measurement [mĕzh**/**ər mənt] **15**
MEASUREMENTS [mĕzh**/**ər mənts] **14**–15
MEASURES [mĕzh**/**ərz] **57**
measure the ingredients [mĕzh**/**ər dhē ĭn grē**/**dē ənts] **57**–A
MEAT AND POULTRY [mēt**/** n pōl**/**trē] **52**
meat and poultry section [mēt**/** n pōl**/**trē sĕk**/**shən] **54**–2
media section [mē**/**dē ə sĕk**/**shən] **98**–11
medical [mĕd**/**ĭ kəl]
   ...charts [–chärts**/**] **87**–20
   ...emergency bracelet [–ĭ mür**/**jən sē brās**/**lət] **83**–14
   ...waste disposal [–wāst**/** dĭ spō**/**zəl] **86**–14
MEDICAL AND DENTAL EXAMS
   [mĕd**/**ĭ kəl ən dĕn**/**təl ĭg zămz**/**] **85**
Medical clinic [mĕd**/**ĭ kəl klĭn**/**ĭk] **84**
MEDICAL CONDITIONS [mĕd**/**ĭ kəl kən dĭsh**/**ənz] **79**
Medical conditions and serious diseases
   [mĕd**/**ĭ kəl kən dĭsh**/**ənz ən sïr**/**ē əs dĭ zē**/**zəz] **79**
MEDICAL EMERGENCIES [mĕd**/**ĭ kəl ĭ mür**/**jən sēz] **82**
medication [mĕd**/**ə kā**/**shən] **80**–11, 12
   ...tray [–trā**/**] **87**–23
medicine cabinet [mĕd**/**ə sən kăb**/**ə nət] **43**–19
medium [mē**/**dē əm] **70**–3
meeting room [mē**/**tĭng ro͞om**/**] **145**–19
memory [mĕm**/**ə rē] **144** ✦
men's store [mĕnz**/** stör**/**] **90** ✦
menu [mĕn**/**yo͞o] **62**–3
MENU, COFFEE SHOP [kö**/**fē shäp**/** mĕn**/**yo͞o] **61**
merchandise [mür**/**chən dīz**/**, –dīs**/**] **152**–24
Mercury [mür**/**kyə rē] **127**–9
messenger [mĕs**/**ən jər] **138**–38
messy [mĕs**/**ē] **11**–16
meter [mē**/**tər] (measurement) **15**, (taxi) **104**–21
meter [mē**/**tər] / [–mē**/**tər]
   gas... [găs**/**–] **48**–14
   parking... [pär**/**kĭng–] **91**–18
mice [mīs] **49**–26
microcassette transcriber [mī**/**krō kə sĕt**/** trăn skrī**/**bər] **142**–4
microfilm [mī**/**krə fĭlm**/**] **98**–5
microfilm reader [mī**/**krə fĭlm rē**/**dər] **98**–4
microphone [mī**/**krə fōn**/**] **164**–4
microscope [mī**/**krə skōp**/**] **119**–4
microwave oven [mī**/**krə wāv**/** ŭv**/**ən] **40**–13
middle-aged [mĭd**/**l ājd**/**] **22**–14
middle initial [mĭd**/**l ĭ nĭsh**/**əl] **4**–3
middle school [mĭd**/**l sko͞ol**/**] **112**–6
midnight [mĭd**/**nīt**/**] **17**–21
midsize car [mĭd**/**sīz**/** kär**/**] **106**–3
mile [mīl] **15** ✦
milk [mĭlk] **148**–C
milk [mĭlk(**/**–)] **54**–35

...shake [–shāk/] **60**–12
milliliters [mĭl/ə lē/tərz] **57** ✦
million [mĭl/yən] **14**
miniblinds [mĭn/ē blīndz/] **43**–11
minivan [mĭn/ē văn/] **106**–10
minute [mĭn/ət] **16**–2
mirror [mĭr/ər] **43**–18, **44**–1
  rearview... [rĭr/vyōō/–] **108**–1
  sideview... [sīd/vyōō/=] **108**–8
missing [mĭs/ĭng] **70**–25
miss the bus [mĭs/ dhə bŭs/] **104** ✦
mistake [mĭ stāk/] **7**–2
mittens [mĭt/nz] **66**–9
mix [mĭks] **58**–K
mixing bowl [mĭk/sĭng bōl/] **59**–31
mobile [mō/bēl] **45**–4
mobile home [mō/bəl hōm/] **34**–8
model (occupation) [mäd/l] **138**–39
model (hobby) [mäd/l] **106** ✦
  ...kit [–kĭt/] **162**–7
  ...trains [–trānz/] **163**–32
models [mäd/lz] **162**–C
modem [mō/dəm, –dĕm] **144**–11
moisturizer [moys/chə rī/zəɪ] **76**–8
molecule [mäl/ĭ kyōōl/] **119**–18
Monday [mŭn/dā, –dē] **18**–2
MONEY [mŭn/ē] **20**
money order [mŭn/ē ör/dər] **20**–16
monitor [män/ə tər] **144**–6
monitors [män/ə tərs] **110**–4
monkey [mŭng/kē] **135**–27
month [mŭnth] **4**–16, **18**–9
monthly statement [mŭnth/lē stāt/mənt] **97**–10
Months of the year [mŭnths/ əv dhə yïr/] **19**
moon [mōōn] **127**–13, 14, 15, 16
moose [mōōs] **134**–1
mop [mäp] **46**–J
mop [(–)mäp(/)]
  dust... [dŭst/–] **47**–17
  wet... [wĕt/–] **47**–16
MORE SCHOOL SUBJECTS [mör/ skōōl/ sŭb/jĭkts] **121**
morning [mör/nĭng] **17**–16
mosque [mäsk] **89**–23
mosquito [mə skē/tō] **132**–23
motel [mō tĕl/] **89**–22
moth [möth] **132**–22
mother [mŭdh/ər] **24**–5, **25**–25
motherboard [mŭdh/ər börd/] **144**–18
mother-in-law [mŭdh/ər ĭn lö/] **24**–13
motorcycle [mō/tər sī/kəl] **91**–19
mountain [mown/tn]
  ...biking [–bī/kĭng] **154**–8
  ...lion [lī/ən] **134**–2
  ...peak [–pēk/] **117**–14
  ...range [–rānj/] **117**–15
  ...time [–tīm/] **17**–27
mouse [mows] (animal) **133**–17, (computer) **144**–8
mouth [mowth] **74**–22
mouthwash [mowth/wäsh/, –wösh/] **77**–23
move [mōōv] **29**–P
move in [mōōv/ ĭn/] **35**–D
Movement [mōōv/mənt] **115**
mover [mōō/vər] **138**–40
movie [mōō/vē] **166**–1
movies [mōō/vēz] **152**–10

movie theater [mōō/vē thē/ə tər] **88**–11
moving van [mōō/vĭng văn/] **106**–14
mow [mō] **39**–C
mudslide [mŭd/slīd/] **102**–6
muffin [mŭf/ən] **60**–14
muffler [mŭf/lər] (clothing) **66**–4, (car part) **108**–11
mug [mŭg] **41**–28
mugging [mŭg/ĭng] **100**–5
multiplication [mŭl/tə plə kā/shən] **118**–3
multi-use knife [mŭl/tē yōōs/ nīf/, mŭl/tī–] **154**–20
mumps [mŭmps] **79**–7
murder [mür/dər] **100**–8
muscle [mŭs/əl] **75**–48
mushrooms [mŭsh/rōōmz/] **51**–26
MUSIC [myōō/zĭk] **120**
musician [myōō zĭsh/ən] **138**–41
music store [myōō/zĭk stör/] **92**–1
mussel [mŭs/əl] **130**–17
mussels [mŭs/əlz] **53**–26
mustache [mŭs/tăsh] **23**–5
mustard [mŭs/tərd] **60**–24
mystery [mĭs/tə rē] **166**–15
nachos [nä/chōz] **60**–10
nail (hardware) [nāl] **150**–29
nail (body) [nāl(/–)]
  ...clipper [–klĭp/ər] **77**–29
  ...polish [–päl/ĭsh] **77**–31
  ...polish remover [–päl/ĭsh rĭ mōō/vər] **77**–32
  ...salon [–sə län/] **91**–25
name [nām] **4**–1, 2, 3, 4, A, C, D
napkin [năp/kĭn] **41**–19, **63**–23
narrow [năr/ō] **71**–45
nasal congestion [nā/zəl kən jĕs/chən] **78**–7
nasal spray [nā/zəl sprā/] **81**–23
NATURAL DISASTERS
  [năch/rəl dĭ zăs/tərz, năch/ər əl–] **102–103**
natural gas [năch/rəl găs/, năch/ər əl–] **126**–3
nature program [nā/chər prō/grăm] **167**–22
near [nïr] **13** ✦
neat [nēt] **11**–15
neck [nĕk] **74**–2
necklaces [nĕk/lə səz] **69**–9
need [nēd] **109**–(54–59)
needle [nēd/l] (sewing) **73**–22, (pine) **128**–12
neighbor [nā/bər] **37**–22
neighborhood [nā/bər hŏŏd/] **90** ✦
Neighborhood Watch
  [nā/bər hŏŏd/ wäch/, –wöch/] **101** ✦
nephew [nĕf/yōō] **24**–18
Neptune [nĕp/tōōn] **127**–2
nerve [nürv] **75**–50
nervous [nür/vəs] **30**–11
nest [nĕst] **132**–5
new [nōō(/–)] **71**–32
  ...moon [–mōōn/] **127**–13
Newfoundland time [nōō/fən lənd tīm/, –fənd–] **17**–31
news [nōōz] **167**–17
newspaper [nōōz/pā/pər] **98**–8
newsstand [nōōz/stănd/] **90**–11
newt [nōōt] **130**–26
New Year's Day [nōō/ yïrz/ dā/] **168**–1
next to [nĕkst/ tōō, –tə] **13**–1, 2
next week [nĕkst/ wēk/] **18**–20
nickel [nĭk/əl] **20**–2
niece [nēs] **24**–17

night [nīt] **17**–20
nightgown [nīt/gown/] **67**–5
night-light [nīt/līt/] **45**–3
nightshirt [nīt/shürt/] **67**–9
night table [nīt/ tā/bəl] **44**–21
nine [nīn] **14**
nineteen [nīn/tēn/] **14**
nineteenth [nīn/tēnth/] **14**
nineteen-year-old [nīn/tēn/yïr ōld/] **22**–8
ninety [nīn/tē] **14**
ninth [nīnth] **14**
nipple [nĭp/əl] **95**–27
noisy children [noy/zē chĭl/drən] **11**–11
nonfiction [nän/fĭk/shən] **98** ✦
noon [noon] **17**–17
no outlet [nō/ owt/lĕt, –lət] **107**–8
no parking [nō/ pär/kĭng] **107**–12
north [nörth] **107, 123, 124**
NORTH AMERICA AND CENTRAL AMERICA
[nörth/ ə mĕr/ə kə ən sĕn/trəl ə mĕr/ə kə] **122**–123
nose [nōz] **74**–21
not [nät(/–)]
...guilty [–gĭl/tē] **99**
...ripe [–rīp] **50**–28
notebook [nōt/bŏŏk/] **3**–24
...paper [–pā/pər] **3**–25
note pad [nōt/ păd/] **143**–36
November [nō vĕm/bər] **19**–35
nuclear energy [noo/klē ər ĕn/ər jē] **126**–8
numbers [nŭm/bərz] **3**–31
NUMBERS AND MEASUREMENTS
[nŭm/bərz ən mĕzh/ər mənts] **14, 15**
nurse [nürs] **94**–C
nurse [nürs(/–)] **84**–10, **87**–22, 24, 29, ✦, **138**–42, ✦
...midwife [–mĭd/wīf/] **86** ✦
...practitioner [–prăk tĭsh/ə nər] **86** ✦
Nurse's station [nür/səz stā/shən] **87**
nursing home [nür/sĭng hōm/] **34**–11
nut (hardware) [nŭt] **150**–31
nuts (food) [nŭts] **50**–23
nylon [nī/län] **70**–19
oak [ōk] **128**–18
obey the law [ō bā/ dhə lö/] **116**–H
oboe [ō/bō] **120**–5
observatory [əb zür/və tör/ē] **127**–19
observe [əb zürv/] **119**–B
obstetrician [äb/stə trĭsh/ən] **86**–1
OCCUPATIONS (A-H) [äk/yə pā/shənz] **136**–137
OCCUPATIONS (H-W) [äk/yə pā/shənz] **138**–139
ocean [ō/shən] **117**–6, **155**–1
o'clock [ə kläk/] **16**–4
October [äk tō/bər] **19**–34
octopus [äk/tə pəs] **130**–4
odometer [ō däm/ə tər] **108**–21
off [öf] **105**–7
OFFICE [ö/fəs] **142**–143
Office [ö/fəs] **37**
office [ö/fəs] **5**–13, 15, 17, **146**–1
...building [–bĭl/dĭng] **89**–24
...manager [–măn/ĭ jər] **143**–25
official [ə fĭsh/əl] **158**–6
oil (cooking) [oyl] **55**–49, **57**–2
oil (petroleum) [oyl(/–)] **109**–55, **126**–6
...gauge [–gāj/] **108**–19
...paint [–pānt/] **163**–24

...spill [–spĭl/] **126**–15
ointment [oynt/mənt] **81**–24, **83**–9
old [ōld] **71**–33
on [än, ön] **13**–8
...the left [–dhə lĕft/] **13**–1
...the right [–dhə rīt/] **13**–2
once a week [wŭns/ə wēk/] **18**–22
one [wŭn(/–)] **14, 15**–1, 2, 3, 4, 5, 11, **16**–4, 15, **20**–1, 12
...o'clock [–ə kläk/] **16**–4
...way [–wā/] **107**–6
one billion [wŭn/ bĭl/yən] **14**
one-eighth [wŭn/ ātth/, –āth/] **15**–1
one-fifteen [wŭn/ fĭf/tēn/] **16**–7
one-fifty [wŭn/ fĭf/tē] **16**–14
one-forty [wŭn/ för/tē] **16**–12
one-fourth [wŭn/ förth/] **15**–2
one-half [wŭn/ hăf/] **15**–4
one-hundred percent [wŭn/ hŭn/drəd pər sĕnt/] **15**–11
one-oh-five [wŭn/ ō fīv/] **16**–5
one-ten [wŭn/ tĕn/] **16**–6
one-third [wŭn/ thürd/] **15**–3
one-thirty [wŭn/ thür/tē] **16**–10
one-twenty [wŭn/ twĕn/tē] **16**–8
onions [ŭn/yənz] **51**–28, **58**–G, H
online catalog [än/līn/ kăt/l ög/, –äg/, ön/–] **98**–9
on time [än/ tīm/, ön/–] **17** ✦
onto [än/too, –tə, ön/–] **105**–6
open [ō/pən] **2**–I
...the presents [–dhə prĕz/ənts] **169**–L
don't... [dōnt/–] **101**–F
opera [äp/rə] **166**–8
operate heavy machinery
[äp/ə rāt/ hĕv/ē mə shē/nə rē] **140**–F
Operating room [äp/ə rā/tĭng room/] **87**
operating table [äp/ə rā/tĭng tā/bəl] **87**–34
Operations (math) [äp/ə rā/shənz] **118**
operator [äp/ə rā/tər] **9**–7
ophthalmologist [äf/thəl mäl/ə jĭst, –thə mäl/–, äp/–] **86**–7
opossum [ə päs/əm, päs/əm] **134**–4
optician [äp tĭsh/ən] **92**–8
optometrist [äp täm/ə trĭst] **81**–34
orange [ör/ənj, är/–] **12**–6
oranges [ör/ən jəz, är/–] **50**–10
orangutan [ə răng/ə tăng/, –tăn/] **135**–40
orbit [ör/bət] **127**–11
orchard [ör/chərd] **148**–16
orchestra [ör/kə strə] **120**–1
orchid [ör/kĭd] **129**–17
order [ör/dər] **62**–D
orderly [ör/dər lē] **87**–18
order puller [ör/dər poŏl/ər] **146**–10
Ordinals [ör/dn əlz, örd/nəlz] **14**
organ [ör/gən] **120**–22
organizer [ör/gə nī/zər] **143**–30
ornament [ör/nə mənt] **168**–19
orthodontist [ör/thə dän/tĭst] **84**–23
orthopedist [ör/thə pē/dĭst] **81**–28
Other instruments [ŭdh/ər ĭn/strə mənts] **120**
otter [ät/ər] **131**–35
ounce [owns] **57**–11
out [owt(/–)] **48**–2
...of focus [–əv fō/kəs] **165**–33
...of the taxi [–əv dhə tăk/sē] **105**–5
OUTDOOR RECREATION [owt/dör rĕk/rē ā/shən] **154**
outfit [owt/fĭt] **64** ✦

outlet [owt/lĕt, –lət] **44**–20, **107**–8, **151**–41
oval [ō/vəl] **118**–9
oven [ŭv/ən] **40**–20, **46**–C, **47**–3
...cleaner [–klē/nər] **47**–3
microwave...[mī/krə wāv/–] **40**–13
over [ō/vər] **105**–2
overalls [ō/vər ölz/] **65**–21
overcoat [ō/vər kōt/] **66**–2
overdose [ō/vər dōs/, ō/vər dōs/] **82**–K
overdrawn account [ō/vər drön/ ə kownt/] **97** ✦
overexposed [ō/vər ĭk spōzd/] **165**–34
overflowing [ō/vər flō/ĭng] **49**–17
overhead [ō/vər hĕd/]
...compartment [–kəm pärt/mənt] **110**–10
...projector [–prə jĕk/tər] **2**–4
overjoyed [ō/vər joyd/] **30** ✦
overnight mail [ō/vər nīt/ māl/] **96**–15
over-the-counter medication
[ō/vər dhə kown/tər mĕd/ə kā/shən] **80**–12
owl [owl] **132**–6
owner [ō/nər] **139**–56
oxfords [äks/fərdz] **68**–20
oxygen mask [äk/sĭ jən măsk/] **110**–14
oysters [oy/stərz] **53**–27
Pacific time [pə sĭf/ĭk tīm/] **17**–26
pacifier [păs/ə fī/ər] **95**–29
package [păk/ĭj] **56**–8, **96**–5
...of cookies [–əv kook/ēz] **56**–20
PACKAGED FOODS [păk/ĭjd foodz/] **56**
packer [păk/ər] **146**–13
packing tape [păk/ĭng tāp/] **143**–42
pager [pā/jər] **9**–16
pail [pāl] **45**–13, **47**–20, **155**–22
pain [pān(/–)]
...reliever [–rĭ lē/vər] **81**–16
paint [pānt] **149**–A, **163**–E
paint [pānt(/–)] / [–pānt/] **151**–20
...pan [–păn/] **151**–45
...roller [–rō/lər] **151**–46
acrylic... [ə krĭl/ĭk–] **162**–47
paintbrush [pānt/brŭsh/] **151**–9, **163**–23
painter [pān/tər] **138**–43
painting [pān/tĭng] **42**–7, **152**–8
pair of scissors [për/ əv sĭz/ərz] **73**–18
paisley [pāz/lē] **70**–13
pajamas [pə jä/məz, –jä/–] **67**–4
palm [päm] (hand) **75**–59, (tree) **128**–15
pan [păn] **40**–24, **59**–5, 13, 26, 28
pancakes [păn/kāks/] **61**–6
pancreas [păng/krē əs] **75**–46
panda [păn/də] **135**–41
panther [păn/thər] **135**–39
panties [păn/tēz] **67**–16
pants [pănts] **64**–8
pantyhose [păn/tē hōz/] **67**–27
papayas [pə pī/əz] **50**–20
paper [pā/pər] (composition) **113**–2
paper [pā/pər] / [–pā/pər]
...bag [–băg/] **55**–22
...clip [–klĭp/] **143**–44
...cutter [–kŭt/ər] **143**–15
...doll [–däl/] **163**–30
...products [–präd/ŭkts] **55**–14
...shredder [–shrĕd/ər] **143**–24
...towels [–tow/əlz] **40**–2, **56**–23

notebook... [nōt/book/–] **3**–24, 25, 26
parade [pə rād/] **168**–2
paragraph [păr/ə grăf/] **113**–5
parakeet [păr/ə kēt/] **133**–15
parallel [păr/ə lĕl/] **118**–21
parcel post [pär/səl pōst/] **96**–14
parent [për/ənt] **94**–1
parents [për/ənts] **24**–4
paring knife [për/ĭng nīf/] **59**–16
park [pärk] **91**–D
park [pärk] **88**–8
parka [pär/kə] **66**–8
PARK AND PLAYGROUND [pärk/ ən plā/grownd/] **153**
parking [pär/kĭng]
...garage [–gə räzh/, –räj/] **89**–26
...meter [–mē/tər] **91**–18
...space [–spās/] **36**–15, **90**–5
parochial school [pə rō/kē əl skool/] **112**–3
parsley [pär/slē] **51**–10
part [pärt] **23**–4
partner [pärt/nər] **6**–J
parts [pärts] **146**–7
Parts of a bird [pärts/ əv ə bürd/] **132**
PARTS OF A CAR AND CAR MAINTENANCE
[pärts/ əv ə kär/ ən kär/ mān/tn əns] **108**–**109**
Parts of a circle [pärts/ əv ə sür/kəl] **118**
Parts of a fish [pärts/ əv ə fĭsh/] **130**
Parts of a flower [pärts/ əv ə flow/ər] **129**
Parts of a square [pärts/ əv ə skwër/] **118**
Parts of a tree [pärts/ əv ə trē/] **128**
PARTY [pär/tē] **169**
Party [pär/tē] **33**
pass [păs] **156**–H
passbook [păs/book/] **97**–5
passenger [păs/ən jər] **104**–7, **110**–23
pass out [păs/ owt/] **7**–O
passport [păs/pört/] **29**–9
pasta [päs/tə] **61**–15
...salad [–săl/əd] **53**–15
pastrami [pə strä/mē] **53**–6
patient [pā/shənt] **84**–3
Patient's room [pā/shənts room/] **86**
patio [păt/ē ō] **39**–6
...furniture [–für/nĭ chər] **39**–5
patron [pā/trən] **62**–5
pattern (clothes) [păt/ərn] **73**–8
pattern maker [păt/ərn mā/kər] **73** ✦
Patterns (fabric) [păt/ərnz] **70**
pause [pöz] **165**–E
paw [pö] **134**–42
pay [pā(/–)]
...taxes [–tăk/səz] **116**–E
...the check [–dhə chĕk/] **62**–I
...the mortgage [–dhə mör/gĭj] **35**–L
...the rent [–dhə rĕnt/] **35**–F
pay phone [pā/ fōn] **9**–42
pay back [pā/ băk/] **20** ✦
pay for [pā/ för/, –fər] **21**–C
PE (physical education) [pē/ē/] / [fĭz/ĭ kəl ĕj/ə kā/shən]
121–11
peaches [pē/chəz] **50**–5
peacock [pē/käk/] **132**–15
peak [pēk] **117**–14
pearls [pürlz] **69**–30
pears [përz] **50**–6

Index

peas [pēz] **51**–19
pedestrian [pə děs/trē ən] **90**–7
   ...crossing [–krö/sĭng] **107**–10
pediatrician [pē/dē ə trĭsh/ən] **86**–4
peel [pēl] **58**–N
peephole [pēp/hōl/] **37**–27
pelvis [pěl/vəs] **75**–55
pen [pěn] **3**–18
pencil [pěn/səl] **3**–20
   ...eraser [–ĭ rā/sər] **3**–21
   ...sharpener [–shär/pə nər] **3**–13, **142**–9
penguin [pěng/wĭn] **132**–12
peninsula [pə nĭn/sə lə] **117**–7
penny [pěn/ē] **20**–1
peppers [pěp/ərz] **51**–7
pepper shaker [pěp/ər shā/kər] **41**–15
Percents [pər sěnts/] **15**
Percussion [pər kŭsh/ən] **120**
perfume [pür/fyōōm/, pər fyōōm/] **76**–5
period [pïr/ē əd] **113**–6
periodical section [pïr/ē äd/ĭ kəl sěk/shən] **98**–6
perm hair [pürm/ hër/] **23**–B
perpendicular [pür/pən dĭk/yə lər] **118**–20
personal check [pür/sə nəl chěk/] **20**–14
PERSONAL HYGIENE [pür/sə nəl hī/jēn] **76–77**
personal identification number (PIN)
   [pür/sə nəl ī děn/tə fə kā/shən nŭm/bər] **97**–B
PERSONAL INFORMATION [pür/sə nəl ĭn/fər mā/shən] **4**
personal radio-cassette player
   [pür/sə nəl rā/dē ō kə sět/ plā/ər] **164**–15
pesticide [pěs/tə sīd/] **49** ✦
   ...poisoning [–poy/zə nĭng] **126**–14
pet [pět(/–)]
   ...food [–fōōd/] **54**–10
   ...store [–stör/] **92**–6
petal [pět/l] **129**–8
petri dish [pē/trē dĭsh/] **119**–6
petroleum [pə trō/lē əm] **126**–6
Pets [pěts] **133**
pharmacist [fär/mə sĭst] **80**–10
pharmacy [fär/mə sē] **80**–9, **90**–2
Phillips screwdriver [fĭl/ĭps skrōō/drī/vər] **150**–26
phone [fōn(/–)] **9**–1
   ...card [–kärd/] **9**–11
photo [fō/tō]
   ...album [–ăl/bəm] **165**–32
   ...shop [–shäp/] **90**–4
photocopier [fō/tə käp/ē ər] **142**–14
photograph [fō/tə grăf/] **44**–7
photographer [fə täg/rə fər] **32**–11
PHOTOGRAPHY [fə täg/rə fē] **164-165**
PHYSICAL DESCRIPTION [fĭz/ĭ kəl dĭ skrĭp/shən] **22**
physically challenged [fĭz/ĭ klē chăl/ənjd] **22**–25
physical therapist [fĭz/ĭ kəl thěr/ə pĭst] **81**–30
physics [fĭz/ĭks] **119**–3
pi (π) [pī] **118** ✦
piano [pē ăn/ō] **120**–16
pickax [pĭk/ăks/] **149**–20
pick up [pĭk/ ŭp/] / [pĭk/ ŭp/–] **94**–G
   ...the children [–dhə chĭl/drən] **27**–O
   ...the receiver [–dhə rĭ sē/vər] **9**–A
pickup truck [pĭk/ŭp trŭk/] **106**–7
picnic [pĭk/nĭk] **153**–D
picnic table [pĭk/nĭk tā/bəl] **153**–8
picture [pĭk/chər]

...book [–bōōk/] **45**–17
...dictionary [–dĭk/shə nër ē] **3**–29
pie [pī(/–)] **61**–21
   ...pan [–păn/] **59**–28
pier [pïr] **155**–16
pierced earrings [pïrst/ ïr/ĭng] **69**–37
pig [pĭg] **133**–8
pigeon [pĭj/ən] **132**–16
pill [pĭl] **81**–26
pillow [pĭl/ō] **42**–20, **44**–9
pillowcase [pĭl/ō kās/] **44**–10
pilot [pī/lət] **110**–12
PIN (personal identification number) [pĭn] **97**–B
pin [pĭn] (jewelry) **69**–36, (sewing) **73**–14
pin [pĭn(/–)] / [–pĭn/]
   ...cushion [–kōōsh/ən] **73**–15
   push... [pōōsh/–] **143**–43
pine [pīn] **128**–10
pinecone [pīn/kōn/] **128**–11
pineapples [pī/năp/əlz] **50**–2
Ping-Pong [pĭng/păng/, –pöng/] **159**–13
pink [pĭngk] **12**–10
pint [pīnt] **57**–3
pipe [pīp(/–)] **151**–16
   ...wrench [–rěnch/] **151**–43
pipes [pīps] **49**–19
pitch [pĭch] **156**–F
pizza [pēt/sə] **60**–7
place [plās(/–)]
   ...mat [–măt/] **41**–20
   ...setting [–sět/ĭng] **63**–14
place of birth [plās/ əv bürth/] **4**–17
PLACES TO GO [plā/səz tə gō/] **152**
PLACES TO LIVE [plā/səz tə lĭv/] **34**
plaid [plăd] **70**–9
plain [plān] **71**–38
plains [plānz] **117**–19
plan [plăn] **169**–A
plane (tool) [plān] **151**–52
PLANE TRIP [plān/ trĭp/] **111**
Planets [plăn/əts] **127**
plant [plănt] **39**–D, **148**–A
plant [plănt] **39**–B, **42**–18
PLANTS [plănts] **128**
plastic [plăs/tĭk] **70**
   ...bag [–băg/] **55**–23
   ...storage container [–stör/ĭj kən tā/nər] **59**–3
   ...wrap [–răp/] **55**–54
plate [plāt] **41**–24, **63**–15, 16, 17
platform [plăt/förm/] **104**–15
platter [plăt/ər] **41**–3
platypus [plăt/ĭ pəs, –pōōs/] **135**–46
play [plā(/–)] **94**–K, **165**–B
   ...an instrument [–ən ĭn/strə mənt] **120**–A
   ...cards [–kärdz/] **163**–H
   ...games [–gāmz/] **162**–C
play [plā] **166**–2
player [plā/ər] **158**–5, **164**–2, 14, 15
PLAYGROUND [plā/grownd/] **153**
playground [plā/grownd/] **36**–6
playpen [plā/pěn/] **95**–11
pliers [plī/ərz] **150**–7
plug [plŭg] **164**–17
plumber [plŭm/ər] **49**–20
plums [plŭmz] **50**–8

plunger [plŭn/jər] **151**–44
Pluto [plōō/tō] **127**–1
plywood [plī/wood/] **149**–16
p.m. [pē/ĕm/] **16**
pneumatic drill [noo măt/ĭk drĭl/] **149**–9
pocket [päk/ət] **73**–4
podium [pō/dē əm] **32**–5
poinsettia [poyn sĕt/ē ə, –sĕt/ə] **129**–23
point [poynt] **2**–F
poison [poy/zən] **82**–J, **147**–3
...ivy [–ī/vē] **128**–25
...oak [–ōk/]**128**–23
...sumac [–soo/măk, –shoo/–] **128**–24
police [pə lēs/]
...officer [–ö/fə sər] **99**–1, **138**–44
...station [–stā/shən] **89**–19
polish [päl/ĭsh]
...nails [–nālz/] **77**–O
...the furniture [–dhə für/nĭ chər] **46**–K
polka-dotted [pō/kə dät/əd] **70**–8
Pollution [pə loo/shən] **126**
polyester [päl/ē ĕs/tər, päl/ē ĕs/tər] **70**
poncho [pän/chō] **66**–18
pond [pänd] **117**–21, **153**–6
pool (game) [pool] **159**–2
pool (swimming) [pool(/–)] **37**–16, **145**–16
...service [–sür/vəs] **145**–17
porch light [pörch/ līt/] **38**–9
porcupine [pör/kyə pīn/] **134**–10
Pork [pörk] **52**
pork chops [pörk/ chäps/] **52**–10
porpoise [pör/pəs] **131**–31
port [pört] **144**–17
portable [pör/tə bəl]
...radio-cassette player [–rā/dē ō kə sĕt/ plā/ər] **164**–2
...TV [–tē/vē/] **164**–7
postage [pō/stĭj] **96**–10
postal [pō/stəl]
...scale [–skāl/] **143**–16
...worker [–wür/kər] **138**–45
postcard [pōst/kärd/] **96**–3
Post-it notes [pōst/ĭt nōts/] **143**–34
postmark [pōst/märk/] **96**–9
post office [pōst/ ö/fəs] **89**–29
pot [pät(/–)] **40**–16, **59**–6
...holders [–hōl/dərz] **59**–29
potato [pə tā/tō]
...chips [–chĭps/] **55**–40
...salad [–săl/əd] **53**–13
potatoes [pə tā/tōz] **51**–21, **61**–11
potty seat [pät/ē sēt/] **95**–10
pouch [powch] **135**–50
POULTRY [pōl/trē] **52**
poultry section [pōl/trē sĕk/shən] **54**–2
pound [pownd] **57**–12
pour [pör(/–)]
...the eggs into the pan [–dhē ĕgz/ ĭn/tə dhə păn/] **58**–D
...the water [–dhə wö/tər] **62**–C
power [pow/ər] **48**–2
...sander [–săn/dər] **150**–9
...switch [–swĭch/] **144**–4
prairie dog [prër/ē dög/] **133**–22
pregnant [prĕg/nənt] **22**–19
PREPOSITIONS [prĕp/ə zĭsh/ənz] **13**
PREPOSITIONS OF MOTION [prĕp/ə zĭsh/ənz əv mō/shən] **105**

preschool [prē/skool/] **112**–4
prescription [prĭ skrĭp/shən] **80**–13
...label [–lā/bəl] **80**–14
...medication [–mĕd/ə kā/shən] **80**–11
President [prĕz/ə dənt] **116**–6
pretend [prĭ tĕnd/] **163**–G
price [prīs(/–)] **21**–6
...tag [–tăg/] **21**–1
principal [prĭn/sə pəl] **5**–14
principal's office [prĭn/sə pəlz ö/fəs] **5**–13
print [prĭnt] **4**–C
print [prĭnt] **70**–10
printer [prĭn/tər] (occupation) **138**–46, (computer) **144**–12
print shop [prĭnt/ shäp/] **91**–22
priority mail [prī ör/ə tē māl/, –är/–] **96**–12
prism [prĭz/əm] **119**–20
prison [prĭz/ən] **99**–G
private school [prī/vət skool/] **112**–2
Problems (clothing) [präb/ləmz] **70**
PROBLEMS, HOUSEHOLD [hows/hōld/ präb/ləmz] **48**–**49**
produce section [prō/doos sĕk/shən] **54**–11
product [präd/ŭkt] **118** ✦
program (computer) [prō/grăm] **144**–21
Programs (TV) [prō/grămz] **167**
projector [prə jĕk/tər] / [–prə jĕk/tər]
carousel slide... [kăr/ə sĕl/ slīd/–] **165**–29
overhead... [ō/vər hĕd/–] **2**–4
prosecuting attorney [präs/ĭ kyoo/tĭng ə tür/nē] **99**–10
protect your wallet [prə tĕkt/ yər wä/lət, –wö/–] **101**–D
proud [prowd] **31**–22
prunes [proonz] **50**–26
pruning shears [proo/nĭng shïrz/] **39**–15
psychiatrist [sī kī/ə trĭst, sə–] **86**–6
PUBLIC SAFETY [pŭb/lĭk sāf/tē] **101**
public school [pŭb/lĭk skool/] **112**–1
public telephone [pŭb/lĭk tĕl/ə fōn/] **91**–21
PUBLIC TRANSPORTATION
[pŭb/lĭk trăns/pər tā/shən] **104**
pudding [pood/ĭng] **61**–20
pull [pool(/–)]
...a tooth [–ə tooth/] **85**–M
...the wagon [–dhə wăg/ən] **153**–A
pullover sweater [pool/ō/vər swĕt/ər] **64**–11
pumps [pŭmps] **68**–16
Punctuation [pŭngk/choo ā/shən] **113**
puppet show [pŭp/ət shō/] **152**–14
puppy [pŭp/ē] **133**–12
purple [pür/pəl] **12**–7
purses [pür/səz] **69**–6
push [poosh] **153**–B
pushpin [poosh/pĭn/] **143**–43
put away [poot/ə wā/] / [poot/ə wā/–]
...the toys [–dhə toyz/] **46**–H
...your pencil [–yər pĕn/səl] **2**–L
put in order [poot/ ĭn ör/dər] **7**–W
put on [poot/ än/, –ön/] / [poot/ än–, –ön–]
...makeup [–māk/ŭp/] **77**–P
...sunscreen [–sŭn/skrēn/] **76**–D
puzzle [pŭz/əl] **45**–22
pyramid [pïr/ə mĭd] **118**–13
quart [kwört] **57**–4
quarter [kwör/tər] (time) **16**, (money) **20**–4
quarter cup [kwör/tər kŭp/] **57**–8
quarter moon [kwör/tər moon/] **127**–15
question mark [kwĕs/chən märk/] **113**–7

Index

quiet [kwī/ət] **11**–12
quill [kwĭl] **134**–23
quiz show [kwĭz/ shō/] **167**–23
quotation marks [kwō tā/shən märks/] **113**–9
quotient [kwō/shənt] **118** ✦
rabbit [răb/ət] **133**–13
raccoon [ră kōōn/] **134**–13
race [rās] **157**–Y
racquetball [răk/ət böl/] **159**–11
radiation [rā/dē ā/shən] **126**–13
radiator [rā/dē ā/tər] **109**–42, 56
radio [rā/dē ō] **44**–16, **108**–31
   ...program [-prō/grăm] **166**–4
radioactive [rā/dē ō ăk/tĭv] **147**–6
radiologist [rā/dē äl/ə jĭst] **86**–5
radishes [răd/ĭ shəz] **51**–5
radius [rā/dē əs] **118**–16
rafting [răf/tĭng] **154**–4
rags [răgz] **47**–6
railroad crossing [rāl/rōd krö/sĭng] **107**–11
rain boots [rān/ bōōts/] **66**–19
raincoat [rān/kōt/] **66**–17
rain forest [rān/ för/əst, fär/–] **117**–1
raining [rā/nĭng] **10**–8
raise [rāz] **2**–A
raisins [rā/zənz] **50**–27
rake [rāk] **39**–F
rake [rāk] **39**–11
ranch [rănch] **34**–12
rancher [răn/chər] **148**–22
RANCHING [răn/chĭng] **148**
rash [răsh] **78**–10
raspberries [răz/běr/ēz] **50**–18
rat [răt] **133**–18
rats [răts] **49**–27
rattle [răt/l] **95**–31
rattlesnake [răt/l snāk/] **131**–38
raw [rö] **52**–24
ray [rā] **130**–6
rayon [rā/än] **70**
razor [rā/zər] **77**–25
   ...blade [-blād/] **77**–26
read [rĕd] **6**–B, **27**–V, **94**–F
Realtor [rē/əl tər] **35**
rearview mirror [rĭr/vyōō/ mĭr/ər] **108**–1
receipt [rĭ sēt/] **21**–5
receive [rĭ sēv/] **96**–D
receiver [rĭ sē/vər] **9**–2
receptionist [rĭ sĕp/shə nĭst] **84**–2, **138**–47
recharging [rē chär/jĭng] **109**–58
record [rĕk/ərd] **98**–15
record [rĭ körd/] (science) **119**–C, (cassette player) **165**–A
Recreation room [rĕk/rē ā/shən rōōm/] **36**
rec room [rĕk/ rōōm/] **36** ✦
rectangle [rĕk/tăng/gəl] **118**–8
recycle [rē sī/kəl] **46**–B, **126**–A
recycling bin [rē sī/klĭng bĭn/] **47**–2
red [rĕd(/–)] **12**–13
   ...hair [-hër/] **23**–14
redwood [rĕd/wōōd/] **128**–1
referee [rĕf/ə rē/] **158**–6
reference [rĕf/rəns]
   ...desk [-dĕsk/] **98**–2
   ...librarian [lī brër/ē ən] **98**–1
refrigerator [rĭ frĭj/ə rā/tər] **40**–9

register [rĕj/ə stər] **116**–F
registered [rĕj/ə stərd]
   ...nurse (RN) [–nürs/] **87**–22
regular price [rĕg/yə lər prīs/] **21**–2
relax [rĭ lăks/] **27**–U
relieved [rĭ lēvd/] **30**–16
religious holiday [rĭ lĭj/əs häl/ə dā/] **19**–44
relish [rĕl/ĭsh] **60**–26
remarried [rē măr/ēd] **25**–27
remote control [rĭ mōt/ kən trōl/] **164**–9
remove [rĭ mōōv/] **97**–F
rent [rĕnt] **28**–I
Renting an apartment [rĕn/tĭng ən ə pärt/mənt] **35**
repair [rĭ për/] **140**–G
repair person [rĭ për/ pür/sən] **48**–10, **138**–48
REPAIRS [rĭ përz/] **48**–49
repeat [rĭ pēt/] **6**–D
report crimes [rĭ pört/ krīmz/] **101**–H
reporter [rĭ pör/tər] **99**–12, **139**–49
Reptiles [rĕp/tīlz] **131**
request [rĭ kwĕst/] **111**–M
rescue breathing [rĕs/kyōō brē/dhĭng] **83**–16
Resident Alien card [rĕz/ə dənt ā/lē ən kärd/] **29**–3
respirator [rĕs/pə rā/tər] **147**–12
Responsibilities (of citizenship)
   [rĭ spän/sə bĭl/ə tēz əv sĭt/ə zən shĭp/] **116**
RESTAURANT [rĕs/tə rənt, –ränt/] **62**–63
restaurant [rĕs/tə rənt, –ränt/] **90**–14
rest rooms [rĕst/ rōōmz/] **5**–8
retire [rĭ tīr/] **29** ✦
return [rĭ türn/] **21**–F
return address [rĭ türn/ ə drĕs/, –ă/drĕs] **96**–7
rewind [rē wīnd/] **165**–D
rewrite [rē rīt/] **113**–D
rhinoceros [rī näs/ər əs] **135**–29
rib cage [rĭb/ kāj/] **75**–53
rice [rīs(/–)] **54**–28, **148**–1
   ...pilaf [–pē/läf, –pĭ läf/] **61**–18
ride [rīd] **91**–E, **157**–W
rides [rīdz] **152**–17
right [rīt(/–)] / [–rīt/]
   ...turn only [–türn/ ōn/lē] **107**–9
   on the... [än dhə–, ön–] **13**–2
right-of-way [rīt/əv wā/] **107** ✦
Rights and responsibilities [rīts/ ən rĭ spän/sə bĭl/ə tēz] **116**
ring [rĭng] **69**–39
rinse [rĭns] **76**–F
rip [rĭp] **70**–23
ripe [rīp] **50**–29
river [rĭv/ər] **117**–3
RN (registered nurse) [är/ĕn/] **87**–22
roast [rōst] **58**–U
roast [rōst(/–)]
   ...beef [–bēf/] **52**–1, **53**–7, **57**–12
   ...chicken [–chĭk/ən] **61**–12
roasting [rō/stĭng]
   ...pan [–păn/] **59**–13
   ...rack [–răk/] **59**–14
robin [räb/ən] **132**–17
rock [räk] **94**–H
rock [räk(/–)] **155**–24
rock band [räk/ bănd/] **120**–2
rocking chair [räk/ĭng chër/] **94**–6
RODENTS [rōd/nts] **133**
roll [rōl(/–)] **56**–11

...of paper towels [–əv pā/pər tow/əlz] **56**–23
roller coaster [rō/lər kō/stər] **152**–15
rollers [rō/lərz] **23**–21
rolling pin [rō/lĭng pĭn/] **59**–30
rolls [rōlz] **54**–30
romance [rō măns/, rō/măns] **166**–16
Roman numerals [rō/mən nōō/mər əlz] **14**
roof [rōōf] **38**–20, **48**–3
roofer [rōō/fər] **48**–8
roof garden [rōōf/ gär/dn] **36**–5
room service [rōōm/ sür/vəs] **145**–12
rooster [rōō/stər] **133**–6
root [rōōt] **128**–5, **129**–3
rope [rōp] **154**–19
rose [rōz] **129**–15
rotary card file [rō/tə rē kärd/ fīl/] **143**–17
rotten [rät/n] **50**–30
rouge [rōōzh] **77**–36
route [rōōt, rowt] **104**–2
router [row/tər] **150**–12
rubber [rŭb/ər]
  ...band [–bănd/] **143**–45
  ...cement [–sə mĕnt/] **143**–38
  ...gloves [–glŭvz/] **47**–4
  ...mat [–măt/] **43**–3
  ...stamp [–stămp/] **143**–40
rug [rŭg] **44**–23
ruler [rōō/lər] **3**–27
run [rŭn] **156**–C
rural area [rōōr/əl ër/ē ə] **34**–4
rye bread [rī/ brĕd/] **53**–3
sad [săd] **31**–20, **167**–28
safe-deposit box [sāf/dĭ päz/ət bäks/] **97**–13
safety [sāf/tē]
  ...boot [–bōōt/] **147**–20
  ...earmuffs [–ïr/mŭfs] **147**–14
  ...glasses [–glăs/əz] **147**–10
  ...goggles [–gäg/əlz] **147**–9
  ...pin [–pĭn/] **73**–24
  ...seat [–sēt/] **109**–39
  ...vest [–vĕst/] **147**–15
  ...visor [–vī/zər] **147**–11
SAFETY, PUBLIC [pŭb/lĭk sāf/tē] **101**
sailboarding [sāl/bör/dĭng] **160**–10
sailboat [sāl/bōt/] **155**–4
sailing [sā/lĭng] **160**–8
salad [săl/əd]
  ...bar [–bär/] **60**–16
  ...dressing [–drĕs/ĭng] **60**–18
  ...fork [–förk/] **63**–24
  ...plate [–plāt/] **63**–17
salamander [săl/ə măn/dər] **130**–27
salami [sə lä/mē] **53**–5
sale price [sāl/ prīs/] **21**–3
salesclerk [sālz/klürk/] **68**–1, **139**–50
salesperson [sālz/pür/sən] **139**–50
sales tax [sālz/ tăks/] **21**–7
salmon steak [săm/ən stāk/] **53**–19
saltshaker [sölt/shā/kər] **41**–14
sand [sănd(/–)] **155**–23
  ...castle [–kăs/əl] **155**–10
  ...dune [–dōōn/] **117**–5
sandals [săn/dlz] **68**–24
sandbox [sănd/bäks/] **153**–15
sandpaper [sănd/pā/pər] **151**–50

sanitation worker [săn/ə tā/shən wür/kər] **139**–51
Saturday [săt/ər dā/, –dē] **18**–7
Saturn [săt/ərn] **127**–4
saucepan [sös/păn/] **59**–25
saucer [sö/sər] **63**–22
sausage [sö/sĭj] **52**–12, **61**–2
sauté [sö tā/, sō–] **58**–H
save [sāv] **126**–B, C
savings account number [sā/vĭngz ə kownt/ nŭm/bər] **97**–6
saxophone [săk/sə fōn/] **120**–7
say [sā] **6**–C
scaffolding [skăf/əl dĭng] **149**–4
scale (weight) [skāl] **43**–26, **84**–7
scales (fish) [skālz] **130**–3
scallions [skăl/yənz] **51**–17
scallop [skăl/əp, skäl/–] **130**–18
scallops [skăl/əps, skäl/–] **53**–25
scanner [skăn/ər] **144**–13
scared [skërd] **31**–24
scarf [skärf] **66**–4, **70**–15
schedule [skĕj/ōōl, –ōō əl] **104**–3
SCHOOL [skōōl] **5**
school **89**–27
  ...crossing [–krö/sĭng] **107**–13
  adult... [ə dŭlt/–, ăd/ŭlt–] **112**–8
  elementary... [ĕl/ə mĕn/trē–] **112**–5
  high... [hī/–] **112**–7
  junior high... [jōōn/yər hī/–] **112**–6
  middle... [mĭd/l–] **112**–6
  parochial... [pə rō/kē əl–] **112**–3
  private... [prī/vət–] **112**–2
  trade... [trād/–] **112**–9
  vocational... [vō kā/shə nəl–] **112**–9
School Registration Form [skōōl/ rĕj/ə strā/shən förm/] **4**
SCHOOLS, TYPES OF [tīps/ əv skōōlz/] **112**
SCHOOL SUBJECTS, MORE [mör/ skōōl/ sŭb/jĭkts] **121**
SCIENCE [sī/əns] **119**
science fiction story [sī/əns fĭk/shən stör/ē] **166**–12
scissors [sĭz/ərz] **23**–19, **73**–18
score [skör] **158**–1
scorpion [skör/pē ən] **132**–31
scrambled eggs [skrăm/bəld ĕgz/] **58**, **61**–1
scraper [skrā/pər] **151**–48
screen [skrēn] **2**–2, **144**–6, **152**–12, **165**–28
screen door [skrēn/ dör/] **38**–8
screwdriver [skrōō/drī/vər] **150**–25
  Phillips... [fĭl/ĭps–] **150**–26
scrub [skrŭb] **46**–L
scrub brush [skrŭb/ brŭsh/] **47**–19
scuba [skōō/bə]
  ...diving [–dī/vĭng] **160**–12
  ...tank [–tăngk/] **155**–8
sculpture [skŭlp/chər] **152**–9
sea [sē(/–)]
  ...anemone [–ə nĕm/ə nē] **130**–21
  ...horse [–hörs/] **130**–23
  ...lion [–lī/ən] **131**–34
  ...urchin [–ür/chən] **130**–20
Sea animals [sē/ ăn/ə məlz] **130**
SEAFOOD [sē/fōōd/] **53**
seal [sēl] **131**–33
seam [sēm(/–)] **73**–11
  ...ripper [–rĭp/ər] **73**–19
Sea mammals [sē/ măm/əlz] **131**
search and rescue team [sürch/ ən rĕs/kyōō tēm/] **103**–17

Index

seashell [sē/shĕl/] 155–21
Seasons [sē/zənz] 19
seat [sēt(/–)] 2–E, 152–11
...belt [–bĕlt/] 109–36
seat [sēt] 62–B
seaweed [sē/wēd] 155 ✦
second [sĕk/ənd] 14, 16–1
...floor [–flör/] 36–2
secretary [sĕk/rə tër/ē] 139–52, 142–3
section [sĕk/shən] / [–sĕk/shən]
   dairy... [dër/ē–] 54–9
   produce... [prō/dōōs–] 54–11
security [sĭ kyōōr/ə tē] 111–C
...gate [–gāt/] 36–13
...guard [–gärd/] 97–4
...system [–sĭs/təm] 36–9
see [sē] 75–A
seed [sēd] 129–1
seedling [sēd/lĭng] 129–2
seesaw [sē/sö/] 153–16
See you [sē/ yə] 8
Selective Service [sə lĕk/tĭv sür/vəs] 116–F
sell [sĕl] 21–B, 140–H
semi [sĕm/ī] 106–15
semicolon [sĕm/ē kō/lən] 113–13
Senate [sĕn/ət] 116–3
Senator [sĕn/ə tər] 116–4
send [sĕnd] 96–B
senior citizen [sēn/yər sĭt/ə zən] 22–12
Senses [sĕn/səz] 75
sentence [sĕn/tns] 113–4
sentence the defendant [sĕn/tns dhə dĭ fĕn/dənt] 99–F
September [sĕp tĕm/bər] 19–33
serious [sïr/ē əs] 167–26
Serious Diseases [sïr/ē əs dĭ zē/zəz] 79
serve (sports) [sürv] 157–N
serve on a jury [sürv/ än ə jōōr/ē, –ön–] 116–G
server [sür/vər] 62–4, 63–6, 139–53
serve the meal [sürv/ dhə mēl/] 62–F
service elevator [sür/vəs ĕl/ə vā tər] 145 ✦
serviceman [sür/vəs măn/, –mən] 139–54
servicewoman [sür/vəs wŏŏm/ən] 139–54
serving dish [sür/vĭng dĭsh/] 41–6
set [sĕt(/–)]
...hair [–hër/] 23–C
...the table [–dhə tā/bəl] 62–A
set of dishes [sĕt/ əv dĭsh/əz] 41–2
seven [sĕv/ən] 14
seventeen [sĕv/ən tēn/] 14
seventeenth [sĕv/ən tēnth/] 14
seventh [sĕv/ənth] 14
seventy [sĕv/ən tē] 14
sew [sò(/–)]
...by hand [–bī hănd/] 73–A
...by machine [–bī mə shēn/] 73–B
...clothes [–klōz/] 140–L
SEWING AND ALTERATIONS [sō/ĭng ən öl/tə rā/shənz] 73
sewing machine [sō/ĭng mə shēn/] 73–10
sex [sĕks] 4–12
shade [shād] 155–11
shampoo [shăm pōō/] 76–9
Shapes [shāps] 118
share [shër] 6–I
shark [shärk] 130–7
shave [shāv] 77–M

shaving cream [shā/vĭng krēm/] 77–27
shears [shïrz] 39–15
sheep [shēp] 133–7
sheet [shēt] 44–13, 14
shelf [shĕlf] 40–8
Shellfish [shĕl/fĭsh/] 53
shelter [shĕl/tər] 34–10
shingles [shĭng/gəlz] 149–19
shin guards [shĭn/ gärdz/] 161–13
ship [shĭp] 146–C
shipping clerk [shĭp/ĭng klürk/] 146–15
shirt [shürt] 64–4, 65–20
shock [shäk] 82–C
shoe [shōō(/–)]
...department [–dĭ pärt/mənt] 68–3
...store [–stör/] 92–10
shoelace [shōō/lās/] 68–14
SHOES AND ACCESSORIES [shōōz/ ən ĭk sĕs/ə rēz] 68–69
shoot [shōōt] 156–I
shop [shäp] 21–A
shop [shäp] 121–10
SHOPPING [shäp/ĭng] 21
shopping [shäp/ĭng]
...basket [–băs/kət] 54–7
...cart [–kärt/] 54–3
...program [–prō/grăm] 167–25
shore [shör] 117–12
short [shört] 22–18, 23–1, 71–35
shorten [shör/tn] 73–D
short-sleeved [shört/slēvd/] 71–30
shorts [shörts] 64–13, 67–3, 12
shortwave radio [shört/wāv/ rā/dē ō] 164–5
shoulder [shōl/dər] 74–10
...bag [–băg/] 69–27
...harness [–här/nəs] 109–37
...pads [–pădz/] 161–21
shoulder-length [shōl/dər lĕngkth/] 23–2
shout [showt] 169–G
shovel [shŭv/əl] 39–13, 149–21
show (puppet) [shō] 152–14
shower cap [show/ər kăp/] 76–1
showerhead [show/ər hĕd/] 43–10
shrimp [shrĭmp] 53–24, 130–19
shutter [shŭt/ər] 38–18
sick [sĭk] 30–14
side [sīd] 118–22
sideburns [sīd/bürnz/] 23–7
sideview mirror [sīd/vyōō/ mïr/ər] 108–8
sidewalk [sīd/wök/] 91–26
sight impaired [sīt/ ĭm përd/] 22–26
sign [sīn(/–)]
...a rental agreement [–ə rĕn/təl ə grē/mənt] 35–C
...your name [–yər nām/] 4–D
sign [sīn] 91–29
signature [sĭg/nə chər] 4–18
Signs [sīnz] 107
silk [sĭlk] 70–15
silk scarves [sĭlk/ skärvz/] 68–4
silver dollar [sĭl/vər däl/ər] 20–6
simmer [sĭm/ər] 58–R
sing [sĭng] 120–B, 169–I
single [sĭng/gəl]
...father [–fä/dhər] 25–25
...mother [–mŭdh/ər] 25–26
sink [sĭngk] 40–6, 43–22, 49–17

sister [sĭs/tər] **24**–8, **25**–30, 32
sister-in-law [sĭs/tər ĭn lö/] **24**–15
sitcom [sĭt/käm/] **167**–18
sit down [sĭt/ down/] **2**–E
situation comedy [sĭch/oo ā/shən käm/ə dē] **167**–18
six [sĭks] **14**
six-pack [sĭks/păk/] **56**–9
six-pack of soda [sĭks/păk/ əv sō/də] **56**–21
sixteen [sĭks/tēn/] **14**
sixteenth [sĭks/tēnth/] **14**
sixth [sĭksth] **14**
sixty [sĭks/tē] **14**
six-year-old [sĭks/yïr ōld/] **22**–4
Sizes [sī/zəz] **70**
skate [skāt] **157**–V
skateboarding [skāt/bör/dĭng] **159**–12
skating [skā/tĭng] **160**–4, 5
Skeleton [skĕl/ə tn] **75**
ski [skē] **157**–V
ski [skē(/–)]
...boots [–boots/] **161**–26
...cap [–kăp/] **66**–10
...mask [–măsk/] **66**–14
...poles [–pōlz/] **161**–25
skiing [skē/ĭng] **160**–1, 3, 7
skin [skĭn] **75**–51
skinless [skĭn/ləs] **52** ✦
skirt [skürt] **64**–10, **65**–25
skis [skēz] **161**–24
skull [skŭl] **75**–52
skunk [skŭngk] **134**–12
skyscraper [skī/skrā/pər] **88** ✦
slacks [slăks] **64**–8
sledding [slĕd/ĭng] **160**–6
sledgehammer [slĕj/hăm/ər] **149**–22
sleeping bag [slē/pĭng băg/] **154**–12
sleepy [slē/pē] **30**–3
sleeve [slēv] **73**–6
sleeveless [slēv/ləs] **71**–29
slice [slīs] **58**–O
slide [slīd] (science) **119**–5, (park) **153**–13
slides [slīdz] **165**–31
slide tray [slīd/ trā/] **165**–30
slim [slĭm] **22**–22
sling [slĭng] **80**–8
slippers [slĭp/ərz] **67**–6
slot [slät] **144**–19
slow [slō] **11**–4
small [smöl(/–)] **70**–2
...town [–town/] **34**–3
smell [smĕl] **75**–C
smog [smäg(/–), smög(/–)] **126**–10
...check [–chĕk/] **109**–57
smoggy [smä/gē, smö/–] **10**–14
smoke detector [smōk/ dĭ tĕk/tər] **37**–25, **45**–11
smoked turkey [smōkt/ tür/kē] **53**–4
snack foods [snăk/ foodz/] **55**–16
snail [snāl] **130**–24
snake [snāk] **131**–38, 39
sneeze [snēz] **78**–B
snorkeling [snör/kə lĭng] **160**–11
snowboard [snō/börd/] **161**–23
snowboarding [snō/bör/dĭng] **160**–2
snowing [snō/ĭng] **10**–9
snowstorm [snō/störm/] **10**–20

soap [sōp(/–)] **43**–23, **76**–2
...dish [–dĭsh/] **43**–24
...pads [–pădz/] **47**–5
soap opera [sōp/ äp/rə] **167**–21
soccer [säk/ər] **158**–12
...ball [–böl/] **161**–12
Social Security card [sō/shəl sĭ kyoor/ə tē kärd/] **29**–5
Social Security number [sō/shəl sĭ kyoor/ə tē nŭm/bər] **4**–15
socks [säks] **67**–15
soda [sō/də] **55**–52, **60**–4
sofa [sō/fə] **42**–19
soft [söft] **11**–6
softball [söft/böl/] **158**–10
Software [söft/wër/] **144**
solar [sō/lər]
...eclipse [–ĭ klĭps/] **127** ✦
...energy [–ĕn/ər jē] **126**–1
...system [–sĭs/təm] **127**
sole [sōl] (fish) **53**–21, (shoe) **68**–12
solid [säl/əd] **70**–6
Solids [säl/ədz] **118**
son [sŭn] **24**–22
son-in-law [sŭn/ĭn lö/] **24** ✦
sore throat [sör/ thrōt/] **78**–6
Sorry. [sär/ē, sör/ē] **8**
sort [sört] **72**–A
soup [soop(/–)] **54**–24
...bowl [–bōl/] **63**–18
...of the day [–əv dhə dā/] **61**–10
soupspoon [soop/spoon/] **63**–29
sour cream [sow/ər krēm/] **54**–37
south [sowth] **107, 123, 124**
soybeans [soy/bēnz/] **148**–3
space [spās(/–)] **127**–22
...station [–stā/shon] **127**–18
spades [spādz] **163**–28
spaghetti [spə gĕt/ē] **54**–27
spare tire [spër/ tīr/] **109**–53
sparrow [spăr/ō] **132**–8
spatula [spăch/ə lə] **59**–19
speak [spēk] **140**–J
speaker [spē/kər] **36**–8
speakers [spē/kərz] **164**–11
specialist [spĕsh/ə lĭst] **86** ✦
speed [spēd(/–)] **144** ✦
...limit [–lĭm/ət] **107**–5
speedometer [spĭ däm/ə tər] **108**–20
spell [spĕl] **4**–A, **6**–E
sphere [sfïr] **118**–14
spices [spī/səz] **55**–46
spider [spī/dər] **132**–30
spinach [spĭn/ĭch] **51**–11
spinal column [spī/nəl käl/əm] **75**–54
spiral notebook [spī/rəl nōt/book/] **3**–26
splint [splĭnt] **83**–11
split skirt [splĭt/ skürt/] **65**–25
sponge [spŭnj] **47**–24
spool of thread [spool/ əv thrĕd/] **73**–17
spoon [spoon] **41**–23, **59**–9
SPORTS [spörts] **158–160**
sports [spörts(/–)]
...car [–kär/] **106**–6
...coat [–kōt/] **64**–6
...shirt [–shürt/] **65**–26
SPORTS EQUIPMENT [spörts/ ĭ kwĭp/mənt] **161**
SPORTS VERBS [spörts/ vürbz/] **156–157**

Index

sprained ankle [sprānd/ ăng/kəl] **78**–18
spray [sprā(/–)]
   …gun [–gŭn/] **151**–19
   …starch [–stärch/] **72**–12
spring [sprĭng] **19**–37
sprinkler [sprĭng/klər] **39**–8
square [skwër] **118**–6
squash [skwäsh, skwösh] **51**–13
squeegee [skwē/jē] **47**–9
squid [skwĭd] **130**–10
squirrel [skwür/əl] **133**–21
stacking tray [stăk/ĭng trā/] **142**–5
stadium [stā/dē əm] **152**–26
stage [stāj] **32**–4
stain [stān] **70**–22
stairs [stërz] **37**–35, **105**–9
stairway [stër/wā/] **37**–26
stall shower [stöl/ show/ər] **43** ✦
stamp [stămp(/–)] **96**–10
   …collection [–kə lĕk/shən] **162**–12
standard [stăn/dərd]
   …time [–tīm/] **17**–32
   …transmission [–trănz mĭsh/ən, –trăns–] **109**
stand trial [stănd/ trī/əl, –trīl/] **99**–D
stand up [stănd/ ŭp/] **2**–D
stand-up comedy [stănd/ŭp/ kăm/ə dē] **166**–5
staple [stā/pəl] **142**–G
staple [stā/pəl] **143**–29
stapler [stā/plər] **143**–28
star [stär] **127**–23
starfish [stär/fĭsh/] **130**–15
start [stärt(/–)] **157**–X
   …school [–skōōl/] **28**–B
starving [stär/vĭng] **30** ✦
state [stāt] **4**–8
station wagon [stā/shən wăg/ən] **106**–8
stay [stā] **101**–B
steak [stāk(/–)] **52**–2, **61**–13
   …knife [–nīf/] **63**–26
steam [stēm] **58**–I
steamer [stē/mər] **59**–4
steel-wool soap pads [stēl/wōōl/ sōp/ pădz/] **47**–5
steering wheel [stïr/ĭng wēl/] **108**–26
steers [stïrz] **148**–21
stem [stēm] **129**–4
stepbrother [stĕp/brŭdh/ər] **25**–33
stepdaughter [stĕp/dö/tər] **25** ✦
stepfather [stĕp/fä/dhər] **25**–28
stepladder [stĕp/lăd/ər] **47**–7
stepmother [stĕp/mŭdh/ər] **25**–31
steps [stĕps] **38**–13, **48**–7
stepsister [stĕp/sĭs/tər] **25**–32
stereo system [stĕr/ē ō sĭs/təm] **42**–14
sterile pad [stĕr/əl păd/] **83**–4
stethoscope [stĕth/ə skōp/] **84**–8
stewing beef [stōō/ĭng bēf/] **52**–3
stick shift [stĭk/ shĭft/] **109**–48
stir [stür] **58**–E
stir-fry [stür/frī/] **58**–W
stitches [stĭch/əz] **83**–15
stock clerk [stäk/ klürk/] **139**–55
stockings [stäk/ĭngz] **67**–26
stomach [stŭm/ək] **75**–41
stomachache [stŭm/ək āk/] **78**–4
stop [stäp] **165**–F

stop [stäp] **107**–3
stopover [stäp/ō/vər] **111** ✦
stopped up [stäpt/ ŭp/] **49**–18
storage locker [stör/ĭj läk/ər] **36**–14
store [stör(/–)] / [–stör/]
   …owner [–ō/nər] **139**–56
   candy… [kăn/dē–] **92**–3
   card… [kärd/–] **92**–7
   convenience… [kən vēn/yəns–] **90**–3
   department… [dĭ pärt/mənt–] **93**–13
   electronics… [ĭ lĕk trän/ĭks–] **93**–18
   jewelry… [jōō/əl rē–] **92**–2
   music… [myōō/zĭk–] **92**–1
   pet… [pĕt/–] **92**–6
   shoe… [shōō/–] **92**–10
   toy… [toy/–] **92**–5
   video… [vĭd/ē ō–] **93**–15
storm [störm] **10**–16, 18, 20, 21
storm door [störm/ dör/] **38**–12
stove [stōv] **40**–18, **154**–16
stow [stō] **111**–H
straight [strāt(/–)]
   …hair [–hër/] **23**–9
   …line [–līn/] **118**–18
strainer [strā/nər] **59**–22
stranger [strān/jər] **101**–F
straw [strö] **60**–20
strawberries [strö/bĕr/ēz] **50**–17
straw hat [strö/ hăt/] **66**–23
stream [strēm] **117** ✦
street [strēt(/–)] **90**–9
   …vendor [–vĕn/dər] **91**–30
streetlight [strēt/līt/] **91**–23
strep throat [strĕp/ thrōt/] **79**–4
stretch [strĕch] **157**–Q
stretcher [strĕch/ər] **87**–28
string beans [strĭng/ bēnz/] **51**–25
string of pearls [strĭng/ əv pürlz/] **69**–30
Strings [strĭngz] **120**
striped [strīpt] **70**–7
stroller [strō/lər] **94**–2
stucco [stŭk/ō] **149**–14
student [stōōd/nt] **2**–3, **139**–57
STUDYING [stŭd/ē ĭng] **6**–7
stuffed animals [stŭft/ ăn/ə məlz] **45**–23
subcompact [sŭb/käm/păkt] **106**–1
subtraction [səb trăk/shən] **118**–2
suburbs [sŭb/ürbz] **34**–2
subway [sŭb/wā/] **104**–9
sugar [shōōg/ər] **55**–48, **60**–21
   …bowl [–bōl/] **41**–12
   …substitute [–sŭb/stə tōōt/] **60**–22
suit [sōōt] (clothing) **64**–2, (diving) **155**–7
summer [sŭm/ər] **19**–38
sun [sŭn] **127**–10
sunbather [sŭn/bā/dhər] **155**–17
sunblock [sŭn/bläk/] **155**–13
sunburn [sŭn/bürn/] **78**–14
Sunday [sŭn/dā, –dē] **18**–1
sunflower [sŭn/flow/ər] **129**–10
sunglasses [sŭn/glăs/əz] **66**–21
sunny [sŭn/ē] **10**–6
sunscreen [sŭn/skrēn/] **76**–6, **155**–13
superintendent [sōō/prĭn tĕn/dənt, sōō/pər ĭn–] **36**–12
supervise people [sōō/pər vīz pē/pəl] **140**–K

supply cabinet [sə plī/ kăb/ə nət] **142**–13
Supreme Court [sə prēm/ kört/] **116**–8
surfboard [sürf/börd/] **155**–5
surfing [sür/fīng] **160**–9
surgeon [sür/jən] **87**–30
surge protector [sürj/ prə tĕk/tər] **144**–10
surgical [sür/jĭ kəl]
   ...cap [–kăp/] **87**–31
   ...gown [–gown/] **87**–32
   ...nurse [–nürs/] **87**–29
surprised [sər prīzd/, sə–] **31**–31
suspect [sŭs/pĕkt] **99**–A
suspenders [sə spĕn/dərz] **68**–2
SUV (sports utility vehicle)
   [ĕs/yōō/vē/] / [spörts/ yōō tĭl/ə tē vē/ĭ kəl] **106**–9
swallow [swäl/ō] **82**–J
swap meet [swäp/ mēt] **152**–22
sweater [swĕt/ər]
   cardigan... [kär/də gən–] **65**–27
   crewneck... [krōō/nĕk/–] **71**–26
   pullover... [pōōl/ō/vər–] **64**–11
   turtleneck... [tür/tl nĕk/–] **71**–28
   V-neck... [vē/nĕk/–] **71**–27
sweatpants [swĕt/pănts/] **64**–15
sweatshirt [swĕt/shürt/] **64**–14
sweep [swēp] **46**–E
sweet peppers [swēt/ pĕp/ərz] **51**–7
swim [swĭm] **157**–T
swimming [swĭm/ĭng]
   ...pool [–pōōl/] **37**–16
   ...trunks [–trŭngks/] **66**–22
swimsuit [swĭm/sōōt/] **66**–26
swing [swĭng] **157**–O
swings [swĭngz] **153**–12
Swiss cheese [swĭs/ chēz/] **53**–11
swivel chair [swĭv/əl chër/] **143**–22
swollen [swō/lən] **78**–16
swordfish [sörd/fĭsh/] **130**–12
SYMPTOMS AND INJURIES [sĭmp/təmz ən ĭn/jə rēz] **78**
synagogue [sĭn/ə gäg/] **88**–9
synthetic materials [sĭn thĕt/ĭk mə tïr/ē əlz] **70**
syringe [sə rĭnj/] **84**–14
syrup [sïr/əp, sür/–] **61**–5
table [tā/bəl] / [–tā/bəl]
   dining room... [dī/nĭng rōōm/–] **41**–17
   night... [nīt/–] **44**–21
   picnic... [pĭk/nĭk–] **153**–8
tablecloth [tā/bəl klöth/] **41**–18
tablespoon [tā/bəl spōōn/] **57**–7
tablet [tăb/lət] **81**–25
table tennis [tā/bəl tĕn/əs] **159**–13
tackle [tăk/əl] **156**–M
taco [tä/kō] **60**–9
tail [tāl] **134**–22
taillight [tāl/līt/] **108**–14
tailor [tā/lər] **73**–9
take [tāk(/–)]
   ...a bath [–ə băth/] **76**–B
   ...a citizenship test [–ə sĭt/ə zən shĭp tĕst/] **116**–C
   ...a message [–ə mĕs/ĭj] **142**–A
   ...a nap [–ə năp/] **94**–L
   ...a picture [–ə pĭk/chər] **32**–D
   ...a seat [–ə set/] **2**–E
   ...a shower [–ə show/ər] **26**–C, **76**–A
   ...medicine [–mĕd/ə sən] **80**–F

   ...ownership [–ō/nər shĭp/] **35**–J
   ...the bus [–dhə bŭs/] **26**–H, **104** ✦
   ...the children to school [–dhə chĭl/drən tə skōōl/] **26**–G
   ...the order [–dhē ör/dər] **62**–E
   ...(your) temperature [–yər tĕm/prə chər] **85**–C
take care of [tāk/ kër/ əv] **140**–L
take in [tāk/ ĭn/] **73**–E
take off [tāk/ öf/] **111**–L
take out [tāk/ owt/] **2**–K, **46**–Q
take out (food) [tāk/ owt/] **62** ✦
talcum powder [tăl/kəm pow/dər] **76**–3
talk [tök] **2**–B, **7**–P, **35**–B, G, **141**–A, I
talk show [tök/ shō/] **167**–20
tall [töl] **22**–16
tambourine [tăm/bə rēn/] **120**–19
tangerines [tăn/jə rēnz/] **50**–13
tank top [tăngk/ täp/] **67**–2
tape [tāp(/–)] **83**–5, **143**–39, 42
   ...deck [–dĕk/] **108**–30
   ...measure [–mĕzh/ər] **73**–13, **150**–22
target [tär/gət] **161**–8
tartar [tär/tər] **84**–17
taste [tāst] **75**–D
taxi [tăk/sē] **104**–18
   ...driver [–drī/vər] **104**–20
   ...license [–lī/səns] **104**–22
   ...stand [–stănd/] **104**–19
TB (tuberculosis) [tē/bē/] / [tōō bür/kyə lō/səs] **79**–13
tea [tē] **60**–5, **61**–24
teach [tēch] **140** ✦
teacher [tē/chər] **2**–5, **5**–2, **139**–58
teakettle [tē/kĕt/l] **40**–17
team [tēm] **103**–17, **158**–3
TEAM SPORTS [tēm/ spörts/] **158**
teapot [tē/pät/] **41**–11
tear [tër] **70**–23
teaspoon [tē/spōōn/] **57**–6, **63**–28
technician [tĕk nĭsh/ən] **86**–8, 16
teddy bear [tĕd/ē bër/] **45**–10
teenagers [tē/nā/jərz] **22**–6
teeth [tēth] **74**–25, **77**–J, K, **85**–I
teething ring [tē/dhĭng rĭng/] **95**–30
telemarketer [tĕl/ə mär/kə tər] **139**–59
TELEPHONE [tĕl/ə fōn/] **9**
telephone [tĕl/ə fōn/] **9**–1, 15
   ...book [–bōōk/] **9**–15
   ...card [–kärd/] **9**–11
   ...number [–nŭm/bər] **4**–11
telescope [tĕl/ə skōp/] **127**–21
television (TV) [tĕl/ə vĭzh/ən] **42**–26, **164**–6
   ...program [–prō/grăm] **166**–3
teller [tĕl/ər] **97**–1
Temperature (weather) [tĕm/prə chər] **10**
temperature (fever) [tĕm/prə chər] **78**–8
temperature gauge [tĕm/prə chər gāj/] **108**–23
ten [tĕn] **14**, **15**–7, **16**–6, **20**–9
tenant [tĕn/ənt] **37**–33
tennis [tĕn/əs] **159**–14
   ...court [–kört/] **153**–7
   ...racket [–răk/ət] **161**–2
   ...shoes [–shōōz/] **68**–22
tent [tĕnt] **154**–10
tenth [tĕnth] **14**
ten-year-old [tĕn/yïr ōld/] **22**–5
termites [tür/mīts] **49**–22

Index

terrified [těr/ə fīd/] **30** ✦
test tube [těst/ toob/] **119**–16
textbook [těkst/book/, těks/–] **3**–22
thank [thăngk] **8**–H
Thanksgiving [thăngks gǐv/ĭng] **168**–15
Thank you [thăngk/ yoo] **8**
theater [thē/ə tər] / [thē/ə tər] **88**–10
...arts [–ärts/] **121**–12
movie... [–moo/vē–] **88**–11
thermometer [thər măm/ə tər] **84**–15
thick book [thǐk/ book/] **11**–7
thigh [thī] **74**–16
thighs [thīz] **52**–21
thimble [thǐm/bəl] **73**–20
thin [thǐn] **11**–8, **22**–22
third [thürd(/–)] **14**
...floor [–flör/] **36**–3
thirsty [thür/stē] **30**–2
thirteen [thür/tēn/] **14**
thirteenth [thür/tēnth/] **14**
thirteen-year-old [thür/tēn/yïr öld/] **22**–7
thirty [thür/tē] **14**
this week [dhǐs/ wēk/] **18**–19
thorn [thörn] **129**–28
thousand [thow/zənd] **14**
thread [thrĕd] **73**–17
three [thrē(/–)] **14**
...times a week [–tīmz/ ə wēk/] **18**–24
three-fourths [thrē/förths/] **15**–5
three-piece suit [thrē/pēs/ soot/] **64**–1
throat [thrōt(/–)] **75**–36
...lozenges [–läz/ən jəz] **81**–21
through [throo] **105**–11
throw [thrō] **156**–D
throw pillow [thrō/ pǐl/ō] **42**–20
throw up [thrō/ ŭp/] **78**–E
thumb [thŭm] **75**–56
thunderstorm [thŭn/dər störm/] **10**–16
Thursday [thürz/dā, –dē] **18**–5
tick [tǐk] **132**–28
ticket [tǐk/ət] **104**–14
tidal wave [tīd/l wāv/] **103**–15
tide [tīd] **155** ✦
tie [tī] **94**–I
tie [tī] (clothing) **69**–40, (sports) **158** ✦
ties [tīz] (clothing) **69**–10
tiger [tī/gər] **135**–37
tight [tīt] **71**–43
tights [tīts] **66**–11
tile [tīl] **43**–9
TIME [tīm] **16–17**
time clock [tīm/ kläk/] **146**–4
Time zones [tīm/ zōnz/] **17**
tire [tīr] **108**–10, **109**–53
tired [tīrd] **31**–33
tires [tīrz] **109**–59
title [tīt/l] **98**–21, **113**–3
toad [tōd] **130**–28
toast [tōst] **33**, **61**–3
toaster [tō/stər] **40**–7
...oven [–ŭv/ən] **40**–15
today [tə dā/] **18**–15
toddler [täd/lər] **22**–3
toe [tō(/–)] **68**–15, **75**–63
...guard [–gärd/] **147**–21

toenail [tō/nāl/] **75**–64
toggle bolt [täg/əl bōlt/] **150**–33
toilet [toy/lət] **43**–17, **49**–18
...brush [–brŭsh/] **43**–16
...paper [–pā/pər] **43**–15
token [tō/kən] **104**–11
tomatoes [tə mā/tōz] **51**–23
tomorrow [tə mär/ō, –mör/ō] **18**–16
tongs [tängz, töngz] **59**–23, **119**–15
tongue [tŭng] **74**–26
too big [too/ bǐg/] **70**–21
TOOLS AND BUILDING SUPPLIES
[toolz/ ən bǐl/dǐng sə plīz/] **150, 151**
too small [too/ smöl/] **70**–20
toothache [tooth/āk/] **78**–2
toothbrush [tooth/brŭsh/] **43**–20, **77**–20
...holder [–hōl/dər] **43**–21
toothpaste [tooth/pāst/] **77**–21
tornado [tör nā/dō] **103**–13
total [tōt/l] **21**–8, **118** ✦
tote bag [tōt/ băg/] **69**–29
touch [tŭch] **75**–E
towel [tow/əl] **43**–8, 12, 13
...rack [–răk/] **43**–8
townhouse [town/hows/] **34**–7
tow truck [tō/ trŭk/] **106**–13
toy [toy(/–)]
...chest [–chěst/] **45**–24
...store [–stör/] **92**–5
toys [toyz] **46**–H, **94**–5
track [trăk] (athletic) **5**–11, (train) **104**–10
track and field [trăk/ ən fēld/] **159**–17
trackball [trăk/böl/] **144**–15
track lighting [trăk/ lī/tǐng] **42**–3
tractor [trăk/tər] **148**–9
...trailer [–trā/lər] **106**–15
trade school [trād/ skool/] **112**–9
traffic light [trăf/ǐk līt/] **90**–6
TRAFFIC SIGNS [trăf/ǐk sīnz/] **107**
tragedy [trăj/ə dē] **166**–11
trailer [trā/lər] **106**–17
train [trān(/–)] **104**–17
...station [–stā/shən] **104**–13
training pants [trā/nǐng pănts/] **95**–24
transcribe [trăn skrīb/] **142**–C
transcriber (medical) [trăn skrī/bər] **142**–4
transfer [trăns für/, trăns/fər] **97**–E
transfer [trăns/fər] **104**–6
translator [trănz/lā/tər, trăns/–] **138**–34
transmission [trănz mǐsh/ən, trăns–]
automatic... [ö/tə măt/ǐk–] **109**
standard... [stăn/dərd–] **109**
TRANSPORTATION, PUBLIC [pŭb/lǐk trăns/pər tā/shən] **104**
trash [trăsh(/–)]
...bags [–băgz/] **47**–12
...bin [–bǐn/] **37**–20
...chute [–shoot/] **37**–24
travel [trăv/əl] **29**–N
travel [trăv/əl]
...agency [–ā/jən sē] **92**–9
...agent [–ā/jənt] **139**–60
traveler's check [trăv/lərz chěk/] **20**–17
tray [trā(/–)] **41**–10, **62**–H, **63**–7
...table [–tā/bəl] **110**–16
treatment [trēt/mənt] **80** ✦

TREES AND PLANTS [trēz/ ən plănts/] **128**
trench coat [trĕnch/ kōt/] **66**–20
triangle [trī/ăng/gəl] **118**–7
tricycle [trī/sĭ kəl] **153**–9
trigonometry [trĭg/ə năm/ə trē] **118**–27
trim [trĭm] **39**–E
tripe [trīp] **52**–8
tripod [trī/päd] **165**–20
trombone [träm bōn/] **120**–12
trout [trowt] **53**–16
trowel [trow/əl] **39**–14, **149**–12
truck driver [trŭk/ drī/vər] **139**–61
TRUCKS [trŭks] **106**
trumpet [trŭm/pət] **120**–13
trunk [trŭngk] (car) **109**–49, (tree) **128**–4, (animal) **135**–47
T-shirt [tē/shürt/] **64**–12, **70**–16, **72**–15, 16, 17, 18
tuba [tōō/bə] **120**–14
tube [tōōb(/–)] **56**–12
...of toothpaste [–əv tōōth/pāst/] **56**–24
Tuesday [tōōz/dā, –dē] **18**–3
tulip [tōō/ləp] **129**–11
tuna [tōō/nə] **54**–25, **130**–9
tuner [tōō/nər] **164**–13
tunic [tōō/nĭk] **65**–22
tunnel [tŭn/əl] **105**–11
turbulence [tür/byə ləns] **111**–N
turkey [tür/kē] **52**–17, **53**–4, **168**–17
turn [türn(/–)]
...left [–lĕft/] **107**–C
...right [–rīt/] **107**–B
turn in [türn/ ĭn/] **113**–E
turnips [tür/nəps] **51**–14
turn signal [türn/ sĭg/nəl] **108**– 4
turntable [türn/tā/bəl] **164**–12
turquoise [tür/koyz, –kwoyz] **12**–4
turtle [tür/tl] **131**–42
turtleneck [tür/tl nĕk/] **64**–7
...sweater [–swĕt/ər] **71**–28
tusk [tŭsk] **135**–48
tuxedo [tŭk sē/dō] **65**–28
TV (television) [tē/vē/] **42**–26, **164**–6
...antenna [–ăn tĕn/ə] **38**–22
tweezers [twē/zərz] **83**–2
twelfth [twĕlfth] **14**
twelve [twĕlv] **14**
twentieth [twĕn/tē əth] **14**
twenty [twĕn/tē] **14**, **16**–8, 9, **20**–10
twenty-five after one [twĕn/tē fīv/ ăf/tər wŭn/] **16**–9
twenty-five to two [twĕn/tē fīv/ tə tōō/] **16**–11
twenty percent [twĕn/tē pər sĕnt/] **15**–8
twenty to two [twĕn/tē tə tōō/] **16**–12
twice a week [twīs/ ə wēk/] **18**–23
twig [twĭg] **128**–1
two [tōō] **14**
two-story house [tōō/stör/ē hows/] **38**◆
type [tīp] **140**–M, **142**–D
Types of entertainment [tīps/ əv ĕn/tər tān/mənt] **166**
Types of material [tīps/ əv mə tïr/ē əl] **70**
Types of math [tīps/ əv măth/] **118**
TYPES OF SCHOOLS [tīps/ əv skōōlz/] **112**
Types of stories [tīps/ əv stör/ēz] **166**
Types of TV programs [tīps/ əv tē/vē/ prō/grămz] **167**
typewriter [tīp/rī/tər] **142**–2
...cartridge [–kär/trĭj] **143**–31
ugly [ŭg/lē] **11**–22

umbrella [ŭm brĕl/ə] **66**–16, **155**–9
umpire [ŭm/pīr] **158**◆
uncle [ŭng/kəl] **24**–11
uncomfortable [ŭn kŭmf/tə bəl, –tər–] **30**–8
under [ŭn/dər] **13**–9, **105**–1
underexposed [ŭn/dər ĭk spōzd/] **165**–35
underline [ŭn/dər līn/] **7**–V
underpants [ŭn/dər pănts/] **67**–17
undershirt [ŭn/dər shürt/] **67**–10
uniform [yōō/nə förm/] **65**–17, **161**–16
UNIVERSE [yōō/nə vürs/] **127**
university [yōō/nə vür/sə tē] **112**–10
unload [ŭn lōd/] **72**–E
unpack [ŭn păk/] **35**–E
unscented [ŭn sĕn/təd] **77**◆
up [ŭp] **105**–9
upset [ŭp sĕt/] **31**–30
upstairs [ŭp/stërz/] **38**◆
Uranus [yōōr/ə nəs, yōō rā/nəs] **127**–3
urban area [ür/bən ër/ē ə] **34**–1
use [yōōz(/–)] **140**–N
...deodorant [–dē ō/dər ənt] **76**–C
user's manual [yōō/zərz măn/yōō əl] **144**–22
U.S. GOVERNMENT AND CITIZENSHIP
[yōō/ĕs/ gŭv/ər mənt ən sĭt/ə zən shĭp/] **116**
U.S. HISTORY [yōō/ĕs/ hĭs/tə rē] **114–115**
Using a pay phone [yōō/zĭng ə pā/ fōn/] **9**
Using the ATM machine [yōō/zĭng dhē ā/tē/ĕm/ mə shēn/] **97**
U.S. MAIL [yōō/ĕs/ māl/] **96**
utilities [yōō tĭl/ə tēz] **35**◆
U-turn OK (sign) [yōō/türn/ ō kā/] **107**–7
vacancy sign [vā/kən sē sīn/] **36**–11
vacation [vā kā/shən] **19**–46
vaccination [văk/sə nā/shən] **80**◆
vacuum [văk/yōōm] **46**–I
vacuum cleaner [văk/yōōm klē/nər] **47**–13
...attachments [–ə tăch/mənts] **47**–14
...bag [–băg/] **47**–15
valedictorian [văl/ə dĭk tör/ē ən] **32**–8
Valentine's Day [văl/ən tīnz dā/] **168**–4
valet parking [văl/ā pär/kĭng] **145**–1
valley [văl/ē] **117**–18
van [văn] **106**–10, 14
vandalism [văn/də lĭz/əm] **100**–1
vase [vās, vāz, väz] **41**–9
vault [völt] **97**–2
VCR (videocassette recorder)
[vē/sē/är/] / [vĭd/ē ō kə sĕt/ rĭ kör/dər] **164**–8
veal cutlets [vēl/ kŭt/ləts] **52**–6
vegetable [vĕj/tə bəl]
...casserole [–kăs/ə rōl/] **58**
...garden [–gär/dn] **148**–12
...peeler [–pē/lər] **59**–15
VEGETABLES [vĕj/tə bəlz] **51**
vegetables [vĕj/tə bəlz] **55**–43
vegetarian [vĕj/ə tër/ē ən] **52**◆
vein [vān] **75**–44
vendor [vĕn/dər] **91**–30
Venus [vē/nəs] **127**–8
vest [vĕst] **65**–24, **66**–13
veterinarian [vĕt/ər ə nër/ē ən] **139**–62
Vice President [vīs/ prĕz/ə dənt] **116**–7
victim [vĭk/təm] **100**◆
video [vĭd/ē ō]
...camera [–kăm/rə] **165**–19

Index

...game system [–gām/ sĭs/təm] **162**–1
...store [–stör/] **93**–15
videocassette [vĭd/ē ō kə sĕt/] **98**–13, **164**–8, 10
view [vyōō] **11**–21, 22
vine [vīn] **128**–22
vineyard [vĭn/yərd] **148**–14
violet [vī/ə lət, vī/lət] **129**–22
violin [vī/ə lĭn/] **120**–8
vise [vīs] **150**–21
visor [vī/zər] **147**–11
vital signs monitor [vīt/l sīnz/ män/ə tər] **87**–21
vitamins [vī/tə mənz] **81**–19
V-neck sweater [vē/nĕk/ swĕt/ər] **71**–27
vocational school [vō kā/shə nəl skōōl/] **112**–9
volcanic eruption [väl kăn/ĭk ĭ rŭp/shən] **103**–14
volleyball [väl/ē böl/] (sport) **158**–14, (equipment) **161**–3
Volume [väl/yəm, –yōōm] **57**
volunteer [väl/ən tĭr/] **87**–19
vomit [väm/ət] **78**–E
vote [vōt] **116**–D
waffles [wä/fəlz, wö/–] **61**–4
waist [wāst] **74**–4
waistband [wāst/bănd/] **73**–3
wait [wāt] **90**–B
waiter [wā/tər] **62**–4
waiting room [wā/tĭng rōōm/] **84**–1
wait on customers [wāt/ än kŭs/tə mərz, –ön–] **140**–O
waitress [wā/trəs] **63**–6
wake up [wāk/ ŭp/] **26**–A
walk [wök] **101**–A, **156**–A
walker [wö/kər] **80**–5, **95**–12
wall [wöl(/–)] **42**–6, **48**–4
...unit [–yōō/nət] **42**–13
wallet [wä/lət, wö/–] **69**–26
wallpaper [wöl/pā/pər] **45**–5
walrus [wöl/rəs] **131**–32
War [wör] **114**
warehouse [wër/hows/] **146**–9
warm [wörm] **10**–2
warning label [wör/nĭng lā/bəl] **80**–15
wash [wäsh(/–), wösh(/–)]
...hair [–hër/] **76**–E
...the dishes [–dhə dĭsh/əz] **46**–M
...the windows [–dhə wĭn/dōz] **46**–D
washcloth [wäsh/klöth/, wösh/–] **43**–14
washer [wä/shər, wö/–] **72**–3, **150**–32
wasp [wäsp, wösp] **132**–18
wastebasket [wāst/băs/kət] **43**–25, **46**–F
watch [wäch, wöch] **69**–34
watch TV [wäch/ tē/vē/, wöch/–] **27**–5
water [wö/tər] **39**–B
water [wö/tər] **117**, **155**–1
...fountain [–fown/tn] **153**–11
...glass [–glăs/] **63**–19
...pollution [–pə lōō/shən] **126**–12
...polo [–pō/lō] **158**–15
watercolor [wö/tər kŭl/ər] **163**–25
waterfall [wä/tər föl/] **117**–2
watering can [wö/tər ĭng kăn/] **39**–17
watermelons [wö/tər mĕl/ənz] **50**–24
waterskiing [wö/tər skē/ĭng] **160**–7
WATER SPORTS [wö/tər spörts/] **160**
wave [wāv] **155**–6
wavy [wā/vē] **23**–10
Ways to pay [wāz/ tə pā/] **20**

WEATHER [wĕdh/ər] **10**
Wednesday [wĕnz/dā, –dē] **18**–4
weed [wēd] **39**–A
week [wēk] **18**–11
weekdays [wēk/dāz/] **18**–12
weekend [wēk/ĕnd/] **18**–13
weigh [wā] **57**–B
weight [wāt] **22**–21, **57**
weightlifting [wāt/lĭf/tĭng] **159**–15
weights [wāts] **161**–19
WEIGHTS AND MEASURES [wāts/ ən mĕzh/ərz] **57**
welder [wĕl/dər] **139**–63
well [wĕl] **30**–15
west [wĕst] **107**, **123**, **124**
western [wĕs/tərn] **166**–9
wet [wĕt(/–)] **72**–17
...mop [–mäp/] **47**–16
...suit [–sōōt/] **155**–7
whale [wāl] **131**–29
wheat [wēt(/–)] **148**–2
...bread [–brĕd/] **53**–2
wheelbarrow [wēl/băr/ō] **39**–16
wheelchair [wēl/chër/] **80**–6
whisk [wĭsk] **59**–21
whiskers [wĭs/kərz] **134**–18
white [wīt(/–)] **12**–14
...bread [–brĕd/] **53**–1
White House [wīt/ hows/] **116**–5
whole [hōl(/–)] **15**–6
...salmon [–săm/ən] **53**–18
wide [wīd] **71**–44
widow [wĭd/ō] **29** ✦
widower [wĭd/ō ər] **29** ✦
width [wĭdth, wĭtth] **15**–17
wife [wīf] **24**–20, **25** ✦
wild animals [wīld/ ăn/ə məlz] **133** ✦
willow [wĭl/ō] **128**–14
win [wĭn] **158** ✦
wind [wĭnd] **126**–2
windbreaker [wĭnd/brā/kər] **66**–24
window [wĭn/dō] **38**–17, **42**–17
...pane [–pān/] **149**–15
...shade [–shād/] **44**–6
windshield [wĭnd/shēld/] **108**–2
...wipers [–wī/pərz] **108**–3
windy [wĭn/dē] **10**–10
wine glass [wīn/ glăs/] **63**–20
wing [wĭng] **132**–2
wings [wĭngz] **52**–20
winter [wĭn/tər] **19**–40
WINTER SPORTS AND WATER SPORTS
[wĭn/tər spörts/ ən wö/tər spörts/] **160**
wipes [wīps] **95**–17
wipe the counter [wīp/ dhə kown/tər] **46**–O
wire [wīr(/–)] **151**–13
...stripper [–strĭp/ər] **151**–37
wish [wĭsh] **169**–J
withdraw cash [wĭdh drö/ kăsh/, wĭth–] **97**–D
witness [wĭt/nəs] **99**–11
wolf [wōōlf] **134**–5
woman [wōōm/ən] **22**–10
wood [wōōd(/–)] **149**–17, **151**–18
...screw [–skrōō/] **150**–28
wooden spoon [wōōd/n spōōn/] **59**–9
woodpecker [wōōd/pĕk/ər] **132**–9

Woodwinds [wood/windz/] **120**
woodworking kit [wood/wür/kǐng kǐt/] **162**–16
wool [wool(/–)] **70**–14
  ...scarf [–skärf/] **66**–4
work [würk/] **26**–K, **140**–P
workbook [würk/book/] **3**–23
Work in a group [würk/ ǐn ə groop/] **6**
working [wür/kǐng] **48**–1
work out [würk/ owt/] **157**–P
Work with a partner [würk/wǐdh/ ə pärt/nər, –wǐth/–] **6**
WORLD [würld] **124**–**125**
worm [würm] **130**–22
worried [wür/ēd] **30**–13
wrap [răp] **169**–D
wrench [rěnch] **109**–50, **151**–42, 43
wrestling [rěs/lǐng] **159**–16
wrinkled [rǐng/kəld] **72**–19
wrist [rǐst] **69**–34, **75**–60
wristwatch [rǐst/wäch/, –wöch/] **69**–34
write [rīt] **2**–G, **113**–A
writer [rī/tər] **139**–64
writing assignment [rī/tǐng ə sīn/mənt] **113**–1
wrong [röng(/–)]
  ...number [–nŭm/bər] **9** ✦
  ...way [–wā/] **107**–4
X-ray [ěks/rā/]
  ...technician [–těk nǐsh/ən] **86**–8
xylophone [zī/lə fōn/] **120**–17
yams [yămz] **51**–22
YARD [yärd] **39**
yard [(–)yärd(/)]
  front... [frŭnt/–] **38**–15
yard (measurement) [yärd] **15** ✦
yardstick [yärd/stǐk/] **151**–15
yarn [yärn] **163**–17
year [yǐr] **4**–16, **18**–8
yellow [yěl/ō] **12**–12
yesterday [yěs/tər dā/, –dē] **18**–17
yield [yēld] **107** ✦
yogurt [yō/gərt] **54**–33, **60**–11
young [yŭng] **22**–13
zebra [zē/brə] **135**–34
zero [zǐr/ō] **14**
ZIP code [zǐp/ kōd/] **4**–9
zipper [zǐp/ər] **73**–16
zoo [zoo] **152**–1
zookeeper [zoo/kē/pər] **152**–3
zoom lens [zoom/ lěnz/] **165**–25
zucchini [zoo kē/nē] **51**–4

Geographical Index

Continents

Africa [ăf/rĭ kə] 125–5
Antarctica [ănt ärk/tĭ kə, –är/tĭ–] 125–7
Asia [ā/zhə] 125–4
Australia [ö strāl/yə] 125–6
Europe [yŏŏr/əp] 125–3
North America [nörth/ ə mĕr/ə kə] 124–1
South America [sowth/ ə mĕr/ə kə] 124–2

Countries and other locations

Afghanistan [ăf găn/ə stăn/] 124–125
Albania [ăl bā/nē ə] 124–125
Algeria [ăl jïr/ē ə] 124–125125
American Samoa [ə mĕr/ə kən sə mō/ə] 124–125
Andorra [ăn dör/ə] 124–125
Angola [ăng gō/lə] 124–125
Argentina [är/jən tē/nə] 124–125
Armenia [är mē/nē ə] 124–125
Australia [ö strāl/yə] 124–125
Austria [ö/strē ə] 124–125
Azerbaijan [ăz/ər bī jän/] 124–125
Bahamas [bə hä/məz] 122–125
Bahrain [bä rān/] 124–125
Bangladesh [bäng/glə dĕsh/, băng/–] 124–125
Barbados [bär bā/dōs] 124–125
Belarus [bē/lə rŏŏs/, byĕl/ə–] 124–125
Belgium [bĕl/jəm] 124–125
Belize [bə lēz/] 124–125
Benin [bə nĭn/, –nēn/] 124–125
Bermuda [bər myŏŏ/də] 122–125
Bhutan [bŏŏ tän/] 124–125
Bolivia [bə lĭv/ē ə] 124–125
Borneo [bör/nē ō] 124–125
Bosnia-Herzegovina [băz/nē ə hĕr/tsə gō vē/nə] 124–125
Botswana [bät swä/nə] 124–125
Brazil [brə zĭl/] 124–125
Brunei [brŏŏ nī/] 124–125
Bulgaria [bŭl gër/ē ə] 124–125
Burkina Faso [bər kē/nə fä/sō] 124–125
Burundi [bŏŏ rŏŏn/dē] 124–125
Cambodia [kăm bō/dē ə] 124–125
Cameroon [kăm/ə rŏŏn/] 124–125
Canada [kăn/ə də] 122–125
Cape Verde [kāp/ vürd/] 124–125
Central African Republic [sĕn/trəl ăf/rĭ kən rĭ pŭb/lĭk]
    124–125
Chad [chăd] 124–125
Chile [chĭl/ē] 124–125
China [chī/nə] 124–125
Colombia [kə lŭm/bē ə] 124–125
Comoros [kăm/ə rōz] 124–125
Congo [käng/gō] 124–125
Costa Rica [kōs/tə rē/kə, käs/–] 122–125
Croatia [krō ā/shə] 124–125
Cuba [kyŏŏ/bə] 122–125
Cyprus [sī/prəs] 124–125
Czech Republic [chĕk/ rĭ pŭb/lĭk] 124–125
Democratic Republic of the Congo [dĕm/ə krăt/ĭk rĭ pŭb/lĭk
    əv dhə käng/gō] 124–125
Denmark [dĕn/märk] 124–125
Djibouti [jĭ bŏŏ/tē] 124–125
Dominica [däm/ə nē/kə] 124–125
Dominican Republic [də mĭn/ĭ kən rĭ pŭb/lĭk] 122–125
Ecuador [ĕk/wə dör/] 124–125
Egypt [ē/jĭpt] 124–125
El Salvador [ĕl săl/və dör/] 122–125

Equatorial Guinea [ē/kwə tör/ē əl gĭn/ē, ĕk/wə–] 124–125
Eritrea [ĕr/ə trē/ə] 124–125
Estonia [ĕ stō/nē ə] 124–125
Ethiopia [ē/thē ō/pē ə] 124–125
Fiji [fē/jē] 124–125
Finland [fĭn/lənd] 124–125
France [frăns] 124–125
French Guiana [frĕnch/ gē ăn/ə, –ä/nə] 124–125
French Polynesia [frĕnch/ päl/ə nē/zhə] 124–125
Gabon [gă bōn/] 124–125
Georgia [jör/jə] 124–125
Germany [jür/mə nē] 124–125
Ghana [gä/nə] 124–125
Greece [grēs] 124–125
Greenland [grēn/lənd, –lănd/] 122–125
Grenada [grə nā/də] 124–125
Guatemala [gwä/tə mä/lə] 122–125
Guinea [gĭn/ē] 124–125
Guinea-Bissau [gĭn/ē bĭ sow/] 124–125
Guyana [gī ăn/ə] 124–125
Haiti [hā/tē] 122–125
Honduras [hän dŏŏr/əs] 122–125
Hong Kong [häng/ käng/] 124–125
Hungary [hŭng/gə rē] 124–125
Iceland [īs/lənd] 124–125
India [ĭn/dē ə] 124–125
Indonesia [ĭn/də nē/zhə] 124–125
Iran [ĭ rän/, ĭ răn/] 124–125
Iraq [ĭ räk/, ĭ răk/] 124–125
Ireland [īr/lənd] 124–125
Israel [ĭz/rē əl, –rā–] 124–125
Italy [ĭt/l ē] 124–125
Ivory Coast [īv/rē kōst/] 124–125
Jamaica [jə mā/kə] 122–125
Japan [jə păn/] 124–125
Java [jä/və] 124–125
Jordan [jör/dn] 124–125
Kazakhstan [kä/zäk stän/] 124–125
Kenya [kĕn/yə, kēn/–] 124–125
Kiribati [kïr/ə băs/] 124–125
Kuwait [kŏŏ wāt/] 124–125
Kyrgyzstan [kïr/gĭ stän/, –stän/] 124–125
Laos [lows, lä/ōs] 124–125
Latvia [lăt/vē ə] 124–125
Lebanon [lĕb/ə nən, –nän/] 124–125
Lesotho [lə sō/tō, –sŏŏ/tŏŏ] 124–125
Liberia [lī bïr/ē ə] 124–125
Libya [lĭb/ē ə] 124–125
Liechtenstein [lĭk/tən stīn/] 124–125
Lithuania [lĭth/ŏŏ ā/nē ə] 124–125
Luxembourg [lŭk/səm bürg/] 124–125
Macedonia [măs/ə dō/nē ə] 124–125
Madagascar [măd/ə găs/kər] 124–125
Malawi [mə lä/wē] 124–125
Malaysia [mə lā/zhə] 124–125
Maldives [möl/dēvz, –dīvz] 124–125
Mali [mä/lē] 124–125
Malta [möl/tə] 124–125
Marshall Islands [mär/shəl ī/ləndz] 124–125
Mauritania [mör/ə tā/nē ə] 124–125
Mauritius [mö rĭsh/əs] 124–125
Mexico [mĕk/sĭ kō/] 122–125
Micronesia [mī/krə nē/zhə] 124–125
Moldova [mäl dō/və, möl–] 124–125
Monaco [măn/ə kō/] 124–125

Mongolia [mäng gō/lē ə] 124–125
Montenegro [män/tə nē/grō, –nĕ/–] 124–125
Morocco [mə räk/ō] 124–125
Mozambique [mō/zəm bēk/] 124–125
Myanmar [myän/mär] 124–125
Namibia [nə mĭb/ē ə] 124–125
Nauru [nä ōō/rōō] 124–125
Nepal [nə pöl/, –päl/] 124–125
Netherlands [nĕdh/ər ləndz] 124–125
New Guinea [nōō/ gĭn/ē] 124–125
New Zealand [nōō/ zē/lənd] 124–125
Nicaragua [nĭk/ə rä/gwə] 122–125
Niger [nī/jər, nē zhër/] 124–125
Nigeria [nī jïr/ē ə] 124–125
North Korea [nörth/ kə rē/ə] 124–125
Norway [nör/wā] 124–125
Oman [ō män/] 124–125
Pakistan [păk/ə stän/] 124–125
Palau [pə low/] 124–125
Panama [păn/ə mä/] 122–125
Papua New Guinea [păp/yōō ə nōō/ gĭn/ē] 124–125
Paraguay [păr/ə gwī/, –gwā/] 124–125
Peru [pə rōō/] 124–125
Philippines [fĭl/ə pēnz/, fĭl/ə pēnz/] 124–125
Poland [pō/lənd] 124–125
Portugal [pör/chə gəl] 124–125
Puerto Rico [pwër/tə rē/kō, pör/tə–] 122–125
Qatar [kä/tär, kə tär/] 124–125
Romania [rō mā/nē ə, rōō–] 124–125
Russia [rŭsh/ə] 124–125
Rwanda [rōō än/də] 124–125
Saudi Arabia [sow/dē ə rā/bē ə, sö/dē–] 124–125
Senegal [sĕn/ə göl/, –gäl/] 124–125
Serbia [sür/bē ə] 124–125
Seychelles [sā shĕlz/, –shĕl/] 124–125
Sierra Leone [sē ĕr/ə lē ōn/, –lē ō/nē] 124–125
Singapore [sĭng/ə pör/] 124–125
Slovakia [slō vä/kē ə] 124–125
Slovenia [slō vē/nē ə] 124–125
Solomon Islands [säl/ə mən ī/ləndz] 124–125
Somalia [sə mä/lē ə] 124–125
South Africa [sowth/ ăf/rĭ kə] 124–125
South Korea [sowth/ kə rē/ə] 124–125
Spain [spān] 124–125
Sri Lanka [srē/ läng/kə, shrē/–] 124–125
Sudan [sōō dän/] 124–125
Sumatra [sōō mä/trə] 124–125
Suriname [sōōr/ə nä/mə] 124–125
Swaziland [swä/zē lănd/] 124–125
Sweden [swēd/n] 124–125
Switzerland [swĭt/sər lənd] 124–125
Syria [sïr/ē ə] 124–125
Tahiti [tə hē/tē] 124–125
Taiwan [tī/wän/] 124–125
Tajikistan [tä jĭk/ə stän/, –stän/] 124–125
Tanzania [tăn/zə nē/ə] 124–125
Tasmania [tăz mā/nē ə] 124–125
Thailand [tī/lănd/, –lənd] 124–125
The Gambia [dhə găm/bē ə] 124–125
Togo [tō/gō] 124–125
Tonga [täng/gə] 124–125
Tunisia [tōō nē/zhə] 124–125
Turkey [tür/kē] 124–125
Turkmenistan [türk mĕn/ə stän/, –stän/] 124–125
Uganda [yōō găn/də] 124–125

Ukraine [yōō/krān, yōō krān/] 124–125
United Arab Emirates [yōō nī/təd ăr/əb ĕm/ər əts] 124–125
United Kingdom [yōō nī/təd kĭng/dəm] 124–125
United States of America [yōō nī/təd stāts/ əv ə mĕr/ə kə]
    122–125
Uruguay [yōōr/ə gwī/, –gwā/] 124–125
Uzbekistan [ōōz bĕk/ə stän/, –stän/] 124–125
Venezuela [vĕn/ə zwā/lə] 124–125
Vietnam [vē/ĕt näm/, –năm/] 124–125
Western Sahara [wĕs/tərn sə här/ə] 124–125
Western Samoa [wĕs/tərn sə mō/ə] 124–125
Yemen [yĕm/ən] 124–125
Zambia [zăm/bē ə] 124–125
Zimbabwe [zĭm bäb/wā] 124–125

Bodies of water
Arabian Sea [ə rā/bē ən sē/] 124–125
Arctic Ocean [ärk/tĭk ō/shən] 122–125
Baffin Bay [băf/ən bā/] 122–125
Baltic Sea [böl/tĭk sē/] 124–125
Barents Sea [băr/ənts sē/] 124–125
Beaufort Sea [bō/fərt sē/] 122–125
Bering Sea [bĕr/ĭng sē/, bïr/–] 122–125
Black Sea [blăk/ sē/] 124–125
Caribbean Sea [kăr/ə bē/ən sē/, kə rĭb/ē ən–] 122–125
Caspian Sea [kăs/pē ən sē/] 124–125
Coral Sea [kör/əl sē/] 124–125
East China Sea [ēst/ chī/nə sē/] 124–125
Greenland Sea [grēn/lənd sē/, –lănd/–] 124–125
Gulf of Alaska [gŭlf/ əv ə lăs/kə] 122–125
Gulf of California [gŭlf/ əv kăl/ə förn/yə] 122–125
Gulf of Honduras [gŭlf/ əv hän dŏŏr/əs] 122–125
Gulf of Mexico [gŭlf/ əv mĕk/sĭ kō/] 122–125
Gulf of St. Lawrence [gŭlf/ əv sānt/ lör/əns, –lär/–] 122–125
Hudson Bay [hŭd/sən bā/] 122–125
Indian Ocean [ĭn/dē ən ō/shən] 124–125
Labrador Sea [lăb/rə dör/ sē/] 122–125
Mediterranean Sea [mĕd/ə tə rā/nē ən sē/] 124–125
North Atlantic Ocean [nörth/ ət lăn/tĭk ō/shən] 122–125
North Pacific Ocean [nörth/ pə sĭf/ĭk ō/shən] 122–125
North Sea [nörth/ sē/] 124–125
Norwegian Sea [nör wē/jən sē/] 124–125
Persian Gulf [pür/zhən gŭlf/] 124–125
Philippine Sea [fĭl/ə pēn/ sē/] 124–125
Red Sea [rĕd/ sē/] 124–125
Sea of Japan [sē/ əv jə păn/] 124–125
Sea of Okhotsk [sē/ əv ō kätsk/] 124–125
South Atlantic Ocean [sowth/ ət lăn/tĭk ō/shən] 124–125
South China Sea [sowth/ chī/nə sē/] 124–125
Southern Ocean [sŭdh/ərn ō/shən] 124–125
South Pacific Ocean [sowth/ pə sĭf/ĭk ō/shən] 124–125

The United States of America
Capital: Washington, D.C. (District Of Columbia)
    [wä/shĭng tən dē/sē/, wö/–]

Regions of the United States
Mid-Atlantic States [mĭd/ət lăn/tĭk stāts/] 123–10
Midwest [mĭd/wĕst/] 123–9
New England [nōō/ ĭng/glənd] 123–11
Pacific States [pə sĭf/ĭk stāts/] 123–7
Rocky Mountain States [räk/ē mown/tn stāts/] 123–8
South [sowth] 123–13
Southeast [sowth/ēst/] 123–13
Southwest [sowth/wĕst/] 123–12
West Coast [wĕst/ kōst/] 123–7

Geographical Index

States of the United States

Alabama [ăl′ə băm′ə] **122–123**
Alaska [ə lăs′kə] **122–125**
Arizona [ăr′ə zō′nə] **122–123**
Arkansas [är′kən sö′] **122–123**
California [kăl′ə förn′yə] **122–123**
Colorado [kăl′ə răd′ō, –ra′dō] **122–123**
Connecticut [kə nĕt′ĭ kət] **122–123**
Delaware [dĕl′ə wĕr′] **122–123**
Florida [flör′ə də, flär′–] **122–123**
Georgia [jör′jə] **122–123**
Hawaii [hə wī′ē] **122–123**
Idaho [ī′də hō′] **122–123**
Illinois [ĭl′ə noy′] **122–123**
Indiana [ĭn/dē ăn′ə] **122–123**
Iowa [ī′ə wə] **122–123**
Kansas [kăn′zəs] **122–123**
Kentucky [kən tŭk′ē] **122–123**
Louisiana [lōō ē′zē ăn′ə] **122–123**
Maine [mān] **122–123**
Maryland [mĕr′ə lənd] **122–123**
Massachusetts [măs/ə chōō′səts] **122–123**
Michigan [mĭsh′ĭ gən] **122–123**
Minnesota [mĭn′ə sō′tə] **122–123**
Mississippi [mĭs/ə sĭp′ē] **122–123**
Missouri [mə zōōr′ē, –zōōr′ə] **122–123**
Montana [män tăn′ə] **122–123**
Nebraska [nə brăs′kə] **122–123**
Nevada [nə văd′ə, –vä′də] **122–123**
New Hampshire [nōō′ hămp′shər] **122–123**
New Jersey [nōō′ jür′zē] **122–123**
New Mexico [nōō′ mĕk′sĭ kō′] **122–123**
New York [nōō′ yörk′] **122–123**
North Carolina [nörth′ kăr′ə lī′nə] **122–123**
North Dakota [nörth′ də kō′tə] **122–123**
Ohio [ō hī′ō] **122–123**
Oklahoma [ō′klə hō′mə] **122–123**
Oregon [ör′ĭ gən, –găn′, är′–] **122–123**
Pennsylvania [pĕn/səl vān′yə] **122–123**
Rhode Island [rōd′ ī′lənd] **122–123**
South Carolina [sowth′ kăr′ə lī′nə] **122–123**
South Dakota [sowth′ də kō′tə] **122–123**
Tennessee [tĕn/ə sē′] **122–123**
Texas [tĕk′səs] **122–123**
Utah [yōō′tö, –tä] **122–123**
Vermont [vər mänt′] **122–123**
Virginia [vər jĭn′yə] **122–123**
Washington [wä′shĭng tən, wö′–] **122–123**
West Virginia [wĕst′ vər jĭn′yə] **122–123**
Wisconsin [wĭs kän′sən] **122–123**
Wyoming [wī ō′mĭng] **122–123**

Canada

Capital: Ottawa [ät′ə wə]

Regions of Canada

Atlantic Provinces [ət lăn′tĭk präv′ən səz] **123 – 6**
British Columbia [brĭt′ĭsh kə lŭm′bē ə] **123 – 2**
Northern Canada [nör′dhərn kăn′ə də] **123 – 1**
Ontario [än tër′ē ō′] **123 – 4**
Prairie Provinces [prë′ē präv′ən səz] **123 – 3**
Quebec [kwĭ bĕk′] **123 – 5**

Provinces of Canada

Alberta [ăl bür′tə] **122–123**
British Columbia [brĭt′ĭsh kə lŭm′bē ə] **122–123**
Manitoba [măn′ə tō′bə] **122–123**

New Brunswick [nōō′ brŭnz′wĭk] **122–123**
Newfoundland [nōō′fən lənd] **122–123**
Northwest Territories [nörth′wĕst′ tĕr′ə tör′ēz] **122–123**
Nova Scotia [nō′və skō′shə] **122–123**
Ontario [än tër′ē ō′] **122–123**
Prince Edward Island [prĭns′ ĕd′wərd ī′lənd] **122–123**
Quebec [kwĭ bĕk′] **122–123**
Saskatchewan [să skăch′ə wən, –wän′] **122–123**
Yukon Territory [yōō′kän tĕr′ə tör′ē] **122–123**

Mexico

Capital: Mexico (City) [mĕk′sĭ kō′ (sĭt′ē)]

Regions of Mexico

Chiapas Highlands [chē ä′pəs hī′ləndz] **123 – 18**
Gulf Coastal Plain [gŭlf′ kō′stəl plān′] **123 – 16**
Pacific Northwest [pə sĭf′ĭk nörth′wĕst] **123 – 14**
Plateau of Mexico [plă tō′ əv mĕk′sĭ kō′] **123 – 15**
Southern Uplands [sŭdh′ərn ŭp′ləndz] **123 – 17**
Yucatan Peninsula [yōō′kə tăn′ pə nĭn′sə lə, yōō/kə tän′–]
    123 – 19

States of Mexico

Aguascalientes [ä/gwəs käl yĕn′täs] **122–123**
Baja California Norte [bä′hä kăl′ə förn′yə nör′tä] **122–123**
Baja California Sur [bä′hä kăl′ə förn′yə sōōr′] **122–123**
Campeche [käm pä′chä, kăm pē′chē] **122–123**
Chiapas [chē ä′pəs] **122–123**
Chihuahua [chĭ wä′wä, –wə] **122–123**
Coahuila [kō′ə wē′lə] **122–123**
Colima [kə lē′mə] **122–123**
Distrito Federal [dĭ strē′tō fĕd′ə räl′] **122–123**
Durango [dōō răng′gō, –räng′–] **122–123**
Guanajuato [gwä/nə hwä′tō] **122–123**
Guerrero [gə rër′ō] **122–123**
Hidalgo [hĭ dăl′gō, ē dhäl′gō] **122–123**
Jalisco [hə lĭs′kō, –lēs′–] **122–123**
México [mĕk′sĭ kō/, mĕ′hē kō] **122–123**
Michoacán [mē/chō ä kän′] **122–123**
Morelos [mö rĕl′ōs] **122–123**
Nayarit [nä′yə rēt′] **122–123**
Nuevo León [nwā′vō lā ōn′] **122–123**
Oaxaca [wə hä′kə, wä–] **122–123**
Puebla [pwĕb′lä] **122–123**
Querétaro [kə rĕt′ə rō′] **122–123**
Quintana Roo [kēn tä′nə rō′] **122–123**
San Luis Potosí [sän′ lōō ēs′ pō/tə sē′] **122–123**
Sinaloa [sē/nə lō′ə] **122–123**
Sonora [sə nör′ə] **122–123**
Tabasco [tə bäs′kō] **122–123**
Tamaulipas [tä/mow lē′pəs] **122–123**
Tlaxcala [tlä skä′lə] **122–123**
Veracruz [vĕr′ə krōōz′, –krōōs′] **122–123**
Yucatán [yōō′kə tän′, –tän′] **122–123**
Zacatecas [zä/kə tä′kəs, sä/–] **122–123**

a cuadros **70**–11
a la autopista **105**–6
a la derecha **13**–2
a la vuelta de la esquina **105**–10
a rayas **70**–7
a través del túnel **105**–11
abadejo **130**–8
abalorios **69**–32
abdomen **74**–3
abedul **128**–8
abeja melífera **132**–26
abogado **138**–36
abogado defensor **99**–4
abordar el avión **111**–F
abra el libro **2**–I
abra tres huevos **58**–A
abrazadera **81**–31
abrazadera en forma de C **150**–6
abrazar **33**–G
abrecosturas **73**–19
abrelatas **59**–1
abrelatas eléctrico **40**–14
abrigo **66**–2
abrigo de invierno **66**–8
abril **19**–28
abrir la puerta **169**–F
abrir los regalos **169**–L
abrocharse el cinturón de
   seguridad **111**–I
abuela **24**–2
abuelo **24**–3
abuelos **24**–1
aburrido(a) **31**–26
acatar las leyes **116**–H
accesorios **68**–**69**, **151**–17
accesorios para aspiradora **47**–14
accidente aéreo **102**–3
accidente automovilístico **102**–2
acebo **128**–19
aceite **55**–49, **109**–55
acera **91**–26
acetona **77**–32
acondicionador **76**–10
acordeón **120**–**121**
acortar **73**–D
acostarse **27**–X
acta de nacimiento **29**–1
actor **136**–2
actriz **136**–2
actuar **163**–G
acuarelas **163**–25
acusado **99**–5
adaptador **164**–17
adelantar **165**–C
aderezo **60**–18
adhesivo **83**–5
adolescentes **22**–6
adolorido(a) **30**–12
adorno **168**–19
aduana **110**–20
adultos **22**–9
aerograma **96**–13
aeromoza **110**–13
aeropuerto **110**
afeitarse **77**–M
África **125**–5

afueras **34**–2
agacharse **157**–R
agallas **130**–2
agarraderas **59**–29
agencia de viajes **92**–9
agenda **143**–27
agente aduanal **110**–21
agente de viajes **139**–60
agosto **19**–32
agradecer a su amigo **8**–H
agrandar **73**–C
agricultor **148**–15
agricultura **148**
agua **155**–1
agua caliente **43**–5
agua en botella **55**–53
agua fría **43**–7
agua oxigenada **83**–8
aguacates **50**–14
aguantar **94**–B
águila **132**–10
aguja **73**–22, **128**–12
agujas de tejer **163**–18
ahogarse **82**–I
ahorrar agua **126**–B
ahorrar energía **126**–C
aire acondicionado **37**–19, **108**–28
aislamiento **149**–19
ajedrez **162**–6
ajíes **51**–8
ajo **51**–29
al lado de **13**–1, **13**–2
al otro lado del agua **105**–3
ala(s) **132**–2, **52**–20
alambre **151**–13
albañil **136**–9
albaricoques **50**–7
alberca **37**–16, **145**–16
albornoz **66**–25
álbum de fotografías **165**–32
alcachofas **51**–20
alcaldía **89**–17
alce **134**–1
alergias **79**–8
aleta **130**–1
aletas **155**–2
alfabeto **3**–30
alfalfa **148**–5
alfiler **69**–36, **73**–14
alfiler de seguridad **73**–24
alfileres para pañales **95**–22
alfiletero **73**–15
alfombra **42**–27, **44**–23
alfombra de goma **43**–3
alfombrilla para baño **43**–27
álgebra **118**–25
algodón **70**–16, **148**–6
alguacil **99**–13
alicates **150**–7
alicates pelacables **151**–37
alimentar **148**–D
alimento para bebé **95**–28
alistarse en el ejército **28**–F
aliviado(a) **30**–16
almacén **146**–9
almejas **53**–28

almidón para rociar **72**–12
almohada **44**–9
almohadilla de tinta **143**–41
alquilando un apartamento **35**
alquilar un apartamento **28**–I
altavoces **164**–11
altiplano de México **123**–15
alto(a) **22**–16
altura **15**–14
ama de casa **137**–32
ama de llaves **138**–33, **145**–15
amalgama **84**–22
amamantar **94**–C
amarillo **12**–12
ambigú **33**–13
América del Norte **122**–**123**
América del Sur **124**–2
ampolla **78**–15
añada las legumbres y las
   hortalizas **58**–Q
añadir el detergente **72**–B
analgésico **81**–16
anaranjado **12**–6
ancho **15**–15
anciana **22**–12
anciano **22**–12
andadera **80**–5
andador **95**–12
andamiaje **149**–4
andar en bicicleta **91**–E
anémona de mar **130**–21
anestesiólogo **87**–35
anfibios **130**–**131**
anfitriona **62**–1
anguila **130**–5
ángulo **118**–24
anillo **69**–39
anillo de dentición **95**–30
animales **152**–2
animales de la granja **133**
animales de peluche **45**–23
animales domésticos **133**
aniversario **19**–42
año **4**–16, **18**–8
anochecer **17**–19
anotar los resultados **119**–C
Antártida **125**–7
antena de tele **38**–22
antiácido **81**–18
antifaz **168**–12
antílope **135**–35
antiparras **147**–10
anunciador **152**–27
apagar las velas **169**–K
aparador **69**–7
aparatos de gimnasia **153**–14
apartamentos **36**–**37**
apellido **4**–4
apio **51**–9
aplaudir **32**–B
aplicación **144**–21
apósito estéril **83**–4
apóstrofo **113**–11
aprender a manejar **28**–E
apretado(s) **71**–43
apto. # **4**–6

Index

arácnidos **132**
araña **132**–30
arándanos **50**–19
arandela **150**–32
árbitro **158**–6
árbol de las pulgas **128**–23
árbol de Navidad **168**–20
árboles **128**
arbusto **39**–20
arce **128**–13
archivar documentos **142**–H
archivero **142**–10
archivista **142**–12
arco **161**–6
ardilla **133**–21
ardilla listada **133**–20
área rural **34**–4
área urbana **34**–1
arena **155**–23
aretes **69**–37, **69**–38
armadillo **134**–8
arquitecto **136**–4
arranque **108**–25
arrastrar el cochecito **153**–A
arreglar los muebles **35**–K
arreglar una caries **85**–L
arreglos **73**
arrendador **37**–32
arrendajo azul **132**–7
arrendatario **37**–33
arrestar a un sospechoso **99**–A
arrojar **156**–D
arroz **54**–28, **148**–1
arrugada **72**–19
arte **121**–1
arteria **75**–43
artes industriales **121**–10
artes marciales **159**–10
artes teatrales **121**–12
artículos de limpieza **47**
artista **136**–5
artista gráfico **137**–29
asalto **100**–7
asar **58**–U
asar a la brasa **58**–V
ascensor **37**–34
asesinato **100**–8
asfixiarse **82**–L, **82**–N
Asia **125**–4
asiento **2**–7, **152**–11
asiento de seguridad para el
    automóvil **95**–13
asiento delantero **109**–35
asiento para niños **109**–39
asiento trasero **109**–38
asistente administrativo **136**–3
asistente del hospital **87**–18
asistente dental **137**–19
asma **79**–11
aspiradora **47**–13
aspirar la alfombra **46**–I
astronauta **127**–17
astrónomo **127**–20
asumir la propiedad **35**–J
asustado(a) **31**–24
atajar **156**–M

ataque **100**–5
atar los cordones de los zapatos **94**–I
atención médica **80**–81
atender a los clientes **140**–O
aterrizar **111**–O
atlas **98**–3
atletismo **159**–17
átomo **119**–17
atractivo(a) **22**–23, **22**–24
atragantarse **82**–L
atrapar **156**–E
atún **54**–25, **130**–9
audífono **81**–33
audífonos **164**–16
audiólogo **81**–32
auditorio **5**–3
auricular **9**–2
Australia **125**–6
auto **55**, **109**–54, **109**–57
autobús **90**–15, **104**–4
automóvil deportivo **106**–6
automóvil grande **106**–4
automóvil mediano **106**–3
automóviles **106**
autor **98**–22, **139**–64
autora **98**–22
aventar **156**–D
avergonzado(a) **31**–25
aves de corral **52**
avión **110**–9
avispa **132**–18
ayer **18**–17
ayudante del camarero **63**–9
ayudante del dentista **84**–19
ayudar a los pacientes **140**–B
ayude a su compañero **6**–J
azadón de pico **149**–20
azafata **110**–13
azafrán **129**–25
azúcar **55**–48, **60**–21
azúcar morena **57**–8
azucarera **41**–12
azucena **129**–24
azul **12**–1
azul claro **12**–3
azul oscuro **12**–2
azul turquesa **12**–4
azulejo **43**–9
babero **95**–8
bacalao **130**–8
bacinica **95**–10
bacinilla **86**–13
bagre **53**–17
bahía **17**–9
bailar **33**–J
bajarle **73**–C
bajo **120**–10
bajo(a) **22**–18
balance **97**–11
balanza **43**–26, **119**–11
balcón **37**–17
balde **47**–20
ballena **131**–29
ballet **166**–7
balompié **158**–12
balón de balompié **161**–12

balón de fútbol **161**–12
balón de fútbol americano **161**–22
baloncesto **158**–8
bañarse **76**–A, **76**–B
banca **153**–10
banco **88**–3, **97**
bancos para almorzar **5**–5
banda de rock **120**–2
bandeja **41**–10, **87**–23
bandeja apilable **142**–5
bandeja de pintura **151**–45
bandeja para asar **59**–13
bandeja para diapositivas **165**–30
bandera **33**–15, **168**–9
bañera **43**–2
bañista **155**–17
baño **43**
baños **5**–8, **43**
banqueta **91**–26
barato **11**–20
barba **23**–6
barbería **88**–15
barbilla **74**–31
barco de transbordo **104**–23
barra **46**–O
barra de caramelo **55**–41
barra de ensaladas **60**–16
barrena **150**–23
barrer el piso **46**–E
báscula **43**–26, **84**–7
base **77**–40
bastón **80**–7
bastones de esquí **161**–25
bata bien **58**–B
bata de baño **67**–8
bata de cirujano **87**–32
bata de hospital **86**–15
bata de playa **66**–25
batatas **51**–22
bate de béisbol **161**–14
batería **109**–43, **109**–58, **120**–18
batidor **59**–21
batidor de huevos **59**–20
batidora eléctrica **40**–25
baúl **109**–49
baúl para juguetes **45**–24
bayas **128**–20
bazar **152**–22
bebé **22**–2
bebedero **153**–11
beber **60**–B
bebidas **55**–15
beige **12**–9
béisbol **158**–9
berenjenas **51**–18
besar **33**–F
betabeles **51**–6
biberón **95**–26
biblioteca **5**–6, **89**–28, **98**
bibliotecario **98**–17
bibliotecario de información **98**–1
bicicleta **153**–4
bien **30**–15
bigote **23**–5
bigotes **134**–18
billar **159**–2

billete **104**–14
billete de transbordo **104**–6
billetera **69**–26, **101**–D
billetes **20**
biología **119**–1
birrete **32**–3
bisonte **134**–6
bistec **52**–2, **61**–13
bistec de salmón **53**–19
bizcocho **54**–32
blanco **12**–14, **161**–8
blanda **11**–6
block de notas con hojas
    adhesivas **143**–34
bloque de pilas secas **165**–22
bloques **45**–15
blusa **64**–9
blusón **65**–22
boca **74**–22
boca de incendio **91**–28
bocina **108**–24
bocinas **164**–11
bodega **146**–9
bola **161**–3
bola de baloncesto **161**–4
bola de boliche **161**–5
bola de señalización **144**–15
boleto **104**–12, **104**–14
boliche **159**–3
bolígrafo **3**–18
bolsa **56**–7, **69**–29, **135**–50
bolsa de aire **108**–16
bolsa de colgar **69**–27
bolsa de harina **56**–19
bolsa de hielo **83**–13
bolsa de papel **55**–22
bolsa para aspiradora **47**–15
bolsa para mareos **110**–15
bolsa plástica **55**–23
bolsas para basura **47**–12
bolsillo **73**–4
bombero **102**–8, **137**–24
bombilla **42**–4
bordado **163**–19
borde de la acera **90**–10
borde de la banqueta **90**–10
borrador para pizarra **3**–17
borre la pizarra **2**–H
bosque **117**–11
bosque húmedo **117**–1
bota de protección **147**–20
botanas **55**–16
botas **68**–18
botas de esquí **161**–26
botas para excursión **68**–21
botas para la lluvia **66**–19
botella **56**–1
botella de refresco **56**–13
botica **90**–1
botiquín **43**–19
botón **73**–21, **86**–10
botones **145**–5
bóveda **97**–2
box spring **44**–26
boxers **67**–12
braguitas de entrenamiento **95**–24

brazalete **69**–35
brazalete para casos de emergencias
    médicas **83**–14
brazo **74**–9
brigadas de búsqueda y rescate **103**–17
brincar **156**–J
brindar **33**–I
brocha **151**–47
broche **76**–18
broche y corchete **73**–23
brócoli **51**–15
buceo con escafandra **160**–12
bueno **11**–17
búfalo **134**–6
bufanda de lana **66**–4
bufet **33**–13
búho **132**–6
bulbo **129**–9
buriladora **150**–12
burro **133**–2
buscando casa **35**
buscapersonas **9**–16
buscar en los anuncios
    clasificados **141**–D
buscar la salida de emergencia **111**–J
buscar su asiento **111**–G
buscar un letrero de "se solicita
    ayuda" **141**–C
buscar un nuevo apartamento **35**–A
busque una palabra **6**–A
butaca **42**–24
buzón **38**–4, **90**–12
buzones **37**–36
cabalgar **157**–W
caballete **163**–21
caballo **133**–4
caballo de mar **130**–23
cabecera **44**–15
cabello **74**–19
cabello a la altura de los hombros **23**–2
cabello castaño **23**–17
cabello corto **23**–1
cabello largo **23**–3
cabello liso **23**–9
cabello negro **23**–15
cabello ondulado **23**–10
cabello rizado **23**–11
cabello rubio **23**–16
cabestrillo **80**–8
cabeza **74**–1
cabezal de la ducha **43**–10
cabina **106**–16
cabina del piloto **110**–11
cable **9**–3, **144**–16
cables para pasar corriente **109**–52
cabra **133**–1
cacerola **40**–16, **59**–6
cacerola a vapor **59**–4
cacerola doble **59**–8
cachar **156**–E
cachemira **70**–13
cachete **74**–29
cachorro **133**–12
cacillo **59**–25
cactus **128**–21
cadena **69**–31, **150**–36

cadena de montaje **146**–8
cadena para puerta **37**–28
cadera **74**–5
caerse **82**–O
café **12**–11, **61**–22
café descafeinado **61**–23
café instantáneo **55**–51
cafetera **40**–11
cafetería **5**–4, **88**–2
cafetín **5**–4
caimán **131**–36
caja **55**–17, **56**–6
caja de cereal **56**–18
caja de fusibles **48**–13
caja de seguridad **97**–13
caja registradora **55**–18
caja toráxica **75**–53
cajera **55**–19, **136**–14
cajero **55**–19, **97**–1
cajero automático **97**–3
cajón **40**–23, **44**–3
cajón de arena **153**–15
cajuela **109**–49
calabacín **51**–4
calabacita **51**–4
calabaza **51**–13
calamar **130**–10
calcetines **67**–15
calcetines hasta la rodilla **67**–25
calculadora **142**–8
cálculo **118**–28
caldera...estropeada **49**–15
calendario **18**–19
calendario para escritorio **142**–6
calentador **108**–29
calentador de agua...no funciona **48**–1
cálido **10**–1
caliente **10**–1
calle **90**–9
calle sin salida **107**–8
callejón **37**–21
callejón sin salida **107**–8
calles de la ciudad **88**–89
calvo **23**–12
calzoncillos **67**–13
calzoncitos de hule **95**–24
cama **44**–8
cama de hospital **86**–11
cámara **165**–24
Cámara de Representantes **116**–1
cámara de video **165**–19
cámara de video y audio **165**–21
camarera **62**–4, **63**–6
camarero **62**–4
camarón **53**–24, **130**–19
cambiar **21**–G
cambiar las sábanas **46**–P
cambiar los pañales **94**–E
cambie su dieta **80**–C
cambio **21**–9
camello **135**–38
camilla **87**–28
camillero **87**–18
caminar **156**–A
caminata **154**–6
camine con un amigo **101**–A

caminito **38**–14
camino para bicicletas **153**–2
camión **90**–15
camión de bomberos **102**–9
camión de la basura **91**–27
camión de mudanza **106**–14
camión de volteo **106**–12
camión semirremolque **106**–15
camionero **139**–61
camiones **106**
camioneta **106**–7, **106**–8
camioneta de servicio **106**–9
camisa **64**–4
camisa de dormir **67**–9
camisa deportiva **65**–26
camiseta **64**–12, **65**–20, **67**–2, **67**–10
camisola **67**–21
camisón **67**–5, **67**–9
campamento **154**–1
cámper **106**–11
campo **5**–12, **34**–4, **148**–7
campo de béisbol **153**–1
caña de pescar **154**–18
Canadá del Norte **123**–1
canal **38**–19
canalón **38**–19
canas **23**–13
canasta **54**–7
cáncer del cerebro **79**–12
cancha de baloncesto **158**–7
cancha de tenis **153**–7
candelero **41**–8
cangrejo **53**–22, **130**–16
canguro **135**–44
cañón **117**–17
cansado(a) **31**–33
cantar "las mañanitas" **169**–I
cantar una canción **120**–B
cantimplora **154**–24
capitán de botones **145**–4
capó **108**–6
capota **108**–6
cápsula **81**–27
cápsula de Petri **119**–6
capullo **129**–6
cara **74**
caracol **130**–24, **155**–21
carbón **126**–4
cardenal **78**–12
cardinales **14**
cardiólogo **86**–3
careta **168**–12
careta de buzo **155**–3
careta del receptor **161**–15
cargador **95**–14
cargador de pilas **165**–23
cargar la lavadora **72**–C
caries **84**–20
carnaval **152**–16
carne **52**
carne de cerdo **52**
carne de cordero **52**
carne de res **52**
carne en conserva **53**–8
carne molida **52**–4
carne para guisar **52**–3

carnicero **136**–11
caro **11**–19
carpa dorada **133**–16
carpeta **3**–24
carpeta de archivos **142**–11
carpintero **48**–12, **136**–13
carrera de fondo **160**–3
carrete de hilo **73**–17
carretilla **39**–16
carretilla de mano **146**–11
carrito **54**–3, **91**–31
carrito de la limpieza **145**–14
carrito de maletas **145**–6
carrusel **110**–18
carta **96**–2
cartapacio para escritorio **142**–7
cartelera **3**–14
carteras **69**–6
cartero **96**–6
cartón **56**–4
cartón de huevos **56**–16
cartucho **162**–2
casa **34**–6, **38**
Casa Blanca **116**–5
casa de muñecas **45**–14
casa móvil **34**–8
casa rodante **34**–8
casados **25**–23
casados nuevamente **25**–27
casarse **28**–L
cascada **117**–2
casco de fútbol americano **161**–20
casco protector **147**–19
caseta **152**–23
caseta de información **93**–22
casete **98**–12
casilla **94**–4
castillo de arena **155**–10
castor **134**–9
casual **71**–37
catarata **117**–2
catarinita **132**–27
catorce **14**
CD ("compact disk") **98**–14
cebollas **51**–28
cebollitas **51**–17
cebra **135**–34
cecina **53**–8
ceja **74**–32
cemento **149**–10
cemento de goma **143**–38
cenar **27**–R
ceñido(s) **71**–43
centavo **20**–1
centímetro **15**–12
centro comercial **92**–93
centro de copias **91**–22
centro de enseñanza preescolar **112**–4
Centroamérica **122**–123
cepillarse los dientes **77**–J
cepillarse…el cabello **76**–I
cepillo **23**–18, **76**–14, **151**–52
cepillo de dientes **43**–20, **77**–20
cepillo de fregar **47**–19
cepillo de frotar **47**–19
cepillo para el inodoro **43**–16

cera para muebles **47**–18
cerca **38**–3, **148**–19
cerdo **133**–8
cerebro **75**–35
cerezas **50**–16
cerezo silvestre **128**–16
cerillos **154**–21
cero **14**
cerradura…estropeada **48**–6
cerrajero **48**–11
cerrojo de seguridad **37**–29
certificado de naturalización **29**–6
césped **39**–21
cesta **42**–2
cesta para el pan **63**–8
cesta para la ropa **43**–1
cesto para la ropa sucia **72**–2
cesto para pañales **95**–23
chaleco **65**–24
chaleco de protección **147**–15
chaleco relleno con plumas **66**–13
chaleco salvavidas **154**–14, **150**–24
chalinas de seda **68**–4
chamaca **66**–7
champú **76**–9
chaqueta **66**–7
chaqueta de cuero **66**–3
chaqueta deportiva **64**–6
chaqueta rellena con plumas **66**–15
charca **117**–21
charola **41**–10
charola de los postres **63**–7
charola para medicamentos **87**–23
chef **63**–11
cheque de viajero **20**–17
cheque personal **20**–14
chequera **97**–7
chícharos **51**–19
chicle **55**–42
chiles **51**–8
chimenea **38**–21, **42**–9
chimpancé **135**–28
chistoso **167**–27
choclos **68**–20
chofer de autobús **104**–8
chofer de taxi **104**–20
choque **82**–C
chuletas de cerdo **52**–10
chuletas de cordero **52**–15
chuletas de ternera **52**–6
chupete **95**–29
chupón **95**–27, **95**–29
ciclismo **159**–4
ciclismo de montañas **154**–8
ciclista **153**–3
ciego(a) **22**–26
cien **14**
cien dólares **20**–12
cien mil **14**
cien por ciento **15**–11
ciencias **119**
ciencias de la computación **121**–4
ciencias domésticas **121**–9
ciento uno **14**
cierre **73**–16
cierre el libro **2**–J

cierre estropeado **70**–24
cierre las puertas con llave **101**–E
cilindro **118**–12
cilindro graduado **119**–10
cima de la montaña **117**–14
cincel **151**–51
cinco **14**
cinco centavos **20**–2
cinco dólares **20**–8
cinco formas de cocinar pollo **58**
cinco para las dos **16**–15
cincuenta **14**
cincuenta dólares **20**–11
cincuenta por ciento **15**–9
cine **88**–11, **152**–10
cinta adhesiva para empacar **143**–42
cinta adhesiva para proteger
    bordes **151**–49
cinta adhesiva transparente **143**–39
cinta aislante **151**–38
cinta de aislar **151**–38
cinta de audio **98**–12
cinta de video **98**–13
cinta métrica **73**–13, **150**–22
cinta para máquina de escribir **143**–31
cinta transportadora **146**–12
cintura **74**–4
cinturón **73**–3
cinturón de hombro **109**–37
cinturón de seguridad **109**–36
cinturones **69**–11
círculo **118**–5
circunferencia **118**–15
ciruelas **50**–8
ciruelas pasas **50**–26
cirujano **87**–30
cita **19**–45
ciudad **4**–7, **34**–1
ciudadanía **116**
clarinete **120**–4
clavel **129**–18
clavelón **129**–13
clavo **150**–29, **150**–30
claxon **108**–24
cliente **62**–5
clínica **84, 87**–20
clínica odontológica **84**
clínicas **84**
clip **143**–44
cloro **72**–8
clóset **44**–4
clutch **109**–45
cobija **44**–12 **67**–7
cobra **131**–40,
cochecito **94**–2, **95**–16
cochera **89**–26
cochino **133**–8
cocina **40, 40**–18, **63**–10
cocina de campamento **154**–16
cocinar **140**–C
cocinar a la parrilla **58**–T
cocine a fuego lento durante una
    hora **58**–R
cocine el brócoli al vapor **58**–I
cocine hasta que estén listos **58**–F
cocinera **137**–17

cocodrilo **131**–37
cocos **50**–22
código de área **4**–10
código de barra **21**–4
código postal **4**–9
codo **74**–15
cojín **42**–20
col **51**–2
cola **55**–20, **134**–22
coladera **59**–22
colcha **44**–11, **45**–2
colchón **44**–25
colección de estampillas **162**–12
colección de monedas **162**–13
colección de timbres **162**–12
coleccionar **162**–A
colegio de enseñanza superior **112**–10
colegio parroquial **112**–3
colgar la ropa **72**–H
colibrí **132**–11
coliflor **51**–16
colinas **117**–16
collar de perlas **69**–30
collares **69**–9
colmillo **135**–48
colocar ladrillos **149**–B
Colombia Británica **123**–2
colonia **76**–5
color naranja **12**–6
colores **12**
colorete **77**–36
Columbia Británica **123**–2
columna vertebral **75**–54
columpios **153**–12
coma **113**–10
comedia **166**–5, **166**–10
comedia de situaciones **167**–18
comedor **41, 62**–2
comejenes **49**–22
comentar sobre su experiencia **141**–I
comenzar **157**–X
comer **60**–A
comestibles preparados **53**
cometa **127**–25
comida congelada **55**–12
comida envasada **56**
comida para mascotas **54**–10
comida rápida **60**
comillas **113**–9
comisaría **89**–19
cómoda **44**–2, **45**–8
cómodo(a) **30**–7
compacto **106**–2
comparecer ante el tribunal **99**–C
comparta un libro **6**–I
compartimiento para el equipaje de
    mano **110**–10
competir en una carrera **157**–Y
composición **113**–2
composición en inglés **113**
comprando una casa **35**
comprar **21**–C
comprar el boleto **111**–A
comprar una casa **29**–O
comprobante de depósito **97**–12
computadora **3**–15

computadora portátil **144**–14
computadoras **144**
con diseño de cuadros **70**–9
con esmog **10**–14
con flores **70**–12
con lunares **70**–8
con problemas auditivos **22**–27
con viento **10**–10
concesionaria de autos **88**–4
concha **155**–21
concierto **166**–6
condenado **99**–14
conducir al trabajo **26**–I
conducir un camión **140**–E
conducto para basura **37**–24
conductor **104**–16
conejillo de Indias **133**–14
conejo **133**–13
confeti **168**–3
confundido(a) **31**–27
congelador **40**–10
congestión nasal **78**–7
congresista **116**–2
conmutador **144**–4
cono **118**–11, **128**–11
conseguir empleo **28**–G
consejero **5**–16
conserje **36**–12, **138**–35
conservación **126**–16
conservar agua **126**–B
conservar energía **126**–C
constelación **127**–24
construcción **149**
construir **162**–C
contadora **136**–I
contaminación **126**
contaminación del agua **126**–12
contaminación del aire **126**–10
contento(a) **31**–32
contestadora **9**–14
conteste una pregunta **6**–H
continentes **124**
contorneador **150**–12
contrachapada **149**–16
contrapuerta **38**–12
contratar a un abogado **99**–B
control para la cama **86**–12
control remoto **164**–9
conversación diaria **8**
convertible **106**–5
convertir **57**–C
convertirse en ciudadano **28**–H
convidar a los invitados **169**–B
copa de vino **63**–20
copie la palabra **6**–F
corazón **75**–38, **168**–6
corazones **163**–29
corbata ancha **71**–44
corbata de moño **69**–40
corbata estrecha **71**–45
corbatas **69**–10
cordillera **117**–15
cordón **68**–14
cordón prolongador **151**–14
cornamenta del ciervo **134**–16
cornejo **128**–16

Index

corno **120**–13
corno francés **120**–15
coro **121**–3
corpulento(a) **22**–20
corral **148**–17
corralito **95**–11
correas **69**–11
correo certificado **96**–11
correo expreso **96**–15
correo prioritario **96**–12
correo urgente **96**–15
correr **156**–C
corrija el error **7**–Z
corrija su ensayo **113**–B
corrosivo **147**–4
corta **71**–35
cortada **78**–13
cortadora de césped **39**–22
cortapapeles **143**–15
cortar el cabello **23**–A
cortar el césped **39**–C
cortarse las uñas **77**–N
cortauñas **77**–29
corte el pollo **58**–M
corte las cebollas **58**–G
Corte Suprema **116**–8
cortinas **42**–16, **44**–5
cosechar **148**–B
coser a mano **73**–A
coser a máquina **73**–B
coser ropa **140**–I
costa oeste **123**–7
costillas de res **52**–5
costo **21**–6
costura **73**, **73**–11
cotejar documentos **142**–F
coyote **134**–3
cráneo **75**–52
crema agria **54**–37
crema antihistamínica **83**–10
crema de afeitar **77**–27
crema humectante **76**–8
crema para el cuerpo **76**–7
creyones **45**–21
crin **135**–49
crisantemo **129**–19
cronómetro de cocina **59**–18
cruce del ferrocarril **107**–11
cruce escolar **107**–13
cruce peatonal **90**–8, **107**–10
cruzar la calle **90**–A
cuaderno **3**–24
cuaderno de espiral **3**–26
cuaderno de tamaño legal **143**–18
cuaderno de trabajo **3**–23
cuadra **107**–2
cuadrado **118**–6
cuadro **42**–7
cuarenta **14**
cuarto **14**
cuarto de galón de leche **57**–4
cuarto de lavado **63**–12
cuarto menguante **127**–15
cuarto para las dos **16**–13
cuarto piso **36**–4
cuatro **14**

cuatro de julio **168**–7
cubeta **47**–20
cubierto **63**–14
cubo **47**–20, **118**–10, **155**–22
cubrecama **44**–11
cucaracha(s) **49**–25
cuchara **41**–23
cuchara de madera **59**–9
cuchara para sopa **63**–29
cucharada de azúcar **57**–7
cucharadita de sal **57**–6
cucharita **63**–28
cucharón **59**–7
cuchilla **150**–11
cuchillo **41**–22, **63**–27
cuchillo de pelar **59**–16
cuchillo de trinchar **59**–12
cuchillo multiusos **154**–20
cuchillo para carne **63**–26
cuelgue el auricular **9**–F
cuello **73**–7, **74**–2
cuello de tortuga **64**–7
cuentas **69**–32
cuento de acción **166**–13
cuento de aventuras **166**–13
cuento de ciencia ficción **166**–12
cuento de horror **166**–14
cuerda **72**–9, **154**–19
cuerda para saltar **153**–5
cuerno **134**–21
cuero **70**–18
cuerpo **74**–75
cuidadoso **147**–24
cuidar niños **140**–L
culebra americana no venenosa **131**–39
cultivador **148**–15
cumpleaños **19**–41
cuna **45**–6
cuna mecedora **45**–19
cuñada **24**–15
cuñado **24**–16
cursos de manejo **121**–5
curva **118**–19
dados **162**–4
damas **162**–5
dar **21**–D
dar de comer **94**–D
dar un discurso **32**–E
dar vuelta a la derecha **108**–4, **108**–18
dar vuelta a la izquierda **107**–B
darse una ducha **76**–A
dátiles **50**–25
datos personales **4**
de compras **21**
de figuras **160**–5
de seis **56**–9
debajo **13**–9
debajo de **13**–7
debajo del puente **105**–1
décimo **14**
decimoctavo **14**
decimocuarto **14**
decimonoveno **14**
decimoprimero **14**
decimoquinto **14**
decimosegundo **14**

decimoséptimo **14**
decimosexto **14**
decimotercero **14**
declaración de aduana **110**–22
decorar la casa **169**–C
dedal **73**–20
dedo del pie **75**–63
dedo hinchado **78**–16
dedos **75**–57
defensa **108**–7
dejar **94**–A
dejar una propina **62**–J
deje un mensaje **9**–E
deletree la palabra **6**–E
deletree su nombre **4**–A
delfín **131**–30
delgado **11**–8
delgado(a) **22**–22
delincuencia **100**
delineador (de ojos) **77**–35
demasiado grande **70**–21
demasiado pequeño **70**–20
dentista **84**–18, **137**–20
dentro de **13**–5
dentro del cuerpo **75**
denuncie los delitos a la policía **101**–H
departamento de zapatos **68**–3
dependiente **139**–50
dependiente de la gasolinera **137**–28
dependiente encargado del despacho
    de mercadería **146**–15
deporte de la patineta **159**–12
deporte de la tabla hawaiana **160**–9
deportes acuáticos **160**
deportes de invierno **160**
deportes en equipo **158**
deportes individuales **159**
deposite monedas **9**–C
depósito de almacenamiento **36**–14
depósito de basura **37**–20
derechos y responsabilidades **116**
derrame de petróleo **126**–15
derrumbe **102**–6
desagüe **43**–4
desastres naturales **102**–103
desayunar **26**–E
descansar **27**–U
descapotable **106**–5
descargar la secadora **72**–E
descosido **70**–23
describiendo objetos **11**
descripción de la ropa **70**–71
descripción del cabello **23**
descripción física **22**
descuidado **147**–23
desechos peligrosos **126**–9
desempacar **35**–E
desfile **168**–2
desierto **117**–4
desinfectante **95**–19
desodorante **76**–4
desordenado **11**–16
despachar **146**–C
despegar **111**–L
despejado **10**–6
despertarse **26**–A

desplantador **39**–14
destornillador **150**–25
destornillador de estrella **150**–26
destrezas laborales **140**
detector de humo **37**–25, **45**–11
detener **165**–F
detenerse **107**–3
detergente para ropa **72**–7
detrás de **13**–3
devolución de botellas **54**–1
devolver **21**–F
día **4**–16, **18**–10
Día de Acción de Gracias **168**–15
Día de Año Nuevo **168**–1
día de fiesta oficial **19**–43
Día de la Independencia **168**–7
Día de las Brujas **168**–10
Día de los Enamorados **168**–4
día feriado legal **19**–43
diabetes **79**–9
diagonal **118**–23
diamantes **163**–27
diámetro **118**–17
diapositivas **165**–31
días de la semana **18**, **18**–12
días feriados **168**
dibujo animado **167**–19
diccionario **3**–28
diccionario gráfico **3**–29
diciembre **19**–36
dicte una oración **6**–N
diecinueve **14**
dieciocho **14**
dieciséis **14**
diecisiete **14**
dientes **74**–25
dietista **87**–25
diez **14**
diez centavos **20**–3
diez dólares **20**–9
diez mil **14**
diez para las dos **16**–14
diez por ciento **15**–7
difícil **11**–24
diga la palabra **6**–C
dimensiones **15**
dinero **20**
diploma **29**–2, **32**–7
diploma universitario **29**–7
dirección **4**–5, **146**–1
dirección del destinatario **96**–8
direccional **113**–E
direcciones **107**
director **5**–14
directorio **93**–19
directorio telefónico **9**–15
disco **98**–15, **144**–5
disco CD–ROM **144**–2
disco flexible **144**–5
disco volador **159**–6, **161**–27
disculparse **8**–I
discuta la lista **6**–L
diseñador **146**–3
diseñar **146**–A
diseños **70**
disfraz **168**–13

disparar **156**–I
dispositivo salvavidas **155**–19
distribuya las hojas **7**–O
división **118**–4
divorciados **25**–24
DJ (el disc jockey) **33**–17
dobladillo **73**–1
doblar la ropa **72**–F
doce **14**
doctor **84**–6, **137**–22
doctora en veterinaria **139**–62
dólar **20**–7
dólar de plata **20**–6
dolor de cabeza **78**–1
dolor de espalda **78**–5
dolor de estómago **78**–4
dolor de garganta **78**–6
dolor de muelas **78**–2
dolor de oído **78**–3
domingo **18**–1
dona **60**–15
dormirse **27**–Y
dormitorio **44**
dormitorio para niños **45**
dos **14**
dos puntos **113**–12
dos veces por semana **18**–23
driblar **156**–K
drogas ilegales **100**–4
ducharse **76**–A
dueña de tienda **139**–56
dueño **37**–32
dueño de la fábrica **146**–2
dulcería **92**–3
dulces **168**–14
duna **117**–5
dura **11**–5
duraznos **50**–5
echar clavados **157**–S
echar una siesta **94**–L
eche los huevos en la sartén **58**–D
economía **121**–6
economía doméstica **121**–9
edad **22**
edad avanzada **22**–15
edad media **22**–14
edificio de apartamentos **34**–5
edificio de oficinas **89**–24
edredón **45**–2
educación de negocios **121**–2
educación física **121**–11
edulcorante artificial **60**–22
efectivo **20**–13
ejotes **51**–25
elabore una lista de ideas **6**–K
electricista **48**–9
electrónica **164**–165
elefante **135**–42
elevador **37**–34
elevador de carga **146**–14
elipse **118**–9
embarazada **22**–19
embrague **109**–45
embudo **119**–12
emergencias **102**–103
emergencias médicas **82**

emitir el veredicto **99**–E
emocionado(a) **31**–23
empacador **146**–13
empezar a ir al colegio **28**–B
empleada de correos **138**–45
empleada de una fábrica de ropa **137**–27
empleada doméstica **137**–31
empleado **5**–18
empleado de almacén **139**–55
empleado de servicios de la higiene
    pública **139**–41
empleado de una casa de
    mudanzas **138**–40
empleado de una guardería **94**–3
empleos **136**–139
empujar el columpio **153**–B
en busca de trabajo **141**
en el taxi **105**–4
en frente de **13**–4
enamorado(a) **30**–19
enamorarse **28**–K
encargado de pedidos **146**–10
encargado del banquete **33**–12
encargado del zoológico **152**–3
encendedor **108**–32
encender las velas **169** H
enchufe **44**–20, **151**–41, **164**–18
encías **74**–24
enciclopedia **98**–18
encierre en un círculo la respuesta **7**–S
encima de **13**–6
energía **126**
energía geotérmica **126**–7
energía hidroeléctrica **126**–5
energía nuclear **126**–8
energía solar **126**–1
enero **19**–25
enfermedades **79**
enfermedades cardíacas **79**–14
enfermedades comunes **79**
enfermedades de la infancia **79**
enfermedades graves **79**
enfermera **84**–10, **138**–42
enfermera quirúrgica **87**–29
enfermera registrada **87**–22
enfermero **84**–10
enfermero con licencia práctica **87**–24
enfermero con licencia
    vocacional **87**–24
enfermo(a) **30**–14
engrapadora **143**–28
engrapar **142**–G
engrase la sartén **58**–C
engrudo **143**–37
enjuagarse...el cabello **76**–F
enjuague bucal **77**–23
enojado(a) **31**–29
enredadera **128**–22
ensalada de col fresca **53**–14
ensalada de papas **53**–13
ensalada de pasta **53**–15
ensalada del chef **61**–9
ensalada verde **60**–8
ensamblar componentes **140**–A
ensayo **113**–2
entrada del garaje **38**–5

Index

entre **13**–10
entregarla **96**–C
entregue su ensayo **107**–C
entrenador **158**–2
entrenar **157**–P
entretenimiento **166**–167
envase especial para remitir un objeto por correo **143**–32
envenenamiento con insecticidas **126**–14
envenenarse **82**–J
enviar una carta por fax **142**–B
enviarla **96**–B
envío por vía terrestre **96**–14
envolver un regalo **169**–D
equipo **158**–3
equipo de primeros auxilios **83**–1
equipo de sonido **42**–14
equipo deportivo **161**
equipo para trabajar en el campo **148**–10
equipo y accesorios **144**
equitación **154**–9
equivalencias **15**
erizo de mar **130**–20
erupción **78**–10
erupción volcánica **103**–14
escala tipográfica **84**–11
escalera **37**–26, **149**–2
escalera automática **93**–21
escaleras **37**–35
escaleras abajo **105**–8
escaleras arriba **105**–9
escalerilla **47**–7
escalofríos **78**–9
escalones **38**–13
escalones...rotos **48**–7
escalope **130**–18
escalopes **53**–25
escamas **130**–3
escarabajo **132**–19
escayola **81**–29
escenario **32**–4
escoba **47**–10
esconderse **169**–E
escorpión **132**–31
escriba en la pizarra **2**–G
escriba su clave en el teclado **97**–B
escriba su nombre **4**–C
escriba un primer borrador **113**–A
escribiente **99**–12
escribir a máquina **140**–M
escribir la dirección en una postal **96**–A
escribir una carta a máquina **142**–D
escritor **139**–64
escritorio **2**–6, **142**–1
escuchar el corazón **85**–D
escuche un casete **2**–C
escuela **5**, **89**–27, **112**–3
escuela de artes y oficios **112**–9
escuela intermedia **112**–6
escuela para adultos **112**–8
escuela primaria **112**–5
escuela privada **112**–2
escuela pública **112**–1
escuela secundaria **112**–7
escuela vocacional **112**–9
escultura **152**–9

escurridor **47**–9, **59**–17
escurridor de platos **40**–3
esfera **118**–14
esgrima **159**–5
esmalte de uñas **77**–31
esmog **126**–10
esmoquin **65**–28
esnórquel **160**–11
espacio **127**–22
espacio de estacionamiento **36**–15
espadas **163**–28
espaguetis **54**–27
espalda **74**–11
espárragos **51**–24
espátula **59**–19, **151**–48
especias **55**–46
espectáculo de marionetas **152**–14
espejo **43**–18, **44**–1
espejo lateral **108**–8
espejo retrovisor **108**–1
esperar a que cambie el semáforo **90**–B
espere el tono de marcar **9**–B
espina **129**–28
espinaca **51**–11
espinilleras **161**–13
esponja **47**–24
esponjas de lana de acero **47**–5
esposa **24**–20
esposas **99**–2
esposo **24**–19
esqueleto **75**
esquí a campo traviesa **160**–3
esquí acuático **160**–7
esquí de descenso **160**–1
esquiar **157**–U
esquíes **161**–24
esquina **91**–17, **107**–1
esta semana **18**–19
estación de bomberos **88**–1
estación de policía **89**–19
estación de trabajo con computadora **143**–21
estación del salvavidas **155**–20
estación del tren **104**–13
estación espacial **127**–18
estacionamiento **89**–26
estacionamiento para minusválidos **107**–14
estacionar el auto **91**–D
estacionar el coche **91**–D
estaciones **19**
estadio **152**–26
estado **4**–8
estado de cuenta mensual **97**–10
estados de ánimo y sentimientos **30**–31
estados de las Montañas Rocosas **123**–8
estados del centro del Atlántico **123**–10
estados del Pacífico **123**–7
estampado **70**–10
estampilla **96**–9
estanque **117**–21
estanque para patos **153**–6
estante **40**–8
estantería **42**–13
estar cansado(a) **30**–3
estar en la escuela **26**–J

estar en shock **82**–C
estar inconsciente **82**–B
estatura promedio **22**–17
estéreo **42**–14
estetoscopio **84**–8
estibador **137**–21
estirarse **157**–Q
estómago **75**–41
estornudar **78**–B
estrado **32**–4
estrella **127**–23
estrella de mar **130**–15
estuche para la cámara **165**–27
estuco **149**–14
estudiando **6**–7
estudiante **2**–3, **139**–57
estufa **40**–18
etiqueta **143**–35
etiqueta de advertencia **80**–15
etiqueta de la receta **80**–14
etiqueta del precio **21**–1
Europa **125**–3
eventos históricos **114**
eventos políticos **114**
evidencia **99**–9
examen de sangre **86**–17
examen sanguíneo **86**–17
exámenes dentales **85**
exámenes médicos **85**
examinar los ojos **85**–F
excursión **154**–6
exhibición **152**–21
experimentar turbulencias **111**–N
explorador **144**–13
explosión **102**–4
expuesto insuficientemente **165**–35
expulsar **165**–F
extensión **151**–14
extintor de incendios **147**–22
extra grande **70**–5
extra pequeño **70**–1
extraer un diente **85**–M
extraer una muela **85**–M
fábrica **146**
fabricar **146**–B
fácil **11**–23
fagot **120**–6,
faja **67**–18
falda **64**–10
falda abierta **65**–25
falta un botón **70**–25
familia **24**–25
fanático **158**–4
farmaceuta **80**–10
farmacéutico **80**–10
farmacia **80**–9, **90**–2
farol **91**–23
fauna marina **130**
fax **143**–23
fea **11**–22
febrero **19**–26
fecha **4**–16, **18**–14
fecha de nacimiento **4**–16
Feliz cumpleaños **169**–I
femenino **4**–14
feria de comida rápida **93**–14

feria del condado **152**–19
ferretería **88**–14
ferry **104**–23
festividad **168**–16
ficha **104**–11
fichero **142**–10
fichero de tarjetas **98**–10
fichero en computadora **98**–9
fiebre **78**–8
fiesta **169**
fiesta religiosa **19**–44
figuras geométricas **118**
figurilla **162**–10
filete **52**–2, **61**–13
filetes de lenguado **53**–21
fin de semana **18**–13
firma **4**–18
firmar un contrato de alquiler **35**–C
firme **4**–D
fiscal **99**–10
física **119**–3
fisioterapeuta **81**–30
flaco(a) **22**–22
flauta **120**–3
flecha **161**–7
fleco **23**–8
flequillo **23**–8
flor **39**–19, **129**–7
flor de Nochebuena **129**–23
florería **92**–12
florero **41**–9
flores **129**
florista **137**–25
floristería **92**–12
foca **131**–33
foco **42**–4
fogata **154**–11
fondo entero **67**–22
forma del seguro **84**–5
formal **71**–36
formas de pagar **20**
fórmula **95**–25, **119**–19
formulario de inscripción escolar **4**
fornido(a) **22**–20
fósforos **154**–21
fotocopiadora **142**–14
fotografía **44**–7, **164**–165
fotógrafo **32**–11
fracciones **15**
frambuesas **50**–18
frasco **56**–2
frasco de mermelada **56**–14
frazada **111**–M
fregadero **40**–6
fregador **40**–6
fregar el piso **46**–L
freír **58**–S
frenillos **84**–24
freno de mano **109**–44
frenos **84**–24
frente **74**–20
fresa **84**–21
fresas **50**–17
frijoles **54**–26
frijoles de soya **148**–3
frío **10**–4

frustrado(a) **31**–28
frutas **50**
fuego **42**–10
fuegos artificiales **168**–8
fuente **41**–6, **92**–11
fuente de agua **153**–11
fuera de foco **165**–33
fuera de la autopista **105**–7
fuera del taxi **105**–5
fumigador **49**–21
funda **44**–10
fútbol **158**–12
fútbol americano **158**–11
gabardina **66**–17
gabinete **40**–1
gabinete de artículos de oficina **142**–13
gabinete de baño **43**–19
gafas de seguridad **147**–10
gafas de sol **66**–21
gafas protectoras **147**–9
galaxia **127**–26
galletas dulces **54**–31
gallina **133**–5
gallo **133**–6
galón de jugo de manzana **57**–5
ganadería **148**
ganadero **148**–22
ganado **148**–13, **148**–21
gancho **72**–11, **150**–34
gancho de ojo **150**–35
ganso **132**–14
garaje **38**–6
gardenia **129**–16
garganta **75**–36
garra **132**–4, **134**–20
garrapata **132**–28
gas natural **126**–3
gasa **83**–6
gasolina **109**–54
gasolinera **88**–12
gatito **133**–10
gato **133**–9
gato hidráulico **109**–51
gaveta **40**–23, **44**–3
gavetero **45**–8
gel para el cabello **76**–11
geografía **117**
geometría **118**–26
gerente **54**–8
gimnasia **159**–8
gimnasio **5**–9, **89**–21
girar **157**–O
girasol **129**–10
giro postal **20**–16
gis **3**–16
globo terráqueo **3**–9
gobierno estadounidense **116**
golf **159**–7
goma de borrar **3**–21
goma de mascar **55**–42
gordo **11**–7
gorila **135**–30
gorra **66**–6
gorra de baño **76**–1
gorra de béisbol **66**–27
gorrión **132**–8

gorro de cirujano **87**–31
gorro para esquiar **66**–10
gotas para los ojos **81**–22
goteo intravenoso **87**–27
gotero **119**–14
grabadora **164**–3
grabar **165**–A
gradas **5**–10
graduación **32**–33
graduado **32**–6
graduandos **32**–1
graduarse **28**–D, **32**–A
grajo azul **132**–7
grande **11**–2, **70**–4
granizada **10**–18
granizo **10**–19
granja **34**–13, **148**–11
grapa **143**–29
grapadora **143**–28
grifo **43**–6, **49**–16
grillo **132**–24
gripe **79**–2
gris **12**–5
gritar "¡sorpresa!" **169**–G
grúa **106**–13, **149**–7
grúa alzacarro **149**–5
grueso **11**–7
guajolote **168**–17
guante **161**–17
guantera **108**–33
guantes **66**–9
guantes de goma **47**–4
guantes de látex **147**–17
guardar el equipaje de mano **111**–H
guardar los juguetes **46**–H
guarde el lápiz **2**–L
guardería infantil **94**–95
guardia **97**–4, **99**–3
guardián **138**–35
guía telefónica **9**–15
guillotina **143**–15
guisantes **51**–19
guitarra **120**–11
gusano **130**–22
habichuelas **54**–26
habitación de los huéspedes **145**–10
habitación del paciente **86**
hablar con el agente de bienes
   raíces **35**–G
hablar con el conserje **35**–B
hablar con los amigos **141**–A
hablar otro idioma **140**–J
hable con la maestra **2**–B
hable con sus compañeros **7**–P
hacer **85**–A, **85**–H
hacer artesanías **162**–D
hacer copias **142**–E
hacer creer **163**–G
hacer ejercicios **27**–W, **157**–P
hacer gárgara **77**–L
hacer la cama **46**–G
hacer la colada **72**
hacer la permanente **23**–B
hacer la tarea **27**–T
hacer labores manuales **140**–D
hacer más corto(a) **73**–D

Index

hacer más largo(a) **73**–C
hacer un cumplido a su amigo **8**–G
hacer un experimento **119**–A
hacer una comida campestre **153**–D
hacer una oferta **35**–H
hacha **150**–3
hacienda **34**–12
haga ejercicios **80**–D
haga un depósito **97**–C
haga un dibujo **6**–M
haga una pregunta **6**–G
hágase acupuntura **81**–G
halibut **53**–20
hamaca **39**–2
hamburguesa **60**–1
hamburguesa con queso **60**–3
harina **55**–45
hebilla del cinturón **69**–41
helado **10**–13, **55**–44
helicóptero **110**–8
hemorragia nasal **78**–17
heno **148**–18
herirse **82**–A
hermana **24**–8
hermanastra **25**–32
hermanastro **25**–33
hermano **24**–9
hermosa **11**–21
héroe de aventuras **163**–31
herramientas **150**–**151**
hibisco **129**–12
hiedra venenosa **128**–25
hielera **155**–11
hiena **135**–31
hierva el pollo **58**–P
hígado **52**–7, **75**–39
higiene personal **76**–**77**
higienista dental **84**–16
hija **24**–21
hijo **24**–22
hilo **163**–17
hilo dental **77**–22
hipertensión **79**–15
hipismo **159**–18
hipopótamo **135**–43
historia de los EE.UU. **114**–**115**
historia médica **87**–20
hockey sobre hielo **158**–13
hogar **42**–9
hogar de ancianos **34**–11
hogaza **56**–10
hogaza de pan **56**–22
hoguera **154**–11
hoja **59**–27, **128**–6, **129**–5
hoja de ingreso **97**–12
hoja de vidrio **149**–15
hojilla **77**–26
holgados **71**–42
hombre **22**–11
hombre de negocios **136**–10
hombreras **161**–21
hombro **74**–10
hongos **51**–26
hora **16**–3, **16**–17
hora de Alaska **17**–25
hora de Hawai–de las Aleutianas **17**–24

hora de montaña **17**–27
hora de Terranova **17**–31
hora de verano **17**–33
hora del Atlántico **17**–30
hora del centro **17**–28
hora del este **17**–29
hora del Pacífico **17**–26
hora estándar **17**–32
horario **104**–3
hormiga(s) **49**–24
hornee a 350° por 45 minutos **58**–L
hornilla **40**–19
horno **40**–20
horno microondas **40**–13
horno tostador **40**–15
horquillas **76**–19
hortaliza **148**–12
hospital **86**–**87**, **88**–7
hotel **88**–5, **145**
hoy **18**–15
huerta **148**–12
huerto **148**–16
hueso **75**–49
huésped **145**–11
huevos **54**–34
huevos revueltos **58**, **61**–1
húmeda **72**–17
húmedo **10**–12
humidificador **80**–2
huracán **103**–12
idioma extranjero **121**–8
iglesia **88**–6
imán **119**–21
impedido visual **22**–26
impedido(a) **22**–25
impermeable **66**–17
imprenta **91**–22
impresor **138**–46
impresora **144**–12
impuesto de ventas **21**–7
incaíbles **76**–19
incendio **102**–7
incómodo(a) **30**–8
industrial **112**–9
infección de la garganta **79**–4
infección en el oído **79**–3
inflamable **147**–2
inflar **109**–59
informal **71**–37
ingeniero **137**–23
inglés como segundo idioma **121**–7
inicial segundo nombre **4**–3
iniciar una conversación **8**–B
inmigración **114**
inmigrar **28**–C
inodoro **43**–17
inodoro...tapado **43**–15
inquilino **37**–33
inscribirse en el ejército **116**–F
insectos **132**
instructora **139**–58
intercomunicador **36**–8
internista **86**–2
intérprete **138**–34
interruptor de la luz **44**–19
intersección **90**–**91**

intestinos **75**–42
introduzca la tarjeta de cajero automático **97**–A
inundación **103**–16
invernadero **152**–5
invierno **19**–40
invitados **33**–14
invitar **169**–B
inyectar anestésico **85**–J
inyéctese **80**–E
ir a la cárcel **99**–G
ir a la universidad **28**–J
ir a prisión **99**–G
ir a una entrevista **141**–H
ir al mercado **26**–L
ir al trabajo **26**–I
ir de campamento **154**–7
ir de compras para **21**–A
ir derecho **107**–A
irse **111**–L
isla **117**–8
izquierda, a la **13**–1
jabón **43**–23, **76**–2
jabonera **43**–24
jamón **52**–9
jarabe **61**–5
jarabe para la tos **81**–20
jardín **38**–15
jardín aéreo **36**–5
jardín de niños **112**–4
jardinero **137**–26, **152**–6
jardines botánicos **152**–4
jarretes de cordero **52**–13
jarro **41**–28
jazmín **129**–21
jefa de oficina **143**–25
jefe de comedor **62**–1
jeringa **84**–14
jirafa **135**–33
joroba **135**–51
joven **22**–13
joyería **69**–8, **92**–2
judías verde **51**–25
jueces **116**–10
juego **152**–18
juego de artesanía en madera **162**–16
juego de disección **119**–7
juego de mesa **162**–3
juego de pants y sudadera **65**–16
juego de platos **41**–2
juego de raqueta **159**–11
juego de video (sistema) **162**–1
juego para construir modelos a escala **162**–7
juego para hacer muñecas **162**–15
juegos **162**–**163**
jueves **18**–5
juez **99**–6
jugador **158**–5
jugar **94**–K
jugar a los naipes **163**–H
jugo de manzana **55**–50
juguetería **92**–5
juguetes **94**–5
julio **19**–31
junio **19**–30

Júpiter **127**–5
jurado **99**–8
koala **135**–45
labio **74**–30
laca **76**–12
lado **118**–22
ladrillos **149**–11
lagartija **131**–41
lago **117**–13
lámpara **41**–5, **44**–17
lámpara de mano **151**–39
lámpara de pie **42**–15
lana **70**–14, **134**–19
langosta **53**–23
lanzar **156**–F
lápiz **3**–20
lápiz de cejas **77**–33
lápiz de labios **77**–37
larga **71**–34
largo **15**–17
lastimado(a) **30**–17
lastimarse **82**–A
lata **55**–40, **56**–3
lata de sopa **56**–15
lavadora **72**–3
lavamanos **43**–22, **49**–17
lavandería **90**–1
lavaplatos **40**–4, **63**–13
lavaplatos se desborda **49**–17
lavar la ropa **72**
lavar las ventanas **46**–D
lavar los platos **46**–M
lavarse…el cabello **76**–E
lazo **69**–40
lea la palabra **6**–B
leche **54**–35
lechera **41**–13
lechina **79**–6
lechosas **50**–20
lechuga **51**–1, **60**–17
lechuza **132**–6
lector de microfilm **98**–4
leer el periódico **27**–V
leer un cuento **94**–F
leggings **65**–23
lengua **74**–26
lenguado **130**–13
leños **42**–12
lente de zoom **165**–25
lentes **81**–35
lentes de contacto **81**–36
lento **11**–4
león **135**–36
león marino **131**–34
leopardo **135**–25
leotardo **67**–1
lesiones **78**
letrero **91**–29
letrero de "se alquila" **36**–11
levantamiento de pesas **159**–15
levantar **94**–G
levantarse **26**–B
levante el auricular **9**–A
levante la mano **2**–A
libra de rosbif **57**–12
librería **92**–4

librero **3**–8, **42**–1
libreta de banco **97**–5
libreta de citas **143**–27
libreta de notas **143**–36
libreta para taquigrafía **143**–36
libro aburrido **167**–29
libro cómico **167**–27
libro de dibujos **45**–17
libro de la biblioteca **98**–20
libro de pintar **45**–20
libro de texto **3**–22
libro interesante **167**–30
libro serio **167**–26
libro triste **167**–28
licencia de manejar **29**–4
licencia de matrimonio **29**–8
licencia del taxi **104**–22
licuadora **40**–12
lienzo **163**–22
liga elástica **143**–45
liguero **67**–19
lijadora eléctrica **150**–9
lima **77**–30
limas **50**–12
límite de velocidad **107**–5
limones **50**–11
limones verdes **50**–12
limpia **72**–16
limpiador **47**–23
limpiador de hornos **47**–3
limpiador de vidrios **47**–8
limpiaparabrisas **108**–3
limpiar el filtro de pelusa **72**–D
limpiar el horno **46**–C
limpiar el mostrador **46**–O
limpiar el piso **46**–J
limpiar la casa **27**–N
limpiar los dientes **85**–I
línea de ensamblaje **146**–8
líneas **118**
lino **70**–17
linterna **151**–39, **154**–22
linterna hecha de una calabaza **168**–11
líquido corrector **143**–33
líquido lavaplatos **47**–21
lirio **129**–20, **129**–24
lisa **71**–38
litera **45**–1
liviana **11**–14, **71**–40
llama **135**–26
llamada de larga distancia **9**–5
llamada internacional **9**–6
llamada local **9**–4
llamar para información **141**–E
llano **117**–19
llanta **108**–10
llanta de repuesto **109**–53
llanura **117**–19
llave **37**–31, **43**–6
llave corrediza **151**–42
llave de tuerca **109**–50, **151**–43
llave gotea **49**–16
llavero **69**–43
llegar **111**–O
llegar a la casa **27**–Q
llenar **72**–C

llenar una solicitud **141**–F
llene el espacio en blanco **7**–R
llene un formulario **4**–B
lleno **11**–9
llevar a los niños al colegio **26**–G
llevar la bandeja **62**–H
llorar **32**–C
lloviendo **10**–8
lluvia ácida **126**–11
lobo **134**–5
loción para después de afeitarse **77**–28
lombriz **130**–22
lote de autos **88**–4
lucha **159**–16
lugar **63**–14
lugar de nacimiento **4**–17
lugar para estacionar **90**–5
lugares para pasear **152**
lugares para vivir **34**
luna llena **127**–16
luna nueva **127**–13
lunes **18**–2
luz de noche **45**–3
luz del freno **108**–13
luz del porche **38**–9
luz delantera **108**–5
luz móvil **42**–3
luz trasera **108**–14
maceta **39**–18
madera **149**–17, **151**–18
madera terciada **149**–16
madero **149**–17
madrastra **25**–31
madre **24**–5, **94**–1
madre soltera **25**–25
maduro(a) **50**–29
maestra **2**–5, **5**–2, **139**–58
maestro **5**–2
magnolia **128**–9
mahones **64**–5
maíz **51**–27, **148**–4
maletera **109**–49
maletero **36**–14
mallas **67**–1
malo **11**–18
malteada **60**–12
mamadera **95**–27
mamíferos **134**–135
mamíferos marinos **131**
mamila **95**–26
mañana **18**–16
mancha **70**–22
mandril **135**–32
manejar en estado de embriaguez **100**–3
manejar un automóvil **90**–C
manga **73**–6
manga corta **71**–30
manga larga **71**–31
mangos **50**–21
manguera **39**–9
maniobra de Heimlich **83**–18
mano **74**–8
manta **44**–12, **111**–M
mantecado **55**–44
mantel **41**–18
mantel individual **41**–20

Index

mantenga el bolso cerca del cuerpo **101**–C
mantenimiento del auto **108–109**
mantequilla **54**–36
manual **144**–22
manual de primeros auxilios **83**–7
manzanas **50**–4
mapa **3**–12
mapache **134**–13
maquillarse **77**–P
máquina de coser **73**–10
máquina de escribir **142**–2
máquina de fax **143**–23
máquina de hielo **145**–18
máquina franqueadora **143**–16
maravilla **129**–13
marcador **3**–19
marcador de tiempo **146**–4
marco de la cama **44**–27
maremoto **103**–15
margarina **54**–39
margarita **129**–14
mariposa **132**–20
mariposa nocturna **132**–22
mariquita **132**–27
mariscos **53**
marmota de las praderas **133**–22
marque el número **9**–D
marque la hoja de respuestas **7**–T
marrón **12**–11, **149**–22
marsopa **131**–31
Marte **127**–6
martes **18**–3
martillar **149**–D
martillo **150**–1
martillo perforador **149**–9
marzo **19**–27
máscara **168**–12
máscara de esquí **66**–14
máscara de oxígeno **110**–14
mascotas **133**
masculino **4**–13
matasellos **96**–9
matemáticas **118**
materiales de construcción **150–151**
materiales peligrosos **147**–7
materias escolares **121**
mayo **19**–29
mayonesa **60**–25
mazo **150**–2
mecánico de automóviles **136**–7
mecánico de reparaciones **138**–48
mecedora **94**–6
mecer **94**–H
mechero de Bunsen **119**–9
media docena de refrescos **56**–21
media hermana **25**–30
media luna **127**–14
mediano **70**–3
medianoche **17**–21
medias cortas **67**–24
medias de malla **66**–11
medias largas **67**–26
medicamento de libre venta **80**–12
medicamento prescrito **80**–11
médico **84**–6, **137**–22

medida(s) **14–15**
medidas **57**
medidas de volumen **57**
medidas para líquidos **57**
medidor de aceite **108**–19
medidor de gas **48**–14
medidor de gasolina **108**–22
medidor de presión **84**–12
medidor de temperatura **108**–23
medio dólar **20**–5
medio fondo **67**–23
medio hermano **25**–29
medioambiente **126**
mediodía **17**–17
mediooeste **123**–9
medios audiovisuales **98**–11
medir **149**–C, **57**–A
medusa **130**–14
mejilla **74**–29
mejillón **130**–17
mejillones **53**–26
melena **135**–49
melocotones **50**–5
melones **50**–15
mensajero **138**–38
menú **62**–3
menú de un café **61**
mercado **54–55**, **89**–20
mercado de pulgas **152**–22
mercancía **152**–24
Mercurio **127**–9
meriendas **55**–16
mes **4**–16, **18**–9
mesa de centro **42**–23
mesa de examen **84**–13
mesa de operaciones **87**–34
mesa del comedor **41**–17
mesa para cambiar pañales **45**–12, **95**–9
mesa para comidas campestres **153**–8
mesa para la cama **86**–9
mesera **63**–6, **139**–53
mesero **62**–4
meses del año **19**
mesetas del Sur **123**–17
mesita **42**–21, **110**–16
mesita de noche **44**–21
meterle **73**–E
metro **104**–9
mezcla para pastel **55**–47
mezcle los ingredientes **58**–K
mezquita **89**–23
microfilm **98**–5
micrófono **164**–4
micrograbadora de transcripción **142**–4
microscopio **119**–4
miércoles **18**–4
mil **14**
mil millones **14**
mil uno **14**
militar **139**–54
minipersianas **43**–11
miniván **106**–10
minuto **16**–2
mirar la garganta **85**–E
mirar la tarjeta sobre emergencias **111**–K
mirar la tele **27**–S

mirar un tablero donde se anuncian trabajos **141**–B
mirilla **37**–27
misterio **166**–15
mitones **66**–9
mocasines **68**–19
mochila **69**–28, **154**–15
mochila de bebé **95**–15
modelo **138**–39
módem **144**–11
modista **73**–2
mofeta **134**–12
molde para pastel **59**–26
molde para torta **59**–28
molde refractario **59**–11
molécula **119**–18
molesto(a) **31**–30
mollejas **52**–23
moluscos y crustáceos **53**
mondongo **52**–8
monedas **20**
monedero **69**–25
monitor **144**–6
monitor para bebés **45**–9
monitor para signos vitales **87**–21
monitores de salidas y llegadas **110**–4
mono **135**–27
monopatinador de nieve **160**–2, **161**–23
montador **136**–6
montaña rusa **152**–15
mopa **47**–16
morado **12**–7, **78**–12
moretón **78**–12
morir **29**–R
morsa **131**–32
mosca **132**–29
mosquito **132**–23
mostaza **60**–24
mostrador **60**–13, **69**–7
mostrador de libros de consulta **98**–2
mostrador de préstamos **98**–16
mostrador para registrarse **110**–3
motel **89**–22
motocicleta **91**–19
motor **109**–41
móvil **45**–4
mozo de campo **148**–20
muchacha de 19 años **22**–8
muchacho de 13 años **22**–7
mudarse **29**–P, **35**–D
mueblería **88**–13
muebles del patio **39**–5
muelle **44**–26, **155**–16
muelle de carga **146**–16
mujer **22**–10
mujer de negocios **136**–10
mujer militar **139**–54
muletas **80**–1
multiplicación **118**–3
mundo **124–125**
muñeca **45**–18, **75**–60
muñeca de papel **163**–30
murciélago **134**–7
muro construido de piedras encajadas sin mezcla cohesiva **149**–18
músculo **75**–48

museo de arte **152**–7
música **120**
músico **138**–41
muslo **74**–16
muslos **52**–21
muy frío **10**–5
nabos **51**–14
nacer **28**–A
nachos **60**–10
nadar **157**–T
nalgas **74**–12
naranjas **50**–10
naranjas mandarinas **50**–13
narciso atrompetado **129**–26
nariz **74**–21
navaja **77**–26
Navidad **168**–18
neblinoso **10**–11
neblumo **126**–10
negro **12**–15
Neptuno **127**–2
nervio **75**–50
nervioso(a) **30**–11
neumático **108**–10, **109**–53
nevando **10**–9
nevera **40**–9
nevera de playa **155**–11
nido **132**–3
nieta **29**–M
nieto **24**–7
nieve **55**–44
nilón **70**–19
niña de 10 años **22**–5
niñera **136**–12
niño de 6 años **22**–4
niño pequeño **22**–3
niño perdido **102**–1
niños **22**–1
nivel **150**–24
no abra la puerta a extraños **101**–F
no estacionarse **107**–12
no hay electricidad **48**–2
no maneje en estado de
  embriaguez **101**–G
no pasar **107**–4
no poder respirar **82**–N
noche **17**–20
nombre **4**–1, **4**–2
noroeste del Pacífico **123**–14
Norteamérica **124**–1
nostálgico(a) **31**–21
noticias **167**–17
noticiero **167**–17
noveno **14**
noventa **14**
noviembre **19**–35
novillos **148**–21
nublado **10**–7
nueces **50**–23
Nueva Inglaterra **123**–11
nueve **14**
nuevos **71**–32
número de cuenta corriente **97**–8
número de cuenta de ahorros **97**–6
número de seguro social **4**–15
número de teléfono **4**–11

números **3**–31, **14**–15
números romanos **14**
nutria **131**–35
obedecer **116**–H
oboe **120**–5
obra de teatro **166**–2
obrero **146**–6
obrero de la construcción **149**–1
observar **119**–B
observatorio **127**–19
obstetra **86**–1
obtener un préstamo **35**–I
océano **117**–6, **155**–1
ochenta **14**
ochenta por ciento **15**–10
ocho **14**
octavo **14**
octubre **19**–34
odómetro **108**–21
oficial **158**–6
oficial de policía **99**–1, **138**–44
oficina **142**–143
oficina de correos **89**–29
oficina del consejero **5**–15
oficina del director **5**–13
oficina principal **5**–17, **146**–1
oftalmólogo **86**–7
oír **75**–B
ojal **73**–12
ojo **74**–27
ojo mágico **37**–27
ola **155**–6
ola de calor **10**–15
oler **75**–C
olla **40**–16, **59**–4, **59**–6, **59**–25
olmo **128**–17
once **14**
Ontario **123**–4
onza de queso **57**–11
onza líquida de agua **57**–1
ópera **166**–8
operaciones matemáticas **118**
operador de maquinaria **138**–37
operadora **9**–7
operar maquinaria pesada **140**–F
opossum **134**–4
óptica **92**–8
optómetra **81**–34
optometrista **81**–34
oración **113**–4
orador invitado **32**–9
oradora estudiantil **32**–8
orangután **135**–40
órbita **127**–11
ordenado **11**–15
ordeñar **148**–C
ordinales **14**
oreja **74**–28
orejeras **66**–12
orejeras de protección **147**–14
organizador **143**–30
órgano **120**–22
orgulloso(a) **31**–22
orilla **117**–12
ornitorrinco **135**–46
orquesta **120**–1

orquídea **129**–17
ortodoncista **84**–23
ortopedista **81**–28
oruga **132**–21
osito **45**–10
oso **134**–11
oso hormiguero **135**–24
ostras **53**–27
otoño **19**–39
óvalo **118**–9
oveja **133**–7
overol **65**–21
paciente **84**–3
padecimientos **79**
padrastro **25**–28
padre **94**–1
padre soltero **25**–26
padres **24**–4
pagar **21**–C
pagar el alquiler **35**–F
pagar impuestos **116**–E
pagar la cuenta **62**–I
pagar la hipoteca **35**–L
pájaro carpintero **132**–9
pájaros **132**
pala **39**–13, **47**–11, **149**–21, **155**–22
palacio municipal **89**–17
palanca de juegos **144**–9
palanca de velocidades **108**–27, **109**–48
paleta de albañil **149**–12
palma **75**–59, **128**–15
palo de golf **161**–1
palo de hockey **161**–11
paloma **132**–16
pan **54**–29
pan blanco **53**–1
pan con ajo **61**–16
pan de centeno **53**–3
pan de trigo **53**–2
panadería **89**–16
panadero **136**–8
pañales de tela **95**–21
pañales desechables **95**–20
pancarta **33**–15
páncreas **75**–46
panda **135**–41
pandereta **120**–19
pandero **120**–19
pandillismo **100**–2
panecillos **54**–30
pañoleta(s) **68**–5
panquecito **60**–14
panqueques **61**–6
pantaletas **67**–17
pantalla **2**–2, **144**–6, **152**–12, **165**–28
pantalla de lámpara **44**–18
pantalla de protección **42**–11
pantaloncillos **64**–13
pantalones **64**–8
pantalones flojos **71**–42
pantalones mezclilla **64**–5
pantera **135**–39
pantimedias **67**–27
pantis **67**–16
pantis bikinis **67**–16
pantorrilla **74**–18

pants **64**–15
pantuflas **67**–6
pañuelo **69**–42
papa asada **61**–14
papas **51**–21
papas fritas **60**–2
papas fritas de bolsa **55**–40
papayas **50**–20
papel de aluminio **55**–55
papel de lija **151**–50
papel higiénico **49**–18
papel membretado **143**–19
papel para cuaderno **3**–25
papel tapiz **45**–5
papelera **43**–25
paperas **79**–7
paquete **56**–8, **96**–5
paquete de galletas dulces **56**–20
paquete de media docena **56**–9
parabrisas **108**–2
parachoques **108**–7
parada de autobús **91**–16, **104**–1
parada de taxis **104**–19
paraguas **66**–16
paralela **118**–21
pararse **107**–3
parásitos intestinales **79**–16
parche de calor **80**–3
pared **42**–6
pared...agrietada **48**–4
parka **66**–8
párpado **74**–33
parque **36**–6, **88**–8, **153**
parque de diversiones **152**–13
parquímetro **91**–18
párrafo **113**–5
parrilla **39**–7, **40**–21
parrilla para asar **59**–14
partes de un árbol **128**
partes de un círculo **118**
partes de un cuadrado **118**
partes de un pájaro **132**
partes de un pez **130**
partes del auto **108**–**109**
participar **162**–B
partida **29**–1
partido de béisbol **152**–25
pasado(a) **50**–30
pasadores **76**–19
pasaje **104**–5
pasajero **104**–7, **110**–23
pasaporte **29**–9
pasar **156**–H
pasar por seguridad **111**–C
pasas **50**–27, **57**–9
pasatiempos **162**–**163**
pascua **129**–23
paseo a caballo **154**–9
paseo en balsa **154**–4
paseo en bote **154**–2
paseos **152**–17
pasillo **54**–5, **145**–13
pasta **61**–15
pasta de dientes **77**–21
pastel **54**–32, **61**–19
pastilla **81**–26

pastillas para el resfriado **81**–17
pastillas para la garganta **81**–21
pastrami **53**–6
pata **134**–20
patas **52**–22
patear **156**–L
patillas **23**–7
patinaje artístico **160**–5
patinaje sobre hielo **160**–4
patinaje sobre ruedas **159**–9
patinar **157**–V
patines de hielo **161**–9
patines de rueda **161**–10
patio **37**–18, **38**–2, **39**–6, **39**
patio de recreo **153**
pato **52**–18, **132**–13
patrón **73**–8
pausar **165**–E
pavo **52**–17, **168**–17
pavo ahumado **53**–4
pavo real **132**–15
pay **59**–28, **61**–21
peatón **90**–7
pecho **74**–13, **74**–14
pechugas **52**–19
pedal del acelerador **109**–47
pedal del freno **109**–46
pediatra **86**–4
pedir del menú **62**–D
pedir un deseo **169**–J
pedir una cobija **111**–M
pedir una frazada **111**–M
pedir una manta **111**–M
pega **143**–37
pegamento **162**–8
pegar **156**–G
peinarse **76**–G
peine **76**–13
peinilla **76**–13
pelador de verduras y hortalizas **59**–15
peldaños **38**–13
pele las zanahorias **58**–N
película **165**–26, **166**–1
película de vaqueros **166**–9
película del oeste **166**–9
peligro de tipo eléctrico **147**–1
peligro por sustancias biológicas **147**–5
pelirrojo(a) **23**–14
pelo **74**–19
pelota **45**–16
pelota de béisbol **161**–18
pelota de vólibol **161**–3
peluquera **137**–30
peluquería **93**–16
pelvis **75**–55
península **117**–7
península de Yucatán **123**–19
peón de labranza **148**–20
pepinos **51**–12
pequeña **11**–1
pequeño **70**–2
peras **50**–6
perca **130**–11
percha **72**–11
perejil **51**–10
perfume **76**–5

perilla de la puerta **37**–30
periódico **98**–8
periquito **133**–15
permanezca en calles bien
    iluminadas **101**–B
perpendicular **118**–20
perro **133**–11
perro caliente **60**–6
persiana **38**–18, **44**–6
persianas **43**–11
persona que empaca la compra **55**–21
persona que realiza ventas por
    teléfono **139**–59
personal del hospital **86**
pesada **11**–13, **71**–41
pesar **57**–B
pesas **161**–19
pesca **154**–5
pescado **53**
pescado congelado **53**–30
pescado fresco **53**–29
pescado frito **61**–17
pescador comercial **136**–15
peso **57**
peso promedio **22**–21
pesos **57**
pestañas **74**–34
pétalo **129**–8
petirrojo **132**–17
petróleo **126**–6
pez espada **130**–12
pezuña **134**–17
piano **120**–16
picadura de insecto **78**–11
picaflor **132**–11
picas **163**–28
pickup **106**–7
pico **117**–14, **132**–1
pie **74**–7
piel **75**–51, **134**–19
pierna **74**–6
pierna de cordero **52**–14
piezas **146**–7
pijama **67**–4
pila **151**–40
pila de abono **39**–10
pilaf de arroz **61**–18
piloto **110**–12
pimentero **41**–15
pimentones **51**–7
pimientos morrones **51**–7
pimpollo **129**–2
piña **128**–11
piñas **50**–2
pincel **163**–23
ping pong **159**–13
pingüino **132**–12
pino **128**–10
pinta de yogurt **57**–3
pintar **149**–A, **163**–E
pintarse... las uñas **77**–O
pintor **138**–43
pintura **77**–31, **151**–20, **152**–8
pintura al óleo **163**–24
pintura de aceite **163**–24
pintura de acrílico **162**–9

pinza para el cabello **76**–17
pinza para ropa **72**–10
pinzas **59**–23, **83**–2, **119**–8
piragüismo **154**–3
pirámide **118**–13
piscina **37**–16, **145**–16, **145**–17
piso **44**–24
pista **5**–11
pista de baile **33**–16
pistola **100**–9
pistola rociadora **151**–19
pizarra **2**–1
pizza **60**–7
placa **108**–15
placa matriz **144**–18
plagas domésticas **49**
plancha **72**–13
planchada **72**–20
planchar la ropa **72**–G
planear una fiesta **169**–A
planetas **127**
planicie de la costa del Golfo **123**–16
planta **38**–1, **42**–18
planta para interiores **129**–29
plantar un árbol **39**–D
plantas **128**
plántula **129**–2
plasticina **162**–14
plástico para envolver **55**–54
plastilina **162**–14
plataforma **104**–15
plátanos **50**–3
platillo **63**–22
platina **119**–5
platito **63**–22
plato **41**–24, **63**–15
plato de verduras y hortalizas al
  horno **58**–Q
plato gira discos **164**–12
plato giratorio **164**–12
plato grande **41**–3
plato hondo **41**–25
plato para el pan y la mantequilla **63**–16
plato para ensalada **63**–17
platón **41**–3
playa **117**–10, **155**
plomero **49**–20
pluma **3**–18, **132**–5
plumero **47**–1
Plutón **127**–1
población **114**
podar el seto **39**–E
podio **32**–5
podrida(a) **50**–30
policía **99**–1
polilla **132**–22
pollo **52**–16
pollo asado **61**–12
pollo cocido **52**–25
pollo crudo **52**–24
polo acuático **158**–15
polvo facial **77**–39
poncho **66**–18
poner la mesa **62**–A
poner una inyección de anestésico **85**–J
ponerla en el correo **96**–B

ponerse protector solar **76**–D
ponerse…maquillaje **77**–P
ponga las palabras en orden **7**–W
póngase de pie **2**–D
popote **60**–20
por el túnel **105**–11
por encima del puente **105**–2
porcelana **43**–9
porcentajes **15**
portacepillos **43**–21
portero **36**–10, **145**–2
postal **96**–3
poste de luz **91**–23
pradera **117**–20
prado **117**–20
precio **21**–6
precio de oferta **21**–3
precio normal **21**–2
preguntar acerca del salario **141**–K
preguntar sobre el horario **141**–F
preguntar sobre las prestaciones **141**–J
preguntar sobre los beneficios **141**–J
prensa de tornillo **150**–21
prensa para ajo **59**–10
preocupado(a) **30**–13
preparación de alimentos **58**
preparar el almuerzo **26**–F
preparar la cena **27**–P
preposiciones **13**
preposiciones de movimiento **105**
prescripción **80**–13
presentar a su amigo **8**–F
presentar un examen de
  ciudadanía **116**–C
presentarse **8**–D
presentarse en la puerta **111**–D
preservación **126**–16
presidente **116**–6
presidente de la Corte Suprema **116**–9
presión arterial alta **79**–15
pretina **73**–3
prima **24**–12
primavera **19**–37
primer lugar **152**–20
primer piso **36**–1
primer premio **152**–20
primero **14**
primeros auxilios **83**
prisma **119**–20
probar **75**–D
problemas **70**
problemas domésticos **48**–49
procesador de alimentos **40**–26
productos de papel **55**–14
productos de pastelería **54**–6
productos enlatados **54**–4
productos para hacer pastelerías **55**–13
profesiones **136**–139
profesora **5**–2
profesora **2**–5
profundidad **15**–16
programa **144**–21
programa de entrevistas **167**–20
programa de juegos **167**–23
programa de preguntas **167**–23
programa de radio **166**–4

programa de televisión **166**–3
programa de ventas **167**–25
programa infantil **167**–24
programa sobre la naturaleza **167**–22
programador de computadoras **136**–16
programas **144**
protección para los dedos de
  pies **147**–21
protector **45**–7
protector de sobrevoltaje **144**–10
protector solar **76**–6, **155**–13
proteja la cartera **101**–D
provincias de las praderas **123**–3
provincias del Atlántico **123**–6
proyector de diapositivas en forma de
  carrusel **165**–29
prueba de esmog **109**–57
pruebas **99**–9
púa **134**–23
público **32**–10
pudín **61**–20
pueblo pequeño **34**–3
puerco **133**–8
puerco espín **134**–10
puerta **36**–13, **110**–5
puerta del garaje **38**–7
puerta mosquitero **38**–8
puerta principal **38**–11
puerto **144**–17
puesto **60**–19
puesto de enfermeras **87**
puesto de helados **93**–20
puesto de periódicos **90**–11
pulga(s) **49**–23
pulgada **15**–13
pulgar **75**–56
pulir los muebles **46**–K
pulirse **77**–O
pulmón **75**–37
pulóver **64**–11
pulpo **130**–4
pulsera **69**–35, **83**–14
puma **134**–2
puño **73**–5
punta **68**–15
punto **113**–6
punto y coma **113**–13
puntos **83**–15
puntuación **113**, **158**–1
punzón **151**–44
puré de papas **61**–11
purificador de aire **80**–4
Quebec **123**–5
quedarse con **21**–E
quehaceres domésticos **46**
quemadura de sol **78**–14
quemar(se) **82**–H
quemarse por el frío **82**–G
queso **54**–38
queso americano **53**–9
queso cheddar **53**–10
queso suizo **53**–11
queso tipo jack **53**–12
quijada **74**–23
química **119**–2
quince **14**

Index

quinto **14**
quiosco **152**–23
quirófano **87**
quitar la maleza de las flores **39**–A
rábanos **51**–5
radiación **126**–13
radiactivo **147**–6
radiador **109**–42, **109**–56
radio **108**–31, **118**–16, **164**–2, **164**–15
radio de onda corta **164**–5
radio reloj **44**–16, **164**–1
radiólogo **86**–5
raíz **128**–5, **129**–3
rallador **59**–2
ralle el queso **58**–J
rama **128**–2, **128**–3
ramillete **129**–27
ramita **128**–1
ramo **129**–27
rana **130**–25
rancho **34**–12
ranura **144**–19
rápido **11**–3
raqueta de tenis **161**–2
rascacielos **89**–25
rasgón **70**–23
raspador **151**–48
rastrillar las hojas **39**–F
rastrillo **39**–11, **77**–25
rasuradora **77**–24
rata **133**–18
rata(s) **49**–27
ratón **133**–17, **144**–8
ratones **49**–26
raya **23**–4, **130**–6
RCP (la resucitación cardiopulmonar) **83**–17
rebane las zanahorias **58**–O
rebobinar **165**–D
rebotar **156**–K
recargar **109**–58
recepción **145**–8
recepcionista **84**–2, **138**–47, **145**–9
receta **80**–13
reciba comentarios **113**–C
recibir la tarjeta de abordaje **111**–E
recibir una descarga eléctrica **82**–F
recibirla **96**–D
recibo **21**–5
reciclar **126**–A
reciclar los periódicos **46**–B
recipiente **45**–13, **56**–5
recipiente de basura **39**–3
recipiente de plástico **59**–3
recipiente de queso fresco **56**–17
recipiente de reciclaje **47**–2
recipiente para desechos médicos **86**–14
recipientes **56**
recogedor **47**–11
recoger a los niños **27**–O
recoger el equipaje **111**–P
recoger la mesa **62**–G
recoja las hojas **7**–Q
recreación al aire libre **154**
recta **118**–18
rectángulo **118**–8

recursos energéticos **126**
red de pescar **154**–17
redacte nuevamente su ensayo **113**–D
redecilla para el cabello **147**–18
refresco **55**–52, **60**–4
refrigerador **40**–9
refrigerante **109**–56
refugio **34**–10
regadera **39**–17
regalos **33**–18
regar las plantas **39**–B
regatear **156**–K
regiones de Canadá **123**
regiones de los Estados Unidos **123**
regiones de México **123**
regiones montañosas de Chiapas **123**–18
registrar el equipaje **111**–B
regla **3**–27
reír **33**–H
reja de seguridad **36**–13
relámpago **10**–17
relicario **69**–33
relleno de espuma **154**–13
reloj **3**–10, **69**–34
reloj de pulsera **69**–34
reloj registrador **146**–4
remitente **96**–7
remolachas **51**–6
remolque **106**–17
removedor de esmalte de uñas **77**–32
renta **35**–C, **35**–F
reparaciones **48**–49
reparador de techos **48**–8
reparador **48**–10, **138**–48
reparar electrodomésticos **140**–G
repartidor **137**–18
repelente de insectos **154**–23
repisa de la chimenea **42**–8
repisa para toallas **43**–8
repita la palabra **6**–D
reportero **139**–49
repose en cama **80**–A
representante de la línea aérea **110**–2
reptiles **130**–131
requisitos para la solicitud de ciudadanía **116**
resbaladilla **153**–13
resfriado **79**–1
residencia universitaria **34**–9
residencia urbana **34**–7
respiración de boca a boca **83**–16
respirador **147**–12
resta **118**–2
restaurante **62**–63
restaurante de comida rápida **90**–14
restregar **46**–L
retire el efectivo **97**–D
retire la tarjeta de cajero automático **97**–F
retroexcavadora **149**–8
retroproyector **2**–4
revise su trabajo **7**–Y
revista **98**–7
revistero **42**–22
revuelva **58**–E
rímel **77**–38

rinoceronte **135**–29
riñón **75**–45
río **117**–3
rizador **76**–15
rizadores **23**–21
rizar el cabello **23**–C
róbalo **130**–11
roble **128**–18
robo **100**–6
roca **155**–24
rociador **39**–8
rociador nasal **81**–23
rodilla **74**–17
rodillo **59**–30
rodillo de pintar **151**–46
roedores **133**
rojo **12**–13
rollo **56**–11
rollo de película **165**–26
rollo de toallas de papel **56**–23
romance **166**–16
rompecabezas **45**–22
romperse un hueso **82**–P
rompevientos **66**–24
ropa **64**–67
ropa interior de invierno **67**–11
ropa sucia **72**–1
roperos **5**–7
rosa **129**–15
rosado **12**–10
rosbif **52**–1, **53**–7
rubor **77**–36
ruedo **73**–1
ruidosos **11**–11
ruta **104**–2
rutinas diarias **26**–27
sábado **18**–7
sábana **44**–13
sábana esquinera **44**–14
sacapuntas **3**–13
sacapuntas eléctrico **142**–9
sacar **85**–M
sacar la basura **46**–Q
sacar sangre **85**–G
sacarle **73**–F
saco para dormir **154**–12
sacudidor **47**–17
sacudir los muebles **46**–A
sala **42**
sala de conferencias **145**–19
sala de emergencia **87**
sala de espera **84**–1
sala de examen **84**–9
sala de operaciones **87**
sala del tribunal **99**–7
salamandra **130**–27
salamandra acuática **130**–26
salami **53**–5
salchicha **52**–12, **61**–2
salero **41**–14
salida de incendios **36**–7
salir del trabajo **26**–M
salir en libertad **99**–H
salmón entero **53**–18
salón de bailes **145**–20
salón de clase **2**–3, **5**–1

salón de uñas **91**–25
salsa catsup **60**–23
salsa de pepino **60**–26
saltamontes **132**–25
saltar **156**–J
saltee las cebollas **58**–H
salto de agua **117**–2
saludar a alguien **8**–A
salvavidas **155**–18
sandalias **68**–24
sandías **50**–24
sandwich de queso a la plancha **61**–8
sangrar **82**–M
sapo **130**–28
saque el lápiz **2**–K
sarampión **79**–5
sarpullido **78**–10
sarro **84**–17
sartén **40**–24, **59**–5
sastre **73**–9
Saturno **127**–4
sauce **128**–14
saxofón **120**-7
seca **72**–18
secador **23**–20
secador de cabello **76**–16
secadora **72**–4
secar los platos **46**–N
secarse el cabello **76**–H
sección de carne **54**–2
sección de productos lácteos **54**–9
sección de publicaciones
    periódicas **98**–6
secoya **128**–7
secretaria **139**–52, **142**–3
secretario **99**–12
seda **70**–15
segundo **14**, **16**–1
segundo piso **36**–2
seguridad en el lugar de trabajo **147**
seguridad pública **101**
seguro **109**–34
seis **14**
seleccione la pareja **7**–X
sello de goma **143**–40
selva tropical húmeda **117**–1
semáforo **90**–6
semana **18**–11
semana pasada **18**–18
semana próxima **18**–20
sembrar **148**–A
semilla **129**–1
Senado **116**–3
senador **116**–4
señale el dibujo **2**–F
señales **107**
señales de tráfico **107**
seno **74**–14
sentar al cliente **62**–B
sentenciar al acusado **99**–F
sentido contrario **107**–4
sentir **78**–D
sentir asco **30**–9
sentirse mareado **78**–C
sentirse satisfecho(a) **30**–6
separar la ropa **72**–A

septiembre **19**–33
séptimo **14**
sequía **103**–10
ser contratado **141**–L
ser juzgado **99**–D
serpiente de cascabel **131**–38
serrucho **150**–4
servicio de correo de los EE.UU. **96**
servicio de directorio **9**–8
servicio de emergencia **9**–9
servicio de estacionamiento **145**–1
servicio en la alberca **145**–17
servicio en la habitación **145**–12
servicio para automovilistas **90**–13
servilleta **41**–19, **63**–23
servir **157**–N
servir el agua **62**–C
servir en un jurado **116**–G
servir la comida **62**–F
sesenta **14**
setenta **14**
seto **39**–1
sexo **4**–12
sexto **14**
shorts de ciclista **67**–3
siembras **148**
siéntese **2**–E
sierra **117**–15
sierra circular **150**–10
sierra de arco **150**–5
siete **14**
siga las instrucciones **7**
signo de exclamación **113**–8
signo de interrogación **113**–7
silenciador **108**–11
silla **2**–7
silla alta **95**–7
silla de playa **155**–14
silla de ruedas **80**–6
silla del comedor **41**–16
silla giratoria **143**–22
sillón **42**–24
sin mangas **71**–29
sinagoga **88**–9
síntomas **78**
sintonizador **164**–13
siquiatra **86**–6
sistema de inyección de
    combustible **109**–40
sistema de seguridad **36**–9
sistema legal **99**
situación de peligro **147**–8
sobre **13**–8, **96**–1, **143**–20
sobreexpuesto **165**–34
sobrina **24**–17
sobrino **24**–18
sofá **42**–19
sofá para dos **42**–25
sófbol **158**–10
sofreír **58**–W
software **144**
sol **127**–10
soldador **139**–63
soleado **10**–6
sólidos **118**
sólo giro a la derecha **107**–9

solo(a) **30**–18
sombra **77**–34, **155**–12
sombrero de paja **66**–23
sombrero(s) **66**–1
sombrilla de playa **155**–9
sonaja **95**–31
sonajero **95**–31
sopa **54**–24
sopa de pollo **58**
sopa del día **61**–10
soplador de hojas **39**–4
soporte **67**–14
soporte para la espalda **147**–16
sorbeto **60**–20
sordo(a) **22**–27
sorprendido(a) **31**–31
sostén **67**–20
suavizante **72**–6
subibaja **153**–16
subirle **73**–D
subraye la palabra **7**–V
suburbios **34**–2
sucesos de la vida **28**–29
sucia **72**–15
sudadera **64**–14
suegra **24**–13
suegro **24**–14
suela **68**–12
suéter cerrado **64**–11
suéter con cuello de cisne **71**–26
suéter con cuello de tortuga **71**–28
suéter con cuello en V **71**–27
suéter de lana tejida **65**–27
sujetapapeles **143**–44
suma **118**–1
supercompacto **106**–1
superintendente **36**–12
supervisar a las personas **140**–K
supervisor de la cadena **146**–5
supervisor de línea **146**–5
sur, el **123**–13
sureste **123**–13
surf a vela **160**–10
surfing **160**–9
suroeste **123**–12
suspensorio **67**–14
sustancias **100**–4
tabla de cortar **40**–27
tabla de picar **40**–27
tabla de surf **155**–5
tabla hawaiana **155**–5
tabla para planchar **72**–14
tablero **108**–17
tableta **81**–25
tablilla **83**–11, **108**–15
tablilla con sujetapapeles **143**–26
tache la palabra **7**–U
tachuela **143**–43
taco **60**–9
tacómetro **108**–20
tacón **68**–13
tacones **68**–17, **71**–46
tacos altos **68**–17, **71**–47
tacos bajos **71**–46
taladrar un diente **85**–K
taladrar una muela **85**–K

taladro **84**–21
taladro eléctrico **150**–8
taladro neumático **149**–9
talco **76**–3
talco para bebé **95**–18
tallas **70**
tallo **129**–4
talón **75**–62
tanque de buceo **155**–8
tanque de gasolina **108**–12
tanteo **158**–1
tapa **59**–24
tapacubos **108**–9
tapete de hule **43**–3
tapones de oído **147**–13
tarde **17**–18, **17**–23
tarea de redacción **113**–1
tarjeta **168**–5
tarjeta de béisbol **162**–11
tarjeta de cajero automático **97**–9
tarjeta de crédito **20**–15
tarjeta de felicitación **96**–4
tarjeta de residente permanente **29**–3
tarjeta del seguro **84**–4
tarjeta del seguro social **29**–5
tarjeta para uso de la biblioteca **98**–19
tarjeta telefónica **9**–10
tarjetero **143**–17
taxi **104**–18
taxímetro **104**–21
taza **63**–21
taza de aceite **57**–2
taza de café **41**–27
taza de harina **57**–10
taza grande **41**–28
tazón **41**–25
tazón de sopa **63**–18
tazón para mezclar **59**–31
té **61**–24
té helado **60**–5
teatro **88**–10
techo **38**–20, **42**–5
techo...gotea **48**–3
teclado **144**–7
teclado electrónico **120**–20
técnico de laboratorio **86**–16
técnico de rayos X **86**–8
técnico médico de emergencia **87**–26
tejado **38**–20
tejas de madera **149**–13
tejer **163**–F
tejido a gancho **163**–20
teléfono **9**, **9**–1
teléfono celular **9**–13
teléfono inalámbrico **9**–12
teléfono público **9**–11, **91**–21
telenovela **167**–21
teleobjetivo **165**–25
telescopio **127**–21
televisión **42**–26, **164**–6
televisor portátil **164**–7
temperatura **10**
templado **10**–3
temprano **17**–22
tenazas **119**–8
tenazas para crisol **119**–15

tenazas para el cabello **76**–15
tendedero **72**–9
tenedor **41**–21, **63**–25
tenedor para ensalada **63**–24
tener 18 años de edad **116**–A
tener calor **30**–1
tener frío **30**–4
tener hambre **30**–5
tener náuseas **78**–D
tener sed **30**–2
tener un ataque al corazón **29**–Q
tener un bebé **82**–D
tener un nieto **29**–M
tener una reacción alérgica **82**–E
teñir el cabello **23**–D
tenis **159**–14
tenis de mesa **159**–13
tercer piso **36**–3
tercero **14**
terminal de la línea aérea **110**–1
terminar **157**–Z
terminar la conversación **8**–C
termita(s) **49**–22
termómetro **84**–15
terraza **38**–16
terremoto **102**–5
testigo **99**–11
tetera **40**–17, **41**–11
tía **24**–10
tibio **10**–2
tiburón **130**–7
tiempo **10**
tienda de aparatos electrónicos **93**–18
tienda de artículos para fotografía **90**–4
tienda de campaña **154**–10
tienda de conveniencia **90**–3
tienda de donas **91**–20
tienda de mascotas **92**–6
tienda de música **92**–1
tienda de regalos **145**–7
tienda de ropa de maternidad **93**–17
tienda de tarjetas **92**–7
tienda de videos **93**–15
tienda por departamentos **93**–13
tierra **127**–7
tiesto **39**–18
tigre **135**–37
tijeras **23**–19, **73**–18
tijeras de podar **39**–15
tijeras para setos **39**–12
timbre **38**–10
timbre para llamar **86**–10
timbre postal **96**–10
tina **95**–23
tintorería **91**–24
tío **24**–11
tipos de cuentos **166**
tipos de entretenimiento **166**
tipos de escuela **112**
tipos de matemáticas **118**
tipos de materiales **70**
tipos de programas de tele **167**
tirantes **68**–2
tiro con arco **159**–1
título **113**–3, **98**–21
tiza **3**–16

toalla de baño **43**–12
toalla de manos **43**–13
toalla de playa **155**–15
toalla para frotarse **43**–14
toalla para platos **47**–22
toallas de papel **40**–2
toallero **43**–8
toallitas húmedas **95**–17
toallitas para la secadora **72**–5
tobillo **75**–61
tobillo torcido **78**–18
tocacintas **3**–11, **108**–30
tocacintas personal **164**–15
tocacintas portátil **164**–2
tocador de disco compacto **164**–14
tocar **75**–E, **165**–B
tocar un instrumento **120**–A
tocino **52**–11, **61**–7
todos los días **18**–21
toga **32**–2
tomacorrientes **44**–20, **151**–41
tomar **26**–C, **94**–L
tomar el autobús para ir al colegio **26**–H
tomar la orden **62**–E
tomar la temperatura **85**–C
tomar un baño **76**–B
tomar un mensaje **142**–A
tomar una cita **85**–A
tomar una foto **32**–D
tomar una placa de rayos X **85**–H
tomar una sobredosis de drogas **82**–K
tomates **51**–23
tome asiento **2**–E
tome líquidos **80**–B
tome medicina **80**–F
tope **40**–22
tormenta **10**–16
tormenta de nieve **10**–20
tormenta de polvo **10**–21
tornado **103**–13
tornillo articulado **150**–33
tornillo de banco **150**–21
tornillo para madera **150**–28
tornillo para máquina **150**–27
toronjas **50**–9
torre de control **110**–7
torta **61**–21
tortuga **131**–42
toser **78**–A
tostada **61**–3
tostador de pan **40**–7
tostadora **40**–7
total **21**–8
trabajador agrícola **148**–8
trabajador portuario **137**–21
trabajar **26**–K
trabajar en una computadora **140**–P
trabaje con un compañero **6**
trabajo en grupo **6**
trabajo en clase **7**
tractor **148**–9
tractor nivelador **149**–6
traductor **138**–34
tragedia **166**–11
trailer **106**–15
traje **64**–2

traje de baño **66**–22, **66**–26
traje de buzo **155**–7
traje de tres piezas **64**–1
tranquilo(a) **30**–10
tranquilos **11**–12
transcribir notas **142**–C
transfiera fondos **97**–E
transporte de equipaje **110**–19
transporte público **104**
trapeador **47**–16
trapear **46**–J
trapos **47**–6
tréboles **163**–26
trece **14**
treinta **14**
tren **104**–17
tren subterráneo **104**–9
trenes a escala **163**–32
trepar a las barras **153**–C
tres **14**
tres cuartos **15**–5
tres veces por semana **18**–24
triángulo **118**–7
tribunal **89**–18
triciclo **153**–9
trigo **148**–2
trigonometría **118**–27
trinchera **66**–20
tripa **52**–8
tripié **165**–20
trípode **165**–20
triste **31**–20
tritón **130**–26
triturador de desperdicios **40**–5
trituradora de papeles **143**–24
trombón **120**–12
trompa **128**–4
trompeta **120**–13
trompón **129**–26
tronco **135**–47
trotar **156**–B
trucha **53**–16
tuba **120**–14
tuberculosis **79**–13
tuberías...congeladas **49**–19
tubo **56**–12, **151**–16
tubo de ensayo **119**–16
tubo de pasta de dientes **56**–24
tuerca **150**–31
tulipán **129**–11
tuza **133**–19
TV **42**–26
un cuarto **15**–2
un entero **15**–6
un medio **15**–4
un millón **14**
un octavo **15**–1
un solo sentido **107**–6
un tercio **15**–3
uña **75**–58
uña del pie **75**–64
una en punto **16**–4
una vez por semana **18**–22
una y cinco **16**–5
una y cincuenta **16**–14
una y cincuenta y cinco **16**–15

una y cuarenta **16**–12
una y cuarenta y cinco **16**–13
una y cuarto **16**–7
una y diez **16**–6
una y media **16**–10
una y quince **16**–7
una y treinta **16**–10
una y treinta y cinco **16**–11
una y veinte **16**–8
una y veinticinco **16**–9
ungüento **81**–24
ungüento antibacterial **83**–9
unidad central de procesamiento **144**–1
unidad de disco **144**–3
unidad de disco duro **144**–20
uniforme **65**–17, **161**–16
unirse al ejército **28**–F
universidad **112**–10
universo **127**
uno **14**
Urano **127**–3
usando el teléfono público **9**
usar desodorante **76**–C
usar hilo dental **77**–K
usar una caja registradora **140**–N
uso del cajero automático **97**
uso del diccionario **6**
utensilios de cocina **59**
uvas **50**–1
vaca **133**–3
vacaciones **19**–46
vaciar **72**–E
vaciar la papelera **46**–F
vacío **11**–10
vale **104**–11
valle **117**–18
vandalismo **100**–1
varicela **79**–6
vaso **41**–26
vaso de agua **63**–19
vaso de laboratorio **119**–13
vaya a un quiropráctico **81**–H
vecina **37**–22
vecino **37**–22
vehículo de doble tracción **106**–9
veinte **14**
veinte dólares **20**–10
veinte para las dos **16**–12
veinte por ciento **15**–8
veinticinco centavos **20**–4
veinticinco para las dos **16**–11
veintidós **14**
vejiga **75**–47
vela **41**–7
velerismo **160**–8
velero **155**–4
velocímetro **108**–20
vena **75**–44
venado **134**–14
venda adhesiva **83**–3
vendaje elástico **83**–12
vendedor **68**–1, **139**–50
vendedor ambulante **91**–30
vender **21**–B
vender automóviles **140**–H
veneno **147**–3

venera **130**–18
venir a la casa **27**–Q
ventana **38**–17, **42**–17
ventana...rota **48**–5
ventas por tele **167**–25
ventilador de techo **41**–4
ventisca **103**–11
ventiuno **14**
Venus **127**–8
ver **75**–A
verano **19**–38
verbos utilizados en los
    deportes **156**–157
verde **12**–8, **50**–28
verde liso **70**–6
verduras y hortalizas **51**
verduras y hortalizas congeladas **55**–43
verduras, hortalizas y frutas **54**–11
vereda **38**–14
verificar la presión sanguínea **85**–B
verificar lo que oye **8**–E
vesícula biliar **75**–40
vestíbulo **145**–3
vestido **64**–3
vestido con peto y tirantes **65**–18
vestido de maternidad **65**–19
vestido de noche **65**–29
vestir **94**–J
vestirse **26**–D
vía férrea **104**–10
viajar **29**–N
viajar en trineo **160**–6
viaje en avión **111**
vicepresidente **116**–7
vida marina **130**–131
video **98**–13
videocasete **164**–10
videograbadora **164**–8
viejos **71**–33
viento **126**–2
viernes **18**–6
viga **149**–3
viga maestra **149**–3
vigésimo **14**
VIH **79**–10
viña **148**–14
violeta **129**–22
violín **120**–8
violoncelo **120**–9
virus de la inmunodeficiencia
    humana **79**–10
visera de seguridad **147**–11
vistosa **71**–39
vitaminas **81**–19
vitrina para la vajilla **41**–1
vivir en los EE.UU. por cinco
    años **116**–B
volante **44**–22, **108**–26
voleibol **158**–14, **161**–3
vólibol **158**–14
voluntario **87**–19
vomitar **78**–E
votar **116**–D
vuelta en U permitida **107**–7
wafles **61**–4
xilófono **120**–17